JOHN M. BROOKE

Naval Scientist and Educator

JOHN M. BROOKE

Naval Scientist and Educator

GEORGE M. BROOKE, JR.

University Press of Virginia

CHARLOTTESVILLE

THE UNIVERSITY PRESS OF VIRGINIA
Copyright © 1980 by the Rector and Visitors
of the University of Virginia

First published 1980

Library of Congress Cataloging in Publication Data

Brooke, George M., Jr.
  John M. Brooke, naval scientist and educator.
  Includes bibliographical references and index.
  1. Brooke, John Mercer, 1826–1906. 2. Naval
biography—United States. 3. Inventors—United States—
Biography. 4. Confederate States of America. Navy—
Biography. 5. Educators—Virginia—Biography.
6. Virginia. Military Institute, Lexington—Biography.
I. Title.
V63.B74B76   359.3'3'10924[B]   79-18559
ISBN 0-8139-0809-4

PRINTED IN THE UNITED STATES OF AMERICA

To Frances, Marion, and Chip

Contents /

Illustrations /

M A P S

Preface /

THE nineteenth century witnessed enormous changes in the leading navies, as steam supplanted sail, iron replaced wood, and ordnance was improved. The United States Navy in the years before the Civil War was slow to respond to these developments, but some progress was made. John Mercer Brooke, who entered the navy in 1841, witnessed this evolution.

The most significant contribution of the navy in these years was its promotion and organization of a number of surveying and exploring expeditions to various parts of the world. Brooke, who had invented an effective deep-sea sounding lead, played a prominent part in an expedition which was active in the North Pacific Ocean and led another into the same region. On these cruises Brooke demonstrated his scientific talents and did important work as an astronomer, hydrographer, and surveyor. He also was given the opportunity in Japan to serve in a quasi-diplomatic capacity at the time that insular country was opened to the West. By the time of the American Civil War, Brooke had established a solid professional reputation as a scientist and inventor.

When Virginia seceded from the Union in 1861, Brooke resigned his commission and offered his services to the Confederacy. In the fledgling Confederate navy, Brooke's abilities were quickly recognized, and he made important contributions in ordnance and the design of armored warships.

That Brooke was an important figure during his twenty-five years of naval service is generally appreciated, as there are frequent references to him in standard works. But the details have been lacking, and the principal purpose of this study is to supply the necessary information, so that the full scope of his activities may be understood.

The Civil War ended Brooke's career as a national figure, although he lived forty-one years after that conflict ended. During most of that period of adjustment for the South, Brooke was a professor at the Virginia Military Institute, a state engineering and scientific college. His work at that institution was of secondary importance. Nonetheless, a study of his life during those years is of value because he participated in the South's struggle to survive. For a time, VMI was a leader in the effort to revive higher education in the defeated region.

Brooke's active life can be divided into three periods: twenty years in the United States Navy, four years in the Confederate navy, and thirty-four years as a professor. But a biography poses problems, not only because Brooke lived so long, but because he was engaged in so many diverse activities. Fortunately, he left thousands of letters, private and official, and a score of journals. These papers, which were in a state of complete confusion, are in the author's possession and serve as the nucleus of this study. There is also a vast amount of information on Brooke's naval career and some relating to his postwar activities at the National Archives in Washington, D.C. I used those records extensively. Also, I found helpful the primary source material in the Manuscript Division of the Library of Congress, the Virginia State Library, the Virginia Historical Society, and the manuscript collections at the University of North Carolina, the University of Virginia, and Duke University. To obtain a background for Brooke's work at VMI, I used the official records of that institution, manuscript and printed.

It is a pleasure after many years to recognize the encouragement and support I have received in writing this book.

First, I wish to acknowledge that my father, Colonel George M. Brooke, U.S.A., awakened within me at an early age an intense curiosity about the eventful and romantic career of my grandfather John M. Brooke, who had died a number of years before I was born.

To the late Professor Fletcher M. Green of the University of North Carolina, I am indebted for professional guidance. He taught me how to reduce a bulky manuscript to manageable size.

The Virginia Military Institute has been cooperative in many ways. Particularly, I wish to thank the Dean of the Faculty, Brigadier General James M. Morgan, for his help in obtaining funds for typing and publication.

Without the assistance of Mr. Joseph D. Neikirk and the VMI Foundation, my efforts might well have been in vain. Through the generosity of Mr. F. H. C. Wachtmeister, the foundation established a sabbatical leave program which enabled me to find the time to complete my research.

The George C. Marshall Research Foundation in Lexington has kindly permitted me to store the Brooke Papers in its vaults and to use its facilities as a place to work.

A great many people assisted me in uncovering useful material. But I would like to mention especially Nelson M. Blake, who assisted me at the National Archives in utilizing effectively the enormous mass of material pertaining to the United States Navy.

I am much indebted to the VMI Civil Engineering Department for their cooperation. Through the department I gained the services of Cadet William Charles Kyle, who prepared the maps.

Innumerable typists have helped me along the way but I am indebted particularly to Patsy Smith and Janet Aldridge at VMI.

Finally, I want to pay tribute to my wife. She endured my moods and gave me constant encouragement. As I never learned to type, she developed that skill and thereby helped translate my scrawl into something other people could read. What more could a husband ask?

JOHN M. BROOKE

Naval Scientist and Educator

I /

BOYHOOD

AND EARLY CRUISES

A Brooke family genealogist once lamented, "The colonial Brookes were either too large or too small to 'care whence they came'; else they would never have allowed their genealogical record to fall into such confusion."[1] It is known, however, that the Virginia Brookes came from England by way of Maryland. The line from Robert Brooke (1654–1712), the first of the Virginia line, to John Mercer Brooke (1826–1906), who is of the sixth generation, is unbroken; hence the latter's paternal ancestry can be traced in the colonial period. Brooke's forbears held responsible positions in public life and intermarried with such established families as the Braxtons, Tunstalls, and Mercers.

Robert Brooke settled on the Rappahannock River and was a "gentleman justice" of Essex County from its formation in 1692 until 1706. One of his sons, Humphrey, was a joint holder of fifteen thousand acres of land in Spotsylvania County, a justice of the peace, and "a Merchant of considerable Note."[2] George Brooke (1728–1782), the eldest son of Humphrey and the great-

[1] St. George Tucker Brooke, "The Brooke Family of Virginia," *Virginia Magazine of History and Biography* 9 (Jan. 1902): 317 (hereafter cited as *VMHB*).
[2] Arnold Motley, Clerk of Essex County, Va., to the author, 14 March 1951; Brooke, "Brooke Family," *VMHB* 14 (1907): 325, 11 (1904): 445.

grandfather of John M. Brooke, played a prominent role in Virginia affairs preceding and during the American Revolution. A patriot, George was a member of the House of Burgesses for six years, the King and Queen County Committee of Safety, and the Virginia Conventions of 1775 and 1776 and was a colonel of the Virginia line. At the time of his death he was treasurer of Virginia.[3] During his lifetime George Brooke enlarged his inherited holdings by the purchase of a rich plantation on the Mattaponi River in King and Queen County. Known as Mantapike, this plantation became the family seat and was of importance as a shipping point for tobacco. George's son Richard (1760–1816) married Maria Mercer, seventeenth child of John Mercer of Stafford County, Virginia.[4]

Richard, a state senator, directed in his will that his land, including Mantapike, be sold so that each of his children should share equally in his estate. Only one of Richard's four sons married. This son, George Mercer Brooke, was a professional army officer and the father of John, the subject of this study. One of Richard's five daughters, Anna Maria Brooke, married her first cousin Colonel William Garnett and was the mother of Mary Elizabeth Selden Garnett, the later naval officer's first wife.

George Mercer Brooke entered the army in 1808, distinguished himself during the War of 1812 in operations around Lake Erie, and at the end of the struggle was a major with the brevet rank of colonel.[5] After the war Brooke was assigned to the Fourth Infantry, which took part in General Andrew Jackson's Florida campaign against the Creeks and Seminoles in 1817–18. Following the Seminole War, the history of the Fourth, like that of other infantry regiments, "was one of continual marching and coun-

[3] John Pendleton Kennedy, *Journals of the House of Burgesses of Virginia, 1766–1776*, 3 vols. (Richmond, 1905–6), 3:3 and passim; Brooke, "Brooke Family," *VMHB* 11 (1904): 338; Louis A. Burgess, ed. and comp., *Virginia Soldiers of 1776*, 3 vols. (Richmond, 1927), 3:1042–45.

[4] Maria's sister, Grace Fenton Mercer, married Muscoe Garnett. These marriages were the first in a series that tied the Brooke and Garnett families together.

[5] Francis B. Heitman, *Historical Register and Dictionary of the United States Army, from Its Organization, September 29, 1789, to March 2, 1903*, 2 vols. (Washington, D.C., 1903), 1:284; William A. Gordon, *A Compilation of Registers of the Army of the United States from 1815 to 1837* (Washington, D.C., 1837), app. pp. 3, 4 (hereafter cited as Gordon, *Registers of the Army*).

termarching, building cantonments and opening military roads through the wilderness." In 1824 Brooke constructed Fort Brooke at the site of present-day Tampa. The fort served as an important supply base in the second Seminole War. Colonel Brooke was promoted to brevet brigadier general in 1824 for ten years' faithful service in grade.[6]

Despite the arduous life that the army demanded, Brooke, a dashing officer whose portrait was painted by both Gilbert Stuart and Rembrandt Peale, found time for romance. In 1819 he married Lucy Thomas of Duxbury, Massachusetts, the seventh of eight children born to Winslow and Abigail Delano Thomas. Lucy's father was a sea captain and the great-grandson of John Thomas, who had been brought up in the home of Edward Winslow, a founder and governor of Plymouth Colony. Lucy was only eight when her father died and her mother was left with the responsibility of rearing the large family. Abigail is said to have been a handsome woman, but very strict.[7]

A miniature depicts Lucy as a striking girl with blue eyes and brown hair tinged with red. All too soon, however, she was forced to assume the responsibilities of motherhood amid the dreary routine and physical hardships of a succession of isolated army camps. For Lucy, army life, though monotonous, was hardly tranquil; the children prevented that, four being born between 1820 and 1826. The last of the four was John Mercer Garnett, who arrived on December 18, 1826, at Fort Brooke on Tampa Bay. Large families posed difficult problems on frontier posts. In addition to the low pay that drove many officers out of the service, the lack of medical facilities made all the more dangerous the "terrible scourges of plague and epidemic that riddle the commands of the frontier."[8] The Brooke family did not escape sickness and death. The eldest boy died three months after birth,

[6] James A. Leyden, "The Fourth Regiment of Infantry," *The Army of the United States: Historical Sketches of Staff and Line with Portraits of Generals-in-Chiefs*, ed. Theodore F. Rodenbaugh and William L. Haskin (New York, 1896), p. 456; George M. Brooke, Jr., "Early Days at Fort Brooke," *Sunland Tribune* (Journal of the Tampa Historical Society), 1 (July 1974): 1–14.

[7] Rosa Brooke Willis, granddaughter of General Brooke, to the author, 23 April 1951.

[8] William Addleman Ganoe, *The History of the United States Army* (New York, 1924), p. 167.

and two other children died within twelve days of each other in 1828.

When John Mercer, the lone survivor, was in his fifth year, a brother named William Neverson was born. Three months after William's birth, Brooke was assigned to command the Fifth Infantry, whose components were stationed at various posts within the present limits of Michigan, Wisconsin, Illinois, and Nebraska. According to family tradition, the parents and their two small sons made the long trip from the southeastern states to Michigan Territory in an army wagon.

General Brooke established his regimental headquarters at Fort Mackinac, Michigan Territory, with units of the Fifth distributed at that post and three others: Fort Winnebago, Fort Brady (Sault Ste. Marie), and Fort Howard (Green Bay).[9] The following year Brooke moved his headquarters to Fort Howard and still later to Detroit Barracks. The Fifth remained in the Northwest until 1845, although its units were constantly being shifted about among the posts mentioned and six others. Such dispersion of forces required much travel by Brooke as the commanding officer, and the rearing of the family devolved more and more upon Lucy. A son was born in 1833 and another in 1835, but both died in infancy. Charles, the eighth and last child, was born in 1837.

The strain of childbearing and the sorrow of death tested all of Lucy's New England faith and fortitude, but she had other griefs as well. Writing from Fort Howard to her husband at Prairie du Chien, where Fort Crawford was located, Lucy gave vent to her feelings. Particularly was she depressed by the pervading loneliness. Little disturbed the humdrum existence on frontier posts except the vexations caused by servants. In letters to her husband Lucy complained of petty thievery and drunkenness among the servants—problems that confronted her continually. Intemperance among officers and men of the regiment was another cause of shame. "I confess my pride is touched to say nothing of my happiness," she wrote.[10]

These annoyances were typical of the service. As in the pre-

---

[9] Gordon, *Registers of the Army*, p. 451.

[10] Lucy Brooke to Gen. George Brooke, 11 Aug. 1837, Brooke Papers, in the possession of the author (hereafter cited as BP).

ceding decade, the tiny army of the 1830s "was assigned more than it could do in peacetime." In 1836 alone, 117 officers resigned from an army whose total officer strength had numbered but 603 in the preceding November. As for the enlisted men, it has been stated that "the down-and-outer, the foreigner, and the adventurer made up to too great a degree the rank and file."[11] Drunkenness, harsh punishments, low pay, and the West Point system contributed to the widespread desertion. Officers could assign enlisted men to perform domestic service, but with such a rough lot to choose from it is not surprising that officers' wives found their patience sorely tested.

Such was the army into which John M. Brooke was born and in such an environment did he lead the active and exciting life of the average army child. When about two years of age he was a large baby with blue eyes, a dimple in each cheek, and the fair coloring of his Massachusetts mother. Of serious mien, he never laughed loudly but is said to have had a sweet smile. Already he showed a tendency toward the gravity and reserve that were to characterize him.[12] A seemingly trivial incident which occurred when Brooke was a small boy made a lasting impression upon him. Having been given a silver watch by a soldier, he was curious to know "what made it tick." Determined to find out, he placed it upon a stone and tapped it. The blow broke open the watch and revealed its inner mechanism. But still Brooke did not know the secret of the watch, so he tapped it again. This solved the riddle, for the mainspring jumped out. In later years Brooke used to say that nothing since had given him "so good an idea of the mechanism of a watch."[13]

The future naval officer did not inhale much salt spray as a young boy, but his home on the Great Lakes did expose him to

[11] Richard L. Watson, Jr., "Congressional Attitudes toward Military Preparedness, 1829–1835," *Mississippi Valley Historical Review*, 24 (March 1948): 615, 617; Emory Upton, *The Military Policy of the United States* (Washington, D.C., 1911), p. 162; Ganoe, *History of the United States Army*, p. 173. Particularly useful studies on army life in this period are: Francis Paul Prucha, *Broadax and Bayonet: The Role of the United States Army in the Development of the Northwest, 1815–1860* (Madison, Wis., 1953); Prucha, *The Sword of the Republic: The United States Army on the Frontier, 1783–1846* (London, 1969); Henry Putney Beers, *The Western Military Frontier, 1815–1846* (Philadelphia, 1935).

[12] Charlotte Garnett Darby to Anna Maria Brooke, 16 Oct. [1871], BP.

[13] Kate Corbin Brooke Diary, 19 Aug. 1874, BP.

ships and sailing. His first real taste of sailing came when his father and an old sailor rigged up a sailboat to use on the Fox River. Moreover, the lad became acquainted with the marvels of steam when crossing the Great Lakes in steamboats. He became an expert swimmer while living at Fort Howard.[14] Young John Brooke and his mother made at least one trip from Fort Howard to her family home in Duxbury. Such visits meant a chance to hear about and perhaps see Lucy's three brothers, who were sea captains sailing from the busy port on Plymouth Bay.

At Fort Howard, John's nurse was an old soldier who had served in Napoleon's armies, and the story goes that the veteran held the youngster spellbound with his tales of military campaigns. In a day when army posts were so small, however, there were few children to play with. But there was Elizabeth St. Clair Denny whose father, Captain St. Clair Denny, acting quartermaster, had graduated from West Point in 1822 and served with the Fifth Infantry ever since. Perhaps Elizabeth was a witness to John's first ordnance experiment. Finding an old umbrella tube, he "stopped the end with wood, pierced a hole for the fuse put it down and got behind the rain barrel and touched it off with a lighted stick." The explosion was sufficient to bring General Brooke out of the house crying, "Merc what are you doing?"[15]

Proper schooling for children was a problem on frontier posts. There were no good teachers in Green Bay, and when John had exhausted the possibilities of the local dame's school, his parents decided a more formal education was necessary for him. They selected Milnor Hall, the Junior Preparatory Department of Kenyon College in Gambier, Ohio, where he matriculated in 1835, at the age of eight. The curriculum was comprehensive, including spelling, reading, writing, geography, arithmetic, English grammar, bookkeeping, Latin and Greek declamation, composition, sacred music, and scriptures, but it is not known whether young Brooke's work was satisfactory.[16] It is established, however, that

[14] Kate Corbin Brooke notes recording conversations with Brooke, 1896, BP; *National Cyclopedia of American Biography*, s.v. "John Mercer Brooke."

[15] Kate Corbin Brooke notes, n.d., BP. As a boy John Mercer Brooke was called Mercer or Merc by his parents.

[16] Elaine L. Weygand, Assistant Registrar, Kenyon College, to the author, 21 March 1951.

on more than one occasion he ran away from the school. The primary reason each time was a bad case of homesickness.

A year or two after John Brooke's return from boarding school, his mother went to Philadelphia, taking her three sons with her. She hoped to restore her failing health through medical treatment. William and Charles were entrusted to a childless couple, and John was registered at Aaron's School in Burlington, New Jersey. It was at this school that the future scientist first saw experiments in physics. The apparatus was excellent and the experiments engendered in him a profound interest. Although his thirst for learning was stimulated, John felt that Samuel Aaron, the master, lacked the necessary force to discipline the larger boys. This criticism was apparently justified, for Aaron was soon impelled to reduce the size of the school and take only small boys. Be that as it may, most of Brooke's formal education before he entered the navy was obtained at Aaron's School.[17]

In Burlington a favorite pastime was to skate on the Delaware River. Once when he was skating with school friends John Brooke saw a girl fall into the freezing water while crossing on a shaky plank from the shore to the firm ice beyond. Rushing to her, John plunged into the water beside the drowning girl and pushed her ashore. But when the girl came to the school the next day to thank him for saving her life, he was too embarrassed to see her.[18]

On Saturdays and holidays John frequently saddled a horse and rode into Philadelphia to see his mother, now an invalid, and his brothers. He was deeply attached to little Charles. But these happy holiday jaunts came to an abrupt end when Lucy Brooke died in 1839, at the age of thirty-four. Less than a year later Charles followed her.[19] Of the eight Brooke children, only John and William were left.

When Lucy died, John Brooke wanted to return to his father, who was then stationed at St. Louis, and the old soldier was anxious for him to do so. Friends on the spot, however, dissuaded him from the step, and he stayed on at the school in Burlington. Although General Brooke wrote regularly and supported him fi-

[17] Kate Corbin Brooke Diary, 24 Jan. 1875, BP.
[18] Ibid.
[19] Ibid., 21 Aug. 1874.

nancially, John saw his father only once or twice after his mother's death, and then for very short periods of time. Except for visits with his brother William, who was five years his junior, he was quite alone.

In April 1841 John Brooke spent the Easter holiday in Philadelphia with the family of General Robert Patterson, a friend of his father's. A strong Democrat, General Patterson at that time was a successful commission merchant and commander of a division of the Pennsylvania militia. He fathered eleven children, of whom six survived infancy.[20] Of these, John Brooke's particular friend was the eldest son, Frank. In Frank's den many an hour was whiled away telling tall stories, speculating rosily on the future, and smoking a vast quantity of cigars.

While at the Pattersons, John Brooke received word that he had been appointed an acting midshipman in the United States Navy and that a warrant dated March 3, 1841, had been forwarded to him. Promptly the enthusiastic youngster wrote the secretary of the navy, "I shall esteem it a favor to be put on duty as soon as practicable." In later years Brooke reminisced to his wife that "a prouder boy never walked the streets of Burlington" than he upon his return to ready himself for a life at sea. General Brooke's efforts to secure the appointment were well rewarded by the gratitude of the youngster who had only recently passed his fourteenth birthday. On April 30, 1841, Brooke received orders to "proceed to Norfolk without delay, and report to Come. Shubrick for duty on board the U.S.S. Delaware."[21] Accordingly, the new acting midshipman proceeded to the Virginia port city, where he stayed with his Garnett relatives.

For the next five years Brooke served on routine cruises. He then entered the newly opened Naval Academy for the standard nine-month course. The young officer learned much about navigation, seamanship, and gunnery and absorbed the rudiments of hydrography and ordnance that would later be important to him.

[20] *Dictionary of American Biography*, s.v. "Robert Patterson (1792–1881)."

[21] Brooke to George E. Badger, 13 April 1841, Officers Letters, 1802–84, Office of the Secretary of the Navy, Record Group 45, National Archives (hereafter RG 45, NA); Kate Corbin Brooke Diary, 24 Jan. 1875, BP; Badger to Brooke, 30 April 1841, Appointments, Orders, and Resignations, 1813–42, RG 45, NA.

Brooke matured quickly, and in many respects his character was molded at this time.

He had entered the navy at a time of transition when the air was pregnant with new ideas. The fifty-year period beginning in 1837 has been called "the naval counterpart of the mechanical revolution in industry." Technological improvements were slow to win favor in naval circles, but by 1841 significant developments were well under way. The gradual substitution of steam for sail and iron for wood profoundly affected naval construction, tactics, and strategy. These fundamental changes were closely interrelated with and accelerated by the introduction of the screw propeller, the explosive shell, rifled ordnance, and the built-up gun.[22] Brooke would witness these developments and contribute to them.

In matters pertaining to personnel, however, resistance to change was entrenched. The navy faced a problem which would plague it until the Civil War—stagnation in the line of promotion. The problem was similar to that which had disturbed the army during Brooke's boyhood. The two basic causes were strict adherence to seniority in promotion and the failure to provide any system of retirement. Disillusionment was marked in the lower grades, for in 1840 there were passed midshipmen who had been in the service for sixteen years.[23] Like others, Brooke would complain of these outmoded practices and, with his somber yet impatient disposition, would at times become discouraged.

It had been the threat of war with Great Britain in 1841 which had given Brooke his chance by raising the appointments of midshipmen to flood tide; he was only one of fourteen midshipmen appointed on March 3, 1841, the last day of President Martin Van Buren's administration. The flood continued as a total of 224 midshipmen were appointed in 1841, the largest number that had ever been appointed in one year. At the end of the year there were 195 passed midshipmen and 262 midshipmen in the navy.[24] This huge influx led to legislation in 1842 limiting future appointments.

[22] Harold and Margaret Sprout, *The Rise of American Naval Power, 1776–1918* (Princeton, N.J., 1946), p. 5.

[23] W. D. Puleston, *Annapolis, Gangway to Quarterdeck* (New York, 1942), p. 38.

[24] Appointments, Orders, and Resignations, RG 45, NA; U.S. Congress, *Senate Documents*, Report of Secretary of the Navy Abel P. Upshur, 9 Feb. 1842, 27th Cong., 2d sess., vol. 2, no. 109, p. 10.

When Brooke made the initial entry in his *Delaware* journal on May 7, 1841, he was two years younger than the average newly appointed midshipman of his day.[25] Not only was he young, but he was small. He had fair skin, ruddy complexion, and dark hair; his intense blue eyes were clear, luminous, and penetrating. He was an active and agile boy, as is attested by his skills as a swimmer and fencer, and he soon demonstrated manual dexterity in the handling of instruments. Intelligent, ambitious and observant, Brooke possessed an inquiring mind and a reflective disposition. These qualities, coupled with an interest in natural phenomena, predisposed him to scientific investigation. Essentially a student, Brooke had little time for pranks, banter, and gossip. Routine bored him and he was impatient toward those who lacked his talents or did not share his views. Through life he would be one to cultivate a few close friends of similar interests rather than seek popularity. Serious by nature without much sense of humor, he must have appeared aloof—even arrogant—to his young contemporaries. On the surface, however, with his natty blue uniform and dirk Brooke was not very different from the usual cocky midshipman of his day. Certainly the youngsters assigned to the *Delaware* had some reason to strut. Their vessel was a 74-gun ship of the line and her destination was rumored to be the Mediterranean, the choicest station of all. The great ships of the line formed the backbone of the navy in the days of wood and canvas.

While John Brooke was learning the regimen for midshipmen and the whims of his superior officers, others were considering the problem of his eventual place in society. Brooke's uncle, Colonel William Garnett of Norfolk, who saw more of Brooke than any other elder kinsman, wrote him a long letter of advice. Colonel Garnett, collector of customs at Norfolk and a prominent Whig, warned his nephew to use "the utmost caution in the selection of your associates." He pointed out that "a state of debt is a state of slavery," and urged Brooke to "study economy, keeping [expenditures] always within your income." Garnett then referred to the inadequacy of his nephew's education, caused by his "premature

[25] Register of Applications for Appointments as Midshipmen, RG 45, NA.

(*10*)

entrance upon public life," and advised that he "lose no opportunity to repair the loss you have thereby sustained." Garnett was especially concerned with education; he was president of the board of trustees of Norfolk Academy and had made the principal address at the laying of the school's cornerstone the year before. Brooke's uncle placed primary emphasis upon technical subjects such as navigation, seamanship, and mathematics. Colonel Garnett's fourth point concerned religion, which he felt was "the Alpha and Omega of our existence." Young Brooke should read a chapter of the Bible daily so that he could learn God's will. Finally, Garnett suggested that the boy call on his superiors for advice "as often as you may feel the necessity for it."[26]

Aboard the *Delaware* educational facilities were poor. Until a permanent school was established at Annapolis, the instruction of midshipmen was haphazard and dependent upon the ship commander. To learn through practical experience was the credo of many veterans who looked back to the fabulous exploits of the navy in the distant past. Endless repetition of practical tasks meant that what was learned was learned well.[27] But naval ships did have libraries, and although most of the books were technical treatises, there were some of a biographical and historical nature.

As a practical matter, it was to the older officers of the *Delaware* that Brooke and his steerage mates looked for advice and instruction. The commanding officer was a capable Pennsylvanian, Captain Charles S. McCauley, who had spent sixteen years at sea, but the officer to whom the youngsters turned most frequently was the first lieutenant, David Glasgow Farragut. Farragut, the adopted son of Commodore David Porter, had gone to sea at ten and in 1841 was a veteran of thirty years' service, half of which time had been spent at sea. An able and inspiring leader, though not of the "spit and polish" school, he made a deep impression on young Brooke, who was filing his first mental notes on the attributes of a competent naval officer. A third of a century later

[26] Garnett to Brooke, 1 June 1841, BP; "The Norfolk Academy, 1840," in Edward Wilson James, ed., *Lower Norfolk County Antiquary*, 2 vols. (1908; rept. New York, 1951), 4:161.

[27] Secretary of the Navy [George E. Badger], "Our Navy," *New York Review* 9 (July 1841): 153.

Brooke recalled "that he never saw greater skill in administering affairs than Farragut displayed in controling and organizing the crew of eight hundred men."[28] It was on this cruise that Farragut was promoted to commander.

Brooke was eager to get to sea, but not until June 4, after a delay of two months, was the *Delaware* towed into Hampton Roads. Then for another two months the officers and crew were drilled on the great guns and with small arms as the ship moved up and down Chesapeake Bay. The addition of four Paixhans guns to the armament and the trial of a new type of patent carriage on two main deck guns quickened interest. Routine gun drill was enlivened by occasional target practice. To facilitate loading the great guns, Farragut designed a contrivance to hoist powder from the magazine to the gun. Captain McCauley ordered a demonstration under simulated battle conditions to test the effectiveness of Farragut's invention and the efficiency of the crew. The results were highly satisfactory: the main deck gun divisions fired three broadsides in four minutes. It was a lucky accident for Brooke on his first cruise to be assigned to a ship where gunnery and ordnance were emphasized, for on most United States warships little time was devoted to those subjects.[29]

Late in September, Brooke received orders detaching him from the *Delaware* and directing him to report at Norfolk for duty aboard the sloop of war *Cyane*, which had been assigned to the Pacific Squadron. He was destined to spend the next three years on the *Cyane*, a very different vessel from the stately old *Delaware*. Three-masted and square-rigged, she mounted twenty-two guns on her single gun deck and carried a crew of 164 men. Eager to make a good impression on the commanding officer, Commander Cornelius K. Stribling, Brooke asked and received permission to exercise sails during the week before the the sloop's departure.[30]

[28] Kate Corbin Brooke Diary, 30 Dec. 1874, BP.

[29] Charles Lee Lewis, *David Glasgow Farragut, Admiral in the Making* (Annapolis, 1941), pp. 222–23; J. M. Brooke Journal of the *Delaware*, 23 July 1841, BP. Farragut was the navy's first admiral, and his superb qualities as a leader were demonstrated in the Civil War. See Daniel J. Carrison, *The Navy from Wood to Steel, 1860–1890* (New York, 1965).

[30] Vessels of the U.S. Navy, RG 45, NA; J. M. Brooke Journal of the *Cyane*, 31 Oct. 1841, BP.

After breakfast on November 1, 1841, a cool, clear day, the *Cyane* "got under weigh and stood out for hampton Roads." By late afternoon many of the officers and seamen were seasick, and the cynical gunner, William H. Mcyers, recorded "Dr. Garnet dying Midn Brooks dead." [31] Two days later, he noted that there was "an awful sight among the Midshipmen." Throughout his career, Brooke was to suffer from seasickness at the beginning of every cruise.

On December 13 the *Cyane* rounded Cape Frio and dropped anchor in the beautiful harbor of Rio de Janeiro, the rendezvous of the Brazil Squadron. No less than five American warships lay at anchor when the *Cyane* came to. In Rio the sloop's hold was stowed with beef and vegetables, her sails were removed, and she was readied for the long trip around Cape Horn to Valparaiso, Chile. As this work progressed Brooke became accustomed to the formalities that surrounded a warship in foreign ports.

The *Cyane* then stood out to sea, heading for Cape Horn. Anticipating the worst, a multitude of preparations were made as the vessel neared the treacherous cape, but she made it through the usual heavy squalls and vicious head winds with no serious incident. Rounding Cape Horn the *Cyane* ran north, stopping at Valparaiso, Arica, and Callao, the seaport for Lima and rendezvous of the Pacific Squadron.

From Valparaiso, Brooke wrote his father that he was pleased with the naval profession. At Arica, which was in dispute between Peru and Bolivia, Brooke witnessed first the Bolivian flag above the town and then the Peruvian. In Callao, a town of five thousand with a large assortment of dram shops, the sailors were given their first liberty since leaving the United States. To officers a principal attraction of the Peruvian city was the Marine Hotel, operated by a courteous Frenchman. Few youngsters owned a complete wardrobe to wear on shore leave, but as never more than half the midshipmen were given leave at one time, an outfit of sorts could be assembled by borrowing. At Callao, Brooke was

[31] Extracts from the Journal of William H. Meyers, Gunner on Board the U.S.S. *Cyane*, 1841–43, on a Cruise to the Pacific and Return (photostatic copy), RG 45, NA. "Dr. Garnet" was Alexander Yelverton Peyton Garnett, Brooke's second cousin.

first called on to tack ship, and "though flustered he gave the orders correctly in a clear voice through the trumpet and was complimented by the boatswain."[32]

On May 15, 1842, the frigate *United States*, flagship of the Pacific Squadron, arrived from the Atlantic coast. She brought Brooke a letter from his father, the first since he had entered the navy more than a year earlier. The general averred that his delay in writing did not proceed "from any want of affection, for you, and William, are seldom absent from my thoughts." He blamed the apparent neglect on the uncertainty of the mails. The letter contained both news and advice. Wrote the general: "You will perceive as I often told you, how necessary it will be, for you, to understand & speak the French & Spanish languages. . . . I therefore hope you will pay the utmost attention to them. I am very well satisfied with your exchange to the *Cyane*, as I know, the Captain Cornelius K. Stribling, very well, & I have the highest opinion of his moral and religious worth, as well as his skilful semanship. You are now in an excellent school both, as it regards your profession, your habits and your intellectual improvement & your character & manners as a gentleman."[33] In subsequent letters the general reiterated the importance of being able to speak French and Spanish fluently, and he also sought to impress upon his son the necessity for economy.

On board the flagship *United States* was Commodore Thomas ap Catesby Jones, younger brother of General Roger Jones, the adjutant general of the army. Dubbed the "Contentious Commodore" by his biographer, Jones was rated an able though not a great officer. Often unpopular and always feared, Jones was a strict disciplinarian and at times tyrannical. The old commodore was quick to take offense and, unhappily, he lacked a sense of humor. Jones was an old hand in the Pacific and in 1826 had concluded an informal commercial treaty with the Hawaiian kingdom. Given the strained relations between the United States and

[32] Charles Robert Anderson, ed., *Journals of a Cruise to the Pacific Ocean, 1842–1844, in the Frigate* United States *with Notes on Herman Melville* (Durham, N.C., 1937), pp. 32 n.24, 125; Puleston, *Annapolis*, p. 40; Kate Corbin Brooke notes from conversations with Captain Brooke, 1896, BP.
[33] Brooke to Brooke, 26 Dec. 1841, BP.

Great Britain and the remoteness of the Pacific station from Washington, Jones's impulsive temperament promised a tempestuous cruise.[34]

Under Commodore Jones the Pacific Squadron consisted of a frigate, four sloops, a schooner, and a storeship. Its cruising ground stretched west to the 180th meridian and northward from the South Pole without limit. Jones was instructed to protect American commercial and whaling interests on the Pacific slope and among the islands of the South Seas. Also, it was his responsibility to keep a weather eye on California and to improve the discipline of his men by frequent drills and maneuvers.[35] In accordance with the last responsibility, Jones took his squadron to sea on May 31 and for two months engaged in fleet maneuvers, a type of training almost ignored in the navy of that day.

Meanwhile, a rumor spread that war had broken out between the United States and Mexico. When the British squadron at Callao put to sea with sealed orders, Jones and the American chargé at Lima suspected that the British were preparing to seize California. To prevent the British from grabbing Monterey, the *Cyane* and Jones's flagship, the *United States*, set sail for that port on September 8.[36]

On October 20 the *United States* and the *Cyane* entered the commodious harbor of Monterey. The British were no place to be seen. The next morning a storming party clambered ashore, and without a shot, the political, military, and social capital of the Mexican province of California fell. The transfer of sovereignty was celebrated by a twenty-six gun salute. But three hours later, according to Brooke's journal, all hands on the *Cyane* were called to muster and read a communication from the commodore stating

[34] Udolpho Theodore Bradley, "The Contentious Commodore, Thomas ap Catesby Jones," Ph.D. diss., Cornell University, 1933.

[35] *Senate Documents*, Report of Secretary of the Navy Upshur, 4 Dec. 1841, 27th Cong., 2d sess., vol. 1, no. 1, pp. 368–69.

[36] All of the correspondence of the Monterey affair is to be found in U.S. Congress, *House Executive Documents*, 27th Cong., 3d sess., vol. 5, no. 166. See also Letters from Officers Commanding Squadrons, RG 45, NA; Brooke Journal of the *Cyane*, BP; Journal of Alonzo C. Johnson, Midshipman aboard the Frigate *United States* (Nov. 3, 1841–June 9, 1844), 20 Oct. 1842, Manuscripts Division, Library of Congress (hereafter cited as MSS Div., LC); Meyers's Journal of the *Cyane*, RG 45, NA; Log of the *Cyane*, Ships' Logs, 1801–1942, RG 24, NA; Bradley, "Contentious Commodore," pp. 143–63.

that as he had received information "that there was no war with Mexico: the Town and Fort of Monterey would be immediately restored to the Mexican authorities." When the Americans "sent to the Mexican authorities 95 lbs. of powder to replace that expended by us while in possession of the fort," it seemed harmony had been restored.

Following the incident, Jones kept his squadron on the move. He boasted to the secretary of the navy that in one eight months' period his squadron "had sailed more and visited more ports, than any former squadron on this station ever before did, in a full cruize of three years."[37] On the *Cyane*, Brooke energetically cultivated his talent for drawing and painting, and on later cruises he often illustrated his journals with sketches and watercolors. Every few months he received letters and bundles of newspapers from his father. Meanwhile the ambitious young officer was laying a solid professional base for his career. When Commander Stribling reported on the character and conduct of the midshipmen serving under him, he commented favorably on eight of them, including Brooke. This was not automatic, for Stribling gave unfavorable reports on four midshipmen.[38] During the cruise the Navy Department also showed its confidence in the young acting midshipman by sending him his midshipman's warrant.

The firm discipline and thorough training demanded by Commander Stribling in time produced an efficient naval unit. At San Diego the officers and crew of the *Cyane* demonstrated the extreme importance of iron discipline, prompt obedience to orders, and careful training. One calm day all of the guns on the *Cyane* "were loosed from their moorings to be painted." Suddenly and without warning the vessel lurched. With a frightful roar the guns hurtled across the deck like a stampede of elephants. According to Brooke, every man sprang to his post "in spite of the horrible danger of going among such irresponsible machines governed only by the swelling and pitching of the sea. The hammocks were thrown in to interrupt their career and every gun was speedily put

[37] Jones to Abel P. Upshur, 1 Feb. 1843, Letters from Officers Commanding Squadrons, RG 45, NA.
[38] Stribling to Jones, 27 May 1842, ibid.

in position and secured." The crew acted so quickly that no damage was sustained.[39]

In July the *Cyane* left the California coast and steered for Honolulu in quest of fresh provisions. In 1843 Honolulu was a thriving city at the crossroads of the North Pacific and was the rendezvous for the great whaling fleets. Brooke was in the Hawaiian city at an historic time, for in the preceding February Lord George Paulet, commanding H.M.S. *Carysfort*, had seized the islands for the British crown, on his own responsibility. In July, Paulet's arbitrary action was repudiated by Rear Admiral Richard Thomas, commanding the British Pacific Squadron, and on July 31 at a picturesque ceremony the Hawaiian flag was raised again. King Kamehameha III ordered a ten-day celebration, and when the *Cyane* arrived on August 4, the gala events were in full swing. The *Cyane* quickly absorbed the festive spirit, sending twelve national flags to the ballroom on shore.

Returning to the coast of California, the *Cyane* cruised for seven months between San Francisco and Valparaiso, finally receiving orders at Callao to proceed to the United States via Cape Horn. Commander Stribling was transferred to the *United States*, and Commander George Nichols Hollins was given command of the *Cyane* for the trip home. Brooke had seen long, hard service under Stribling, and before the latter left the *Cyane* he gave Brooke a strong letter of recommendation. It reads: "I have great pleasure in stating, that during the period of two years and eight months that you have been under my command, your general attention to duty and correct conduct as a gentleman, have been such as to merit and obtain my approbation of your character and conduct, both as an Officer and Gentleman."[40]

Before leaving Callao some of the officers had a final fling. Brooke accompanied the *Cyane* gunner Meyers and Midshipman Thomas Roney on a jaunt to Lima; it was a feast day with troops parading, music, and the tramp of cavalry. The young men "spent the day very pleasantly," and after attending the theater, they

[39] Kate Corbin Brooke Diary, 12 Sept. 1874, BP.
[40] Stribling to Brooke, 6 June 1844, BP.

repaired to a hotel where they indulged in an elegant supper with champagne.[41]

On the homeward voyage Brooke made very brief and often incomplete entries in his journal. The *Cyane* made straight for Cape Horn, and soon the daily entries referred to nothing but weather conditions and adjustments of the sails. Rounding the Horn in July, the dead of winter below the equator, was a man-killing job which allowed no respite. Richard Henry Dana once noted that July was "the worst month of the year there; when the sun rises at nine and sets at three, giving eighteen hours night, and there is snow and rain, gales and high seas, in abundance." On arrival at Norfolk, Commander Hollins gave Brooke a letter of recommendation stating that "during the time you have served on board this Ship under my command your gentlemanly and of-ficerlike conduct and strict attention to duty have met with my en-tire approbation."[42] On October 5 orders were prepared de-taching Brooke from the *Cyane* and granting him three months' leave.

Brooke stayed in Norfolk with the Garnetts while arranging plans through the mail for a reunion with his father and brother William; General Brooke was stationed in Detroit and William was attending school in Kingston, Rhode Island. John Brooke had not seen his father since leaving Green Bay as a boy. As matters worked out, John and William spent a few days visiting their Thomas relatives in Duxbury, Massachusetts, and then joined their father in New York City. The general took Brooke to a tailor to have him outfitted, but there is no evidence that Brooke ever took any particular pride in the way he dressed. Later, after a sec-ond visit to Duxbury, Brooke rejoined his father in Washington. After this reunion, the general lived for six more years, but Brooke never saw him again.

Returning to Norfolk to await his next assignment, young Brooke, now eighteen, began to think of the examination that he must pass before advancing to the grade of passed midshipman. Such examinations were given periodically, and generally, youths

[41] Meyers, Journal of the *Cyane*, 6 June 1844, RG 45, NA.

[42] Richard Henry Dana, *Two Years before the Mast* (1840; Modern Library ed., New York, 1936), p. 298; Hollins to Brooke, 10 Oct. 1844, BP.

who had entered the service in the same year took the examinations together. Midshipmen on distant stations, however, could not always return to the United States in time to take the examinations and were forced to wait a year or more. As the time for the examination drew near, it was, therefore, a matter of concern where a midshipman was stationed. The navy maintained several temporary schools staffed by professors of mathematics to prepare unassigned midshipmen for the examinations. As both midshipmen and professors were subject to call by the Navy Department, the student body and faculty underwent constant change at these schools and no regular system of instruction could be prescribed.

Commodore Charles Morris, chief of the Bureau of Construction and one of General Brooke's close friends, believed that there was no school like a warship at sea, and he strongly urged that John Brooke go to sea rather than mark time at a school ashore waiting for the examination. Morris thought it probable "that the examination will be deferred until '47," but that in any event, "the young men go, to the school, generally too soon." Commodore Lawrence Kearny, another of the general's friends, "perfectly coincided in opinion with Comdre Morris."[43]

While awaiting orders in Norfolk, Midshipman Brooke became more restless every day. His anxiety was augmented by a lack of funds, and he gained slight solace from his father's promise to send him $100 "if possible." Impatient for an assignment, Brooke began to consider any form of naval service that might be available, rather than to wait for assignment to the *Congress*—a frigate bound for the Mediterranean—which his father had arranged at his request. In alarm, the general wrote that his son should "not think of going aboard the Southampton & never touch, a store ship; you might as well, try the merchant service at once."[44]

During the spring of 1845 while he was fretting in Norfolk, Brooke continued a lively correspondence with his old friend Frank Patterson, who was working for his father in Philadelphia. The two shared similar interests. Patterson, who had spent the summer of 1843 in the West, reported that hunting had been ex-

[43] General Brooke to Brooke, 31 March 1845, BP.
[44] Ibid., 22 April 1845.

cellent and that he had shot a bull elk the first day. Around Norfolk, Brooke found hunting a poor imitation of that on the Pacific coast. Patterson was completely sympathetic, exclaiming: "You speak of a want of gaiety and vigor, any man who has dropped a buck & received notice to quit from a grissly bear & than descends to robin stalking! Oh fie! I wonder yr eye has not faded & yr legs dwindled!" Patterson did not always comprehend his friend's use of slang, once writing: "I am glad to hear that you are 'hard up' but wd. be much better pleased if [I] knew what in the devil you meant by it."[45]

General Brooke finally promised his son that he would ask Commodore W. Compton Bolton to have him assigned temporarily to the receiving ship *Pennsylvania* at Norfolk. The orders came through, and on May 13 the restless midshipman reported for duty aboard that vessel. Though she was the largest ship in the navy, the *Pennsylvania*, like receiving ships at other stations, was not considered a vessel "in commission for Sea Service."[46] A receiving ship absorbed recruits into the navy and held them until they were assigned to some warship in commission. But in the summer of 1845, when Brooke was on the *Pennsylvania*, there was little for the ship to do because of the temporary suspension of enlistments. The navy was in the doldrums as the merchant service, with higher pay and shorter cruises, attracted the best trained seamen and left the navy the scum.

On the *Pennsylvania* Brooke received perfunctory instruction from the professor of mathematics. Matthew Fontaine Maury's *Navigation* had recently been adopted as the "Text Book of the Navy," and midshipmen were required "to make themselves acquainted with at least so much of Mathematics, Nautical Astronomy, and the other kindred branches of Navigation, as is therein contained."[47] Professors of mathematics were charged with execution of the order. Personal diligence, however, was a midshipman's only guarantee of knowledge. Forewarned, Brooke had obtained two months before assignment to the *Pennsylvania* a

[45] Patterson to Brooke, Dec. 1843, 6 March 1845, BP.
[46] Directives (Circulars and General Orders), 1798–1895, Office of the Secretary of the Navy, RG 45, NA.
[47] Order issued by Secretary of the Navy John Y. Mason, 4 Sept. 1844, ibid.

copy of *Outlines of Naval Routine* by Lieutenant Alexander Fordyce of the Royal Navy and had made extensive use of it. Perhaps the greatest benefit he received aboard the receiving ship was the opportunity to serve under David Farragut again. But Brooke was impatient on the receiving ship; he wanted sea service.

The waiting ended when Brooke received an order detaching him from the receiving ship as of October 1 and directing him to report to the frigate *Columbia* bound for the Brazil station. Before leaving the *Pennsylvania* he secured another recommendation from Farragut. "It affords me great pleasure to be able to state to your next commanding officer," wrote Farragut, "that your conduct while under my command, both as an Officer and a Gentleman have merited my highest commendation." He added that "it will afford me great pleasure at all times to be associated with you on duty."[48]

The *Columbia* was the flagship of Commodore Lawrence Rousseau, newly appointed commander of the Brazil Squadron, which was charged with the protection of American commerce along the east coast of South America from Rio de Janeiro to the mouth of the Rio de la Plata. Rousseau, a veteran of thirty-six years' service, was "the first officer west of the Alleghenies ever selected to command a squadron." He was an old friend of General Brooke's and the latter wrote his son that he had been "much gratified, to learn, by the papers, that the Columbia, was to be Comdre Rousseau's flagship," for there was not an officer in the navy "with whom, I should prefer you, to sail." Lest Brooke take advantage of the commodore's kind nature, his father warned that "instead of its making you, the least inattentive, to your duties . . . it should be, the very reverse."[49] The ship's captain was Robert Ritchie, a tough disciplinarian. Brooke was the ranking midshipman on the *Columbia*, which had a crew of four hundred.

The run to Rio de Janeiro was marred by the outbreak of smallpox. By the time the *Columbia* reached the Brazilian port thirty-eight cases of the disease had been diagnosed aboard, and the epidemic took four lives. Brooke, fortunately, escaped the

[48] Farragut to Brooke, 1 Oct. 1845, BP.

[49] *Senate Documents*, Report of Secretary of the Navy George Bancroft, 1 Dec. 1845, 29th Cong., 1st sess., vol. 1, no. 1, p. 645; Brooke to Brooke, 16 Oct. 1845, BP.

disease. The next month, the *Columbia* and the sloop *Saratoga* sailed for Montevideo where the Colorados and Blancos were engaged in a civil war. The British and French gave active support to the Colorados, landing troops at Montevideo and proclaiming a blockade of all ports held by the Blancos. The United States recognized the blockade and followed a policy of strict neutrality. The observant Brooke witnessed the internecine fighting and the foreign intervention. At that time there was an uprising within the city and a reign of terror. Commodore Rousseau sent ashore a guard of twelve marines for the protection of American lives and property and prepared to send in the entire marine guard of the flagship. But in the end, reinforcement was not necessary.[50]

The *Columbia* stayed in port for unusually long periods of time performing routine duties. The captain's policy of granting almost no shore leave made morale low. Although corporal punishment was a mainstay on naval vessels, few captains resorted to it as often as Ritchie. Testifying before a court of inquiry some years later, Brooke stated that Ritchie had "oppressed his junior officers and punished the men indiscriminately." Of a sensitive nature, the young officer did not feel that flogging was the best way to enforce discipline.[51]

On May 12, 1846, the United States Congress declared war on Mexico, but news of the outbreak of hostilities did not reach the Brazil station until July 9. Brooke, however, had been forewarned in letters from Colonel Garnett and his father. In February, Uncle William had written that "our affairs with Mexico seem to threaten war more than at any period since the annexation of Texas." This letter arrived two months ahead of news of the war declaration. General Brooke, writing in March, had expressed the view that though the situation was tense the United States would settle the boundaries of Texas and secure California without going to war with its southern neighbor. Knowledge of the war had

[50] Fleet Surgeon Benjamin K. Tinslar to Rousseau, 6 Jan. 1846, Rousseau to the Secretary of the Navy, 20 Jan., 2 Feb., 25 April 1846, Letters from Officers Commanding Squadrons, RG 45, NA; Brooke Journal of the *Columbia*, 10 Jan. 1846, BP; Charles Edward Chapman, *Republican Hispaniç America: A History* (New York, 1938), pp. 341–46.

[51] Brooke Journal, 23 Oct. 1857, BP. For a comparison of punishments on all warships during this period, see *Senate Documents*, Report of the Secretary of the Navy Mason, 6 Feb. 1849, 30th Cong., 2d sess., vol. 3, no. 23, pp. 1–341.

little effect upon the *Columbia*. The immediate result was the exercise of one gun in each division for the next three days; then activity settled back into the old routine. The squadron's function remained unchanged, as, in the words of the secretary of the navy, it "secured protection to American commerce within the limits of its operations." In modern parlance, the men of the Brazil Squadron were going to sit out the war.[52]

Midshipman Brooke, however, remained on the Brazil station only two months after news of the war reached Rio, for Secretary of the Navy George Bancroft issued the following circular: "As the number of midshipmen of the date of 1841, being one hundred and eighty six is larger than can be conveniently examined at one time, and as the number of the date of 1842 is too small to form a separate class, all those appointed between January 1841 and July 1842 inclusive, will be ordered to report for examination in such numbers and at such times as the interests of the service will allow. In order however that an equal chance may be afforded to all, the numbers of relative merit will not be assigned, until all within those dates shall have had an opportunity of being examined."[53] Promotion to the rank of passed midshipman depended upon passing the examination, and Brooke's relative rank would be determined by his grade.

With such a large number of aspirants and promotion so slow, relative rank established at the beginning of his career could have lifelong effects for Brooke. Promotion above passed midshipman was based entirely on seniority; this examination was the only time when he could expect to benefit directly from hard work and native intelligence. Brooke was eager to get back to the States in order to "bone up." In June he was authorized "to return to the United States in the first public vessel coming from the Brazil station, or if you prefer it, you may return at your own expense in a private vessel, without waiting for a public one."[54]

This authorization must be credited to Colonel Garnett, who

[52] Garnett to Brooke, 28 Feb. 1846, Brooke to Brooke, 28 March 1846, and Brooke Journal of the *Columbia*, 8–10 July 1846, BP; *Senate Documents*, Report of Secretary of the Navy Mason, 5 Dec. 1846, 29th Cong., 2d sess., vol. 1, no. 1, p. 378.

[53] Circular to Midshipmen, Feb. 26, 1846, Circulars and General Orders, RG 45, NA.

[54] Bancroft to Brooke, 20 June 1846, Letters to Officers, RG 45, NA.

had asked his congressman to intercede with Secretary Bancroft for Brooke's relief. The naval school at Annapolis had just recently been established by Bancroft, and according to newspaper reports it had a model steamship and other apparatus of a most useful nature to midshipmen preparing for the examination. The intensity and scope of the tests had been substantially increased, and the portion devoted to steam navigation was comprehensive. It was Uncle William's conviction that those midshipmen who had a chance to study at Annapolis before the examination would enjoy a pronounced advantage over those who did not.

The day after receiving his orders, Brooke left Rio on the *Anahuac*, an American bark loaded with a cargo of coffee. With him Brooke carried a letter of recommendation from Rousseau stating that "your conduct while under my command has been highly satisfactory." Reaching New York on October 25, Brooke proceeded immediately to Norfolk. There, Brooke received orders to report to "Commander [Franklin] Buchanan for attendance at the Naval School" in Annapolis, Maryland.[55] He reported on November 10, 1846, apparently a few weeks after classes had begun. The new school on the Severn, which came to be called the Naval Academy, was located on the site of an old army post. It was small and crude when Brooke enrolled, but under the capable leadership of Commander Buchanan, a strict disciplinarian of forty-five, it was assuming an air of permanence. Nine buildings and a gatehouse had been transferred to the navy for the school, and the superintendent had converted them into midshipmen's barracks, recitation rooms, and a mess hall. Brooke lived in Brandywine Cottage, originally a brick bakehouse, named by a group of midshipmen "who had sailed around Cape Horn in the Brandywine prior to arriving at Annapolis."[56] In 1846 about one-third of the midshipmen who had joined the navy in 1841 matriculated at the academy, and still more would enter in 1847 and 1848. During the school year 1846–47, when Brooke was at Annapolis, there were some fifty-six midshipmen enrolled. The ages of the midshipmen ranged from thirteen to twenty-eight; Brooke was nineteen.

[55] Rousseau to Brooke, 12 Sept. 1846, John Y. Mason to Brooke, 27 Oct. 1846, BP.
[56] Puleston, *Annapolis*, p. 57.

The curriculum for the nine-month course was rugged. Despite his late arrival, however, Brooke's grades were well above average and improved steadily. From November to April his unweighted weekly average climbed from 5.75 to 8.4 on the basis of 10 as a perfect mark. Generally speaking, he did his best work in those subjects in which there were frequent recitations. Perhaps he considered those scheduled at less frequent intervals of lesser importance. Brooke showed his steadiest improvement in mathematics, but he also showed a striking improvement in gunnery after getting off to a poor start. He excelled in natural philosophy (physics), astronomy, and grammar.[57] Brooke also found time to draw caricatures of his professors; his sketches of William Chauvenet, who taught navigation and mathematics, and Arsene Girault, professor of French, have survived.

At the academy there was little to distract Brooke from the prescribed course of study. Although the school was subject to navy regulations and the specific orders of the superintendent, military routine was dispensed with. Buchanan did insist that instructors and students alike comport themselves as gentlemen. Insubordination, improper conduct, and a lack of mental ability were all causes for prompt dismissal. The midshipmen at Annapolis did not wear uniforms or march to class. They were allowed to visit Annapolis, but that sleepy little town offered scant diversion.

By February, Brooke had hit his stride and was working very hard. In fact, he was working so hard that he neglected his correspondence, and his father, now commander of the Western Division of the army, inquired whether he was "sick, or angry, or studying, to[o] hard." General Brooke wrote his son frequently from New Orleans, admonishing him not to underestimate his classmates and to "study just as hard as if every one of them, was a Sir Isaac Newton."[58] Brooke was progressing satisfactorily in his studies, but his financial situation remained as critical as ever.

---

[57] No records of early grades are preserved at the United States Naval Academy. Among the Brooke Papers, however, is a record Brooke kept at Annapolis which shows his weekly grades in mathematics, philosophy, chemistry, gunnery, grammar, French, and astronomy.

[58] Brooke to Brooke, 24 April, 23 Feb. 1847, BP.

His father reminded him that debt "has been the cause of the destruction of many, of the cleverest fellows, in the world" and that "a man, does not feel like a gentleman, when he is subject, to be dunned every moment, in the day." Uniforms were a heavy expense to junior officers in the navy, and as the time for Brooke's examination drew near, General Brooke promised to notify Owen and Evans, military and naval tailors in Washington, D.C., that he would pay for any uniforms his son should need. In June the general sent $100 to cover such expenses and offered to send more money if necessary.

After the months of intensive preparation Midshipman Brooke was examined by the Board of Naval Examiners early in July 1847. On July 21 he was notified by Commodore Thomas ap Catesby Jones, president of the board, that he had passed. Two years later, when all the results were in for the midshipmen who had entered the service in 1841, the record showed Brooke standing thirty-fifth among the 136 who passed the examination; 50 men failed. Brooke was given the relative stand determined by his examination grade.[59]

[59] This information was adduced from a study of United States *Navy Registers* and the printed records of the United States Naval Academy Graduates Association.

II /

FURTHER CRUISING,

MARRIAGE, AND THE

COAST SURVEY

As a new passed midshipman John Brooke had little time to reflect on his elevated status or to consider how he would spend his additional $300 annual pay. Along with the news that he had passed the examination came orders to report to the steamer *Princeton* at Philadelphia, which he did the next day. Assignment to the iron-hulled frigate *Princeton*, under orders to the Mediterranean, gave Brooke the chance to study at close range the operation of one of the newest and finest ships in the navy. Launched in 1843, this revolutionary vessel was regarded as one of the wonders of the age. The first warship in the world to utilize the screw propeller successfully, she combined the mobility of steam locomotion with the adequate deck space and firepower of the sailing vessel. She was also the first warship to burn anthracite coal, a fuel which did not produce the dense clouds of black smoke that had hitherto betrayed the approach of steamers. Nonetheless, the *Princeton* was a full-rigged ship, and her steam engines, placed safely below the water line, were designed to be used as an auxiliary source of power. On the *Princeton*, commanded by Commander Frederick Engle, Brooke applied the lessons in steam navigation he had learned at Annapolis. He was fortunate indeed to be included in the ship's small complement of 151 officers and men, of whom 6 were midshipmen or passed midshipmen.[1]

While at Annapolis, John had believed he was in love with Mary Roy, whom he later described as the "prettiest girl in Maryland." Little is known of the romance. In the future there were shadowy references to this beauty, but apparently the affair died a natural death when Brooke shipped out of Annapolis. Not many months later Mary became engaged, and General Brooke, who had not married until he was a field-grade officer and opposed early marriages, was noticeably relieved. "I hear Miss Rob is engaged, to midshipman Jones," he wrote. "So much the better for you, & I am pleased you got out of that scrape."[2]

The *Princeton*'s hasty departure presented to Passed Midshipman Brooke a situation that showed his enterprising nature. He had turned over his dirty clothes to a washerwoman, but as the hour for sailing drew near, he found he did not have the two dollars necessary to pay her. Being in his own words "extravagant and reckless," Brooke feared his shipmates would be reluctant to lend him the money. Embarrassed by his predicament, he resolved to raise the money through a wager. Standing on the ladder of the port gangway with another officer, he abruptly asked his companion what he would give him to jump overboard. No sooner had the unwary officer said, "Twenty dollars," than Brooke, shaking his hand to seal the pledge, made the plunge. When asked to pay up, the surprised officer reluctantly produced sixteen dollars from his locker. Brooke told his victim that he only wanted two dollars to pay his laundress. As a matter of fact, the conscientious young officer considered the two dollars a loan and later repaid it.[3]

The *Princeton* sailed from Philadelphia for Gibraltar on July 23, 1847. Technically, she was a part of the Mediterranean

[1] Complement of Officers and Men Allowed on the U.S. Ship *Princeton*, Circulars and General Orders, RG 45, NA.
[2] Brooke to Brooke, 2 Feb. 1848, BP.
[3] Kate Corbin Brooke Diary, 21 Aug. 1874, BP.

Squadron commanded by Commodore George C. Read, who carried his flag on the frigate *United States*, but Engle did not effect a junction with Read for nine months. Instead, on his own responsibility, he played a lone hand in the Mediterranean and reported directly to the secretary of the navy. Leaving Gibraltar early in September, the *Princeton* was extremely active, visiting twenty ports in the next three months. As a steamer she was able to do the work of more than three sailing sloops of war, but the short supply of anthracite coal on the station was a constant source of annoyance. In these years the Mediterranean Squadron had no regular rendezvous and had to obtain supplies from store ships sent out from the United States. Because the Mexican War was still raging, the *Princeton*'s commander had been ordered to be especially vigilant for Mexican privateers, but during Brooke's service on the steamer not a single privateer was seized. Spain adhered steadfastly to the Treaty of 1795 and its "honorable conduct" was a source of considerable satisfaction to Secretary of the Navy John Young Mason.[4]

On September 30, three weeks out of Gibraltar, the *Princeton* dropped anchor at Genoa, having visited Almeria, Oran, Xavia, Barcelona, and Marseilles. At Genoa, Brooke conducted experiments in mesmerism and clairvoyance. The subject was the steward of the officers' mess, Nathaniel Bishop, "a mulatto about 26 years of age, in good health but of an exciteable disposition." As Brooke later explained, "The first experiment was of the magnetic or mesmeric sleep which overpowered him in thirty minutes from the commencement of passes made in the ordinary way accompanied with a steadfast gaze and effort of will that he should sleep. In this state he was insensible to all voices but mine unless I directed or willed him to hear others, he was also insensible to such amount of pain, or what would have been pain to another as one might inflict without injury."[5]

Brooke had previously witnessed experiments in mesmerism that he had regarded as "satisfactory," but he had never accepted clairvoyance. In fact, he had always considered clairvoyance as

[4] Engle to Mason, 19 Nov., 7 Sept. 1847, Letters from Officers Commanding Squadrons, RG 45, NA; Mason to Engle, 24 Sept. 1847, Confidential Letters Sent, RG 45, NA.
[5] Brooke to Francis Wayland, [27 Oct. 1851] (copy), BP.

"nothing more than a sort of dreaming produced by the will of the operator." Aboard the *Princeton*, however, Brooke made tests in clairvoyance that convinced him of the validity of this strange power. Once again Bishop was the subject. The steward's accurate and confident answers to difficult questions, shortly after coming out of a mesmeric sleep, had induced Brooke and his fellow officers to believe that Bishop might be clairvoyant. Perhaps the most dramatic experiment to verify this belief was conducted one evening aboard the steamer in the harbor of Genoa when the captain was on shore. Brooke "asked Bishop in the presence of several officers where the Capt. [Engle] then was." Bishop replied, "At the opera with Mr. Lester the Consul." Then Brooke inquired what the captain was saying. After appearing to listen, Bishop said, "The Capt. tells Mr. Lester that he was much pleased with the port of Xaira, that the authorities treated him with much consideration." When Engle returned one of the officers remarked that they had been listening to his conversation on shore. "Very well," Engle rejoined, "what did I say?" The officer repeated the conversation. "Ah! who was at the opera," Engle exclaimed. "I did not see any of the officers there." Brooke wrote later that the officer "then explained the matter, the Capt. confirmed its truth, and seemed very much surprised as there had been no other communication with the shore during the evening."[6]

The practical surgeons of the *Princeton* ridiculed the experiments and remained dubious. Some were persuaded by an experiment in telling time. While one of the surgeons stood alone—about ten feet from Bishop and Brooke—with a watch concealed in his hands, Bishop described the watch in detail and specified accurately the positions of the minute and second hands. When the wily doctor stopped the second hand, Bishop immediately called attention to the fact. The surgeon is said to have been convinced, exclaiming "that twas contrary to reason but he must believe." Brooke wrote his cousin Lizzie Garnett, "By the bye I could have heard some news from home for I magnetised our mess

[6] Ibid.

boy and proved the worth of clairvoyance so conclusively that the doctor a *sceptic* exclaimed I must believe although it appears contrary to reason." [7]

Three years after Brooke had conducted these investigations he described them to President Francis Wayland of Brown University at the latter's request. Wayland found Brooke's letter relating his experiences so extraordinary that he read it to his class in intellectual philosophy. And for Brooke he elucidated with enthusiasm his own views of clairvoyance: "the subject is one of very unusual interest. It opens to our view a range of facts of the most remarkable character and wholly at variance with our established notions. It was formerly laid down as an axiom that no knowledge of the external world could be given us except through the medium of the senses. It is now admitted by the highest authorities that in certain abnormal states of the mind cognition may take place without any action of the organs of sense." [8]

The Mediterranean cruise gave Brooke the chance to witness another revolution, this time the 1848 revolution in the Kingdom of the Two Sicilies. The target was Ferdinand II, derisively called "King Bomba." The *Princeton* arrived at Messina in January, and for the next two months divided her time between that port and Palermo. Although Engle's orders enjoined him to follow a neutral course, his sympathies lay with the rebels. On January 29 the American warship found herself in the midst of the fighting when the rebels launched an attack on the city of Messina. As the revolt spread, the royal forces evacuated the city and took up positions in the Citadel and other strongpoints. The rebels, or "the people" as the Americans called them, surged into Messina and hoisted the revolutionary flag in the public square. Some of the *Princeton*'s men were in Messina when the king's forces opened up with shell, grape, round shot, and musket fire from the surrounding forts. Commander Engle, who was in the city, reported that for fifteen minutes the grape dropped so fast around him that he could not reach his boat. The *Princeton* was in a vulnerable position, too, for she lay "steam down directly between the Citadel and Town"

[7] Ibid.; Brooke to Garnett, c. Nov. 1847, BP.
[8] Wayland to Brooke, 5 Nov. 1851, BP.

with firing on both sides. Surprisingly the steamer was not hit.[9]

From February 1 to March 10 the fighting continued intermittently, at times warming up with spirited exchanges of gunfire. The overall damage to the city was frightful, with as many as thirty-eight heavy shot entering a single house. Brooke wrote Lizzie Garnett: "Our Messinese friends have been horribly treated. Twenty thousand Neapolitan and mercenary troops, stormed their city; and the cowardly scoundrels, revenged themselves upon the inhabitants for their desperate resistance, by bombarding and cannonading the town for eight hours after its surrender. Six thousand refugees were crowded onboard one French ship of the line. The firing was most destructive." It was during these exciting days at Messina that Passed Midshipman Brooke began to keep a watch on the *Princeton*. The ship's log for February 21, 1848, reads: "From 8 to Mid calm and clear. Lieut Middleton left the ship on leave—flood made at 9—J. M. Brooke."[10]

At Messina the excitement gradually died down and a preliminary truce was negotiated between the royalists and the rebels. With harmony apparently restored, the *Princeton* shaped a course for Naples, arriving on March 20. Writing of the revolutionary activity in Naples, Brooke predicted that "at some unexpected moment there will be an outburst, and I think the people would do right if they hung the King and his advisers at the palace door, and massacred without exception every soldier in the Army: thus establishing the rights which these tyrants withold from them."[11]

Because the steamer needed repairs, Engle resolved to remain in the general vicinity while awaiting the arrival of Commodore Read in the *United States*. The junction was made in Leghorn Roads on April 3, and Brooke was transferred from the *Princeton* to the *United States*, flagship of the Mediterranean Squadron. The transfer to the "Old States" was recorded in that ship's log by Lieutenant John Rodgers, the officer of the watch. Thus began a

[9] Mason to Engle, 26 April 1848, Confidential Letters Sent, RG 45, NA; Engle to the President of the Comitato di Publica Sicurezza, 8 Feb. 1848 (copy), Engle to Mason, 30 Jan. 1848, Letters from Officers Commanding Squadrons, RG 45, NA.

[10] Engle kept Mason fully informed, writing him on 9 Feb., 16 Feb., 7 March, and 21 March (Letters from Officers Commanding Squadrons, RG 45, NA); Brooke to Garnett, 10 Sept. 1848, BP; Log of the *Princeton*, 27 Nov. 1846–31 Oct. 1848, RG 24, NA.

[11] Brooke to Garnett, 10 Sept. 1848, BP.

lifelong friendship between Brooke and Rodgers which was to deepen as the years passed.

Commodore Read, whom Brooke characterized as "that amiable old gentleman," did not practice Catesby Jones's policy of keeping his squadron on the move.[12] While Brooke was assigned to her, the *United States* spent 214 out of 275 days in Mediterranean ports.[13] Most of the nine months' period was spent in the Italian ports of Leghorn, Messina, Palermo, Syracuse, and La Spezia. Commodore Read made no attempt to mold the ships of his command into an effective striking force through fleet maneuvers.

The day Brooke transferred to the *United States*, that vessel left Leghorn and headed south along the coast for Naples. While she lay anchored in the Bay of Naples, Vesuvius was in an active state of eruption. Writing to Lizzie Garnett, Brooke described "the glowing crater of Vesuvius from which the red lava flows in sluggish streams, reminding one of the entrance to that place of which the preachers speak in such melting terms."[14]

Late in May the frigate cast anchor in the harbor of Messina again, where she lingered for nearly a month, ready to give aid to American citizens should they need it. Although in April the revolutionary parliament in Sicily had proclaimed Bourbon rule over the island at an end, the struggle was far from over. The wily King Ferdinand was merely waiting for a chance to withdraw his concessions. When the Neapolitan parliament convened on May 15, the king took advantage of a dispute to launch a counterrevolution. The *United States* did not intervene in the hostilities, and on June 23, with the situation still in a state of flux, she sailed for Leghorn.[15]

In August the *United States* was back in the Bay of Naples, where she remained for three weeks. Brooke visited Pompeii. As he stepped into the deserted streets of the ancient city he found

[12] Ibid.

[13] This fact was determined by a study of the log of the *United States*, 1 Aug. 1847–24 Feb. 1849, RG 24, NA.

[14] Brooke to Garnett, 10 Sept. 1848, BP.

[15] Pietro Orsi, *Modern Italy, 1748–1922* (London, 1923), pp. 177–78. In the long run the revolution of 1848 failed in the Kingdom of the Two Sicilies and the Bourbons were restored.

his mind struggling in vain "to realize, that seventeen hundred years have passed since the current of life ran through them." He imagined himself a stranger "in a living Roman city." To Lizzie he described enthusiastically the forum, temples, theaters, shops, and the street of tombs. Brooke concluded that "nothing that could be associated with beauty, or that admitted of emblematical design escaped the artist."[16]

In January 1849 the frigate sailed from Cadiz for Porto Praia, homeward bound. On February 18 she dropped anchor off Norfolk and Brooke was detached and given three months' leave. Brooke, now twenty-two, spent his leave in Norfolk with the Garnetts. It was his first real vacation since the return of the *Cyane* from the Pacific five years earlier. Norfolk was regarded as a hospitable town by Brooke's naval contemporaries and "geniality and kindness to young officers were the rule."[17] The relaxed atmosphere of the Virginia port was a pleasant change from the harsh discipline aboard a man-of-war. But to young Brooke the days in Norfolk meant chiefly an opportunity to pursue his courtship.

Brooke had for some time been corresponding with his first cousin, Mary Elizabeth Selden Garnett, known as Lizzie, who was his own age. A typical southern girl of the upper class, she had two brothers and three sisters, all considerably older than she. As the baby of the family, Lizzie had been the pet of the household and was particularly close to her father, William Garnett. Though her formal education was sketchy, she had an interest in literature, particularly novels and poetry. Her letters, however, disclose an ignorance of punctuation and a weakness in spelling. From all accounts Lizzie Garnett was by nature a light-hearted girl who had a sense of humor and loved a bit of gossip. Yet she had a serious side marked by a strong love for her family and a reverence for God. As she grew older, the serious side of her nature tended to dominate. Lizzie had deep blue eyes, an exceedingly fair skin, and regular features, and we have the assurance of her sister Charlotte that despite a severe case of scarlet fever when a child she was not without "good looks."[18]

[16] Brooke to Garnett, 10 Sept. 1848, BP.

[17] Daniel Ammen, *The Old Navy and the New* (Philadelphia, 1891), p. 31.

[18] Charlotte Garnett Darby to Anna Maria Brooke, 16 Oct. [1871], BP. Charlotte was one of Lizzie's three sisters, and Anna Maria Brooke was Lizzie's daughter.

Further Cruising, Marriage, and the Coast Survey

When Brooke had first gone to sea Lizzie had given him a watch guard which she had made, and eight years later he was still wearing it. For some years after 1841 the cousins had exchanged letters, but the correspondence lapsed until Brooke renewed it shortly after arriving at Gibraltar; later, while at sea off Stromboli, he began a second letter. Lizzie Garnett's letters in reply, written in a sprightly style, reveal a fun-loving disposition. She was never one to commit herself too far on paper, but she fired her cousin's hopes with the assurance that her feelings toward him were of "a very friendly nature."

After Brooke's transfer to the *United States*, he wrote Lizzie a long letter from the Bay of Naples. Its neatness and style suggest that, at the very least, he was attempting to make a good impression. The fact that the letter was copied meticulously in a notebook indicates a more serious purpose. In his opening sentence the young suitor expressed regret that he had not written more often, because he had thereby deprived himself "of the pleasure attendant upon the reception of your letters." Though he tried to be amusing and debonair, he was not very successful, for it was not his nature. However, though the style is stilted, the letter is informative. Brooke indicated an impatience to return to Norfolk.[19]

The arrival of the frigate at Norfolk in 1849 gave Brooke an opportunity to reinforce his words with action. He did not falter, for the earnest young man had realized that he was in love. Sensitive and introspective, he had found separation from a loved one hard to bear. While in the Mediterranean he seems to have reached a decision on marriage, and when the *United States* anchored off Norfolk, Brooke did not leave the issue in doubt. The first night in port he informed his cousin John Ludlow that he intended to propose to Lizzie.[20]

Lizzie, though she was strongly drawn to Brooke, found the answer difficult. She was deeply religious, and for a long time she had felt that it was unwise for a devout church member to marry a person who was not religious. At this stage of his life Brooke, though not indifferent to religion, was a serious doubter who could not reconcile revealed religion with reason. Moreover, the

[19] Brooke to Garnett, 10 Sept. 1848, BP.
[20] Lizzie to Brooke, 26 Dec. 1855, BP.

rough life on a warship was not conducive to religious meditation. But Lizzie Garnett's heart won out. After all, Brooke seemed young enough to mold. Even so, she suffered misgivings and contemplated with sorrow the impending separation from her family and friends. She did not look on marriage as the first step toward everlasting bliss as her cousin did, but once she gave her word she was steadfast. No date was set for the wedding, although Brooke indicated a decided preference for short engagements.

Brooke was too busy courting to write his father until eleven days after his detachment from the *United States*. When he finally got around to writing, he reported his engagement. The general "was much surprised" for he had not "the least suspicion of such a thing." The gruff old officer, now sixty-three, who less than two years earlier had vigorously condemned early marriages, neatly reversed his former position. "I like early marriages," he wrote, "as I believe it confirms good & even, sometimes corrects bad habits, & will induce econnimy, or that proper reflection of your circumstances, which should be always exercised." He did point out that "it is a very serious matter, either to make, or break off, a match," and immediately offered to contribute "with pleasure" $250 per year to the young couple's support.[21]

Brooke had been assigned to the brig *Washington* for work on the Coast Survey in the Chesapeake Bay area. With Lizzie's consent and his father's blessing to his marriage assured, the young lover did his best to carry out his new duties. On shipboard, he wrote Lizzie almost daily and complained because she wrote him only once a week. When he worried that she might be sick, she replied that engaged people were no more likely to become sick than other people. Brooke also offered his fiancée his opinion of books he had read and of the general value of reading. He noted that to read works in history was not only informative but amusing, and he lamented that she did not regard reading as being "very improving."

Early in October, Lizzie stated that she would be ready to marry in a month. But she was not an enthusiastic bride, and declared that "marriages now a days are doubtful affairs." She

[21] Brooke to Brooke, 19 March 1849, BP.

even questioned "the happiness of marriages generally." Brooke, on the other hand, was certain that the event portended nothing but joy.

The wedding took place at the Garnett home on November 6, 1849, according to the Episcopal service. It is recorded that the "bride looked very lovely and modest and the groom very handsome." Usually so solemn, Brooke surely smiled on this occasion. En route to their new home in Washington, D.C., the twenty-two-year-old bride "was taken for John's sister as persons thought she looked too young to be a married lady."[22]

In the capital, where Brooke compiled data for the Coast Survey during the winter, the young couple lived frugally. But General Brooke helped them, and knowing Washington well he believed that his gifts combined with Brooke's pay and allowances should enable the couple "to live genteely, & with the best company, which should never, be lost sight of." The young officer's resolve to practice economy prompted his father to explain, "I am well pleased, at your intention of economy, and expect, that your acts, will prove the truth of your professions." Then, and we can almost hear the sigh of relief, the old soldier, who had tried his best to be a real father despite manifold obstacles, suggested that "it will not be hereafter necessary for me to say much, on this subject, or any other, where morality, is concerned, as you now have, a Father in law, who, if he extends his advice to you, as he does to Dick [Garnett], and should you stand in need of it, I have no doubt, but what you will derive the greatest benefits."[23] During their few months in Washington the bride and groom were "as happy as mortals can be." They had entrée to the social life of the city, for General Brooke did his best to pave the way for them. The general urged his son to "find out the House where Genl. [George] Talcott, [Jr.,] of the Ordnance, boards . . . & endeavour to obtain lodgings there . . . [where] you will meet with best society particularly among the Army & Navy officers." Where the

[22] George Holbert Tucker, comp., *Abstracts from Norfolk City Marriage Bonds (1797–1850) and Other Genealogical Data* (n.p., 1934), p. 198; Charlotte Darby to Anna Brooke, 16 Oct. [1871], BP.

[23] Brooke to Brooke, 24 Nov., 25 Nov. 1849, BP. Richard Brooke Garnett, one of Lizzie's two brothers, was a graduate of West Point in the Class of 1841, and was for many years General Brooke's aide at a succession of army posts.

young couple settled down is not known, but Brooke did see quite a bit of General Talcott, whom General Brooke described as "without doubt, the very best officer, regarding, ordnance duties & gunnery, both theoretically & practically, in the U.S. or you may say, any where else." From Talcott, Brooke could "obtain the most valuable information upon these subjects, as well, as others, which will be, of great service to you, in your profession."[24] It could have been from just such a contact that Brooke developed his marked interest in ordnance that was to manifest itself at a later date. But for the present, hydrographic work would be his specialty.

In Washington, Brooke had been directed to report to the surveying brig *Washington*, which was part of the hydrographic party commanded by Lieutenant Samuel Phillips Lee. Lee was continuing the hydrographic survey of Chesapeake Bay and "the in and offshore work on the outer coast of Maryland and Virginia" and revising the sailing directions of the Chesapeake generally.[25]

Brooke's service on the Coast Survey was routine. In 1849 the Survey, under Superintendent Alexander Dallas Bache, was active on the Atlantic and Gulf coasts and had begun operations on the Pacific slope. Naval officers, army officers, and civilians were all utilized, with civilians furnishing the permanent nucleus. The naval officers served as navigators and performed the hydrographic work. A majority of Brooke's brother officers served at one time or another on the Coast Survey, but over the years the relationship between the Navy Department and the Survey—which was under the Treasury Department—became strained. Lieutenant Lee probably spoke for most navy men when he complained that "if the C. S. (the present organization of it) is not a privateer, it certainly is a pirate as regards the Navy—on board of which pirate we work the craft for a small share of the inside credit & with a large share of discredit."[26]

Professionally this was an important year in Brooke's life, for

[24] Brooke to Brooke, 24 Nov. 1849, BP.

[25] Complement of the U.S. Surveying and Gun Brig *Washington*, Circulars and General Orders, RG 45, NA; *Senate Executive Documents*, Report of A. D. Bache, Superintendent of the Coast Survey, Oct. 1849, 31st Cong., 1st sess., vol. 5, no. 5, p. 34.

[26] Lee to Brooke, 5 March 1850, BP.

under the kindly guidance of Lee he learned much about surveying and hydrographic work.[27] There is no evidence that Brooke
showed particular interest in scientific studies at this time, but
there is proof that he performed his assigned duties well. The
roots of Brooke's later scientific achievements go back to this
period.

As early as 1844 Superintendent Bache had directed that when
sounding, hydrographers secure bottom samples for analysis.
Brooke was quickly initiated. Off Point Lookout, where the Potomac flows into Chesapeake Bay, Lee ordered the whole crew of
the *Washington* to sound. Brooke described the technique to Lizzie:
"Today I went in a boat at 6 in the morning and pulled two miles
to a station signal on the bay shore; there I commenced by running the boat while a man threw the lead every fifteen seconds,
straight out into the bay; then parallel to the shore for about a
quarter of a mile; then straight back to the shore parallel to the
line run in coming out, and so on, until sunset; anchoring once in
a while to obtain tumblers of mud [from the bottom]. . . . In
steering great care must be taken, and what with that, looking
through instruments, and the glare of the sun, ones eyes are not in
condition to write much by candlelight. Mosquitos, gnats, and
other pests are abundant annoying us excessively." But there was
compensation in being near Lizzie. "If it were not that I am bent
upon remaining near you," he wrote, "I should prefer some duty
more agreeable than sitting all day cramped up in a boat." As a
whole, these months on the Coast Survey were an exceedingly
happy time.[28]

Early in June, Brooke was transferred to the surveying steamer
Legaré where he was under the direct command of Lieutenant Lee.
The *Legaré*, a vessel of iron construction, was a most inefficient
steamer. Early in the season she had begun "to show great
weakness in the machinery, the condenser, the propeller, and the
coupling of the propeller, all becoming more or less disordered or

[27] There are many letters from Lee in the Brooke Papers over a period of more than 30
years in which Lee expressed a keen interest in Brooke's activities. Also, he strongly recommended Brooke for positions of considerable responsibility.

[28] Robert Ervin Coker, *This Great and Wide Sea*, rev. ed. (Chapel Hill, N.C., 1949), p.
40; Brooke to Lizzie Garnett, 23 May 1849, BP.

giving away entirely." Such defects prevented Lee's party from attaining peak efficiency. Brooke had an exceedingly low opinion of the craft, "the most miserable attempt at a steamer, that I ever had the pleasure of seeing." The boat's crew, all transferred from the *Washington* to the *Legaré*, were so discontented with the new vessel that they even preferred "rowing about to remaining on board."[29]

Despite the disagreeable characteristics of the *Legaré*, Brooke liked his fellow officers "very much," particularly gregarious, carefree John Madigan, Jr., a passed midshipman from Maine, and Passed Midshipman William D. Whiting, whose new bride was ensconced in a farmhouse nearby. The boat's crew formed a motley group of "individually amusing characters." Among them were an erstwhile whaler, a former soldier of the Mexican War, and the nephew of a Catholic bishop. They made, in Brooke's words "a hard party."[30]

In July the *Legaré* moved through Hampton Roads to the Atlantic bound for Lewes, Delaware. Lewes, near Cape Henlopen, would serve as a base for the survey work on the Atlantic coasts of Delaware and Maryland. For a few days, until the arrival of the regular shore party, the men on the *Legaré* were employed making observations. Seated on the beach among numerous sand flies Brooke interspersed letter writing to Lizzie with sextant observations at ten-minute intervals. Spare time was used to fish and catch sharks. On one occasion Brooke caught two large sharks and observed that he would not expose himself "outside the breakers at Cape May for a fortune." Aboard the cumbersome steamer again, the young officer took turns working ship. Brooke joked that by the time he was finished he should "be qualified to command a Mississippi steamer." The leaky vessel was employed constantly during July with little diversion being offered the men on the forlorn coast. Bad weather restricted operations to Lewes part of the time, but Brooke did not think the town "very fashionable." In fact, he found the society "decidedly of a mixed character" and the children "les enfants terrible." It impressed him, however,

---

[29] *Senate Executive Documents*, Report of Bache, Superintendent of the Coast Survey, Oct. 1849, 31st Cong., 1st sess., vol. 5, no. 5, pp. 34–35; Brooke to Lizzie Garnett, 16 June 1849, BP.

[30] Brooke to Lizzie Garnett, 10 June, 16 June 1849, BP.

that the women bathed in the surf frequently, even though the sailors did "not keep sober onshore." Brooke found dips refreshing and urged Lizzie to indulge in this pleasure.[31]

Lizzie was the center of his world, but Brooke did give some thought to his father in San Antonio and to his brother at Brown University. "Oh! if father will only come North next summer," he confided to Lizzie, "I shall be delighted, it will be what sailors call a deadweather, since the Secty of the Navy cannot refuse me leave to visit him, and of course you will be with us." A few days later he wrote wistfully: "I hope above most things that father will come on next summer. He is getting old now and it is a long time since I saw him."[32] A letter from his brother William led Brooke to assert that "Willie is decidedly the finest boy that I know and will I hope turn out an able lawyer."[33] As the older brother, John Brooke always felt responsible for William's welfare.

In September 1849 Brooke finally received his warrant as a passed midshipman. The last group of those who had entered the navy in 1841 had completed the course of study and examinations at Annapolis, and the whole class had been rated relatively according to academic grades. Brooke was informed by the secretary of the navy that his rank as passed midshipman had been made retroactive to August 10, 1847.[34] Elated, Brooke noted that "the last batch only put one ahead" of him, while placing fifteen behind him.

With the outside work done, Brooke was shifted in November to the Coast Survey office in Washington, but the close work on charts soon affected his eyes and required that he be given sick leave. At this juncture, Lee, who felt a real affection for Brooke, wrote that he felt him capable of fitting himself "to fill any professional post" and that he intended to retain him on the Survey. By April, Brooke's eyes were much better, but plans for the Coast Survey in the new season were still up in the air.

Soon Brooke's plans for another pleasant year on the Coast Survey were rudely shattered by orders assigning him to the brig

[31] Ibid., 13 July, 19 July, 29 July 1849.
[32] Ibid., 20 Sept., 22 Sept. 1849.
[33] Ibid., 20 Sept. 1849.
[34] William Ballard Preston to Brooke, 29 Sept. 1849, BP.

Porpoise bound for the African station.[35] These orders were unexpected and unwanted. Brooke's only consolation was that he had won a staunch friend in S. P. Lee, who expressed "deep regret" at Brooke's detachment from his party. To Brooke the African assignment spelled out the pain of separation; he found it difficult to think of his long-term best interests. His first reaction was expressed in a brief note he wrote Lizzie shortly after going aboard the *Porpoise:* "I did not anticipate such intense agony though God knows the prospect was terrible. I have made a vow that if it *is possible* I will never go to sea again." Later in the day Brooke wrote Lizzie a final letter to be taken ashore by the pilot boat. In this letter the unhappy young man asserted twice that he would not go to sea again and twice that he intended to resign; he concluded with the flat statement that "no power can keep me in the Navy."[36]

The *Porpoise*, under the command of Lieutenant James L. Lardner, "got under way from Lynhaven bay" on June 9, and though Brooke wrote several letters to his wife in the days following, not until two weeks had passed did he compose one cheerful enough to send. Meanwhile, the other officers seemingly had adapted themselves quickly to life on shipboard and in the evenings made merry with boxing and with music supplied by a fiddle and tambourine. Brooke began to emerge slowly from his cocoon, but he did not relent of his determination to resign. At Madeira he wrote a letter to his father and included in it his resignation to be forwarded to the secretary of the navy. He also enclosed in a letter to Lizzie "a resignation to be sent to the Dept. in case you happen to be as miserable as I am." Brooke intended, furthermore, to present his resignation to Commodore Francis H. Gregory, the commander of the African Squadron, whenever Lardner caught up with the flagship. In any event, because of his relatively high rank as a passed midshipman and Lieutenant Lardner's seeming warm regard for him, Brooke expected to be designated master of a homeward-bound vessel soon after the *Porpoise's* arrival on the African station. On the voyage Brooke had many conversations with Lardner on a variety of topics, and after one

[35] Index to Orders Issued to Officers (Key to Orders), 1828–51, Office of the Secretary of the Navy, 3 May 1850, RG 34, NA.
[36] Brooke to his wife, two letters, 9 June 1850, BP.

long talk on inventions he concluded that he was "building up" with Lardner as he had with S. P. Lee.[37]

On July 25, forty-six days after leaving Norfolk, the *Porpoise* dropped anchor at Porto Praia in the Cape Verde Islands, where she spent four days stowing provisions. The brig then headed down the coast to the Gulf of Biafra, stopping at various ports along the way. Like other vessels of the African Squadron, she was charged with protecting American commerce on the west coast of Africa and suppressing the slave trade.[38]

On the African station Brooke found the "crowded apartments" of the brig stifling. For example, he once wrote his wife: "We have rain and heat all day, the steerage is like an oven . . . the brig rolls, the air suffocates." But Brooke's health remained good. Writing letters to Lizzie, making entries in his journal, mending his oiled clothes, and cultivating a beard gave Brooke some variety from the monotony of standing watch. In the evenings while others sang sorrowful, long-winded ditties, Brooke embarked upon a reading of the New Testament. Particularly did he like Luke, the Gospel that Lizzie found "so affectionate in style and manner." He was disgusted with the "commonplace nonsensical conversations" in the wardroom and, as he recorded in his journal, could "find not one congenial spirit onboard."[39]

Arriving at Monrovia, Brooke was "pleased with the appearance of comfort," but he found that as elsewhere "the rich make use of the poor." It was his opinion "that such negroes as have kept bar rooms and have been otherwise practised in dealing with the world are well suited for the colony but the servants in coming out only change a white master for a black one." Brooke, however, had a high regard for the Kroomen who were employed by warships off the coast of Africa "as messengers, interpreters, boatmen, and in communicating with the shore, in bringing off provisions, wood, water, etc., and in all those services of exposure to the climate which the constitution of the white man is incapable of

[37] Ibid., 17 July, 7 July 1850.

[38] The duties of the squadron, which had been established by the Webster-Ashburton Treaty of 1842, are described in detail in *House Documents*, 27th Cong., 3d sess., vol. 5, no. 192, pp. 1–4; *House Executive Documents*, 35th Cong., 2d sess., vol. 9, no. 104.

[39] Brooke to his wife, 6 Aug. 1850, BP; Brooke's *Porpoise* Journal, 2 Oct. 1850, BP.

bearing." The Kroomen, who bore such names as Pea Soup and Frying Pan, owned slaves and regarded the "white negroes," as they termed the black colonists from America, "with great contempt."[40]

At Cape Coast, Brooke visited the grave of the English poet and novelist Letitia Elizabeth Landon, better known as L.E.L., who had died in tragic circumstances in 1838. Brooke liked Miss Landon's romantic yet melancholy poetry and "found something very touching in her life story." In her poetry Miss Landon had expressed a wish to be buried "where the flowers grow," Brooke observed, but instead she had been buried in the center of the parade ground with "a few flags of burnt brick marking the spot."[41] Brooke also saw the vicious African king of Appolonia, Quacco Acco, confined in the castle prison for his many brutal crimes, one of which was nailing his mother and sister to the walls of his house. Wrote Brooke: "We looked at him through the bars of his prison. . . . proud of the notice taken of him he advanced to the grated window and leaned upon his elbow, affording a good view of his person; he regarded us with a malignant stare. I can only compare the expression of eye to that of a serpent, yet more brutal and sluggish. I should really experience pleasure in seeing him hanged."[42] Acco was only the most notorious of the prisoners.

At Prince's Island in the Bight of Biafra, Brooke enjoyed himself "more than at any other place on the coast." Especially did he like the hospitality of the Femiras, owners of a large plantation who lived in a spacious Portuguese-style house with long piazzas on two sides. At the Femiras's home Brooke was guest at two memorable dinners—at one of which he was introduced to stewed

---

[40] Brooke to his wife, 8 Aug., 13 Aug. 1850, BP; *Senate Documents*, 28th Cong., 2d sess., vol. 9, no. 150, pp. 3–4; Brooke to his wife, 15 Nov. 1850, BP.

[41] *Encyclopedia Britannica* (1951 edition), s.v. "Letitia Elizabeth Landon." Letitia was born in England in 1802, and when about 13 years of age she began contributing to various journals. In 1838 she married George Maclean, governor of the Gold Coast, but was not happy; an earlier engagement had apparently been broken off by scandalmongers. She died from an overdose of prussic acid 4 months after her marriage. See Brooke's *Porpoise* Journal, 26 Aug. 1850, and Brooke to his wife, 26 Aug. 1850, BP.

[42] Brooke's *Porpoise* Journal, 26 Aug. 1850, BP.

monkey. In appreciation of her many kindnesses Brooke presented Madame Femira with a caricature he had sketched.[43]

By this time Brooke had certain convictions about the Negro race, ideas arrived at from contacts with the Kroomen on board and the natives in the towns along the coast, superimposed upon his occasional exposure to the slave society in the southern states. He described his ideas in some detail in his journal and letters. His favorable first impressions of Monrovia were modified by subsequent contact when he "saw, no beast of burden, nothing in the shape of cart or wheelbarrow—no agricultural implements—and no one at work save the carpenters, and a few road makers." But he did witness slavery. The blacks from the interior, called bush Negroes, were used as slaves by the natives of the coast. Brooke thought this natural, because "the bush Negroes are stupid and only fit to be slaves otherwise they would not remain in subjection." In Brooke's opinion, Negroes were "naturally inferior and as a race can not arrive at anything like the perfection of government or civilization at least in this era of the world. What they will become in the course of 1 000 000 000 000 000 years I could not say though perhaps they will change somewhat."[44]

The *Porpoise* returned to Porto Praia, the base for supplies, in October. The cruise to the Bight of Biafra had lasted a little less than three months, and even though the African station was rated as insalubrious the health of the officers and crew had remained good. The *Porpoise* had seized no slavers; indeed, from 1843 through 1857 the U.S. African Squadron captured only nineteen vessels.[45] By contrast, the British patrol was far more effective. Brooke's explanation was that "our Capts will not take the responsibility as Government does not support them as with the English." Brooke had a strong aversion to the slave trade, stating that "of all associations I think that of kidnapping prejudices me most against Africa." He labeled the unsuccessful efforts of the United

---

[43] Ibid., 6 Sept. 1850.

[44] Brooke to his wife, 15 Nov. 1850, BP.

[45] Log of the *Porpoise*, RG 24, NA; *House Executive Documents*, 35th Cong., 2d sess., vol. 9, no. 104, pp. 31–82. Six of the 19 vessels were seized between January 1845 and July 1846, while Commodore Charles W. Skinner was in command of the African Squadron.

States to suppress the slave trade "a perfect farce." A look at the record corroborates Brooke's pessimistic view. It was estimated that in the eleven-year period ending in 1849, some 685,000 slaves were carried from Africa to the American market in spite of the efforts of the naval squadrons.[46]

When Brooke finally caught up with the squadron's flagship, the *Portsmouth*, at Porto Praia, he lost no time in applying to Commodore Gregory for a transfer to the Coast Survey. The ten letters Brooke received from Lizzie at this time did nothing to lessen his dissatisfaction with a naval career. Gregory promptly disapproved Brooke's request on the ground that the latter's services in his present position were important. Nothing daunted, the unhappy officer informed the commodore that he would resign; that he had written his father to that effect; and that he wished to go home as soon as possible. Gregory, who had known General Brooke before the impatient youngster was born, was sympathetic and promised that after the *Porpoise* had returned from a short trip to the Gambia he would "do all in his power" to get Brooke home. Gregory's position was complicated by a shortage of officers in the squadron.[47]

On October 26 the *Porpoise* sailed for Bathurst, at the mouth of the Gambia River, to inquire about several American citizens reportedly held captive by the Moors. In consequence of Lardner's arrest of the brig's first lieutenant, Brooke was ordered to assume the duties of acting master. Though elevated to the wardroom, Brooke admitted to no accompanying elevation of spirit; his new duties, however, did awaken in him a sense of responsibility. He was struck forcibly by the fact that the safety of the vessel depended upon a single timepiece, and he noted that "an error of one minute would make a difference of 15 miles in the determined position." Brooke was acutely conscious of the fact that with a low coast and hazy sky, he could not see the land at a distance greater than six miles. On the run to Bathurst, Brooke's flagging interest

[46] Brooke to his wife, 2 Aug. 1850, BP; *An Exposition of the African Slave Trade from the Year 1840, to 1850, Inclusive*, published by direction of the representatives of the Religious Society of Friends, in Pennsylvania, New Jersey, and Delaware (Philadelphia, 1851), p. 148.
[47] Gregory to Brooke, 23 Oct. 1850, Brooke to his wife, 26 Oct. 1850, BP.

in the naval profession revived slightly, and he wrote that had he not three watches to deter him and the firm determination to resign, he would study again "the whole theory of navigation," for he had forgotten most of what he had learned at Annapolis.[48]

At Gambia, Captain Lardner was unable to obtain any information on the American captives, so he headed back to Porto Praia. Near the end of the return trip death struck in the wardroom. Lieutenant Henry P. Robertson, the first lieutenant placed under arrest at Porto Praia, had been sick since leaving that port. The day the *Porpoise* returned to her base, Robertson died. Hit hard by the death, Brooke lamented that "taking one from such a small compass death makes a strong impression," and with Robertson gone the wardroom looked "like a tomb." The same day Brooke surrendered to Commodore Gregory his warrant as a passed midshipman with a letter of resignation. He had long since resolved to resign, "but learning that no one was to be ordered in Robertson's place," he acted sooner than he otherwise would have done.[49]

The shorthanded commodore, although talking to Brooke "in the most kindly manner," refused to accept the resignation, for he had "no power or authority" to do so. He did, however, forward Brooke's warrant and letter directly to the secretary of the navy. Brooke's blunt letter merely said: "I hereby tender my resignation for your acceptance." The commodore's action left Brooke up in the air. Brooke grew increasingly bitter and blamed the navy for all his woes; his letters to his wife during this period make sorry reading.[50]

Lizzie, for sound practical reasons, disapproved of Brooke's resigning. In General Brooke's view, Lizzie's reasons did "honor to her head & heart" and proved that his son had "a partner in this life, whose strong affection for her husband, & excellent judgement, is worthy of all admiration." Father and wife presented a united front. Brooke was intensely mortified to learn of this strong

---

[48] Gregory to the Secretary of the Navy, 14 Dec. 1850, Letters from Officers Commanding Squadrons, RG 45, NA; Brooke's *Porpoise* Journal, 26 Oct., 30 Oct. 1850, BP.

[49] Brooke's *Porpoise* Journal, 5 Nov. 1850, BP.

[50] Gregory to Brooke, 6 Nov. 1850, BP; Brooke to the Secretary of the Navy, 6 Nov. 1850, Officers Letters, RG 45, NA.

opposition to his proposed course of action and retreated—but not gracefully.[51]

In November while the *Porpoise* was still at Porto Praia, word was received of the abolition of flogging in the navy.[52] Captain Lardner was reluctant to accept the new law until he received official confirmation, and when a sailor ran afoul of regulations a few days later he was flogged. Brooke, however, thought the abolition of flogging was "the best step taken since I entered the Navy."[53] His stand was contrary to that of nearly all of the senior officers of the navy.[54] Congress provided no substitute for flogging, and many naval officers feared that without it there would be no way to enforce discipline among the incorrigible elements. But the navy survived, and history has proved that Brooke and those who shared his conviction were right.

The long months on the African coast—months during which the deadly routine was relieved but infrequently by strange and colorful sights ashore—hardened and matured Brooke. Early in the cruise he assured Lizzie that he intended "now calmly to think over the matter and see if I cannot become a Christian." Apparently his reflections were unrewarding, for four months later in his journal he branded the observance of a fast day by one of the passed midshipmen as "disgusting nonsense and fanaticism." To Brooke, man was not created in the image of God; on the contrary, he insisted that the longer he lived the lower sank his opinion of the human race. "We are all asses emphatically," he cynically announced.[55] Gone were references to reading the Bible and such works as Baron Alexander von Humboldt's *Kosmos.* Instead, he began to examine Lieutenant Matthew Fontaine Maury's pilot charts and was delighted to find how well they agreed with his own observations on the *Porpoise.*

Brooke's curt letter of resignation passed across the desk of Secretary of the Navy William A. Graham, who rejected it on the

[51] Brooke to Brooke, 13 Oct. 1850, BP.

[52] The law, passed as a rider on the naval appropriation bill, 28 Sept. 1850, provided for the abolition of flogging aboard all public and private vessels of the United States.

[53] Brooke's *Porpoise* Journal, 19 Nov., 13 Nov. 1850, BP.

[54] Among the few senior officers who opposed flogging were Uriah P. Levy, John A. Dahlgren, and Robert F. Stockton.

[55] Brooke to his wife, 11 Aug. 1850, and Brooke's *Porpoise* Journal, 17 Jan. 1851, BP.

ground that "officers on duty on distant service, cannot be permitted to resign without assigning sufficient reasons for it." This should have ended the matter, but Brooke's friends and relatives were fearful lest he promptly produce "sufficient reasons." They sought to forestall such a step. At this point the hand of fate intervened and shoved Brooke along the road to adult responsibility. On March 9, 1851, General Brooke, in command of the Military Department of Texas, died unexpectedly after a siege of dysentery. Upon learning of General Brooke's death, William Garnett at once informed the secretary of the navy that unless his son-in-law returned home immediately to make provision for his brother's education, the latter would be compelled to discontinue his studies.[56] Brooke was ordered home.

Oddly enough, just at the time his recall was being ordered in Washington, Brooke had come to see the error of his ways. He had not yet learned that his resignation had been refused, but letters from Lizzie and Colonel Garnett had persuaded him that his true course was to remain in the navy. He was now quite frantic and sought desperately to recover his warrant through writing letters to Commodore Charles Morris, General Roger Jones, Commodore Henry E. Ballard, and Lieutenant S. P. Lee. Now that his eyes had improved, he hoped particularly that Lee could get him reassigned to the Coast Survey. Brooke was penitent for having written cruel letters to Lizzie that caused her anguish, but he found it more difficult to apologize to his father-in-law, to whom he wrote nine letters without mailing any. Brooke wrote Lizzie that he was "fully aware now" that he must depend upon himself "in every respect." The next day he received an appointment as acting lieutenant of the *Porpoise* which further mollified him.[57] It had been a hard but necessary lesson, because for years Brooke had leaned, perhaps unconsciously, on his father's considerable influence and financial support. Though he did not know it, the lesson had been learned none too soon. Not until May 14, more than

[56] Graham to Brooke, 24 Jan. 1851, Letters to Officers, RG 45, NA; Garnett to Graham, 22 March 1851, Miscellaneous Letters Received, 1801–84, Office of the Secretary of the Navy, RG 45, NA.

[57] List of Acting Appointments made in the African Squadron by Commodore Francis H. Gregory, Letters from Officers Commanding Squadrons, RG 45, NA.

two months after the event, did Brooke learn of his father's death. At first he feared that his own precipitate resignation had killed his father, but he found solace in an understanding letter from Lizzie who foresaw such an interpretation and assured him that it was not true.

The day after Brooke received at Porto Praia the sad intelligence of his father's death, he was informed by Commodore Elie A. F. Lavallette, Gregory's successor, that he would go home on the *Portsmouth*. This he did, arriving at Boston on June 25, 1851. The most agonizing period of his life was behind him. Ignoring his Thomas relatives in Duxbury, Brooke started for Norfolk the following morning, where he learned that the department had granted him three months' leave and confirmed his appointments as acting master and acting lieutenant on the *Porpoise*. This meant additional pay.

Brooke had spent only a year on the coast of Africa, but the cruise marked a turning point in his life. There would be no more routine cruises. Upon his return to the United States, Brooke chose a different road from that selected by most of his naval contemporaries. By concentrating on scientific work, he hoped to win recognition in his profession while enjoying more time ashore with his wife.

III /

THE DEEP-SEA SOUNDING

LEAD AND FIRST

VOYAGE OF EXPLORATION

THE immediate problem confronting John Brooke on his return to Norfolk in June 1851 was the settlement of his father's estate, which he felt required his presence in the United States for some time. While still on leave in Norfolk, he wrote to the secretary of the navy requesting that he be assigned to the Naval Observatory in Washington.[1] The request was granted, and on October 15 Brooke reported to Lieutenant Matthew Fontaine Maury.

The Naval Observatory, called originally the Depot of Charts and Instruments, had been established in 1830 to safeguard and preserve navy charts and instruments (such as chronometers) when they were not actually in use.[2] Enlarging its duties to in-

---

[1] Brooke to William A. Graham, 21 Aug. 1851, Officers Letters, RG 45, NA.

[2] Gustavus A. Weber, *The Naval Observatory: Its History, Activities, and Organization* (Baltimore, 1926), p. 10. The depot had soon been drawn into astronomical work and acquired a 30-inch transit telescope. After 1844 the title Depot of Charts and Instruments fell into disuse and the names Naval Observatory or National Observatory were used. See Charles Lee Lewis, *Matthew Fontaine Maury, Pathfinder of the Seas* (Annapolis, 1927), p. 45.

clude astronomical work, the observatory had been placed under the Bureau of Ordnance and Hydrography, whose chief when Brooke arrived was the venerable Commodore Charles Morris, second-ranking captain in the navy.

Matthew Fontaine Maury, Brooke's immediate superior, was superintendent from 1844 to the Civil War. Although his predecessors had done good work, it was Maury who gave the Naval Observatory a worldwide reputation. Although not neglecting astronomy, he leaned toward work in hydrography and meteorology, and "really laid the foundations for the systematic hydrographic work of the Navy Department." He compiled data for a comprehensive chart of the North Atlantic showing the tracks of vessels, the direction of prevailing winds, the currents, and the temperature of the water. This project was completed in 1847 with the publication of his *Wind and Current Chart of the North Atlantic.*[3]

In time Maury greatly expanded his activities and sought the cooperation of American warships and merchant ships throughout the world in completing specially prepared abstract logs. Gradually, he overcame the reluctance of merchant captains to share their trade secrets, and by the time Brooke joined the observatory, more than one thousand American navigators were cooperating. Charts of other oceans were published as information became available. A large part of the staff at the Naval Observatory was engaged in compiling information and preparing charts; Brooke joined in these activities. The charts served a very useful purpose even though they were prepared in the twilight of the sailing era. The work of the observatory in astronomy was important, also. By 1855 one hundred thousand stars had been closely observed.[4]

Brooke was fortunate indeed to be at the Naval Observatory under Maury, for he received thorough training in hydrography, astronomy, and meteorology, which he could have acquired no place else. Furthermore, he developed the scientific approach so essential for the voyages of exploration on which he was soon to

[3] Weber, *Naval Observatory*, p. 17.
[4] Lewis, *Maury*, pp. 55, 49.

embark. And the mental stimulation, after the torpor of the African cruise, cannot be gainsaid.[5]

In 1851 the Naval Observatory was located in a new building at Twenty-third and E streets, Northwest. Brooke and his wife found comfortable quarters at Mrs. Herbert Bryant's boarding-house at the corner of New York Avenue and Fifteenth Street, in the shadow of the White House. It was a convenient location and just far enough from the Naval Observatory to give Brooke a little exercise as he picked his way along the unpaved streets, flanked by occasional low wooden houses and massive public buildings in various stages of construction. Henry Adams described the Washington of that day as a southern village with "unfinished Greek temples for workrooms, and sloughs for roads."[6] Perhaps the best symbol of the nation's capital was the stubby shaft of the Washington Monument rising slowly above the Potomac to the south.

In his new work Brooke found much to interest him. He learned that his views on winds and currents, based on nearly ten years' sea service, agreed well with those expounded at the observatory. With his taste for scientific inquiry already whetted, Brooke resolved to improve his qualifications by hard study. His quarters at Mrs. Bryant's encouraged study and reflection in his free time. Such devotion to book learning was, apparently, unusual in the navy. "It so rarely happens," his uncle William Garnett noted, "from all I can learn, that young Navy officers at the Observatory, or indeed, any where else, manifest the least desire to improve themselves; or in fact, to do one iota more than to escape observation or censure, for neglect of duty, that one who pursues a different course, is very apt to render himself quite conspicuous."[7]

It was Brooke's good fortune that several men at the observatory who were carried in the *Navy Register* as "Professors of Math-

---

[5] The variety and amount of work performed at the Naval Observatory in the early fifties is shown in a report submitted by the superintendent to the chief of the Bureau of Ordnance and Hydrography: *Senate Executive Documents*, Maury to Lewis Warrington, 6 Oct. 1851, 32d Cong., 1st sess., vol. 2, no. 1, pt. 2, pp. 160–61.

[6] *The Education of Henry Adams: An Autobiography* (Boston, 1918), p. 99.

[7] Garnett to Brooke, 9 Nov. 1851, BP.

ematics" were true scientists of considerable ability. Among the people with whom Brooke was most closely associated were Professor Ruel Keith and Passed Midshipmen George P. Welsh and Andrew W. Johnson. Only one officer was junior to Brooke. Congenial surroundings and stimulating work did much to improve Brooke's outlook on life. He overlooked no opportunity to win a reputation. Colonel Garnett, who had the instincts of a politician, was "well pleased to find" that Brooke had "become convinced of the policy of cultivating the acquaintance of those with whom" he was "compelled to have official relations, as well as with those between whom" and his "father, there existed friendly relation[s], and in many instances mutual acts of kindness."[8]

A matter of growing interest at the Naval Observatory was deep-sea soundings. Sounding in moderate depths with a hand lead and hemp line, such as Brooke had done on the Coast Survey, was well established. When the lead struck bottom, the shock of impact was transmitted through the line, or the line ceased to run out. The lead could be armed by covering its base with soft tallow to which the sediment from the bottom adhered. Recovery of the lead proved that the bottom had been sounded and gave some indication of its composition. The techniques so satisfactory for depths up to approximately one thousand fathoms, however, failed in the deep sea. And this was a serious matter, for the greater part of the sea is more than two thousand fathoms deep. In sounding the deep sea there were two basic problems: the inability to detect when the lead reached bottom and the inability to recover the lead. At great depths the sheer weight of the conventional hemp line caused it to run out after the lead struck bottom. A light line, on the other hand, was easily broken and was pulled willy-nilly by the currents.[9]

The problem of detecting when the lead struck bottom was finally solved. A strong light twine was developed for use with the standard thirty-two-pound round shot. The twine was strong

[8] *Navy Register of the United States for the Year 1851*, p. 68 and passim; Garnett to Brooke, 9 Nov. 1851, BP.

[9] C. Wyville Thomson, *The Depths of the Sea, an Account of the General Results of the Dredging Cruises of H.M.S.S. "Porcupine" and "Lightning" during the Summers of 1868, 1869, and 1870*, 2d ed. (London, 1874), p. 207; Matthew Fontaine Maury, *Explanations and Sailing Directions to Accompany the Wind and Current Charts*, 7th ed. (Philadelphia, 1855), p. 129.

enough not to be snapped during descent and yet sensitive enough to indicate when the shot struck bottom. But positive proof that the shot had reached bottom was lacking, for the new method required that the sounding line be cut and the lead left on the bottom after each cast. It was presupposed that the shot could not be recovered, for if the line were "small enough for the weight to drag down, the line would not be strong enough to haul the weight up again; and if the line were strong enough to haul the weight up, then the weight would not be heavy enough to drag the line down." Yet, unless the shot was recovered, there was no proof the bottom had been plumbed nor any sample to indicate the nature of the bottom. Simple though this problem seemed, it had defied solution for centuries.[10]

At this juncture John Brooke, who had been at the Naval Observatory six months, proposed to Maury a contrivance by which "the shot might be detached as soon as it touched the bottom, and specimens brought up in its stead." This was in the usual course of business, for Maury noted: "I was in the habit of consulting him; he often assisted me with his reflections." Brooke's plan called for a knife to be attached to a movable rod passing through the shot in such a way that the shot would be detached when it reached bottom, yet the rod could be recovered with a sample of the ocean's floor. Maury deemed the invention feasible. But on reflection Brooke decided it would be difficult to keep such a blade sharp and that it would be undesirable to have an open knife kept close to sounding lines. So he discarded this plan.[11]

Next, Brooke thought of suspending the shot from a hinged metal arc which would be tripped when a rod passing through the shot struck the bottom. The principle was similar to that of the iceman's tongs. Utilizing a small perforated brass ball and two pieces of light wire for an arc, Brooke conducted the experiment before Maury and "nearly every officer attached to the Observatory." Nearly thirty years later Brooke still remembered the smile

[10] Maury to Capt. Duncan N. Ingraham, 16 Jan. 1857, Letters Received Relating to Hydrography, RG 45, NA; Maury, *Explanations and Sailing Directions*, p. 129.

[11] Maury, *Explanations and Sailing Directions*, p. 129; Brooke to George E. Belknap, 1 Dec. 1880, BP; Brooke to Maury, 12 March 1856, Letters Received, 1840–85, and Maury to Brooke, 21 March 1856, Letters Sent (Letter Book, Record, or Records), 1842–62, Records of the Naval Observatory, RG 78, NA.

that illumined the great oceanographer's face. When Maury was satisfied as to the practicability of the plan and understood precisely the form it was to take, he directed Brooke to have William R. Greble, the machinist or instrument maker at the Naval Observatory, construct a model.[12]

The apparatus was of simple construction. It consisted of a round shot with a hole bored or cast through the center and a comparatively light, close-fitting metal rod which was inserted into the hole so that each end projected a few inches beyond the shot. During the descent of the apparatus the position of the rod was perpendicular to the ocean floor. The lower end of the rod was hollowed out and filled with soft tallow or grease, so that the specimen from the bottom of the sea would adhere to it. Attached to the upper end of the rod was a hinged arm moving in a vertical plane. The outer end of the arm was notched, forming two fingers. There was a hole in the upper finger to which the sounding line was fastened. Over the lower finger the ends of a sling were looped. This sling passed vertically around the ball, holding it in position on the rod. When the rod struck the ocean bottom its descent was arrested, but inertia carried the shot down the rod. Simultaneously the deep-sea line slackened, terminating the upward pull on the movable arm. As the shot plunged to the bottom, it pulled the arm in a downward arc on its axis, disengaging the sling and releasing the shot. The rod with the specimen in the bottom could then be reeled into the boat.[13]

Greble, the instrument maker, suggested using two movable arms instead of one, and careful drawings were made with this ap-

[12] Brooke to Maury, 12 March 1856, Letters Received, Naval Observatory, RG 78, NA; Brooke to George E. Belknap, 1 Dec. 1880 (copy), BP; Maury to Brooke, 21 March 1856, Letters Sent, Naval Observatory, RG 78, NA.

[13] For descriptions and illustrations of the Brooke apparatus in its original and its improved form, see Maury, *Explanations and Sailing Directions*, p. 129 and plates VII and VIII; Thomson, *Depths of the Sea*, pp. 211–14; Bureau of Navigation, "Brooke's Sounding Apparatus," in *General Instructions for Hydrographic Surveys of the United States Navy and for Writing and Editing Sailing Directions and for Keeping Remark Books* (Washington, D.C., 1868), pp. 61–63; George Washington Littlehales, "Growth of Our Knowledge of the Deep Sea," *Popular Science Monthly* 43 (May 1893): 42–43. For additional discussions of the Brooke apparatus, see George E. Belknap, "Something about Deep-Sea Sounding," *United Service* 1 (April 1879): 167 and passim; *House Reports*, Report of Committee on Naval Affairs, 5 March 1858, 35th Cong., 1st sess., Report no. 143, p. 2.

parent improvement. Brooke explained the modification to Maury. When the drawings for the two-arm Brooke lead—sometimes called apparatus or detacher—were completed, Maury submitted them together with a description to the chief of the Bureau of Ordnance and Hydrography and requested that "a few 32 lb. shot, or 32 lb. lead balls be cast and fitted as per Mr. Brooke's plan, and sent to sea for trial." This was done, and the experiments at sea were successful. Lieutenant William R. Gardner, Passed Midshipmen Welsh, Johnson, and Jonathan Carter, and Professor Keith had followed Brooke's experiments with interest; and Brooke explained to them the operation of his new sounding apparatus and Greble's contribution. This was fortunate, because a disagreeable controversy developed later with Greble about the essential characteristic of the invention and to whom the credit should go. Brooke maintained that the significant feature of his invention was the idea of the hinged arm to be tripped when the rod struck bottom, and that the number of arms was a secondary matter. Brooke's position was sustained by Charles G. Page, a patent examiner in the Department of the Interior, who ruled that the "essential characteristic" was the suspending of the weight from a hook which could be tripped. The Patent Office stated that the number of arms was "not at all material."[14]

In time, use would demonstrate that with two arms the apparatus often failed to act at depths greater than two and one-half miles and occasionally even at moderate depths. Proper use of the device required a knowledge of the principles involved and positive care to adjust the two arms at exactly the same level so that they would trip simultaneously. Because of its shortcomings, use of the two-arm model was discontinued after a few years, and the navy adopted the one-arm model that Brooke had originally proposed.

The primary functions of the Brooke lead were to prove that bottom had been reached and to bring back samples of the ocean floor. Nonetheless, the sensitivity of the Brooke instrument, and the fact that a small line could be used with a detachable weight,

[14] Brooke to Maury, 12 March 1856, Letters Received, and Maury to Charles Morris, 15 May 1852, Letters Sent, Naval Observatory, RG 78, NA; Charles G. Page to Brooke, 24 March 1856, quoted by Brooke in letter to George E. Belknap, 9 May 1879 (copy), BP.

made it much easier than formerly for a skilled operator working from a small boat to discern exactly when the bottom had been reached. But the Brooke apparatus was not infallible in measuring depth, and Brooke never claimed that it was. As Maury put it in a report to his chief, Brooke's invention "proposes to bring up specimens of the bottom—not to tell the depths, and is applicable to every plan for bringing up specimens that, to my knowledge, has ever been tried. The depth is told by the time and rate according to which the shot sinks." [15]

The long-range results of the invention were stupendous. The most spectacular immediate result was the impetus it gave to the Atlantic cable. By 1852, when Brooke invented his sounding lead, some fourteen thousand miles of telegraph line had been put up in the United States, and the Associated Press was paying at least $70,000 a year "for news to the various lines leading to New York." Also, a few months before Brooke's invention, great interest had been aroused by the laying of telegraphic wires between England and France. [16] The practicability of laying a cable between Europe and America rested solely upon the evidence furnished by the Brooke lead. It laid bare the secrets of the sea bottom and demonstrated that no currents would disturb the cable on the ocean floor.

In so far as the navy was concerned, the value of Brooke's invention was perhaps summarized best by Maury in a report to the chief of Ordnance and Hydrography. Maury wrote: "The excellency of Brooke's machine consists in its simplicity, its economy, and in the fact that, excepting the twine, every man-of-war, of whatever nation, is already provided with everything requisite for assisting us in carrying out this plan of deep sea soundings. A cannon ball and a rod of wood or iron which the armorer or boatswain can prepare and attach in a few minutes—that's all." [17]

After tests, the Bureau of Ordnance and Hydrography issued general instructions for the use of the Brooke lead. Large twine,

[15] Maury to Duncan N. Ingraham, 16 Jan. 1857, Letters Received Relating to Hydrography, RG 45, NA.

[16] Washington *Daily National Intelligencer*, 31 May 1852; Washington *National Intelligencer*, 16 Oct. 1851.

[17] Maury to Ingraham, 16 Jan. 1857, Letters Received Relating to Hydrography, RG 45, NA.

one-tenth of an inch in diameter, furnished in reels of five thousand fathoms, was to be used. Experiments had demonstrated that the sixty-four-pound shot was more satisfactory than the thirty-two-pound shot first utilized.[18]

Certainly the Brooke lead stimulated deep-sea soundings in the United States Navy. From data obtained by it, Maury was able to prepare the first bathymetrical map of the North Atlantic, showing contour lines in thousands of fathoms.[19] This map was included in Maury's *Physical Geography of the Sea*, the first great textbook of oceanography. Much of the information in it on great depths and the ocean bottom would not have been available but for the Brooke lead. From the first, Maury gave the invention Brooke's name, and as such he designated it in published drawings and descriptions. Although deep-sea sounding—even with a light line and detachable weight—was a difficult and tedious operation, the time saved by reeling in without a weight far more than compensated for the cost of the weight left on the bottom. Even today, when sonic sounding is commonplace, if specimens from the bottom are desired, there is no way to get them other than to sound with a line and detachable weight.

At the Naval Observatory, like other officers, Brooke performed a variety of tasks in the fields of oceanography, astronomy, and meteorology. His interest in astronomy is suggested by the fact that he bought a book of his own on the subject to study at home. Just three months after his arrival in Washington, Brooke prepared an analysis of hurricanes which showed much reflection. Several theories had been proposed to explain the circular and progressive movement of hurricanes, but Brooke noted they were all defective because none took into account the significant fact that in the Northern Hemisphere hurricanes rotate counterclockwise, while in the Southern Hemisphere they rotate clockwise.[20] With reference to air currents, Brooke noted that the belt of equatorial calms where the northeast and southeast trades con-

[18] Instructions for using the sounding twine, issued by Commodore Charles Morris, chief of the Bureau of Ordnance and Hydrography, 17 Dec. 1853, reproduced in Maury, *Sailing Directions*, p. 125.

[19] Coker, *This Great and Wide Sea*, p. 23.

[20] Memorandum by Brooke, 28 Jan. 1852, Letters Received, Naval Observatory, RG 78, NA.

verge is not along the equator but almost always north of it, the southeast trades sometimes advancing five to seven degrees north of the line but never retreating more than two degrees south. He suggested that the cause was the great deserts of Africa and Arabia, lying north·of the line, which act as reflectors.[21]

Brooke worked hard at the Naval Observatory and studied at home. The first few months of his tour of duty in Washington seem to have been among the happiest of his life. Lizzie's good humor was just what a person of Brooke's serious nature needed. But the dream came to an end. Aunt Anna, Lizzie's mother, became desperately ill in the early summer, and Lizzie had to go home to Norfolk for an indefinite period. Brooke maintained bachelor quarters at Mrs. Bryant's and wrote frequently. The intense July heat of the capital, however, equaled that of the African coast, and at times he complained that he could not "study or do anything but gasp for breath." Soon he lamented that he could not study at all while separated from his wife.

Many officers at the Observatory took leave during the summer, and Maury was gone for an indefinite period. The work piled up and Brooke noted that "most of the officers will slack up but I shall only work the harder so as to have something to show when he returns." Greatly admiring Maury and having an inquisitive, scientific turn of mind, he anticipated a long scientific career under the great oceanographer. But such was not his lot, for abruptly he was directed to report to the steam frigate *Powhatan* for duty with the East Indian Squadron. While on that cruise the squadron commander, Commodore Matthew Calbraith Perry, would take the frigate on his historic mission to Japan. But for Brooke, this was not to be; his work at the Naval Observatory had not gone unnoticed. On February 1 his orders to the *Powhatan* were revoked, and he was appointed an acting master in the navy and directed to proceed to New York "for duty as a Lieutenant on board the Tender Fenimore Cooper," which would participate in a voyage of exploration into the North Pacific Ocean.[22]

[21] Rough draft of a 19-page article in the Brooke Papers. Internal evidence suggests that Brooke wrote it at the observatory.

[22] John P. Kennedy to Brooke, 1 Feb. 1853, Appointments, Orders, and Resignations, Records of the Bureau of Naval Personnel, RG 24, NA.

Brevet Colonel George M. Brooke. Portrait by Gilbert Stuart

Lucy Thomas Brooke, c. 1820

John M. Brooke as a young officer in the
United States Navy, c. 1852

Lizzie Garnett Brooke

The *Cyane*'s third cutter, apparently painted by Brooke while he was serving on her from 1841 to 1844. Sent by Brooke to Lizzie Garnett during their courtship.

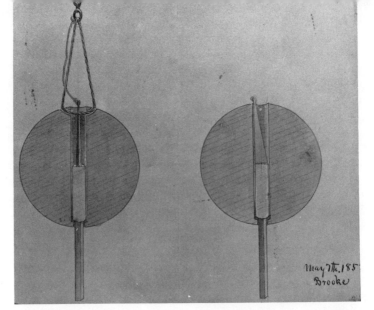

Brooke's first design for a deep-sea sounding lead, with a knife to cut the line

Brooke's drawing of the single-armed deep-sea sounding lead that he designed

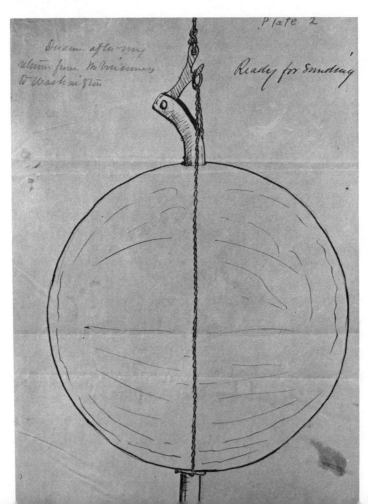

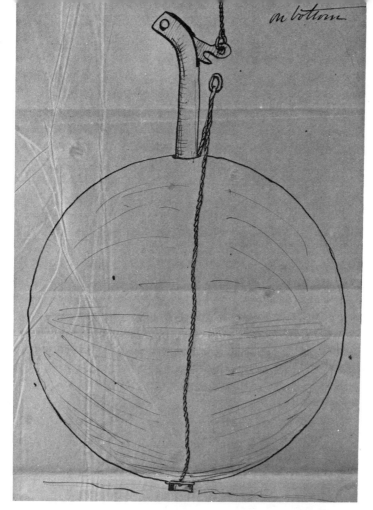

Brooke's drawing of his deep-sea sounding lead as the sling disengaged

The two-arm Brooke sounding lead in operation. From C. Wyville Thomson, *The Depths of the Sea*, 2d ed. (London, 1874), p. 213.

The artist Edward Kern

The *Vincennes* cheering the launch on her departure from
Shimoda for Hakodate, Japan, 1855

The launch of the *Vincennes*

Joseph Heco

The *Fenimore Cooper* in the harbor of Honolulu.
Reproduced from a broken glass positive

The *Fenimore Cooper* off the southern coast of Japan

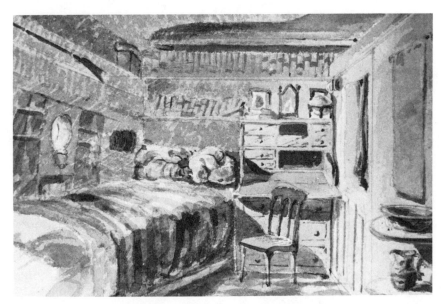

Brooke's painting of his cabin on the *Fenimore Cooper*, 1858–59

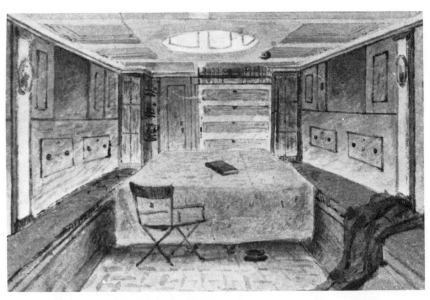

The chart room of the *Fenimore Cooper*, painted by Brooke

French Frigate Shoal, apparently painted by Brooke in 1858

Quarters of Lieutenant John M. Brooke and crew of the *Fenimore Cooper* at Yokohama, Japan

Lieutenant John M. Brooke, c. 1859. The picture was apparently taken in Japan.

Manjiro Nakahama, late in life

Officers of the *Kanrin Maru* (from left): Captain Katsu Rintaro; unidentified; Ono Tomogoro, the astronomer

[Overleaf]
The *Kanrin Maru*, from silk print

The expedition to the North Pacific Ocean was one of several dispatched by the American government in the 1850s to explore and survey far-flung areas of the globe. Even before the fifties the navy had sent out occasional expeditions. The most famous, that led by Lieutenant Charles Wilkes into the South Pacific, has been called "our first great government scientific expedition."[23] The roots of the exploring and surveying expedition to the North Pacific, which set out in 1852, lay in the expanding and unpredictable whaling industry of New England. Whaling in the Arctic seas exceeded in value the entire trade with the Orient, but heavy losses were sustained because there were no adequate charts.[24] Merchants and shippers demanded systematic surveys of the North Pacific and the China seas, which were strewn with unmarked dangers. In addition, there was a need for coaling stations.

In response Congress authorized an expedition "for the reconnaissance and survey for naval and commercial purposes of such parts of Behring Straits, of the North Pacific Ocean and of the China Seas as are frequented by American whaleships" and trading vessels. It appropriated $125,000 "for the building or purchase of suitable vessels." Commander Cadwalader Ringgold, a Marylander of thirty-three years' service, was selected to head the expedition. An accomplished surveyor, he had commanded the *Porpoise* on the Wilkes expedition. Although only a commander in rank, all "the rights and powers of a Commander of a Squadron" were conferred upon him. All naval officers senior to Ringgold were enjoined by Ringgold's instructions from interfering with his command except "under the most urgent circumstances."[25]

Before John Brooke got to sea, Lieutenant S. P. Lee, Brooke's commander on the Coast Survey, wrote to Lieutenant Maury: "I call to ask you to see Ringgold to get Brooke transferred from the Powhatan to the Vincennes, for he is too valuable an officer to go

---

[23] Coker, *Great and Wide Sea*, p. 46.

[24] In a report to the Senate dated 5 April 1852, Secretary of the Navy William A. Graham quoted numerous extracts from Maury's report of 3 Dec. 1851. Secretary Graham's report to the Senate appears in the Washington *Daily National Intelligencer* for 7 April 1852.

[25] Secretary of the Navy John P. Kennedy to Commodore Charles Morris, 24 Sept. 1852, Letters Received relative to Hydrography from the Secretary of the Navy, 1852–53, RG 45, NA.

in the Schooner [*Fenimore Cooper*]. His qualifications you know are of a high order, both as an officer & a man of science; To great capacity for duty & fidelity in its discharge, he unites qualities valuable to a Comdr. whom he will support clear of all cliqueism, you cannot recommend him too highly & I hope you will arrange this matter."[26] Brooke was duly transferred to the *Vincennes*, Ringgold's flagship.

It was expected that the five-vessel expedition would be gone at least three years and subject to all types of weather from the equator to the polar seas. A tight budget necessitated careful planning. The flagship *Vincennes*, commanded by Lieutenant Henry Rolando, was one of the "staunchest and best sloops-of-war" in the navy.[27] It had also sailed on the Wilkes expedition. The bark-rigged, propeller-driven *John Hancock*, Lieutenant John Rodgers commanding, was the only steamer in the expedition. The *Porpoise* was the brig in which Brooke had cruised off the coast of Africa. The smallest vessel of the squadron was the tiny schooner *Fenimore Cooper*, with a complement of twenty men and one gun. This New York pilot boat had been purchased by the government to serve as the tender. The fifth vessel was the *John P. Kennedy*, a merchantman which had been converted into a storeship for the cruise. It was intended that she carry coal and provisions to the Bering Strait, so that the other vessels would not be interrupted in their labors by a lack of supplies.[28]

The squadron lacked rank, Commander Ringgold being the only officer above the grade of lieutenant. All four lieutenants commanded vessels, and of the eighteen passed midshipmen, fourteen were acting lieutenants and four were acting masters. All eighteen performed the duties of a higher and more responsible grade than their own. There was only one midshipman in the squadron.[29] A corps of civilian scientists accompanied the expedi-

[26] Lee to Maury, 20 Jan. 1853, Letters Received, Naval Observatory, RG 78, NA.

[27] *Senate Executive Documents*, Report of Secretary of the Navy John P. Kennedy, 4 Dec. 1852, 32d Cong., 2d sess., vol. 2, pt. 2, no. 1, p. 298.

[28] Allan B. Cole, "The Ringgold-Rodgers-Brooke Expedition to Japan and the North Pacific, 1853–1859," *Pacific Historical Review* 16 (May 1947): 154.

[29] *Navy Register of the United States Navy for the Year 1854*, p. 117. A complete list of the officers and civilian scientists aboard the *Vincennes*, the *John Hancock*, the *Porpoise*, and the *Fenimore Cooper* at the start of the expedition can be found in Frederic Donald Stuart, Jour-

tion, including Fred D. Stuart, draftsman and assistant astronomer, and Edward M. Kern, assistant artist and photographer. All the scientists were under Brooke's supervision. Kern, a lanky six-foot bachelor from Philadelphia, who was four years Brooke's senior, brought to the expedition a number of useful skills. A member of the Philadelphia Academy of Natural Sciences, he had accompanied Charles Frémont on the latter's third and fourth expeditions to the American West. Under Frémont's tutelage he had developed his talents as a surveyor and topographer. Also, as a naturalist, he had collected and classified specimens for his scientific friends and learned taxidermy. But he is chiefly remembered as an artist, and the sketches he made with the North Pacific expedition as with Frémont were of great value. Also, when feasible, he used the extensive daguerreotype equipment he took with him. Brooke and Kern had similar scientific and artistic interests and shared a love of adventure and a zest for travel. Although Kern had periods of gloom and seemed to attract bad luck, he was by nature more optimistic than his southern friend. His gloom was leavened by a sense of humor and a love for practical joking, whereas Brooke's fits of depression were relieved principally by hard work.[30]

Three weeks after Brooke began making preparations, Ringgold notified Secretary of the Navy John Pendleton Kennedy that Sidney Coolidge, "a young gentleman of Cambridge Mass. well versed in Astronomy and the Sciences," had been strongly recommended to him by Lieutenant Charles H. Davis, superintendent of the Nautical Almanac. Ringgold felt that the astronomical duties of the expedition required "great care and attention," and he asked permission to hire Coolidge, a Harvard graduate, at a salary of $800 a year. The request was approved.[31]

Before Coolidge reported for duty, Ringgold informed the secretary that it was essential "to make a series of very careful observa-

nal of a Cruise in the U.S. Ship *Vincennes,* Flagship of the Expedition to the North Pacific Ocean, Comdr. Cadwalader Ringgold Commanding during the Years 1853, Naval Records Collection of the Office of Naval Records and Library, RG 45, NA.

[30] See Robert V. Hine, *Edward Kern and American Expansion* (New Haven, 1962), p. 102 and passim.

[31] Ringgold to Kennedy, 26 Feb. 1853, Letters from Officers Commanding Expeditions, RG 45, NA.

tions with the Astronomic and other instruments of the Expedition; in order to give careful rates to the chronometers, as well as to test the various instruments, and also to practice the officers." Ringgold noted on the Wilkes expedition the matter had been deemed of such importance that Wilkes himself had directed the operation. Ringgold wanted the tests made in Norfolk by an officer of his own selection. The officer would also superintend the erection of a temporary transit house. From the first, Ringgold apparently had Brooke in mind for these duties, but before formal orders were issued, he discussed the matter with Brooke and gained his assent. Ringgold then ordered him to submit to Captain S. D. Breese, commanding the Norfolk Navy Yard, "the dimensions of the Transit House, and request him to afford you such facilities as will enable you to erect it as soon as possible." Brooke was to keep himself "in readiness to participate in the Astronomic and other Scientific duties about to be commenced at that place." Brooke reported to Captain Breese in Norfolk on March 12.[32]

After a few days of hard work, Brooke advised Commander Ringgold, who was in New York readying the ships of his squadron, that he anticipated completion of the transit house on March 21. Ringgold posthaste wrote Maury and requested that the transits, zenith telescopes, some chronometers, and any other instruments Brooke might desire be sent to Norfolk. About the same time, Brooke asked Maury to dispatch three or four chronometers at once and the rest of the instruments as soon as possible "to avoid loss of time." In advance Brooke thanked Maury for any suggestions he might offer and expressed the desire to help the observatory in any way that he could while on the expedition. Maury promptly dispatched an officer with the instruments in his possession and asked Brooke to observe and report on an eclipse of the moon scheduled to occur near the end of the year.

Meanwhile, Ringgold with Brooke's knowledge wrote Maury requesting that Professor Keith of the observatory be ordered to Norfolk. "I would feel much pleased to know," wrote Ringgold, "that the Oby lent its aid and experience in making our first standard point." Maury responded promptly that he did not think

[32] Ringgold to Kennedy, 3 March 1853, ibid.; Brooke to his wife, 8 March 1853, Ringgold to Brooke, 9 March 1853, BP.

"Brooke wants any instructions from anybody, and I cannot spare Mr. Keith, though I would if I thought he could help Mr. Brooke out of any difficulties that he cannot get out of himself." To this Ringgold replied: "I am delighted with your remarks in regard to Brooke, and think as you do, that there is little connected with the duties he is engaged in, that he does not perfectly understand." So it came about that Brooke without assistance erected the transit house and tested thoroughly the astronomical and other instruments upon which the success of the expedition depended.[33] For six weeks Brooke prosecuted his duties assiduously, and when the expedition vessels arrived early in May he reported to Commander Ringgold "that everything was in readiness for observing with the transits & zenith telescopes etc."

Some chronometers had been acquired in New York and Boston and were brought to Norfolk by the vessels of the expedition. It was necessary to test them and determine their rates. These tedious duties devolved upon Brooke. But Ringgold felt the loss of time "was of less importance than the uncertainty and irregularity, which might be supposed very properly to exist in untried instruments." At this juncture Sidney Coolidge finally arrived. By then, Brooke had in fact become astronomer of the expedition and Ringgold told him that he "was to superintend all the astronomical work, to be excused from watch and to direct things as might appear advantageous."[34] Henceforth Coolidge, like Fred Stuart, was Brooke's assistant.

Brooke was the only naval officer on the expedition given purely scientific duties. Unimpressive looking and retiring in his ways, Brooke at twenty-six had already begun to attract through his intelligence, and willingness to assume responsibility, the support of influential men. Perhaps the best description of his duties is one he himself wrote. "I had entire charge of that essential part of the work—the determination of the positions of primary stations by astronomical observation, and the measurement, chrono-

[33] Ringgold to Maury, 24 March [1853], Letters Received, Maury to Ringgold, 25 March 1853, Letters Sent, and Ringgold to Maury, 29 March 1853, Letters Received, Naval Observatory, RG 78, NA.

[34] Brooke Journal, 17 May 1853, BP.

metrically of differences of longitude between them. Every observation upon which those determinations were dependent was made by myself." Secretary Kennedy regarded the astronomic work of the expedition as vital and expressed the hope that one or more standard meridians could be established at the Bonin, Loochoo (Ryukyu), or Aleutian Islands. Such meridians, he wrote Ringgold, "would be of great advantage, as it would enable you to correct the extensive surveys with those points by a series of small meridian distances, . . . almost entirely preventing the errors which grow out of the necessity of conveying time." John Brooke was also assigned hydrographic duties on the expedition. He was promised warm support, and Ringgold expressed to Maury "much interest in the experiments for deep sea soundings."[35]

At the end of May, the *Vincennes*, the *John Hancock*, the *Porpoise*, and the *Fenimore Cooper* dropped down Hampton Roads preparatory to sailing. The *John P. Kennedy* was scheduled to follow in two weeks from New York. Finally, on June 11, the squadron, minus the storeship, stood to sea. It was Ringgold's intention that the squadron sail to the East Indies with brief stops at the Cape Verde Islands and the Cape of Good Hope, but a few days after departure, a bad leak in the *Porpoise* made it necessary to take the squadron to Madeira.[36]

Discipline was a problem on the expedition, primarily because of a lack of junior officers to perform such routine but important tasks as "the superintendence of the decks and the care and vigilant supervision of the spirit room and Hold." Early in the cruise the problem was highlighted on the *Porpoise* when it was discovered the spirit room had been raided and several of the men were drunk, including the boatswain's mate, master at arms, and ship's

[35] Brooke to Adm. Thornton Jenkins, 15 Sept. 1881 (copy), BP; Kennedy to Ringgold, 28 Feb. 1853, Confidential Letters Sent, RG 45, NA; Ringgold to Maury, [1853], Letters Received, Naval Observatory, RG 78, NA.

[36] Ringgold had opposed successfully Secretary Kennedy's plan for the expedition to double Cape Horn and proceed to the Bering Strait by way of the Sandwich Islands. It had been Kennedy's intention for the expedition to operate in the high latitudes from June until October during each year of the cruise and during the remainder of the year to survey and explore in the warmer latitudes along the coasts of Japan, in the China seas, amid the East Indies, and along the route from California to China. Kennedy had been unduly optimistic, hoping that Ringgold could get away early in 1853 and reach the polar seas in June.

steward. As flogging had been banned, the offenders were lashed to an eyebolt and kept on bread and water.[37]

John Brooke began the cruise with a firm resolve to be cheerful. He executed his assigned duties zealously and studied hard. Principally he studied astronomy, but he allotted some time to meteorology and kindred sciences. As always, Brooke was an exceedingly keen observer of all kinds of natural phenomena and he displayed an intense curiosity in many fields of science, including zoology and botany, that did not relate directly to his duties. When the sea was sufficiently calm, he sounded the depths for temperature and tested the efficacy of various types of deep-sea thermometers. Commander Ringgold was particularly anxious to prove by experiment the existence of an isothermal line of depth. But no attempt was made to measure the depth of the deep sea on the run to Madeira.

When the *Vincennes* left Norfolk, the responsibility of winding, comparing, and rating the chronometers had been entrusted to Brooke, and he placed them "in the cabin packed in two rows of boxes raised about three feet above the deck and forming a semicircle abaft the mizzenmast." Five days after leaving Hampton Roads, the young officer noted that the temperature in the chronometer cases had risen five degrees. Further observation convinced him that the chronometer rates were materially affected by sudden changes in temperature and to a lesser extent by the vibration and rolling of the ship. Fortunately such errors tended to balance. Head seas were also a constant source of worry and quite definitely affected the chronometers. The results were better than Brooke expected, and during the passage to the Orient only one or two chronometers had to be rejected because of excessive errors.[38] Important as such work was, the usual line officer would have found it exceedingly boring.

The squadron made Madeira in twenty-eight days, anchoring at Funchal. The condition of the *Porpoise* proved to be so bad that

[37] Ringgold to Secretary of the Navy James C. Dobbin, 9 May 1853, Letters from Officers Commanding Expeditions, 1818–85, Office of the Secretary of the Navy, RG 45, NA; Lt. Frank A. Roe, *Porpoise* Journal, 18 June 1853, Roe Papers, Naval Historical Foundation Manuscript Collection, MSS Div., LC.

[38] Astronomical Report submitted to Lt. Commanding John Rodgers, 20 March 1855, BP.

the expedition's commander made a special report to the secretary of the navy on the subject, stating that at the Brooklyn Navy Yard "many important repairs were neglected." [39] Fate would prove her to be a hard-luck vessel. Brooke found little time for pleasure at Funchal, for he was busy with his instruments. The day the *Vincennes* anchored, he rushed ashore to select a site for sextant observations in order to check the rates of the chronometers. On the cruise Brooke went ashore for observations whenever the *Vincennes* put into port. Ordinarily, rates were checked by equal altitudes obtained with Gambey's sextant, but when the larger instruments were mounted ashore, Brooke took transits of the sun and stars. At Madeira his principal duty was taking sextant observations to check the chronometers. The best chronometer on the expedition proved to be one made by T. S. Negus and Company of New York and purchased by the government for $325, which many believed an excessive price at the time. The Negus chronometer was thought a distinct credit to the "young and enterprising" Americans when in competition with "the most distinguished manufacturers in Europe." [40]

On July 18 the *Vincennes*, the *Porpoise*, and the *Fenimore Cooper* sailed in company for the Cape Verdes. Aboard the vessels were several natives of Madeira who had signed on to escape the poverty of the island. The dull voyage southward to Porto Praia consumed ten days. The heat, humidity, and lack of wind made it perhaps the most depressing part of the entire cruise. Brooke as usual was busy with the chronometers and casts to determine temperature of the water. One cast with a Saxton thermometer produced a "very interesting" result: at a depth of 450 fathoms the same minimum temperature was found as had been obtained in the Gulf Stream at 575 fathoms. [41] For a time Brooke was inclined to the erroneous view that below a certain depth the temperature of the water is constant.

The first attempts to reach the bottom with the deep-sea lead

[39] Ringgold to Dobbin, 13 July 1853, Letters from Officers Commanding Expeditions, RG 45, NA.

[40] Stuart's *Vincennes* Journal, 9–18 July 1853, RG 45, NA. Stuart devotes 11 long detailed pages to the Madeira visit.

[41] Brooke's Abstract Log of the *Vincennes*, 26 July 1853, RG 45, NA.

were made on this leg of the cruise. Unfortunately, the tests were made from the ship rather than from a small boat. On the first test, Maury's large twine was used with a thirty-two-pound shot. After 390 fathoms had run out, it appeared bottom had been reached, but when the attempt was made to recover the line, it parted. On the second trial the line parted as soon as the lead was lowered into the water. On the third attempt with the thirty-two-pound shot, it again appeared bottom had been reached at 390 fathoms. This time the line and shot were recovered, but the arming had been washed away. There was no evidence that bottom had been reached. On the last attempt, a twenty-five-pound shot was bent onto a thick hemp rope, but "the line being light and buoyant its descent was so slow as to render the time of its reaching the bottom uncertain." Once more the arming washed away.[42] These failures could be attributed in part to the drift of the ship. Three valuable lessons were learned: soundings should be made from boats; the arming should be firm enough not to wash off; and heavy hemp rope was useless, if one desired to ascertain when bottom had been reached. It was also evident that even with Maury's twine and Brooke's lead, deep-sea sounding required skill and patience. On each of the following days casts were made of 575 and 680 fathoms with no bottom. Brooke was dispirited by his failure.

During these days the color of the ocean had changed from blue to a yellowish-green hue. There was wide speculation aboard the *Vincennes* as to the cause of the peculiar color. Brooke attributed it to the "diatomacae," or plankton, suspended in it, as did William Stimpson, the expedition's naturalist, while Dr. William Grier, the surgeon, held the "meteorological condition of the atmosphere" responsible. John Van McCollum, an acting lieutenant, thought the strange color was caused by light reflected from a bottom of white sand, but Commander Ringgold inclined to the opinion that the outflow of the large African rivers was the principal cause.[43] The discussion illustrates the sketchy knowledge of

[42] Ibid., 22 July 1853; Stuart's *Vincennes* Journal, 22 July 1853, RG 45, NA.

[43] Brooke's Abstract Log of the *Vincennes*, 22 July, 25 July 1853, RG 45, NA. Brooke and Stimpson seem to have been right. A modern authority states that "in certain areas . . . waters from the deep rise to the surface and become the seat of a large outburst of planktonic life which imports a distinct tint of green to the water" (Coker, *Great and Wide Sea*, p. 86).

the day and the variety of theories postulated on a seemingly simple matter. Commander Ringgold thought the matter of scientific importance. "We often suddenly passed," he reported, "from the ordinary clear blue water into green, of a very decided colour, indicating Soundings—but although various casts were obtained at different depths, our efforts to reach bottom were unavailing."[44]

During the early months of the cruise Brooke held his emotions on a leash and got along well with the squadron commander. From Madeira he wrote: "Capt. Ring. treats me with great kindness." Near the end of July after many weeks of close association with Ringgold, Brooke was enthusiastic: "Capt. Ringgold is the best man I ever sailed with,—that is with my present opportunity of judging." So it was with his messmates. After a month at sea Brooke called them "very agreeable." McCollum was desperately in love and could talk of little else, but Brooke found him as always "a great companion." Brooke was also close to Acting Master Robert R. Carter, a Virginian from Shirley and the only one in the mess "inclined to be religious."

Brooke was delighted to find at least one officer of a religious nature, for on this long cruise he was relying upon religion, no doubt at Lizzie's urging, and hard work to pull him through. At first, he found religion "a great comfort" and affirmed repeatedly his intention to join the church when he returned home. He regretted not having done so before he left Norfolk. At this period Brooke alluded often to reading the Bible and the Reverend Henry Blunt's *Lectures on St. Paul.* But after the squadron left Madeira, Brooke's resolution weakened and his letters referred less and less frequently to religion. The reading of religious works seems gradually to have gone by the board.

On September 12 the *Vincennes* dropped anchor in Simon's Bay near the Cape of Good Hope. The flagship found the *John P. Kennedy,* which had sailed alone from the United States, already there. The *Fenimore Cooper* and the *Porpoise* arrived within the next five days, and with the appearance of the *John Hancock* on September 20, the whole squadron was together for the first time.[45]

[44] Ringgold to Dobbin, 28 July 1853, Letters from Officers Commanding Expeditions, RG 45, NA.

[45] Stuart's journal gives a detailed description of Simonstown and also of Cape Town 20 miles north. Brooke apparently did not visit Cape Town.

For Brooke, Simon's Bay meant more observations. Promptly he erected a transit house, "a snug little box of hooks and staples," on shore close to the home of the British commodore commanding the Cape Squadron, and "obtained a good set of equal altitudes." After building the transit house, Brooke fretted for five days awaiting an opportunity to take ashore the large transit and the zenith telescope. In the meantime he called on two British lieutenants who were engaged in a survey of the coast of South Africa. Brooke recorded that it had seldom been his good fortune to meet two more agreeable men. A pleasant interlude was a dinner with the American vice-consul to Simonstown, who treated him to Cape antelope and good Constantia wine.

Because one of the four regular watch officers was sick, Brooke was pressed into service at Simonstown as a watch officer for the first time on the expedition. Thereafter, he was frequently called upon for such duty despite Ringgold's desire to exempt him. There was no help for it. As Ringgold had pointed out before sailing, the expedition was desperately shorthanded. In fact, there were only eight line officers aboard the flagship in all grades, and these included Commander Ringgold and Lieutenant Rolando, the flag captain. The six remaining officers were all passed midshipmen, including Brooke, astronomer of the expedition, and Carter, acting master. Passed Midshipmen McCollum, Andrew F. Monroe, David P. McCorkle, and Thomas Scott Fillebrown were the regular watch officers. When one of the regular watch officers was sick—and they seemed to be sick often—either Brooke or Carter was put on watch, and if two officers were sick, both Brooke and Carter were called upon, despite their regular duties.

Brooke finally landed the transit and zenith telescopes ten days after the *Vincennes* dropped anchor in Simon's Bay. He was now in sole charge of the astronomical instruments, with one sailor, Wheelan by name, to assist him. Coolidge, now known by the men as "Quick Silver Jack" from the frequency with which he appeared on deck swinging his thermometers, had been placed in charge of the meteorological instruments. Coolidge's duties were divorced entirely from Brooke's. With the transit in meridian, Brooke followed the stars nightly in their courses, and each day at noon, he shot the sun with the sextant as the fiery orb crossed the meridian. When the winds blew, observation was difficult, and in bad weather no observations at all could be made. Between observations, mathematical computation kept Brooke busy much of the time. Oddly, despite the continual use of mathematics in his work, Brooke never liked the subject. The budding scientist had a room in the hotel at Simonstown which he used when he worked ashore, far into the night when return to the vessel was impractical.

Brooke spent many hours alone in the transit house. When times were slack he sketched, brooded, and smoked an unconscionable number of cigars. He blamed the latter for a pain in his chest, and he confessed that he smoked "twelve or thirteen one right after the other." His excuse was that he felt "lonely and sad" if he didn't smoke. Brooke had ceased to chew tobacco when the expedition left the States, and he now resolved to reduce his smoking. Judging by his pictures it was at this time that he apparently began to lose some of his hair, but there is no mention of it in his correspondence. He was a proud young man. At times Brooke brooded as of old and wished he were out of the navy, but he did not write of resigning.

Lizzie had moved to Lexington, Virginia, to live with her sister Louisa, who was married to Thomas Hoomes Williamson, a professor at the Virginia Military Institute. Lizzie had not been well and complained of pains in her chest; the symptoms suggested consumption. Brooke worried about the reduced circumstances of her parents, William and Anna Garnett, after the colonel lost his job when a Democrat was elected president. Gradually, he "rebelled as it were against God and tried to lose consciousness by mingling with the irreligious men of the ship."[46]

Harassed and worn out by bothersome problems concerning his crew and the deplorable condition of his ships, Commander Ringgold underwent a change. Slowly he began to crack under the strain, but for a time Brooke retained a high regard for him. Brooke's first altercation with the commander arose over the location of the chronometers on the *Vincennes*. Brooke was dissatisfied with their position and felt they should be moved nearer the

[46] Brooke Diary, 20 Dec. 1865, BP.

center of motion of the ship. He so expressed himself to Ringgold and too freely on occasion to others, when Ringgold continued to do nothing about it. Brooke was called on the carpet. Toward the end of the colloquy Ringgold "regained his usual good humor," but the chronometers stayed where they were. After some weeks in port, there was a noticeable change in the commander's demeanor and the disintegrating morale of the squadron reflected it. The true scientific purpose of the expedition was forgotten as attention was riveted upon routine and trifling details. The whole venture gave evidence of coming apart at the seams.

After weeks of labor, Brooke finally completed his observations and at sunrise on November 1 took down the transit house. Now that his labors were done, the young scientist was impatient to be on his way. To him Simonstown had meant little more than hard work and the projection of the date for return home still further into the indefinite future. Though he had been there nearly two months, he had not received a single letter. He was at a loss to account for that. Besides, Brooke had spent all his money and had even had to go to the purser for an advance. The young officer admitted to extravagance, but that was only part of the story. He had been required to live ashore much of the time, and Simonstown was one of the most expensive ports in the world.

On November 9, early in the morning watch, with a fresh and fair breeze, the *Vincennes* set out on the long voyage to Sydney, Australia, following a course between 45° and 50° south latitude across the Indian Ocean. Plans called for the vessels of the expedition to rendezvous in the South China Sea. The *Vincennes* ran into rough weather, and for more than a week heavy seas and contrary winds kept her north of the forty-fifth parallel. Brooke called the passage from Simonstown to Sydney one of "an unusually tempestuous character." For many days the *Vincennes* scudded under close-reefed main topsail. Heavy seas were encountered all the way, and once a wave was observed which was "computed to be not less than forty-five feet in vertical line from base to summit." The log of the *Vincennes* shows she traveled the 6,321 miles from Simonstown to east Tasmania at an average speed of 171 miles per day. The maximum speed attained by the sturdy sloop was eleven knots.

During the hectic passage to Australia, Brooke performed his regular duties and stood watch. While still near the Cape of Good Hope he attempted to sound the depths, but on the first attempt, "the circumstances were unfavorable inasmuch that the ship had considerable motion so much indeed as to render the lowering of a boat dangerous."[47] An attempt to sound from the ship failed. Brooke tried again four days later from a boat on a smooth sea. After three and a half hours and at a depth of 7,040 fathoms (determined by timing) Brooke believed that the lead had struck bottom, because the line had ceased to run out. When some five hundred fathoms of line had been recovered, a new boat crew relieved the old one. However, with night approaching and the commander impatient to get on, the new crew jerked the line and it snapped.[48] Though Brooke was bitterly disappointed that no specimen had been obtained, Ringgold, at least, seems to have been satisfied that bottom had been reached, for he related to Maury that "off Cape Good Hope, deep sea sounds in 8000 faths were secured and bottom, no mistake, with Brooke's invention."[49] No further efforts were made to sound for depth until the Indian Ocean had been traversed.

Brooke's principal responsibility was maintaining the chronometers, and during the voyage he was "curious to observe the effect of change in temperature upon our chronometers together with the motion of the ship both of which are in extreme." Upon arrival at Sydney the commander was "pleased that the chronometers appear to be so little out"; in the main the causes of error had canceled out one another. But Brooke saw "nothing to be pleased at except that the position in which they have been kept (location) motion & change of temperature has not thrown them beyond all limits." Brooke concluded philosophically that if the commander was satisfied, he was.[50]

[47] Brooke's Abstract Log of the *Vincennes*, 11 Nov. 1853, RG 45, NA. The Agulhas Current made it a slow and difficult task to round the Cape of Good Hope from west to east.

[48] Log of the *Vincennes*, 15 Nov. 1853, RG 24, NA; Brooke's Abstract Log of the *Vincennes*, 15 Nov. 1853, RG 45, NA; Brooke's *Vincennes* Journals, 15 Nov. 1853, BP; Stuart's *Vincennes* Journal, 15 Nov. 1853, RG 45, NA.

[49] Ringgold to Maury, 27 March 1854, Letters Received, Naval Observatory, RG 78, NA. The line was affected by a strong current setting to the northward.

[50] Brooke's *Vincennes* Journals, 25 Dec. 1853, BP.

Christmas evening the revolving light of Botany Bay was sighted, and the next day the sloop furled her sails in Sydney harbor. The *Vincennes*'s arrival at Sydney "was hailed . . . with acclamation," and Commander Ringgold reminded the secretary of the navy that the ships of the North Pacific expedition were the first American warships to visit Sydney in eleven years. In the interim vast changes had taken place, accelerated by the rush to the Australian goldfields, and thousands of Americans had congregated in the land down under. Sir Charles Augustus Fitz Roy, governor of New South Wales, stated that the Americans as a rule were law-abiding people. Commander Ringgold recommended to the department frequent visits of American warships to prove to the government of New South Wales that the United States was interested in its citizens and to give the Americans confidence and encouragement.[51] The officers of the expedition were elected "honorary members of the Australian Club."[52] Brooke believed the harbor of Sydney with its "deep water sheltered cover and fine scenery" to be the finest he had ever seen. The Americans were pleased to learn that there was a growing trade between Sydney and American ports, with Boston apparently in the lead.

John Brooke did not find the people of Sydney as attractive as the buildings and scenery. "Now with regard to the people," he wrote, "I have been struck by the preponderance of the lower classes you see very few who are not coarse or common looking people, yet some of the females are quite pretty." But Brooke did meet some nice people. He was particularly attracted to a Jewish family by the name of Phillips, whom he met through Fred Stuart. The father resembled an old patriarch, and well he might, for he had sired twenty-two children, fourteen of whom were living. Phillips was a kind and generous host, and Brooke did not remember ever having been more cordially received. In fact, he "felt more at home than ever before when away from the United States." But it was Miss Nancey, an eighteen-year-old daughter,

[51] Ringgold to Dobbin, 28 Dec. 1853, 10 April 1854, Letters from Officers Commanding Expeditions, RG 45, NA.

[52] Stuart's *Vincennes* Journal, 26 Dec. 1853, RG 45 NA. Stuart noted that toward the south the city's streets extended for nearly 5 miles. The stores were filled with a variety of costly articles, and there were several fine hotels, a theater, and many new churches. Though not paved, the streets had sidewalks and curbstones.

who elicited Brooke's warmest praise. "I have seen pleasant faces and graceful persons," he wrote, "but hers were both charming beyond description, her face was artless, cheerful, and expressed the sweetest character." Archly, he observed that "her most exquisite figure was irresistable." Brooke even secured the buckle from one of her gloves as a keepsake! And in his journal, he concluded: "I do like the Jews more and more."[53]

Brooke, with Stuart to assist him, made his observations at Fort Macquarie, and though the site had been used by the Wilkes expedition, it was now old and dilapidated, Stuart terming it "an eye sore to the good people of Sydney." Although the *Vincennes* remained at Sydney nearly two weeks, weather conditions were unfavorable for observation. Still, Brooke regarded the results as satisfactory. He recorded his routine at Sydney: "I generally start before breakfast with Mr Stuart, go to Fort Macqarie where there a[re] four or five cannon and two or three soldiers. Stay there until 10 o clock lo[u]nging about on the grass or taking sights according to the clearness of the sky. Then I go to town to get some breakfast at the French Cafe smoke a *segar*, walk about looking at all the ladies I can find worth looking at. At 2 I go to the fort again for more sights about four o'clock I return to the town to get dinner and walk about until the sun set boat comes on shore."[54] Certainly Brooke had little reason to complain about his duties at Sydney.

The accuracy of the chronometers made it possible to determine the longitude of Sydney with "great precision." When H.M.S. *Calliope* ushered in the new year by firing a gun at mean midnight, as determined by the British chronometers, Brooke found the expedition chronometers differed by only two-fifths of a second. Brooke was in much better spirits when the *Vincennes* left Sydney for he knew that the chronometers ran well enough for him "to earn a little reputation."[55]

On January 8, 1854, with a stiff breeze at her back, the *Vincennes* "stood handsomely out" of the harbor. It was with some regret and a thin purse that Brooke saw Sydney fade away in the

[53] Brooke's *Vincennes* Journals, 1 Jan. 1854, BP.
[54] Brooke to his wife, 31 Dec. 1853, BP.
[55] Ibid., 8 Jan. 1854.

distance. At least he had a copying machine to show for his expenditures, which he hoped would make it easier to write his long letters. As for intangible assets, his pleasant memories of the Phillips family would never die.

From Botany Bay, the *Vincennes* steered for the Coral Sea, which Ringgold in anticipation declared was "the most intricate and dangerous of any portion of the Pacific Ocean."[56] Brooke wrote that there were parts of it from which no ship had ever returned; the dangers were reefs "almost indiscernable to the eye, lying just even with or immediately under the surface of the water." Ringgold's objective was to dispel the mysteries of this little-known sea, expose its dangers, and indicate safe avenues through it for American merchantmen bound for China. Progress was slow as frequent soundings were made; yet the sea was "as glassy as a mirror" and belied the reefs with which parts of it were strewn. Brooke found it "a pure and beautiful blue so deep and intense" that it resembled lapis lazuli. Ringgold suggested that the name of the deeper portion of the Coral Sea be changed to Blue Sea, and Brooke felt the change would be appropriate.[57] But the investigations of the *Vincennes,* as revealed in the journals and log, added strength to Brooke's assertion that the Coral Sea was "the most dangerous one known to mariners."[58]

In the Coral Sea the *Vincennes* explored particularly the passages through the Solomon and Santa Cruz Islands, observing the winds and currents carefully. As hydrographer, Brooke was responsible for the observation of currents. Moreover, when the sloop left Sydney, Ringgold had ordered him "to assist the Master in observing when near land and engaged in determining positions for surveying purposes." This meant that in addition to his own specific scientific duties Brooke was given a full share in the important and arduous surveying activities of the *Vincennes.* Running north to the Carolines, Brooke and the other surveyors found that many reefs laid down upon the charts did not exist.[59]

[56] Ringgold to Dobbin, 28 Dec. 1853, Letters from Officers Commanding Expeditions, RG 45, NA.

[57] Blueness of the sea generally indicates a paucity of suspended material in the water. The bluest areas are in truth the deserts of the ocean.

[58] Brooke to his wife, 8 Jan. 1854, BP.

[59] Brooke's Abstract Log of the *Vincennes,* 10 Jan. 1854, and Stuart's *Vincennes* Journal, 26 Feb.–3 March 1854, RG 45, NA.

The Deep-Sea Sounding Lead and First Voyage of Exploration

Leaving the Carolines the sloop passed rapidly through the Marianas and then steered west for the coast of China by way of the Bashi Channel, taking angles and bearings as she went. Brooke was kept occupied for he had sole management of the chronometers, soundings for temperature, deep-sea soundings, and the astronomical instruments. In addition, he kept watch frequently. As a result of his multifarious duties, the naval scientist often fell behind in his journal entries. With good reason he stated that his duties were various and required "much time."

The cruise from Sydney produced results. In the Coral Sea the water was smooth and the temperature of the air, though high, was even. Such conditions were ideal for chronometers. In the vicinity of the Carolines, the waters were "equally smooth," and the winds were steady and moderate. These general conditions continued all the way to Hong Kong, and Brooke reported at that port that in the passage from Sydney "the chronometers ran together for a much longer time than on any of the preceding passages." [60]

Near the Solomon Islands, Brooke for the first time measured the depth of the sea successfully. He transmitted his enthusiasm to his journal: "This day witnessed the successful operation of my contrivance to procure specimens of bottom from considerable depths. At 2150 faths. the apparatus struck bottom the shot or leaden weight was disengaged and the rod or piston came freely up bringing with it abundant evidence of bottom. . . . Adhering to it was a coating of calcareous mud of great tenacity the arming was lowered and even the mark made by the leaden shot in slipping off remained. . . . The line was of 15 thread and . . . the shot weighed about 40 lbs. The apparatus was put over from a boat at 10^h 11^m reached bottom at 11^h07 its velocity diminishing very regularly. I took it in hand myself and started it fairly on the way up then one hand at the reel wound away. A quartermaster or myself kept hand constantly on the line to see that no undue strain was brought upon it, in veering the line was nearly or rather exactly up and down, there was barely any swell the air came in faintest cats paws. . . . At 1^{hr} 45 P M the sounding was finished and exceedingly well pleased I returned to the ship." [61]

[60] Astronomical Report submitted by Brooke to Rodgers, 20 March 1855, BP.

[61] Brooke's *Vincennes* Journals, 31 Jan. 1854, BP. The sounding was made in latitude 12°59′ south, longitude 162°58′ east.

Nearing the Asiatic coast, the *Vincennes* fell into the path of the China clippers. One morning at daylight the lookout espied two sails on the eastern horizon. They came up fast and were recognized as "the famed clippers of our country." The *Vincennes* signaled a desire to speak and the leading clipper bore up. "The splendid appearance of the clipper as she neared us excited universal admiration her long sharp and beautiful lines ever fairly shown," exulted Brooke. With every sheet home and her sails so taut the yard bowed, the mighty clipper was an impressive sight. Finally, on March 20, 1854, after a run of seventy-one days from Sydney, the *Vincennes* arrived at Hong Kong.

IV /

WITH THE NORTH

PACIFIC EXPEDITION

At Hong Kong, Brooke found letters dated up to January 1 awaiting him. News that Lizzie remained in poor health was disturbing and he passed a sleepless night. From her he received a copy of *Practical Piety; or, the Influence of the Heart on the Conduct of the Life* by Hannah More. This little book, with chapters on "Self-Examination" and "Christian Watchfulness," was sent with the inscription that John read it attentively for his wife's sake.[1] During the six months he was in Hong Kong, Brooke heard from home frequently, for clippers arrived almost daily from New York or San Francisco. The ocean greyhounds made the run from New York in 107 days, and those from the West Coast averaged roughly 37 days.

Commander Ringgold expected to caulk the *Vincennes* at Hong Kong, stow provisions, and give the crew a respite from the long cruise, but he believed the work would take little time. While the vessels were under repair, he pushed the preparation of charts. The North Pacific expedition's small store of optimism was soon used up, for it found itself engulfed in a variety of knotty problems it had not anticipated. China was in ferment resulting from the Taiping Rebellion; the outcome of Commodore Perry's negoti-

[1] The book is in the possession of the author.

ations in Japan was still uncertain; some of the vessels of the expedition needed extensive repairs; and sickness crippled the squadron, aggravating the shortage of junior officers and making a shift of personnel necessary.

By midsummer Commander Ringgold fell victim to "intermittent fever" and was incapacitated. At this juncture Commodore Perry returned to Hong Kong from his mission to Japan, having secured the Treaty of Kanagawa, Japan's first treaty ending its seclusion. Finding affairs of the North Pacific expedition "in a state of confusion" and Ringgold in a highly nervous state, he relieved Ringgold of his command and turned over the North Pacific expedition to Lieutenant John Rodgers, Ringgold's second in command. Perry was strongly influenced in his actions by the statements of Dr. William Grier, chief surgeon of the North Pacific expedition.[2] Though Brooke was at his shore observatory during Ringgold's critical illness, he was pleased at Perry's action. The astronomer had lost faith in the old expedition commander but had enormous respect for the abilities of John Rodgers.

Two days after the *Vincennes* arrived at the British colony, Brooke had gone ashore to select a location for the transit. He chose a site on the side of a mountain which included "a splendid house" with a garden and terrace. Soon Brooke landed "the two best transits one zenith telescope and the [regular] telescope, transit house etc."[3] It was confusion worse confounded when the instruments reached the wharf, but eventually the coolies were arranged into some semblance of order, and they set off in a procession up the winding path with bamboo creaking and boxes rattling. The transit house was quickly erected, and Brooke took up his vigil on shore with his man Wheelan, a boy from Madeira named Pombo, and four marines who were assigned quarters in the building. The astronomical duties were entirely in Brooke's hands now, for at Hong Kong, Sidney Coolidge resigned from the expedition because there were insufficient duties to utilize his specialized skills and Fred Stuart returned to the United States.

Glenelly, Brooke's spacious new home high above the city,

[2] Perry to Dobbin, 9 Aug., 1854 (copy), Grier to Rodgers, 1 Aug. 1854, Letters from Officers Commanding Expeditions, RG 45, NA.

[3] Brooke's *Vincennes* Journals, 25 March 1854, BP.

was far removed from the discomfort, noise, and confusion of the ship. The mansion reminded Brooke of the castle of Otranto, and, like a castle, it had mysterious night noises that echoed down its "lofty halls." The house had five large rooms on the ground floor, the same number above, one or two small rooms, and wide halls. In his room Brooke had a bedstead, table, and wicker chair. The veranda flanking the building on three sides was "cool and pleasant." Glenelly was encircled by beautiful gardens. Here Brooke compared chronometer rates with the *Vincennes* by signal; in his work he was left alone.

In the evening Brooke walked often through the Chinese section of the island, where there was "a good deal to be seen that is interesting." He recorded that the Chinese of Hong Kong were a shrewd race and "very hard bargainers." But their tools were antiquated by Western standards. Brooke was surprised to see spectacles in common use and he noted the lenses were oval rather than round. Of particular interest were the shaved heads of the men from whose crowns dangled the "pendant queues," which were coiled around the neck when in the way. The women, who were "very short and broad," were dressed in "flowing trousers" and wore "their hair made up on the back of the head like the handle to a pitcher." The saving grace of the Chinese was their disposition. "Never saw I more good humored people," wrote Brooke. "In fact the only attraction possessed by the majority of females" was their evident amiability.[4]

Comfortable as the observatory was, it had its drawbacks; they were the demerits of Hong Kong. In March the skies were overcast and there was much sleet and rain. In fact, there were only three or four clear, pleasant days during the whole month. The change of the monsoons made it impossible to obtain a series of observations that "would justify their application to the chronometers, for purpose of careful correction" of the charts. In April the weather became even more changeable with sudden and extreme variations.[5] Oppressively hot, humid days were interspersed with cold, damp ones. Again it was next to impossible

[4] Ibid., 15 April 1854.

[5] Roe's *Porpoise* Journal, 1–30 April 1854, Roe Papers, Naval Hist. Foundation, MSS Div., LC.

to take a series of observations that would permit correction of the chronometers.

By June 22 Brooke's work seemed to be progressing. But the surface calm was deceptive. In July, Brooke discovered that the observations he had made "during the first part of the June lunation" were defective. The Ys of the transit were "unstable" and would not remain adjusted. This was the transit that Wilkes had taken on his expedition and it was badly worn. Brooke concluded that it was "a very poor instrument indeed although the glasses are passable." He valued the zenith telescope but little more, and between the clouds and "inherent defects" of the instrument he could accomplish little. "Take it all in all we have the most worthless set of old instruments for astronomical purposes that was ever gotten up," Brooke confided to his journal.[6] The work of the expedition was being vitiated by the stinginess of the government.

When Brooke finally completed his observations, Rodgers ordered him to rejoin the flagship at Macao. Aware that Brooke was dissatisfied with the location of the chronometers on the *Vincennes*, Rodgers authorized him to select a better position. Brooke chose the place in the port steerage amidships where the motion was least perceptible, "and such precautions were adopted as the experience of the most successful Hydrographers suggested."[7] From experience Brooke accepted the theory that variation in temperature was the principal source of error in chronometers.[8]

The new squadron commander was determined to resume surveying work at the earliest possible moment, for there had been delays far beyond what anyone in the United States could have reasonably anticipated. Even though the end of the monsoon

[6] Brooke's *Vincennes* Journals, 5 July, 20 July 1854, BP.

[7] Brooke to Rodgers, 3 April 1861, Letterbook, BP.

[8] In the Brooke Papers there is an extract from Lt. Henry Roper's "Remarks on the Modes of Determining Longitude," *Nautical Magazine and Naval Chronicle* (1839), p. 324. Roper wrote: "It seems generally admitted that the principal cause of the variation of the rates of chronometers, is change of temperature; and accordingly in several ships care has been taken to keep the temperature of the chronometer room, as nearly constant as possible by artificial means. The fact of a change of rates, following a change of temperature, has been repeatedly noticed; it has been observed however, that the change of rate is not in general simultaneous with the change of temperature but takes place some time afterwards." Lieutenant Roper of the Royal Navy was secretary to the Royal Astronomical Society.

spelled a sharply rising danger from typhoons, Rodgers resolved to sally forth into the China seas. With the *Porpoise* and the *Vincennes*, he intended to proceed to the Bonins and the Marianas. When those islands had been surveyed, the two vessels could begin a survey of the islands of Japan. Upon completion of this assignment the *Vincennes* and *Porpoise* were to rendezvous in Hong Kong with the *John Hancock* and *Fenimore Cooper*, preparatory to extended cruising in the northern seas. The *John P. Kennedy* had been condemned as "unfit for sea service" and transferred to the East India Squadron.

While preparations for sea were made aboard the *Vincennes*, Brooke applied for command of the *Fenimore Cooper*. The vacancy had come about when Lieutenant Henry K. Stevens was transferred from the schooner to the *John Hancock*. Rodgers deliberated for a week and finally refused the request on the ground that Brooke had been chosen for the expedition because of his technical skills. Rodgers was careful to point out that he regarded Brooke's position as astronomer "no less useful and no less honorable" than that of a ship commander. The rank-conscious Brooke was not completely satisfied and complained in a letter to Lieutenant Maury, in the latter's words, that "it is unpleasant however to have ones junior put overhead." He even asked Maury to intercede in his behalf. Maury, though sympathetic, believed Brooke was of more value where he was.[9]

Brooke was very busy after his return to the *Vincennes* and made several trips ashore to secure equal altitudes. Since the departure of Stuart and Coolidge there had been no one except Brooke qualified to make astronomical observations and computations. Hence, on August 31, Anton Schönborn, the mathematical instrument maker, was appointed assistant astronomer on Brooke's recommendation. Presumably Brooke had to acquaint Schönborn with the status of work already done and perhaps teach him how to use the instruments. Before Ringgold departed

[9] Brooke to Rodgers, 26 Aug. 1854, Miscellaneous correspondence, official orders, etc., 4 April 1853–18 Dec. 1855, Box 3, Rodgers Family Papers, 1788–1944, Naval Hist. Foundation, MSS Div., LC; Rodgers to Brooke, 2 Sept. 1854, BP; Brooke to Maury, 3 Sept. 1854, Letters Received, Naval Observatory, RG 78, NA, microfilm copy, BP; Maury to Brooke, 21 May 1855, Letters Sent, Naval Observatory, RG 78, NA.

for the United States, he requested all "data necessary to the construction of preliminary charts of routes of Porpoise & Vincennes." Brooke supplied this information.

Brooke also prepared a long personal report for Lieutenant Maury in which he reviewed the astronomical and hydrographical work of the expedition up to departure from Hong Kong. This report supplemented two routine reports of experiments in deep-sea soundings and a table of temperatures at various depths transmitted to the Navy Department. Brooke wrote that from his experience in the Indian Ocean and the Coral Sea he was "inclined to believe that there is no depth from which specimens of the bottom may not be obtained." In his reply Maury exulted that the specimens from the Coral Sea contained "real gems in the way of infusoria" and urged Brooke to "let us have more deep, deep soundings."[10]

Departure of the *Vincennes* and the *Porpoise* was planned for September 9, but high winds and a threatening sky postponed it until the twelfth. By noon that day the vessels, loaded with chickens, ducks, and geese, were clear of the land. The force, though much reduced in size, was in "far more buoyant spirits than before Ringgold left." Brooke was delighted with the new location of the chronometers and noted that their motion was "entirely different from the violent irregular jerking motion of the cabin."[11]

The two ships set an eastward course for the Bonins, across the South China Sea. The passage into the Pacific was tempestuous, as the vessels were beset constantly by "hard gales high and short seas with a strong current against" them. During the northeast monsoon a strong current in the Bashi Passage made it exceedingly difficult to beat out into the Pacific. Rodgers had selected a trip to the northward in the teeth of the monsoon, despite such hazards, because the crews had been weakened by the hot, unhealthy weather of South China and needed a change. Fortunately the *Vincennes* escaped the vortex of the typhoons "that swept over the China Seas" while she clawed her way eastward against the prevailing winds. On September 29, after seventeen

[10] Brooke to Maury, 3 Sept. 1854, Letters Received, and Maury to Brooke, 21 May 1855 (copy), Letters Sent, Naval Observatory, RG 78, NA.
[11] Brooke's *Vincennes* Journals, 12 Aug. [Sept.] 1854, BP.

hectic days, the flagship glided into the comparatively calm Pacific alone, for a week earlier she had parted company with the *Porpoise*. With relief the crew observed a flock of sparrows alight in the rigging.

With resumption of the cruise Brooke was given more than his share of work. Atop his special duties in astronomy and hydrography, he was again called on to stand watch. He was convinced that some of the regular watch officers were skulking and would not have gone on the sick list if he had not been on board. On the other hand, his scientific duties were perhaps simplified by the use of Maury's abstract log, which had recently been recommended by the maritime conference in Brussels. Rodgers gave Brooke a copy and instructed him to keep it "carefully in accordance with the order of the Hon*ble* Secretary of the Navy."[12]

In a way Brooke began to enjoy the cruise. The difference was in commanders. John Rodgers, an old acquaintance, had long since won Brooke's respect. Close cooperation over many months transformed mutual respect into deep friendship. Of all the commanders Brooke ever had, he admired Rodgers the most. And twenty-five years later a friend wrote Brooke that Rodgers "used to speak of you in terms of great respect and admiration."[13] The writer added that Rodgers "was always a great worker himself and appreciated that quality in others."

After a zigzag passage of twenty days, the *Vincennes* reached the Bonins where Brooke made extensive surveys and observations. At the head of the bay were two prominent peaks "named East and West paps." One morning Brooke, with Kern as his assistant, led a party up West Pap, the higher of the two peaks, and Monroe led another party up East Pap. Brooke's party carried an eprouvette (a small cannon) weighing fifty-four pounds, a theodo-

---

[12] Rodgers to Brooke, 2 Oct. 1854, BP.

[13] George E. Belknap to Brooke, 12 July 1879, BP. Before the Bering Strait expedition, Rodgers had received considerable surveying experience with the Coast Survey. In the Civil War, on the Union side, he won the thanks of Congress and promotion to commodore for his exploits. See J. Russell Soley, "Rear-Admiral John Rodgers, President of the Naval Institute," *Proceedings of the United States Naval Institute*, 8, no. 2 (1882):251–65, and "In Memoriam—Rear Admiral John Rodgers, United States Navy, Chairman of the Light-House Board, 1878–1882," copy in BP. A good biography is Robert Ervin Johnson, *Rear Admiral John Rodgers, 1812–1882* (Annapolis, 1967).

lite and stand, a barometer, a chronometer, and two signal flags. Brooke was armed with a rifle, and each man carried his own drinking water. The other party was similarly equipped. The ascent was aided by a pioneer who cleared a path with an axe. When the surveying parties reached the summits of the two peaks, the distance between the peaks was determined by firing the eprouvettes and "by triangulation from the shore on which a base line was measured." Brooke described the method used to determine the distance by sound. "The ship ran up her flag to the mainmast head dipped it. hoisted and fired and so on six discharges[;] with watch to the ear the beats were counted from flash to report. When she hauled down, I fired six times with warning, then Monroe fired six times." When the distance between the peaks had been ascertained, the theodolite was erected and angles were measured to "all prominent objects." As Kern had little opportunity to sketch the landscape during the day, Brooke and his party remained on West Pap overnight.[14] At sunset the second day Brooke and his party returned to the ship.

The *Vincennes* remained at the Bonins two more weeks. Brooke conducted his astronomical observations on a sandy beach overgrown with shrubbery, particularly hibiscus, the only location "clear of water and yet protected from the winds." Fortunately Brooke's instruments were not up when a terrific typhoon suddenly struck. Brooke noted later that the storm was "of such fury as to cause the *Vincennes* to drag with four anchors down lower yards and topmast struck" while confined "in harbor nearly surrounded by high mountains."[15]

At Port Lloyd in the Bonins the *Vincennes* loaded a supply of water, wood, and turtles and on November 6 headed to sea. Eleven days later she anchored in the harbor of Naha on the island of Okinawa, largest island in the Ryukyu, or Loochoo, Islands.[16]

[14] Brooke's *Vincennes* Journals, 23 Oct. 1854, BP.

[15] Undated draft of an article by Brooke, BP.

[16] This island chain consists of 55 islands stretching southwest from Japan nearly to Formosa. The islands separate the East China Sea from the Pacific Ocean. The islands enjoyed a semi-independent status for centuries. Although under the suzerainty of China, the king of the Ryukyus was also a vassal of the lord of Satsuma, one of the greatest of Japanese feudal lords. The natives of the islands are related to the Japanese. Surgeon Grier noted that Naha was "made up of quite a number of narrow irregular streets, with the ex-

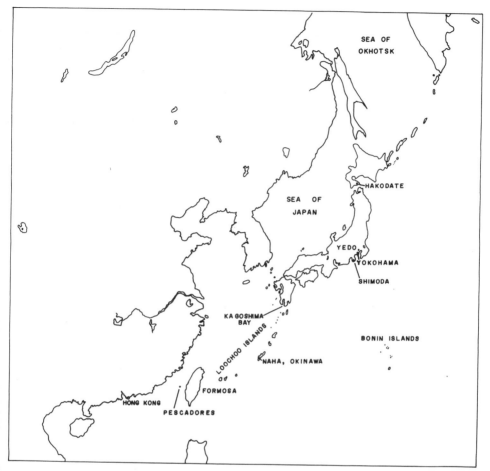

Japan and East China Sea

For observations Brooke selected a site near the landing at Tumai, the same site Perry had used for his coal depot. Brooke's astronomical instruments—a transit, zenith telescope, and portable declinometer—were housed in a bamboo shack thatched with grass. This building, which had served Perry as a coal shed, was used as a residence by Brooke and "some of the scientific corps." Good results were secured at the observatory; indeed, Brooke later reception of a few of the principal ones, which are wide and strait." The houses were enclosed by stone walls 4 or 5 feet thick (Grier's *Vincennes* Journal, 12 Dec. 1854, RG 45, NA).

(*1 0 3*)

ported that his astronomical observations obtained at Okinawa were "better than any before obtained and are to be preferred."[17] The scientific work aroused the natives' curiosity, but they volunteered no information on their own institutions.

Soon friction developed between the American commander and the government of Loochoo. Two principal complaints were the lack of facilities for the repair of the *Vincennes* and the indifference of the native government to the report of a wrecked American vessel on the south side of the island. There were other complaints: the delivery of wood and water was delayed; pilots were never furnished; and fresh beef was not supplied every four or five days as promised. Rodgers interpreted these maneuvers as violations either of Commodore Perry's recent treaty or of agreements the Okinawans had made with Rodgers.[18] The government of Loochoo, it seemed, believed "that by not furnishing any supplies and offering no facilities for repairs they will prevent vessels from coming to their Island." Rodgers resolved on a show of force. The Americans landed a force of fifty sailors, the marines, and a fieldpiece; so escorted, he intended to "march to Shendi [Shuri] and see the Regent in the palace."[19] Brooke, eager to see the interior of the regent's palace, asked permission to accompany the party. Rodgers consented.

The streets lay deserted as the well-armed Americans approached the open gates of the capital. Brooke described the scene in his journal. "Arrived at the palace gates a halt was called and the Captain accompanied by Roe, Fillebrown, Dr. Nichol, Kern and myself with Mr. Moreton as interpreter entered. . . . We passed through several gates barred with iron and beneath several arches containing rooms from which persons were looking down upon us. . . . We did not enter the principal building inasmuch . . . [as] it was probably the residence of the Regent, but were

[17] Astronomical Report submitted by Brooke to Rodgers, 20 March 1855, BP.

[18] John Rodgers's unbound journal no. 3 (Hong Kong, 1854), Box 1, Rodgers Family Papers, Naval Hist. Foundation, MSS Div., LC; Brooke's *Vincennes* Journals, 12 Dec. 1854, BP.

[19] Brooke's *Vincennes* Journals, 12 Dec. 1854, BP. Shuri was the scene of heavy fighting during the Second World War and was captured by the U.S. Marines. The castle on the hill is strongly fortified.

satisfied to seat ourselves in the Council Hall. . . . Seats were brought for all. . . . A venerable man, second to the Regent, made his appearance and we were informed that the Regent was in the country. A relation of the Regent . . . next came and took his seat on the right of the first. . . . Pipes & tobacco tea and cakes were brought. Capt. Rodgers made known the grounds of complaint and everything was amicably arranged."[20] The Reverend Mr. Moreton, a missionary, described Rodgers's dramatic action as "the best thing which had ever been done in Lew Chew."[21] Certainly it was effective. When the party returned to the beach, "long lines of men were passing wood to the waters edge." By ten the next morning the *Vincennes* had been filled with wood, water, and provisions, and it was necessary to refuse some supplies because space was lacking. But to protect American interests in the future, Rodgers urged the appointment of an American consul to Okinawa.

On December 13 the *Vincennes* sailed. Five days later, near the coast of China, she fell in with the clipper *Nightingale*, eleven days from Hong Kong. The clipper bore bad news; the *Porpoise* had not put back to Hong Kong and nothing was known of her. It was nearly three months since the *Vincennes* and the *Porpoise* had parted company near the Pescadores. Everyone felt "the most intense solicitude," and Brooke noted "the general desire of all the watch officers, and I also desire it is to go at once to the China Seas and search for her or her wreck." But Rodgers ruled otherwise and steered for Japan. The next day all were still much depressed and Brooke reiterated his belief that an intense search should be made. He could not understand why Rodgers did not make the search and stated, "this is the only occasion on which I find fault with our commander."[22] No trace of the *Porpoise* was ever found.

On December 28 the *Vincennes* entered Kagoshima Bay in southern Japan. As Perry's treaty had only opened Shimoda and Hakodate, both on a limited basis, Rodgers resolved to use Kago-

[20] Brooke's *Vincennes* Journals, 12 Dec. 1854, BP.

[21] Rodgers's unbound journal no. 3 (Hong Kong, 1854), Box 1, Rodgers Family Papers, Naval Hist. Foundation, MSS Div., LC.

[22] Brooke's *Vincennes* Journals, 18 Dec. 1854, BP.

shima Bay as the testing ground for boldly "pushing the Treaty to its fullest extent."[23] A policy of bluff was adopted. Brooke recorded that "as we neared the shore we saw the Japanese skipping along over the rocks to intercept us at the landing; but we anticipated them by giving way lustily, so that by the time they arrived we were in possession of a large flat rock suitable to our purpose" of making observations. There were twenty or thirty Japanese in the group, "each wearing two swords, a long and a short one." Though the Japanese were consumed with curiosity and eager to examine the Americans and all their belongings, "they continually waved their hands towards the ship, and by all the means in their power" urged the intruders to leave the land. Brooke made his observations, "not a little annoyed" by his audience, while Rodgers entertained the natives with a pistol. Charles Wright, the botanist, came on shore and furnished some comic relief. He was collecting weeds, which the Japanese thought "a funny thing," and as he stumbled among the rocks the Japanese roared with laughter. All day the natives crowded around the industrious Americans, but they remained civil and polite.[24] On succeeding days Brooke returned for observations to the flat rock, which was whitewashed so that it could be more easily recognized.

The new policy—one which the *Vincennes* had "rather *forced,* by giving a liberal construction to the Treaty"—paid dividends.[25] The people became very polite indeed, and whenever Brooke went ashore for observations, the Japanese bowed and no longer made signs for him to return to the ship. They remained firm, however, in their refusal to trade.

Prior to departure Rodgers forwarded a communication "to the 'Minister of foreign affairs of Japan,' to the effect that a certain

[23] Roe Notebook, 1 Jan. 1855, Roe Papers, Naval Hist. Foundation, MSS Div., LC. In 1837 the *Morrison,* an American merchantman, had been dispatched from Macao to Japan to return seven shipwrecked Japanese to their homeland. At Kagoshima the *Morrison* was driven off by gunfire.

[24] Brooke's *Vincennes* Journals, 29 Dec. 1854, BP. Brooke's detailed impressions of the Japanese at Kagoshima Bay are important, for this was the first time Americans had landed in the great southern bay. Rodgers discussed the same incident at length and his account agrees substantially with Brooke's; see Box No. 1, Rodgers Family Papers, Naval Hist. Foundation, MSS Div., LC.

[25] Roe Notebook, 1 Jan. 1855, Roe Papers, Naval Hist. Foundation, MSS Div., LC.

amount of sun taking was a necessity with surveying vessels, and that we must land to observe in Japan, and hinting that there would be trouble if local officers interfered with our procedings." This communication was sent in anticipation of the expedition's projected trip to Japan in the spring.[26]

From Kagoshima the *Vincennes* ran to Tanega-shima, to the southeast. In contrast to Kagoshima, the people of Tanega-shima did not seem to be afraid, nor did they oppose an examination of their island. Rodgers remarked the natives treated the Americans "very kindly," but he added that he always "made it a point to be very civil and have abundance of arms."[27]

South of Tanega-shima the *Vincennes* reached an anchorage off Kikaiga-shima, then known as Harbor Island, in the Amami Group, halfway between the southern Japanese island of Kyushu and Okinawa. At the approach of the *Vincennes* "horns were blown cattle were driven away men women and children ran about in confusion."[28] Going ashore, Brooke was followed by the villagers, who carried clubs, and he noted that there was "not a female to be seen."

From Kikaiga-shima, the *Vincennes* clawed her way through heavy squalls to O-shima. As none of the natives ventured out to meet the ship, Brooke went ashore. In his journals he recorded a threatened confrontation as he approached the village. "Indeed having to pass an angle of rock, projecting nearly to the water, the chief men, wishing to turn me back, placed their inferiors like so many pickets to bar my advance. They bore shoving, but not the sight of a revolver, which in all parts of that country produces excellent effects. They made way. When I returned to my place of observation they brought me tea." In the China Seas the expedi-

[26] Brooke's *Vincennes* Journals, 6 Jan. 1855, BP. Rodgers's communication is published in Allan B. Cole, ed., *Yankee Surveyors in the Shogun's Seas: Records of the United States Surveying Expedition to the North Pacific Ocean, 1853–1856* (Princeton, N.J., 1947), pp. 48–49.

[27] Rodgers's unbound journal no. 3 (Hong Kong, 1854), Box 1, Rodgers Family Papers, Naval Hist. Foundation, MSS Div., I.C. This island, the largest of the Osumi Group, is about 25 miles in length, with a total area of 176 square miles.

[28] Ibid. This small island was also called Bungalow. It was thought the name Bungalow derived "from a clump of trees upon the northern slope of the ridge which resembles a building of that description." Frank Roe described the island as a tableland about 200 feet high.

tion was alert, as always, for scientific data. Near O-shima an "abundance of sperm and other whales" were sighted—on one day twenty were observed.[29]

Leaving O-shima, the *Vincennes* crowded on all sail for Hong Kong, which she raised on the morning of January 30, 1855, after an absence of four months and nineteen days. It was none too soon—the provisions were nearly exhausted and the crew was subsisting largely on rice.

Brooke's computation revealed that the chronometers had gained only "one second and four tenths, over their applied rates." These results were remarkable under the circumstances, for during the 141 days required for the winter cruise, the condition of the sea was recorded as "very rough" on 25 days. The mean temperature of the chronometers varied from 65 degrees at Kagoshima to 84.8 degrees at Hong Kong. The longest interval between observations was the forty-six days between Hong Kong and Port Lloyd; the shortest was the nineteen-day interval between Port Lloyd and Okinawa. The heavy weather encountered, particularly to the east of Harbor Island and O-shima, caused excessive motion, "but the position of the chronometers near the center of motion preserved them in a great measure from its effects."[30]

Upon arrival in Hong Kong, Brooke immediately went ashore to make observations. Then he turned to the "great number" of personal letters that had accumulated during his absence. They reported "all well at home." A few days later Brooke received another large batch of letters from his wife and "an immense number of papers of last year from my kind friend Lieut. S. P. Lee," by clipper from California. So long as he remained at the British colony Brooke enjoyed regular mail service.

Upon the return of the *Vincennes* to Hong Kong, John Rodgers received official confirmation of his appointment as squadron commander. He was ordered to execute his mission as rapidly as pos-

[29] Brooke's *Vincennes* Journals, 22 Jan. 1855, BP; Rodgers to Maury, 5 March 1855, Correspondence between Maury and Rodgers re Exploring Expedition, 1855, Box 6, Rodgers Family Papers, Naval Hist. Foundation, MSS Div., LC. Also known as Amami-O-shima, it is the largest island in the Amami or Oshima island group, composed of about twenty islands in the Ryukyus.

[30] Astronomical Report submitted by Brooke to Rodgers, 20 March 1855, and Chart for Determination of Longitude of Basic Points, BP.

sible, "using the most rigid economy in the expenditure of public money," and cautioned to limit the activities of his vessels "strictly to the purposes for which they have been fitted out, leaving the objects of diplomacy and protection of American Commerce and Citizens in China to the vessels of the squadron on that Station."[31] In preparation for the voyage north, Rodgers wrote a letter which would be delivered to the governor of Shimoda in the spring requesting permission to survey the coast of Japan. With more optimism than was justified he boldly proclaimed that he "dare not anticipate the consequences of a refusal." Commodore Perry had already informed the Japanese that such a survey was intended "in order to ascertain the line of the coasts, learn what harbors existed available in case of storms, or of wrecks of the numerous whaleships in those regions."[32]

Meanwhile, Brooke worked at his observatory on Morrison Hill in Hong Kong for two full months. Much depended on his skill, for, as he wrote years later, he "had the entire charge of that essential part of the work—the determination of the position of primary stations by astronomical observation, and the measurement chronometrically of differences of longitude between them." In his work Brooke had the full support of Rodgers, who commented to Maury: "Our observations turn out very well—Brooke deserves the credit, as he has done all the work—His success considering every thing has my warmest thanks—We have worked against the weather—He takes all the observations for chronometer rates, moon culminations, zenith telescope, magnetic dip intensity and declination[;] he regulates the lamp sticks in the chronometer room, and in a word makes all the nice observations."[33]

From the beginning of the expedition the *Vincennes* had been

[31] Dobbin to Rodgers, 18 Nov. 1854, Correspondence between Maury and Rodgers re Exploring Expedition, 1855, Box 6, Rodgers Family Papers, Naval Hist. Foundation, MSS Div., LC.

[32] Rodgers to Secretary of State, Empire of Japan, 7 Feb. 1855, in Cole, *Yankee Surveyors*, pp. 49–52; S. W. Williams to Rodgers, 26 Feb. 1855, Miscellaneous orders and letters to Rodgers, Box 3, Rodgers Family Papers, Naval Hist. Foundation, MSS Div., LC.

[33] Brooke to Adm. Thornton Jenkins, 15 Sept. 1881 (copy), BP; Rodgers to Maury, 5 March 1855, Correspondence between Maury and Rodgers re Exploring Expedition, 1855, Box 6, Rodgers Family Papers, Naval Hist. Foundation, MSS Div., LC.

shorthanded in officer personnel, and now as she headed into the little-charted North Pacific she had one less officer than when she had limped into Hong Kong a year earlier. The year had brought about a considerable turnover. Of the officers who had arrived in Hong Kong aboard the *Vincennes* in 1854, only Brooke and Scott Fillebrown remained. Ringgold and Rolando were gone, and in their places were John Rodgers and Frank Roe. Of the four regular watch officers of Ringgold's regime, only Fillebrown was left, and he was in "delicate health." John H. Russell, who had sailed to Hong Kong in the decrepit *Kennedy*, had been assigned to the flagship, and Brooke was given the job of training him in navigation. Unfortunately, at the very time Brooke's scientific duties were multiplied, increasing demands were made upon him for routine tasks. To distribute the load the officers served in five watches, with everyone taking a turn.

With the crew it was different. Brooke was struck by the "superior character" of some of the sailors shipped at Hong Kong— men who had been lured into the navy by the increase in pay. Recording that "our men generally are small and such characters as the sharp witted Captains of our swift clippers would not employ," he wished that the *Vincennes* had forty men like those taken on at Hong Kong. Brooke expected much from the change in pay policy, believing that the United States Navy would in time "have the best seamen in the world." [34]

Some signs were auspicious. Morale aboard the flagship was high as she nosed northward through the Formosa Strait. Brooke exulted that he had "a good supply of sounding twine" and seven deep-sea sounding leads. Russell learned fast, and a few days after departure Brooke recorded that he was pleased with his facility in taking observations. Moreover, the sailmaker, Richard Berry, was given a sextant to assist in surveying and navigation.

Fifteen days after leaving Hong Kong, the *Vincennes* arrived at Naha in the Loochoo Islands. The *Fenimore Cooper* followed the flagship in, but it was learned that the steamer *Hancock* had come and gone and was at present engaged in a survey of a nearby island group. Itarashiki Satonushi and several other officials, all

---

[34] Brooke's *Vincennes* Journals, 15 April 1855, BP.

wearing yellow hatchee-matchees, or official headdresses, clambered aboard the flagship. Itarashiki had been the official court interpreter during the *Vincennes*'s first visit; Brooke had a high regard for his ability and thought his inquiries were "very pointed" and "his perceptions acute." The commander entertained the visitors in the cabin.[35]

On the day the *Vincennes* anchored off Loochoo, or Okinawa, Rodgers proposed to Brooke that he take the launch of the *Vincennes* and survey Japan's east coast from Shimoda to Hakodate, the two ports that had been opened by the Perry treaty. "I accepted the proposition," Brooke noted in his journal, "and hope he will not change his mind. It would be interesting indeed." Such a survey was badly needed. The east coast of Japan was "comparatively unknown." From the limited observations of prominent points made by navigators and the interpolations from the crude charts of the Japanese, the bare outline of a chart had been constructed. But that was all. Essential information such as "the depth of water, character of bottom, and sketches of the land by which navigators recognize particular harbors, or points of coasts, were wanting." Geographic knowledge was sketchy indeed. For example, European estimates of the area of Japan ranged from 9,000 to 266,000 square miles, and of the total population from 15,000 to 50,000,000.[36]

At Naha, Brooke found it necessary to take observations for the chronometers, and he was forced to work on the Sabbath against his predilections. Pressed for time, he had to attend personally to the rating of all the *Vincennes*'s chronometers. Moreover, the sun varied so in brightness within a short time that Brooke was compelled to change the colored glasses of his sextant "many times during the taking of complete sets of equal altitudes." Finally he obtained a four-day interval, which he regarded as "al-

---

[35] Ibid., 17 April 1855. Brooke expressed these impressions, which he had formed during his earlier visit to Loochoo, to Rodgers as they neared the island the second time.

[36] Brooke's *Vincennes* Journals, 21 April 1855, BP; J. M. Brooke, "Coasting in Japan," *U.S. Nautical Magazine and Naval Journal* 5 (Dec. 1856): 197; Shunzo Sakamaki, "Western Concepts of Japan and the Japanese, 1800–1854," *Pacific Historical Review* 6 (March 1937): 11. In fact, with an area of about 143,000 square miles, Japan was a little smaller than California. At the time, Japan's population was about 30 million.

together too short for a good rate," but it was the best that he could do.[37]

On April 23 the *Vincennes* got away at an early hour, moving rapidly to the northward. The plan called for the three vessels of the expedition to survey carefully the string of islands running toward Kyushu, the southern Japanese island. By the end of the month the *Vincennes* was on the west side of O-shima. Rodgers, continuing the survey, measured a short base by sound—a method of which Brooke disapproved. Brooke did not admire the inhabitants of O-shima, noting that they looked and dressed like the Loochooans but were dirty. While the *Vincennes* and the *Hancock* were anchored off the northwestern tip of the island, Rodgers decided the time was appropriate to display the benefits of Western civilization. He "ordered the *Hancock* to get up steam and several officers with three boats crews to arm and dress for a visit" to the town three miles from the anchorage. The steamer left in style with three cutters in tow. Meanwhile, Brooke went ashore for observations with two assistants who had buckled on their swords. Having completed his observations, Brooke, accompanied by his "faithful body guard and a dozen or two of the natives," set off on foot for a nearby village. He too adopted a bold policy, and as on previous occasions his resolute attitude impressed the natives.[38]

By the time the *Vincennes* had reached Tanega-shima, the last island before Kyushu, the plans for the proposed launch expedition from Shimoda to Hakodate were set. Rodgers had determined that Brooke should make a "running survey of the coast and examine all harbors or roadsteads that may be found." Rodgers intended to request permission from the Japanese to conduct the survey and to apply for a native to serve as interpreter and assistant pilot. Since there was a distinct possibility the Japanese might refuse permission if asked directly, Brooke suggested that Rodgers merely notify the authorities that the launch was going, as though it were perfectly natural, and request an interpreter who could inform the natives along the coast of the beneficent purpose of the voyage.[39]

[37] Brooke's *Vincennes* Journals, 26 April 1855, BP.
[38] Ibid., 5 May 1855.
[39] Ibid., 9 May 1855.

Brooke's enthusiasm was fanned by the prospect of the voyage in the launch. As the *Vincennes* neared Shimoda, Brooke's interest became still "more strongly excited." "Japan is before us," he noted in his journal. On May 12 the snowcapped peak of Mount Fuji was descried. The next day, eleven months after Commodore Perry's departure and fifteen months before the arrival of Consul General Townsend Harris, the *Vincennes* and the *John Hancock* dropped anchor at Shimoda.[40] Hardly had the *Vincennes* arrived, when a boat of American build was seen approaching "from the inner harbor." "There were three people in it dressed in European costume, two were at the oars, the third steering. With the glass it was concluded that the former were Americans and the latter a Russian." The conjecture proved correct as H. H. Doty and William C. Reed, whom Brooke labeled "pioneers of American progress," and a passed midshipman from the wrecked Russian frigate *Diana* scrambled aboard the flagship. The position of Reed and Doty was peculiar. With their families and several other Americans they had hastened from California "to establish a rendezvous for whale and other ships" under the protection of Perry's treaty. However, the treaty actually "contained no provisions for commercial intercourse betwen the two countries."[41] With their supplies the Americans were domiciled in a temple, and according to Reed it had been "an everlasting job to get those idols and images turned around."[42] The vessel in which the Americans had arrived in Japan, the schooner *Caroline E. Foote,* had promptly departed for Petropavlovsk on the Kamchatka peninsula with a number of Russians from the wrecked *Diana.*[43]

In the meantime the Japanese had pressed the American traders to depart when their vessel returned. Reed had opposed such a retreat, and his stubborn disposition had precipitated an al-

[40] Perry's squadron sailed from Shimoda on 28 June 1854. Harris arrived in Japan on 21 Aug. 1856.

[41] Brooke's *Vincennes* Journals, 13 May 1855, BP; Chitoshi Yanaga, "The First Japanese Embassy to the United States," *Pacific Historical Review* 9 (June 1940): 114. This affair is discussed in Cole, *Yankee Surveyors,* pp. 14–17.

[42] Reporting to Secretary of the Navy Dobbin, Rodgers noted that there were "ten Americans residing in the Temple of Yokushen, five Gentlemen, three ladies, and two Children" (Cole, *Yankee Surveyors,* p. 57).

[43] The *Diana* had been in Shimoda harbor at the time of an earthquake and had foundered.

tercation with the Japanese. He made a bold speech to the officials and had shocked them when he threatened to write the emperor. Such was the situation when the *Vincennes* arrived. The incident led Rodgers to urge the United States to establish an American consul at Shimoda and to acquire extraterritorial rights.[44]

In the wake of the Americans and the Russian came Japanese officials in a long red-lacquered boat. The Japanese were "well dressed," though one who wore a distinctive pair of flowing trousers was immediately dubbed "Calico Jack." The Japanese repaired to the cabin, where Rodgers "informed them among other things that he would ask the prince of the country for permission to Survey the coast of Japan and he intimated quietly that he would be exceedingly pleased to have the permission but that if he did not receive it he would still" do so.[45] The American felt that without such an examination of the coastline, the Treaty of Kanagawa, which permitted "American vessels in distress to enter any of the ports of Japan, would be a mockery." Obvious though this appeared to Western eyes, it seemed that the Japanese, content with their own primitive charts, "had not thought of this necessity."[46]

Two days later Rodgers and the ship's officers, accompanied by an armed guard of sailors and marines, called on the governor of Shimoda. Negotiations were conducted through an interpreter who was studying English with the aid of a Webster's dictionary left by the Perry expedition.[47] Rodgers introduced the question of the projected survey of the foggy and rockbound northeast coast. To make the proposition more attractive, he offered to assign any natives designated by the Japanese government "as interpreters

[44] As a matter of fact, this right had already accrued to the United States under the most-favored-nation clause of the Treaty of Kanagawa, for in February a Russian admiral at Shimoda had concluded a treaty which in substance granted extraterritoriality. Rodgers believed that the American consul at Shimoda, who would be the highest officer accredited to the Japanese government, should decide cases involving American citizens and should, therefore, personally refrain from commerce because the Japanese looked down on traders.

[45] Brooke's *Vincennes* Journals, 13 May 1855, BP.

[46] Brooke, "Coasting in Japan," p. 196.

[47] Grier's *Vincennes* Journal, 17 May 1855, RG 45, NA; Allan B. Cole, "The Ringgold-Rodgers-Brooke Expedition to Japan and the North Pacific, 1853–1859," *Pacific Historical Review* 16 (1947): 158.

and observers of the character of the survey."[48] He also offered to supply the Japanese government with copies of the charts. In his negotiations Rodgers strove "to sooth the jealousy of the Japanese," while maintaining "without any reservation the right to survey." The Shimoda officials gave no direct reply but referred Rodgers to Yedo (Tokyo), the shogun's capital, for authority to execute this venture.[49]

Before leaving Hong Kong, Rodgers had prepared a written request for permission to survey which he now forwarded to the shogun. He was determined that adequate surveys should be made, as it was his belief that a ship in distress had the same right to enter a foreign port as a person had to enter a residence marked "no admittance" when a lion was roaming the streets.[50] But the Japanese government would not be hurried.

Meanwhile, in a sheltered cove in the Bay of Shimoda the ship's carpenter and his crew fitted the *Vincennes*'s launch for her voyage. The launch was a tiny craft, twenty-eight feet long and seven and one-half feet wide, spreading 160 square yards of canvas.[51] As the gunwale was only fourteen inches above the waterline when the boat was fully loaded, a canvas weather cloth was raised as a bulwark around the launch to give a foot and a half more height, without much increase in weight. It was a wise precaution: "Her poop, forecastle and weather clothes enabled her to withstand seas which without those additions would have swamped her."[52] All in all the little craft was well fitted out, and when the job was done, she resembled a minature sloop.

Brooke, the artist Edward Kern, and the volunteer crew of thirteen were well-armed with a variety of weapons including a twelve-pounder brass howitzer, because no one knew how they might be received by the Japanese on the coast. Regular navy rations for fourteen days were issued; it was hoped that should the

[48] Brooke, "Coasting in Japan," p. 196.

[49] Cole, *Yankee Surveyors*, p. 55; Cole, "Ringgold-Rodgers-Brooke Expedition," p. 158.

[50] Rodgers' unbound journal No. 3 (Hong Kong, 1854), Box 1, Rodgers Family Papers, Naval Hist. Foundation, MSS Div., LC.

[51] Brooke, "Coasting in Japan," p. 197; see also the Brooke Journals.

[52] Brooke to Rodgers, 22 June 1855, Cole, *Yankee Surveyors*, p. 98.

need arise further supplies could be obtained from the natives.[53] As it turned out, the Japanese authorities responded negatively to Rodgers's request, insisting that under the Treaty of Kanagawa American vessels were allowed to enter "no other harbors than those of Simoda, and Hakodadi, except in storm or distress."[54]

But the Japanese reply had no effect on Brooke. Since time was running out for the vital survey of the Bering Strait in 1855, that impatient officer had already sailed from Shimoda on May 28. Three cheers from the *Vincennes* had speeded the launch—affectionately called the *Vincennes Junior*—on her way through a rough and irregular sea infested with tide rips. The rips would pose the greatest danger of the voyage, "for in them small vessels became unmanageable and the sea boils like a cauldron." Beyond Shimoda lay adventure in an open boat, an adventure that has been described as "one of the most daring exploits in the annals of naval exploration."[55] The voyage meant Brooke's first responsible command.

Brooke resolved on a "big stick policy" from the beginning, because such a policy had worked in his previous contact with Orientals. Moreover, Western observers had "generally disparaged" Japan's military and naval might.[56] During the voyage the launch put into shore on several occasions—always a risky business. "By repeatedly camping on shore the Americans strained the interpretation of the provision in Perry's treaty which permitted vessels in emergency to find haven in nontreaty ports."[57] At such times there was considerable intercourse with

[53] In an undated entry in his *Vincennes* Journals, Brooke lists the officers and men who "composed the crew of the Launch on her voyage from Simoda to Hakodadi, Coast of Japan 1855." See also Brooke, "Coasting in Japan," pp. 197–98; Cole, "Ringgold-Rodgers-Brooke Expedition," p. 159; Alexander Wylie Habersham, *My Last Cruise; or, Where We Went and What We Saw* (Philadelphia, 1857), p. 257.

[54] Three Japanese officials to Rodgers, c. 1 June 1855, Cole, *Yankee Surveyors*, p. 66.

[55] Brooke, "Coasting in Japan," p. 204; Cole, "Ringgold-Rodgers-Brooke Expedition," p. 159.

[56] Sakamaki, "Western Concepts of Japan," p. 10. Western writers "while admitting the propensity of the Japanese to fight bravely and 'die in heaps' believed: that . . . two frigates were 'amply adequate' for a strict blockade of Edo [Tokyo] and the port of Matsumae (now Fukuyama, in the Hokkaido), [and] that 'a vessel of twenty guns, well manned, and judiciously and cautiously directed, might bid defiance to their whole naval force.' "

[57] Cole, "Ringgold-Rodgers-Brooke Expedition," p. 159.

the Japanese, whom Brooke found "a very humorous people" who laughed "at everything comical." The manner in which the launch was received at different Japanese towns varied markedly and seemed to depend mainly upon the disposition of the local authorities. But in general the Japanese theory about supplies was simple: they were only permitted to supply what was needed, and the Americans naturally could not need what they did not consume immediately. Brooke attributed the difference in treatment at various ports to the fact that the ruling authorities were "bitterly opposed to intercourse with foreigners," whereas the people themselves seemed ready and willing for such dealings.[58] Actually it was to be explained by the varying reactions of the daimyos (feudal lords) to the treaty signed by the shogun.

Brooke and his doughty crew visited ports never before entered by foreigners as they sedulously gathered data for a chart of the coast. Wherever the launch ventured, the natives exhibited curiosity. The people themselves, when not cowed by officials, manifested a spirit of friendliness and extended favors for which they expected no remuneration. Even at a secluded retreat in northern Honshu, where the people were unusually timid and reserved, fear was soon dissolved by some jests, and the Japanese threw wood on the fire, offered water, and handed the Americans their pipes. Brooke was convinced, however, that as a rule much of the respect the Japanese demonstrated "was due to the display of a good supply of offensive weapons."[59]

Satiated with adventure, the launch rounded Cape Shiriya on June 17 and headed for Tsugaru Strait, the treacherous channel lying between Honshu and Hokkaido.[60] Here, nature had saved one more thrill for the "Thunderer of the Seas," as Brooke called the launch. Ahead lay a reef of rocks with seething waters at its base. Basking on the rocks was a herd of seals. Hoping to secure a specimen for the naturalist, Brooke, with the wind at his back, headed straight for the reef, intending to bring the seals within

[58] Brooke, "Coasting in Japan," p. 341.

[59] Ibid., *U.S. Nautical Magazine and Naval Journal* 6 (April 1857): 29.

[60] Roe Notebook, Naval Hist. Foundation, MSS Div., LC. According to Roe, "a strong current sets from the sea of Japan East . . . into the Pacific at a speed of 4 to 5 knots, against a contrary wind and sea."

range and then, after firing, to luff up and pass around the end of the reef. Running seven knots under all sail, the launch neared its prey. "Suddenly," Brooke wrote later, "we discovered that the troubled water indicated a ledge of broken rocks, over which it swept like a mill race." At this moment of peril the seals were forgotten and the vessel was brought into the wind. "It was too late" to clear the danger, for the strong current was sweeping the launch broadside on. There was only one chance: to run the boat over the ledge. "Hard up the helm and let her go through," commanded Brooke. "The main-boom swung broadly off, the boat rose on a swell, gathered way, and with the combined speed of the current and that given by her sails, dashed right in among the boiling eddies. 'Starboard! port! steady!' were the only words uttered as rock after rock was seen in the depths below." A crash was expected any moment until with vast relief the waters were seen to darken. The *Vincennes Junior* had passed through unscathed.[61]

Across the broad Tsugaru Strait lay Hakodate. At length the outline of the *Vincennes* was descried, then the *John Hancock*, and finally the *Fenimore Cooper*. The sun dipped beneath the western sky, and as darkness closed in, a lantern was hoisted to the masthead. Sharp gusts of wind forced a furling of the sails "and for the last time the oars were manned." As the lights of the squadron grew bright, a signal gun was fired. It was a dramatic moment when the *Vincennes* quartermaster heard the heavy sweep of the oars and hailed the launch. "As the answer went, we heard the sound of many feet, and the words 'the launch! the launch has come!' "[62] The entry in the flagship's log for June 17, 1855, was brief: "At 11 the Launch arrived after an absence of 20 days on a Surveying Expedition. All well." Dr. Grier noted that "Mr. Brooke reports that he was kindly treated by the natives along the coast." Alexander W. Habersham stated that the week's delay in the launch's arrival had been a source of worry.[63] The day after her arrival the *Vincennes Junior* was unrigged and hauled aboard the parent ship. The job was done.

[61] Brooke, "Coasting in Japan," 6:37–38.
[62] Ibid., p. 39.
[63] The *Vincennes* arrived at Hakodate on 6 June. This was three weeks after the expected time of arrival that Rodgers had given to Secretary Dobbin before leaving Hong Kong.

During the cruise of twenty-one days Brooke had examined and partially surveyed the 450-mile east coast of Japan from Shimoda to Hakodate. A running survey of the entire coast was made, except for about fifty miles, and Brooke reported that data had been obtained for the location of all important points. He found that from Cape Nojima to the Bay of Sendai there were no secure harbors and discovered that on that stretch of coast the soundings were regular and a constant southeast swell prevailed. North of the Bay of Sendai Brooke found the coast was "a series of harbors," with the land well watered and wooded. There the currents near the coast generally "set to the Southward." The naval scientist was happy to have secured typical specimens of the bottom from every section of the coast. He found that between Shimoda and Hakodate there were neither outlying rocks nor shoals, and a ship could approach to within a mile of the shore without danger. Only the fear of holding up the *Vincennes* in her departure for the northern seas had prevented a closer survey of the coast and its harbors.[64] Rodgers was well pleased with the work and complimented Brooke "exceedingly." Later he told Russell that the cruise of the launch "was the most gallant and best thing yet done by the Expedition."[65] Praise enough! And in writing of the adventure to Secretary James C. Dobbin, Rodgers said that the launch had made "a most successful surveying voyage." To Maury the expedition commander reported that Brooke had done "a gallant thing with success."[66]

Brooke's respite was brief, but while recovering from the rigors of the voyage he had a couple of days to size up the situation in Hakodate, where the authorities were more unbending than those in Shimoda and placed "a constrained interpretation upon the treaty."[67] Then he turned to his scientific duties. During his absence Schönborn had compared and wound the chronometers, and Russell had taken over Brooke's astronomical duties. Back on the job, Brooke went ashore with Schönborn to the mouth of a small creek where Russell had attempted observations

[64] When he rejoined the *Vincennes*, Brooke made a preliminary report to Rodgers. A copy of this report, dated 22 June 1855, can be found in Cole, *Yankee Surveyors*, pp. 87–98.

[65] Brooke's *Vincennes* Journals, 18 June, 29 June 1855, BP.

[66] Rodgers to Dobbin, 23 June 1855, Cole, *Yankee Surveyors*, pp. 125–29; Rodgers to Maury, 25 June 1855, Letters Received, Naval Observatory, RG 78, NA.

[67] Brooke's *Vincennes* Journals, 18 June 1855, BP.

without success and got "a very good set of altitudes for time." He continued the observations with the sextant with satisfactory results, until the *Vincennes* left Hakodate. In his astronomical work Brooke was assisted by Edwin Carnes and Beverley Kennon, from other vessels of the expedition, who made observations for the determination of the latitude of Hakodate. At that port "it was utterly impossible to carry on magnetic observations of any kind," owing to the physical composition of the black sand that covered the beaches.[68]

Finally, on June 26, with a light east wind and fog, the *Vincennes* ran out of the harbor of Hakodate headed for Petropavlovsk on the Kamchatka Peninsula. At that Russian port, which had been attacked by the English and French during the Crimean War and was almost deserted, Rodgers and Brooke dined with Captain Martineff of the Russian army. Martineff turned over to the Americans an old Cossack who was familiar with the language of the Chukchi Indians, inhabitants of the Asiatic coast of the Bering Strait where the *Vincennes* proposed to go. The Cossack was soon named Dobra (good) by the sailors, because that was the only word he used in expressing his admiration of the ship's equipage.

While at Petropavlovsk, Rodgers developed plans "to establish a party at some point on the western shores of Behring Straits" to make observations and gather scientific data while the *Vincennes* sailed in the Arctic Ocean. It was his intention that Brooke should command the shore party.[69] As his plans matured, Rodgers resolved to land the party at the strait of Senyavina, which separates the island of Arakamchechen from the southeastern coast of the Chukotski Peninsula on the Siberian coast. When the flagship left Petropavlovsk for the north, this proposed landing party would be the subject of frequent discussion between Rodgers and Brooke.

On July 3 the *Vincennes* sailed for the Bering Strait, running north across the Bering Sea where Brooke made several deep-sea soundings. In the most successful cast, bottom was reached at 2,700 fathoms (over three miles) and a specimen of greenish mud

[68] Roe Notebook, Naval Hist. Foundation, MSS, LC.

[69] Rodgers selected the Siberian rather than the Alaskan coast for Brooke's party because he believed clearer weather would be found there. See Brooke's *Vincennes* Journals, 3 Aug. 1855, BP.

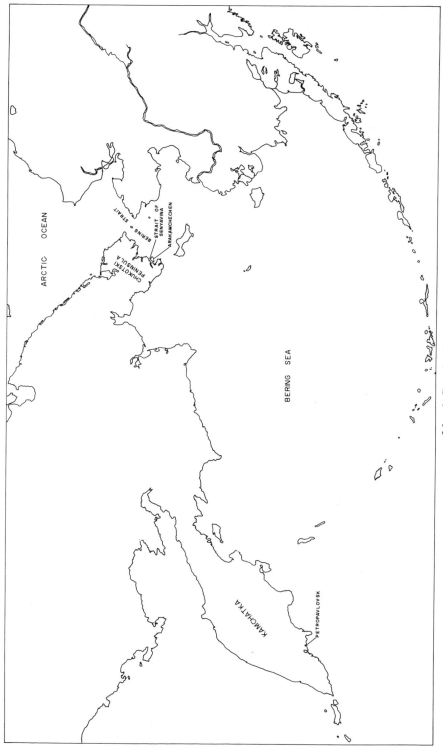

ARCTIC OCEAN

CHUKOTSKI PENINSULA

BERING STRAIT

STRAIT OF SENYAVINA

ARAKAMCHECHEN

BERING SEA

KAMCHATKA

PETROPAVLOVSK

North Pacific Ocean

was recovered to prove it. This was the greatest depth from which a specimen had ever been secured.[70] The cast was made from the *Vincennes* because the thick fog rendered it "too dangerous" to sound from a boat. Fortunately, the water was so smooth that it was satisfactory to sound from the ship. The specimen was placed under the microscope and "*spiculae*" (small calcareous bodies) were detached. It was then put away carefully for future examinations by Professor Jacob Bailey of West Point.

The soundings were hampered by mechanical defects. Some brass rings for the apparatus made in China proved defective as they detached the shot before bottom was reached. During this period Brooke improved his sounding device. His journal indicates his excitement when the improvement brought results: "I wished to get a good specimen of the bottom. the preceding cast was imperfect in that respect as but a very small quantity of the sediment adhered to the rod. My plan was to put the barrels of goose quills firmly in the lower end of the rod. I put four in and at 1700 faths. two of them were entirely filled and I believe the others also but a small hole opening into the rod above them a current of water washed their contents out. As soon as we recovered our specimen, a greenish sediment[,] it was put under the microscope and we saw, I believe we are the first, living animals from that great depth. to be certain that they came not from the upper waters we cut a quill in two and from the middle portion of the sediment which was firmly packed we selected a specimen and in it we found the animals, infusoria most abundant."[71] Subsequent experiments demonstrated that the quills worked "admirably." As soon as recovered they were corked at both ends and placed in alcohol. Brooke gave the armorer the job of making a cup to be attached to the arming rod for the purpose of bringing up large specimens of the bottom.

[70] Log of the *Vincennes*, RG 24, NA. See also Brooke's *Vincennes* Journals, BP. Twenty-four years later Capt. George E. Belknap, commandant of the Pensacola Navy Yard, in a letter to Brooke alluded to this cast. He quoted Sir Wyville Thomson, who in *The Depths of the Sea* claimed "a sounding made from H.M.S. Porcupine—in 1869 [fourteen years after Brooke's cast in the Bering Sea]—in 2400 fathoms as being the most reliable deep water cast made up to that time." Belknap pointed out that Thomson's claim was "completely at fault" (Belknap to Brooke, 6 Feb. 1879, BP). Belknap himself won a considerable reputation for his Pacific soundings in the *Tuscarora* during the 1870s.
[71] Brooke's *Vincennes* Journals, 26 July 1855, BP.

In the Bering Sea the sun rarely showed itself. The days were gloomy and increasingly long. When the *Vincennes* crossed the international date line above 60° north latitude, Brooke noted that "as to daylight we have enough of that for the night is only from 11 to 1." Soon, however, the incessant fog of the Bering Strait made it impossible to get observations, and no one knew exactly where they were.

Off the southern entrance to the strait of Senyavina, the *Vincennes* had its first contact with the natives of the Chukotski Peninsula when three bidars, or walrus-skinned boats, filled with Chukchi came alongside. Brooke observed the natives closely and filled his journal with copious notes. The natives were in quest of tobacco, needles, and thread. In exchange for these items they gave the sailors walrus teeth and small harpoons tipped with ivory. Men, women, and children were addicted to tobacco, and though they preferred chewing it, "they found not the slightest difficulty in smoking segars or cheroots." So eager were they for the weed that they readily traded their weapons for as little as half a plug.[72]

In fog and rain with the temperature in the forties, the *Vincennes* anchored in Glassenappe Harbor, where the vessel was soon overrun with more than a hundred men, women, and children from a small village nearby. Rodgers and Brooke moved promptly to select a spot on an island, which lay east of the strait of Senyavina, for Brooke's party to encamp. The site selected was ideal for an encampment, being a meadow land "luxuriantly carpeted with grass and adorned with blue white and yellow blossoms." The snow had melted and pools of water stood in the plain while high mountains rose abruptly in the background.

In the Chukchi village Brooke noticed the natives' huts were wigwams of hide stretched over a framework of wood and whalebone. In each hut cooking utensils and other implements made of whalebone hung from the frame. The fire, over which were suspended iron kettles, occupied the center of the dwelling. A small sleeping compartment was partitioned off from the rest of the interior.

Rodgers sent for the headman of the village, Car-oor-garh, and

[72] Ibid., 2 Aug. 1855. Brooke's observations were confirmed by later visitors. Further information on the Chukchi can be found in·Rodgers's report to Secretary Dobbin, 19 Oct. 1855, Box 3, United States Navy Miscellaneous Papers, MSS Div., LC.

informed him that he intended to "put a party onshore to remain until the return of the ship, and that if it was kindly treated until then he would give the old man some tobacco." [73] This "Nestor of the tribe" was advised further that should the party be hurt, the ship upon its return would levy retribution—rather an empty threat as the natives could move inland, but it seemed to impress the old Chukchi. After consulting with the villagers, Car-oor-garh gave his consent for a party to land. For more than a hundred years these freedom-loving people had resisted Russian advances into this eastern tip of Siberia. [74]

To seal the bond of friendship with the natives Rodgers and Brooke gave them small presents of tobacco. Brooke was amused particularly by women asking him "for a little piece for the pica-ninny, that word for child being in use among them." He found their fondness for tobacco "really astonishing" and surmised it was not a cultivated taste for all seemed to enjoy it, from the youngest to the oldest. The Chukchi, incidentally, did not recognize the sovereignty of the czar and in fact had a low opinion of the Russians generally. [75]

Brooke and Rodgers knew that in the late eighteenth century a party under Joseph Billings had passed along the Chukotski Peninsula and had been "badly treated by the natives." The prevailing view of navigators was that the Chukchi were not above suspicion. Rodgers had proposed initially that Brooke take a whaleboat and a guard of six men, but Brooke had maintained that such a force was inadequate. Should the *Vincennes* fail to return or get stuck in the ice, it would be Brooke's responsibility to organize a relief expedition. If it became necessary to seek help he wanted a force large enough to divide into two parts, "one to go by Sea down the coast and the other by land to the nearest Russian settlement." [76]

After his conversations with the Chukchi, Rodgers became anxious and told Brooke that "he doubted the propriety" of leaving any party at that location, as there were more natives than he had anticipated. Brooke insisted that it was so important to get the

---

[73] Brooke's *Vincennes* Journals, 4 Aug. 1855, BP.
[74] Hine, *Edward Kern*, pp. 120–21.
[75] Brooke's *Vincennes* Journals, 4 Aug. 1855, BP.
[76] Ibid., 16 July 1855.

magnetic and astronomical observations that the risk should be assumed. Having secured Brooke's promise to keep a sharp lookout
and "to regard the natives as treacherous so as not to be surprised," Rodgers assented. He later remarked that "in the marked
prudence and firmness of Mr. Brooke I had a strong assurance
that I should find the party safe upon my return from the
North."[77]

At an early hour the next day the landing of provisions, tents,
instruments, and weapons began. Provisions for two months were
supplied.[78] One problem on the Siberian coast was the lack of
wood, so this need was filled by the *Vincennes*. The transit house
was sent ashore and such spars, sails, and other materials as could
be spared "for building a commodious house."[79] Brooke had had
many volunteers for the shore party. The ten selected included
Kern, the artist; Stimpson, the naturalist; Wright, the botanist;
three sailors; three marines; and Dobra, the Cossack interpreter.[80]
There was no one to translate Dobra's Russian into English. The
party was not as large as Brooke had recommended; but Rodgers
could only spare one whaleboat, the cutter, to serve as a means of
escape, and a small iron dinghy for utility. Though small, the
party was armed with a twelve-pounder howitzer, fifty-three
rounds of canister and shell, three carbines, three muskets, three
rifles, and about a thousand cartridges. Kern was in effect the second in command and would be in charge whenever Brooke left the
camp. Not only was Kern a seasoned explorer with many of the
same skills as Brooke, but he had also demonstrated leadership.

[77] Ibid., undated entry; Rodgers to Secretary of the Navy Dobbin, 19 Oct. 1855, Box
3, U.S. Navy Misc. Papers, MSS Div., LC.

[78] The following provisions were sent ashore: 400 pounds pork, 400 pounds beef, 96
pounds flour, 96 pounds rice, 48 pounds pickles, 584 pounds bread, 84 pounds sugar, 42
pounds coffee, 24 pounds butter, 24 pounds cheese, 17 gallons beans, 5¾ gallons molasses,
5¾ gallons vinegar, 18¾ gallons spirits, 34 pounds preserved meats, 14 pounds potatoes, 33
pounds candles (List of provisions sent ashore at Brooke's camp in the strait of Senyavina, 5
Aug. 1855, BP).

[79] For observation on shore Brooke had the small transit, the large zenith telescope, the
regular telescope, and various magnetic instruments. Two tents were furnished to house
the instruments (Brooke's *Vincennes* Journals, 6 Aug. 1855, BP).

[80] Ibid., 5 Aug. 1855. The seamen were Salvadore Pelkey, William Wieland (Wheelan?), and Frank Howard. The three privates of marines were Charles Bear, James Barbier,
and Charles Rogier (Log of the *Vincennes*, 5 Aug. 1855, RG 24, NA; see also Brooke's *Vincennes* Journals, BP).

On Frémont's third expedition the artist had for a time been in command of Fort Sutter.[81]

The camp was fortified by a wall of provision barrels filled with gravel and covered over with earth; port holes were cut in the wall on all four sides for the use of the howitzer; and a trench was dug around the wall for further protection. The fort was as formidable as time and limited means allowed. The construction fascinated the villagers, the children even helping to unload the stores. Brooke judged the natives to be honest and independent, and he resolved to make friends with them. "Savage indeed is the man," he wrote, "who is not susceptible to kindness."

Brooke was satisfied that he had everything necessary to accomplish his mission, but a shadow clouded the undertaking. Grumbling was heard in the wardroom of the *Vincennes* that Brooke would win a reputation while leaving routine service to other officers. The same complaint had been voiced before the launch cruise, and Brooke paid little attention to it. It was the old story of the jealousy of the line officer for the scientific specialist. In Brooke's opinion any credit gained at the strait of Senyavina would accrue to the whole North Pacific expedition.

The plan called for Rodgers to take the *Vincennes* as far north "as the ice will permit" but to return within a month.[82] On the evening of August 6 Brooke landed the last of the supplies at the camp, called "Brookeville" in the ship's log, and the next morning the *Vincennes* sailed for the Arctic on the most hazardous leg of the cruise. For the ordeal she carried two hundred men and a three months' supply of wood and provisions.[83] John Brooke celebrated his first full day ashore by buying five white fox skins for Lizzie from a visiting bidar.

As was his way, Brooke noted carefully the physical character-

[81] Hine, *Edward Kern*, pp. 30–37.

[82] Rodgers to Brooke, 6 Aug. 1855 (copy), Letters from Officers Commanding Expeditions, RG 45, NA.

[83] The Arctic Ocean "is a small polar sea hemmed in by continental land masses. . . . Throughout much of its extent, the surface temperatures are well below the freezing point of fresh water. It is characteristically an area of sea ice, 5 to 9 feet in thickness, but as a result of the pressure of moving ice floes, the ice may become piled up to a depth of 15 feet or more. Even in the summer the Arctic is never half free of ice" (Coker, *Great and Wide Sea*, pp. 135–36). It was a dangerous sea for a wooden sailing vessel to explore.

istics, dress, and customs of the natives, and with their aid he compiled a glossary of Chukchi words. The Americans discovered that the natives liked sugar, were unenthusiastic about pickles, and abhorred salt. Chukchi food was "oily and abounding in carbon" which led them to consume prodigious quantities of water after each meal. Brooke thought the "brewers of London had a scarcely greater capacity." The natives repeatedly offered Brooke culinary delicacies, such as raw whale meat, but he did not find their food "inviting to the appetite." No condiments were used. The Chukchi never bathed, which Brooke attributed to the cold climate. Every night some of the natives assembled outside the fort. They were "always ready for any amusement" and frequently staged a dance, or at least a performance of sorts. Some of their demonstrations were fantastic. The girls liked to promenade with the marines "in military style and step before the camp." But all was not dignity. It was not unusual for the girls to seize an unsuspecting American and "romp in the wildest manner imaginable." It was all in fun and the girls were as quick to defend their virtue as their more civilized sisters across the sea. The sailors taught the Chukchi how to play "hunt the slipper" and the game was played with zest. The natives were a generous people. Besides supplying the camp regularly with claytonia, an antiscorbutic, they gave personal presents; Brooke received a pair of moccasins and even a kayak.

Before many days had passed a flare-up requiring diplomacy on Brooke's part occurred. It was a test case. Stimpson complained that the natives were becoming impudent, and he had come near shooting one. The naturalist, accompanied by two enlisted men, had gone to a lagoon near the camp to seek specimens. A prominent native who had hit the rum cask too freely joined Stimpson's party, and after embracing the enlisted men he sought to pay his respects to Stimpson in the same manner. The humorless naturalist rebuffed him; at this, the Chukchi shoved the American and knocked him down. Stimpson was furious that the enlisted men had not shot the native at this juncture. Taking a longer view, Brooke noted that "such a step would have been absurd and the sailor[s] knew it." Brooke held that Stimpson by his stiff attitude had been as much to blame as the Chukchi, and he refused to accept Stimpson's demand that the native be ordered out of camp when he next appeared. Brooke resolved that the appropriate course was to call himself upon the offending native when the latter had sobered up. The matter was settled amicably in that way.

A week after the *Vincennes*'s departure, Brooke placed the magnetic instruments and resumed the tedious round of observations. A major problem was to get the declinometer in working order so that he could make half-hourly readings. Observation was difficult, for the weather was often cloudy and rainy with stiff winds from the east. Nonetheless, Brooke was able to rate the chronometers for six days by transit.[84]

In the main the health of the shore party remained good. Even though the approach of fall cut off the claytonia supply, scurvy held off for the time being. Only one case of sickness occurred at Brookeville. Dobra fell violently ill on September 1 and suffered so intensely that he asked for pen and paper to make out his will. Brooke and Kern diagnosed Dobra's rapid pulse, flushed, dry skin, and labored breathing as a violent cold. That morning the old fellow had followed the example of the Americans and bathed in the snow water of the lagoon. Brooke and Kern decided "vigorous remedies" were in order. While Kern applied mustard plasters to Dobra, Brooke "cupped him with two tumblers." The amateur doctors bathed the old man's feet in hot water and revived him with a whiskey toddy. Moving swiftly, they next placed a heated rock at his feet "and then piled blankets and furs upon him." In less than ten minutes Dobra was in a deep sleep. When he awoke at midnight Kern was ready to administer the coup de grace to the evil spirits. Over voluble resistance Dobra was forced to take a dose of castor oil. The next day the old Cossack was well again, and he insisted that he owed his life to Kern and Brooke.[85]

September 6, 1855, was a day of high excitement at the camp. It marked the return of the *Vincennes*, right on schedule. It was a grand moment, Brooke noted, when just at dinner time "Carrorga and the natives with cries of the Ship! the Ship! informed us that the Vincennes was rounding the point." Brooke saluted the broad

[84] Chart for Determination of Longitude of Basic Points, BP.
[85] Brooke's *Vincennes* Journals, 1 Sept. 1855, BP.

pendant with thirteen guns, and Rodgers acknowledged the honor with a salute of three guns. As soon as the ship anchored, Brooke hastened aboard to report. There was much to talk over with Rodgers, and it was late before Brooke got among his messmates. He recorded that "it makes ones heart jump to meet shipmates after these little seperations." Brooke learned that at least a third of the ship's crew had scurvy. In its haste to get to the Bering Sea before the season was well advanced, the *Vincennes* had traveled north "too soon to find even the earliest plants of spring." Lime juice had retarded the disease but had not prevented it.[86] Rodgers's Arctic voyage had been extremely hazardous but successful. In a letter he wrote Brooke from St. Lawrence Bay, Rodgers claimed that he had gone farther north than any previous explorer.[87] On his return voyage Rodgers had surveyed St. Lawrence Bay.

The return of the *Vincennes* brought Car-oor-garh his reward. The ship's log reveals that two muskets and bayonets, one pistol, 105 musket ball cartridges, 200 pistol ball cartridges, 300 percussion caps, and 5 pounds of priming powder were expended from the gunner's department at this time, "the whole being a present to the Indian Chief, for attention & service rendered to our camp." The expedition commander also gave the patriarch the promised tobacco, a huge kettle, and other things.

Meanwhile scurvy made vicious inroads, and the surgeon urged Rodgers to proceed at once to the nearest port where fresh provisions could be secured. However the commander, extremely anxious to complete the survey of the strait of Senyavina, continued operations for several days. As a partial offset the surgeon increased the crew's allowance of lime juice. Efforts were made to get greens, but the season was over. Only sorrel was available, Brooke noted, and the natives could not spare more than a pail of that a day. As soon as Brooke learned of the prevalence of scurvy he volunteered to lead a party to a Chukchi village in the hope

[86] Ibid., 6 Sept. 1855.

[87] This letter was not received by Brooke until 13 Sept. 1855, a week after Rodgers's return. A full description of the *Vincennes*'s work in the Bering Strait and the Arctic Ocean is given in Rodgers's 12-page report to Secretary of the Navy Dobbin, 19 Oct. 1855, Box 3, U.S. Navy Misc. Papers, MSS Div., LC.

that some fresh meat could be procured. Rodgers accepted Brooke's offer and ordered him to depart in the launch with all speed. Accompanied by Dobra, Brown (a sailor who translated for the Russian), and a Chukchi, Brooke started out the next morning with a supply of such articles as he thought the natives would exchange for their reindeer. Not arriving at the landing place until after dark, Brooke's party spent a miserable night off the land. Calling on the chief the next day, Brooke learned to his chagrin that the Chukchi would trade only two reindeer, but he did obtain a few claytonia roots for the sick. With time running short, the party was obliged to return to the ship with its modest purchases.[88]

During Brooke's absence, Rodgers had been shot in the ankle accidentally. While he was going ashore to make some observations, his pistol had slipped from its holster and fired. Though the ball had penetrated the bone and the surgeon had been unable to remove it, the wound escaped infection.

A week after the return of the *Vincennes*, Brooke broke camp. The villagers gathered around, regretful to see the Americans go. It was the end of an epoch in their isolated lives. Brooke confessed "an attachment to the place that makes itself felt." But the man who was really distressed was Barbier, the marine cook. He had fallen in love with a pretty native girl, Engar, and wanted to stay behind, so he said, to civilize the natives and keep a register of scientific data. Brooke, who was impressed by Barbier's ability and sincerity, promised to forward his application to the squadron commander.[89] Of all the Chukchi, Brooke formed the strongest attachment to Al-ing hai-cow, the patriarch's son. They had made short excursions together, and Brooke had been astonished at the skill with which the young native had handled the dinghy. When Brooke departed, he gave his friend his kayak, a knife, beads, buttons, shot, and percussion caps and powder.

[88] Grier's *Vincennes* Journal, 7 Sept. 1855, RG 45, NA; Brooke's *Vincennes* Journal, 10 Sept. 1855, BP.

[89] Barbier averred that he could eventually make his way to Washington with his report, which would "add greatly to the results of the expedition." The whole affair is covered fully in Brooke's *Vincennes* Journals, BP. Whether Barbier remained at Glassenappe is not known.

In the forenoon of September 17, 1855, with a fresh wind filling her sails, the *Vincennes* stood out of Glassenappe Harbor, sounding and angling as she went. One last bit of business remained—a careful survey of the west entrance of the strait of Senyavina. This done, the ship headed due south into the Bering Sea, San Francisco bound. En route Brooke stood guard with Fillebrown, Russell, Roe, and James C. Davis.

It took the *Vincennes* twenty-five days to reach San Francisco. Sailing through the Aleutians by the Amutka Pass the sloop steered to the southeast and followed the great circle the rest of the way. Nothing of importance happened in the course of the passage. All were eager to sight the Golden Gate, the strait leading into San Francisco Bay, and complained that the *Vincennes* could not do better than ten knots. Although Brooke had endured his separation from home far better than in days of yore, he began to look forward to letters from Lizzie—it had been nine months since he had heard from home—and to speculate on the vast changes wrought in San Francisco since he had seen it last in 1843. In midmorning, October 13, 1855, the *Vincennes* anchored at San Francisco.

The men of the expedition could take pride in their performance. Certainly hearts on the *Vincennes* beat a little faster when Californians in passing steamers cheered them lustily. Rodgers confided to his friend Maury that "we are satisfied with our results, for we have not willingly let anything pass which it was in our power to grasp." For Brooke, Rodgers had nothing but praise, calling him "a regular trump."[90] The work of the expedition did not go unnoticed in Washington. In his annual report to the president, Secretary Dobbin stated: "Commander Rodgers and his officers are entitled to the highest commendation for the ability and energy with which they have prosecuted the work to which they were assigned."[91] Despite old orders to "continue the Survey," Rodgers considered it neither "proper or just or expedient"

[90] Rodgers to Maury, 19 Oct. 1855, Letters Received, Naval Observatory, RG 78, NA.

[91] *Senate Documents*, Report of Secretary of the Navy Dobbin, 3 Dec. 1855, 34th Cong., 1st and 2d sess., 3:9. Rodgers was promoted commander on 14 Sept. 1855, in the big shake-up of that year which placed many officers, including Matthew F. Maury, on the reserve list.

to leave United States territory until his command was substantially bolstered, and he so informed the department.

The delay in San Francisco while Rodgers waited for instructions was made less irksome for Brooke by the news that he had been promoted to lieutenant. His name stood second on a list of sixty appointed to that rank.[92] Brooke's high stand resulted from his diligence at Annapolis. The origin of the promotions went deeper. After years of effort the Navy Department had finally obtained necessary legislation to renovate the service by the elimination of deadwood. Under authority of "an act to promote the efficiency of the Navy," a naval board of fifteen officers had combed the officers' list and after "careful examination" had found 201 officers from captain to passed midshipman "incapable of performing promptly and efficiently all their duty both ashore and afloat." The removal of these officers from the active list opened wide the floodgates of promotion. Many ambitious officers benefited, Brooke among them.[93]

For three and a half months the *Vincennes* remained in California, dividing her time between San Francisco and Mare Island Navy Yard, reported the preceding December to be in "a rapid process of construction." The yard was under the command of Brooke's old friend Captain David Glasgow Farragut, who, with his wife, entertained Brooke.

Brooke now found time to catch up with lagging correspondence and to prepare reports. He wrote at least one letter on deep-sea sounding for publication in the newspapers and worked on an article describing the cruise of the launch. This article, entitled "Coasting in Japan," appeared in the *U.S. Nautical Magazine and Naval Journal* as a narrative in five parts, beginning with the issue of December 1856. He also exchanged letters with Maury on deep-sea sounding and explored the possibility of improved methods.[94]

Lizzie wrote regularly from Lexington, and her understanding

[92] Commissions, 22 Oct. 1855, RG 24, NA.

[93] The subject is discussed in Secretary Dobbin's annual report to the President, 3 Dec. 1855, *Senate Documents*, 34th Cong., 1st and 2d sess., 3:9–10.

[94] Brooke to Maury, 19 Dec. 1855, Letters Received, Naval Observatory, RG 78, NA, microfilm copy, BP.

letters contained both wit and humor. But she chided John for being a poor correspondent, complaining that he had written her but nine sheets from the time the *Vincennes* left Hong Kong until it arrived in San Francisco, a total of 189 days. She realized that when ashore John was busy with observations, but she saw no reason for the shortness of his sea letters except "want of inclination." Lizzie was pleased that the Farraguts had entertained him. She had "high respect" for Farragut, and thought Mrs. Farragut "kind & sociable" but "a great gossip not at [all] to be relied upon." Lizzie reported that Colonel Garnett was working overtime in an effort to secure Brooke compensation from Congress for his sounding lead under a recommendation of President Franklin Pierce that rewards be bestowed "upon the authors of all useful inventions, who had failed to receive for themselves any remuneration."[95]

On December 5, 1855, Secretary of the Navy Dobbin, finding that the funds appropriated for the expedition had "long since been exhausted" and that there were no officers available to reinforce the expedition, ordered Rodgers to proceed home in the *Vincennes* by such route as he deemed "advisable." Rodgers ordered Brooke to travel to Washington independently and wrote Dobbin that Brooke, having performed his "peculiar duties . . . faithfully and intelligently," could now make an important contribution by preparing his observations for publication. Brooke's presence in Washington would speed publication.[96]

The return to the Atlantic coast was a lark. Brooke found "the scenery . . . beautiful and the company . . . agreeable." In fact, he declared that he never enjoyed himself more in his life than he "did *coming home* by the Nicaragua route."[97] He traveled to San

[95] There are 9 long letters in the Brooke Papers from Lizzie to her husband embracing the period 25 Dec. 1855–2 Feb. 1856. The letters were sent either to San Francisco or Valparaiso, and most did not arrive until after Brooke had left. But they are valuable in that they comment on Brooke's activities in San Francisco and give insight into Lizzie's character and interests. There are no letters in the Brooke Papers written by Brooke to his wife at this time. It is evident, however, that he did write and that his tone was often cynical or depressed. At one point Lizzie was constrained to tell John that "tis useless to curse in your letters, at least if a person cant help saying an oath, they can help writing one."
[96] Dobbin to Rodgers, 5 Dec. 1855, Cole, *Yankee Surveyors*, pp. 158–59; Rodgers to Dobbin, 26 Jan. 1855, Letters from Officers Commanding Expeditions, RG 45, NA.
[97] Brooke to his wife, 14 June 1858, BP.

Juan del Şur, Nicaragua, in one of Commodore Vanderbilt's American Atlantic and Pacific Ship Canal steamers which since 1851 had been cutting into the lucrative business of William H. Aspinwall's Pacific Mail. Brooke walked the twelve miles "from the shores of the Pacific to Virgins Bay" at the western end of Lake Nicaragua.[98] There he probably took one of Vanderbilt's shallow-draft river steamers which ran from Virgins Bay to San Juan de Norte on the Atlantic. From Nicaragua to New York, Brooke traveled on the *Star of the West*.

On March 1, 1856, thirty days after leaving San Francisco, John Brooke reported to the secretary of the navy in Washington. He had ended a cruise of three years, during which he had circumnavigated the globe. He was granted two weeks' leave.

---

[98] Brooke to Adm. Daniel Ammen, 4 June 1891 (copy), BP. For a good description of the Nicaragua crossing at this time, see William Harwar Parker, *Recollections of a Naval Officer, 1841–1865* (New York, 1883), pp. 164–65.

V /

CATCHING UP LOOSE

ENDS IN WASHINGTON

From Washington, Brooke rushed to join Lizzie in Lexington, Virginia, where she was living with her sister and brother-in-law, the Thomas Hoomes Williamsons. The three-year separation had been exceedingly long! It was a new experience to travel to the Shenandoah Valley, for after earlier cruises John had met his wife at her parents' home in Norfolk. Lizzie had written that the new railroad was being rapidly pushed south of Staunton, so that Brooke could take the train from Washington to a little beyond Staunton, then transfer to the stage.

At the expiration of his leave, Brooke was ordered to "report to the Chief of the Bureau of Ordnance and Hydrography for special duty at the Naval Observatory in connection with the preparation of the charts for Commander Rodgers' Expedition."[1] There was quite enough for Brooke to do, because data had been compiled for the preparation of charts of many places, including the islands south of Japan, the Japanese coast, the Sea of Okhotsk, and the Bering Strait. Information had been secured, also, for the correction of the plotted positions of reefs and other dangers on existing charts. To hasten publication, Rodgers had written Secre-

[1] Secretary of the Navy Dobbin to Brooke, 17 March 1856, Appointments, Orders, and Resignations, Records of the Bureau of Naval Personnel, RG 24, NA.

(*135*)

tary Dobbin from Honolulu requesting the appropriation of $15,000 for immediate needs.

Upon Rodgers's arrival in July 1856, Brooke was given the responsibility of preparing both the chart based upon his survey in the launch and the computation of longitudes derived from his chronometer readings. By April 1858 Brooke's chart of the coast of Japan from Shimoda to Hakodate and four others of the expedition had been engraved and published.[2]

Two years later when Brooke returned to Washington following a cruise to Japan, he would find the work of the North Pacific expedition still incomplete. Both Captain Ringgold and Commander Rodgers had a hand in the work, each being responsible for the results obtained while he had commanded the expedition. Mutual dislike between the two officers had not slackened, with the result that the project as a whole suffered. For example, when Ringgold wanted some chronometer data, which was in Brooke's possession, he contacted Secretary Isaac Toucey. Toucey in turn wrote to Rodgers and Rodgers to Brooke. But the trouble was not only a matter of red tape: the arbitrary division of work between the proud expedition commanders created confusion. Ringgold, for instance, requested the notebooks containing chronometer comparisons and corrections made on board the *Vincennes* during his regime, but Brooke refused to comply on the ground that such a step "would involve mutilation of the books and the breaking up of the series." The readings taken under Ringgold's direction, particularly those between Sydney and Hong Kong, were unreliable and of value only when used in conjunction with those taken later under Rodgers.[3]

The report of the North Pacific expedition was unfinished

---

[2] *Senate Documents,* Report of Secretary of the Navy Isaac Toucey, 12 April 1858, 35th Cong., 1st sess., vol. 12, no. 52, p. 1.

[3] Brooke to Rodgers, 3 April 1861 (copy), BP. The data on the passage from Sydney to Hong Kong were vulnerable on three counts: (1) the interval between observations was 77 days, whereas 30 to 35 days was considered a long interval by authorities; (2) "the mean temperature of the two rating intervals was nearly equal, whilst on the passage it was some fourteen degrees higher" (for accuracy it was necessary that there be different temperatures at the ends of the measured distance); and (3) the ratings at Sydney had been completed in 5 days, whereas it was generally believed such a series of ratings should extend over a 7-day period.

when the Civil War broke out in 1861, although forty-five general sailing charts had been engraved and published. During and after the Civil War the work was suspended, and in the Chicago fire of 1871 most of the biological collections, drawings, and reports were destroyed. The project was never finished, one reason why this important expedition is not better known.

In August 1856, Brooke asked for one month's leave to join Lizzie in Lexington, where she had remained while her husband was on duty in Washington. When Brooke's leave expired, Lizzie, who was pregnant, accompanied him back to the capital. On December 12, 1856, their first child, Anna Maria Brooke, was born. Years later a friend, who had been a boy at the time, recollected clearly the "excitement" at the Brooke household on that important occasion.[4] A nurse named Frances, apparently a Negro slave, was hired two months later to care for Anna.[5] Later Lizzie returned to Lexington with the baby.

In Washington, Brooke demonstrated that his interest in invention was not confined solely to the problem of plumbing the depths of the sea. He was dissatisfied with the conventional mechanism for attaching boats to their tackles by ringbolts fore and aft. Hooking and unhooking the usual mechanism often were difficult, and the speed of the vessel had to be checked, if not stopped, because in a seaway lowering usually was not feasible. With the conventional arrangement there was danger that the boat when afloat might become accidentally unhooked. Particularly there was the chance that the foretackle might become disengaged and the boat swing free before the after tackle could be disconnected. A guard had to stand by to see that the bolt did not become unhooked except by hand. Brooke invented a simple device, which he patented August 5, 1856, that overcame these difficulties. For the conventional ring and hook Brooke substituted a ball and socket arrangement. The Brooke boat hook had several outstanding features. It was not only easy to attach the tackle to the boat, but it was less likely that the boat would be accidentally unhooked if a wave struck its bottom as it was hoisted into the ship. The

[4] Lewis R. Hamersly to Brooke, 21 Oct. 1879, BP.

[5] Brooke's account book shows that a Mr. or Mrs. Bell was paid periodically for Frances's services.

Brooke device, utilizing a swivel, automatically eliminated all twists in the tackle. By a simple adjustment it was easy to release the boat immediately upon contact with the water if desired. Accidental reattachment was impossible. In the eyes of the editors of the *U.S. Nautical Magazine and Naval Journal*, Brooke's improvement for attaching boats to their tackles was "a labour and life saving improvement, commending itself to the nautical fraternity."[6]

In November 1857 Brooke entered into an agreement with Charles Mortimer of Charleston, South Carolina, editor of the *Southern Quarterly Review*, to transfer to Mortimer the patent for his invention for $1,500, should the editor find a buyer. In that year the *Southern Quarterly Review* was forced to suspend publication, and, no doubt, Mortimer was anxious to augment his income. The editor failed to sell the invention immediately; and while Brooke was making arrangements to leave Washington in the spring of 1858 for another cruise in the Pacific, he defined more clearly his transfer agreement with Mortimer. Under the new terms Brooke "assigned, Sold, and set over" to the editor all rights to the boat device for $1,500.[7] Mortimer promised to pay Brooke $150 at once and the remaining $1,350 from his profit should he sell the invention. But the South Carolinian was unable to find a buyer during Brooke's two years' absence.

Upon his return to Washington in 1860 Brooke developed from his patented boat hook an improved detaching hook, or cat hook. The cat hook, for raising or lowering weights, had various uses on shipboard, such as catting anchors and detaching boats from their tackles when the ship was underway. The inventor believed that his device possessed "the most marked superiority" over other cat hooks in use and, further, that it was better than the established devices "for letting go anchors from iron steamers and other vessels."[8] Brooke filed the specification for his patent with the Patent Office on April 4, 1861; but before that agency

[6] "Brooke's Improvement for Attaching Boats to Their Tackles," 5 Aug. 1856, BP; "Brooke's Improved Attachment for Boats," *U.S. Nautical Magazine and Naval Journal* 3 (Oct. 1856):44–45. This article describes the device in detail and includes 4 drawings to explain its operation.

[7] Assignment of patent rights for Boat Machine to Charles Mortimer of Charleston, S.C., c. April 1858, BP.

[8] Brooke to Robert D. Minor, 5 Nov. 1866 (copy), BP.

could act, he had resigned his commission and left Washington. Nonetheless, a patent was issued to Brooke on May 28, 1861, for a period of seventeen years. A good friend, probably John Rodgers or Samuel P. Lee, picked up the papers for him and preserved them throughout the Civil War. In the fall of 1865 Brooke was given the patent papers, but he took no steps to capitalize on the invention until he received his pardon in August 1866.

While in Washington, Brooke was ordered to Brunswick, Georgia, to help select a site on Blythe Island for the establishment of a naval depot. In 1856 Secretary of the Navy Dobbin had informed the Senate that from Kittery, Maine, to Norfolk, Virginia, navy yards were spaced along the coast from sixty to four hundred miles apart, but from Norfolk to Pensacola there was a huge gap of nearly two thousand miles. Dobbin believed it prudent, therefore, for the government to build a naval station "for *repairing* ships and furnishing supplies" between the two southern bases. When Congress authorized the purchase of a site on Blythe Island at Brunswick for a base, the secretary of the navy appointed a commission consisting of three naval officers, Captain James McIntosh of Georgia, Commander Henry J. Hartstene of South Carolina, and Brooke, and a civil engineer, Calvin Brown, to pick the best location on the island. Brooke's orders directed him to report without delay to Captain McIntosh at Brunswick.[9]

The commission was slow to move, and Brooke, who missed his family, was impatient. Finally, everyone arrived and the work began. By March 10, 1857, the reconnaissance was done, and the other members sat around while Captain McIntosh decided upon the best site. Brooke, becoming more restless by the minute, thought the chairman was "very timid" and noted that "every old countryman who comes in tells him something to render him undecided." According to Brooke, the only suitable site was the one they had first chosen. During the next three days, while McIntosh was arriving at his decision, several people invited Brooke to dine; but he had left his trunk with his clothes at the hotel room in Savannah and was unable to accept the hospitality.

[9] Dobbin to Brooke, 19 Feb. 1857, Appointments, Orders, and Resignations, Records of the Bureau of Naval Personnel, RG 24, NA.

The Commission selected a site with relatively deep water and a broad channel located on the southeast corner of Blythe Island. The nearly level upland of twenty-four hundred acres of rich soil appeared well adapted to the growth of timber. Fresh water could be obtained by sinking wells. The commission recommended the purchase of the whole island rather than only that part needed for the depot so that "the operatives would be protected from the extortion of land owners; there would be less danger to public property from fire; and the live-oak could be successfully cultivated."[10]

In his report to the president at the end of the year, the new secretary of the navy, Isaac Toucey, stated that the government had purchased eleven hundred acres on the southern part of the island from the owners for $130,000 after the state of Georgia had ceded jurisdiction to the United States. Later, in response to a Senate resolution, Secretary Toucey explained that the department had dispatched a civil engineer to Blythe Island to make detailed surveys "with a view of submitting a plan for the naval depot and estimates adequate to its completion." There the matter rested, for the United States Treasury had no money "which can be applied for that purpose without diverting it from other indispensable objects."[11]

Things were not moving fast enough for the state of Georgia. In December 1858 the Georgia legislature passed a resolution instructing that state's representatives and senators in Congress to "use their best exertions to obtain, an appropriation from the Treasury of the United States sufficient for the erection and construction of a naval depot on Blythe Island." The Georgia resolution induced the United States Senate to inquire again of Secretary Toucey as to the status of the project. The secretary reported that the situation was unchanged.[12]

The period during which Brooke was stationed in Washington

[10] Report of Commission appointed to select a naval depot at Blythe Island, Brunswick, Ga., 13 March 1857 (copy), BP.

[11] *Senate Documents*, Report of Secretary of the Navy Toucey, 13 May 1858, 35th Cong., 1st sess., vol. 12, no. 57, 2 pp.

[12] *House Miscellaneous Documents*, Resolution of the Legislature of Georgia in reference to a naval depot on Blythe Island, near Brunswick, 18 Jan. 1859, 35th Cong., 2d sess., vol. 1, no. 34, p. 1; *Senate Executive Documents*, Report of Secretary of the Navy Toucey, 29 Jan. 1859, 35th Cong., 2d sess., vol. 7, no. 24, p. 1.

was one of expansion and development in the United States Navy. In March 1857 Congress authorized the construction of five shallow-draft steam sloops of war; Brooke was appointed to the board to select a model. Thirteen models were exhibited by the outstanding builders in the country. Brooke noted that "the vessel most generally admired" was of the old style and he did not like it at all, but it is not known whether this model or some other was chosen. When Brooke and his associates had selected the model, construction was begun.

In the summer of 1857 Brooke was called before several courts of inquiry as a witness. The weeding out of officers in 1855 had evoked howls of protest. Secretary Dobbin felt constrained in 1857 to appoint a special court of inquiry to investigate petitions for reinstatement. The court was instructed to consider in each case "the physical, mental, professional, and moral fitness of the officers for the naval service." Secretary Toucey increased the number of courts to three in order to expedite proceedings. Brooke was called to testify in the cases of Commanders Murray Mason, Robert Ritchie, and Cadwalader Ringgold, Lieutenants Henry Rolando and Augustus H. Kilty, and former Passed Midshipman William R. Mercer. He testified vigorously against Ritchie and Ringgold, who was defended by two able lawyers, including Charles M. Conrad, former secretary of war.

Of the six officers in whose cases Brooke testified, the three commanders, Ritchie, Ringgold, and Mason, were restored to the active list.[13] No change was made in the status of the other officers. It is interesting to note that Matthew Fontaine Maury was restored to the active list at this time with the rank of commander. His case, which had its origin in the jealousy of the line officer for the scientist, had evoked a furor.

On the cruise in the *Vincennes* Brooke had learned much about chronometers. In Washington he studied his chronometer findings and prepared graphs depicting the law of change for each chro-

---

[13] With restoration to active duty status on a retroactive basis Ritchie and Ringgold became captains; Mason remained a commander. On 23 Jan. 1858, the Washington *Daily National Intelligencer* listed 33 officers whose restoration to active duty had been recommended by the courts of inquiry and confirmed by the Senate. Moreover, 6 officers who had been dropped from the service were placed on the reserved list.

nometer. He found that the chronometer selected as the standard was affected no less than seven and one-half seconds in its daily rate by a change in temperature of twenty-four degrees Fahrenheit. In terms of longitude this was nearly two miles. The influence upon the mean daily rate of all the *Vincennes*'s chronometers by such a temperature change amounted to half a mile of longitude. With such knowledge it was possible to apply corrections provided the time interval between observations for rates was not more than thirty-five days.[14] Brooke's interest is shown by a letter he wrote to Hilton P. Barrand in London, in which he explained his methods: "As the chief source of error in chronometrical measurements is to be found in the neglect to notice the influence of temperature, the chronometers of the Vincennes . . . were placed in an apartment near the center of motion of the ship where by means of thick baize curtains and lamps lighted or extinguished as occasion required an equable temperature was preserved or a very gradual change permitted during the passage from port to port."[15]

Anticipating Lizzie's return to Washington late in 1857, Brooke rented a small furnished cottage. Although he valued privacy, he determined to share the house with Lieutenant and Mrs. George P. Welsh, as he was afraid to leave Lizzie alone. Welsh and Brooke were old friends, having served together at the observatory, and Welsh had supported Brooke with a strong letter at the time of the Greble controversy. When October came, Brooke moved into the cottage and then went to meet Lizzie and Anna at Goshen, "the nearest point of railroad to Lexington." The leaves were just beginning to turn. Reunited with his family once more, John hired a cook named Eliza at $7 per month and went to the market every day. After two weeks of housekeeping he was certain he preferred it to boarding, though he worried about the insufficiency of his navy salary. It was a bonanza when the government paid him $256 in back pay. Promptly he ordered a gold watch for Lizzie and a silver one for himself at a total cost of $101.

[14] Brooke to Rodgers, 3 April 1861 (copy), BP. The appropriate correction for each particular measurement could be applied where the rates had been determined "at different temperatures at the extremes of a measured distance and the mean daily temperature within the chronometer case during the passage has been carefully observed and recorded."

[15] Brooke to Barrand, 29 March 1858 (copy), BP.

Another matter that concerned Brooke was compensation for his deep-sea sounding lead. From 1854 to 1861, through relatives and friends, he tried to get compensation from the government. The navy maintained that as Brooke's invention lay in the field of general science, the question of compensation should be directed to Congress.[16] His father-in-law's application to Congress in 1855 for such a compensation had not been acted upon. In 1856 Brooke applied for a patent on the Brooke lead but was informed by the Patent Office that the law did not permit the issuance of a patent for an invention in public use two years before the inventor made application.[17] That Brooke had not been in the country for three years was not considered a pertinent factor. When the House Committee on Naval Affairs in 1856 recommended that Brooke be given $2,500, it was too late in the session for further action to be taken. In 1860, when Brooke returned to Washington from his second voyage to the Far East, he renewed his efforts—this time by having his request tacked to the navy appropriation bill as an amendment. At long last he got results. Congress authorized compensation in the amount of $5,000, and on February 21, 1861, President James Buchanan signed the bill.[18]

Brooke was betwixt and between as to how he should invest the $5,000. With the Union already broken in two and the Upper South hesitating, it was no easy decision. William Brooke warned his brother not to buy a house in Washington until he was sure "the Border States will not secede," for William believed that the Border States would break their connection with the Union "before many months have elapsed." Cousin Alex Tunstall in Norfolk believed that as a permanent investment "United States, or Virginia State Stock [bonds?] would be judicious." The question

[16] Representative John Letcher to Secretary of the Navy Dobbin, 18 April 1854, Miscellaneous Letters Received, 1801–84, Office of the Secretary of the Navy, RG 45, NA; Charles Morris to Dobbin, 19 April 1854, Letters sent to the Secretary of the Navy and to Bureaus, RG 37, NA; Dobbin to Letcher, 20 April 1854, Miscellaneous Letters Sent ("General Letter Book"), 1798–1886, Office of the Secretary of the Navy, RG 45, NA.

[17] Charles Mason to Brooke, 26 July 1856, quoted in "Lieut. Brooke's Claim," Brooke Papers.

[18] The bill was no. 864. See *Journal of the House of Representatives*, 3 March 1857, 34th Cong., 3d sess., p. 689; *Congressional Globe*, 11 Feb. 1861, 36th Cong., 2d sess., p. 842, 19 Feb. 1861, p. 1034, 26 Feb. 1861, p. 1205.

was when to invest. "If Virginia secedes as I hope she will," wrote Alex, a few days before the bombardment of Fort Sumter, "her stock might temporarily decline, but ultimately would, I think, advance." Brooke held off until Virginia seceded; then, he recalled later, "as a good Constitutional patriot ought to have done I invested it in Confederate bonds which I have not since seen."[19]

While stationed in Washington working on the charts of the North Pacific expedition, Brooke worked to improve his deep-sea lead. Perhaps his interest had been fired when Professor Bailey of West Point proposed to name a beautiful species "Asteromphalus Brookei, in honor of Lieutenant Brooke."[20] In any case, at this time Brooke's original one-arm model was adopted by the navy in place of the two-arm model when the latter proved unreliable. Also, it became apparent that the lead often had been carelessly made. A primary source of error had been the engraving in Maury's *Sailing Directions*. Brooke noted that the engraving "is incorrect and doubtless many failures have occurred in its [the Lead's] use from copying that form." Maury sent a draftsman to Brooke "to obtain a drawing of the deep sea sounding lead with one arm," and Brooke lent the draftsman a model explaining exactly how it operated. Brooke also furnished Maury a description of the one-armed model to accompany the new edition of *Sailing Directions*.[21] Brooke emphasized the need of a light rod and a small but strong twine. The description explained the use of goose quills in the tube at the lower end of the rod to capture specimens and the valve near the top of the tube through which the water could escape during descent. Brooke's experiments in the *Vincennes* had demonstrated the utility of these improvements. After the Civil War the Bureau of Navigation issued a pamphlet entitled *The General Instructions for Hydrographic Surveyors of the United States Navy*, which included a drawing of Brooke's one-arm model. The

[19] Brooke to Brooke, 1 March 1861, Tunstall to Brooke, 8 March 1861, Brooke to Rep. John Randolph Tucker, 14 March 1876 (copy), BP.

[20] *House Reports*, Report of House Committee on Naval Affairs, 3 March 1857, 34th Cong., 3d sess., Report No. 260, p. 7. Jacob Whitman Bailey (1811–1857), appointed professor of chemistry, mineralogy, and geology at West Point in 1838, was a pioneer in the field of microscopy. He was a renowned botanist and wrote many scientific articles.

[21] Brooke's Washington Journal, 18 Oct. 1857, BP.

accompanying description was an almost verbatim copy of that which Brooke had sent Maury in 1857.

Despite the unequivocal acceptance of Brooke's lead in naval circles before the Civil War, the residue of hatred and jealousy which that conflict engendered nearly shunted it into oblivion for a time. During the war and for some years thereafter the United States Navy was indifferent to deep-sea sounding. There was a corresponding "letting-up of work in deep water" by foreign governments, also.[22] Not until the seventies did the United States Navy display a renewed interest, when Captain George E. Belknap was instructed to sound across the North Pacific. By then Brooke's lead "had been virtually discarded—both in the service and by the Coast Survey." George Belknap did not know why "except that for the same reason that some bigoted fanatics and asses . . . wanted to ignore and discard all the work done by Maury and under his superintendence—because of the War."[23] Moreover, the friction between the navy and the Coast Survey continued, and the latter was reluctant to utilize equipment designed at the Naval Observatory. The success that attended Belknap and various British navigators who employed Brooke's detacher or modifications of it restored it to its rightful position as the only apparatus that could recover specimens from the deep sea. The instrument again came into its own. In 1877 an American naval officer wrote that Brooke's detacher was "universally employed" and described it as "the most successful instrument of the kind ever invented."[24]

John Brooke was always open to new ideas. Even while perfecting his deep-sea lead he was cogitating on the possibility of echo sounding. Writing to Maury in 1857, he proposed bouncing sound waves off the ocean floor to determine depth, suggesting that if a bell were struck "just beneath the surface of the water" the ear would hear the echo "with the aid of a partially submerged *water-trumpet.*" The principal obstacle appeared to be the accurate

[22] George E. Belknap, "Something about Deep-Sea Sounding," *United Service* 1 (April 1879): 173–74.

[23] Belknap to Brooke, 12 July 1879, BP.

[24] Theodore F. Jewell, "Deep Sea Sounding," *Papers and Proceedings of the United States Naval Institute* 4 (1878): 44–45.

measurement of elapsed time, but Brooke believed that the mean of six or seven observations by a skilled observer could fix the interval within three hundredths of a second, which he translated to a probable error of seventy-two feet a mile. He predicted that "by *reflected* sound" a surveyor could "construct a map of the bottom of the sea." Unfortunately, Brooke, absorbed in his regular duties, got little or no encouragement from Maury.[25]

Brooke's prediction would be fulfilled in the 1920s when Harvey C. Hayes, a research physicist of the United States Navy, developed a sonic depth finder, which performed the function Brooke had suggested.[26]

Related to Brooke's interest in deep-sea sounding was the laying of the Atlantic cable. The latter was perhaps the most spectacular marine accomplishment of the 1850s. In 1849 certain American naval vessels under the direction of the Naval Observatory began systematic deep-sea soundings in the Atlantic.[27] On the basis of these inconclusive investigations, Maury suggested the existence of a plateau stretching across the North Atlantic from Newfoundland to Ireland. Maury called this nearly level area the Telegraph Plateau.[28] But no specimens had been recovered to indicate the character of the bottom or to prove positively that bottom had been reached. At this juncture, in 1852, Brooke invented

[25] Brooke to Maury, 12 July 1857 (copy), BP. The method was not as new as Brooke seemed to think. Leonardo da Vinci long before had discovered that sound traveled through water and had conducted experiments in that field of physics. Some years before Brooke the French scientist Jean François Arago proposed that sound waves be used to measure the depth of the sea. Brooke was apparently unaware that in 1854 while Brooke was in the Pacific, Maury had failed in an attempt to measure the depths by sound (Thomas H. Whitcroft, "Sonic Sounding," *United States Naval Institute Proceedings* 69 [Feb. 1943]: 216).

[26] Hayes's instrument was not nearly so crude as that Brooke had suggested nearly 70 years earlier, but the basic principles were the same. Hayes's instrument "consists chiefly of means of making a sound on the ship, with the sound waves directed toward the bottom of the ocean, a delicate receiving apparatus to catch the echo from the bottom, and a highly accurate and delicate clock mechanism to measure the time interval in small fractions of a second. Knowing the velocity of sound in water, the depth can be calculated very closely. The 'sound' is not necessarily audible to the ears: supersonic waves may be more effective" (Coker, *Great and Wide Sea*, pp. 70–71). For an interesting description of Hayes's work, see Whitcroft, "Sonic Sounding," pp. 217–21.

[27] *Senate Executive Documents*, Report of Secretary of the Navy Dobbin, 1 Dec. 1856, 34th Cong., 3d sess. vol. 3, no. 5, p. 409; see also Lewis, *Maury*, p. 67.

[28] Maury is generally given credit for suggesting the Telegraph Plateau. See Lewis, *Maury*, p. 76. But there is little unanimity of opinion in this matter. Cf. *House Journal*, 30th

his deep-sea lead. The next year, Lieutenant Otway Henry Berryman in the *Dolphin* used the Brooke lead in the North Atlantic "with great success." Berryman forwarded his specimens of the bottom to Maury and to Professor Bailey at West Point. Microscopic examinations revealed that the specimens did not contain "a particle of sand or gravel mixed with them," but were "mites of sea-shells as perfect and unworn as when they were alive." These findings supported by further investigation proved that the bottom of the North Atlantic in the area sounded was composed of nonabrasive substances and was unaffected by currents. Soundings with Brooke's lead also showed that a plateau some four hundred miles in width stretched from Cape Race, Newfoundland, to Cape Clear, Ireland. As early as February 1854, Maury was able to assert that a cable was feasible in the North Atlantic so far as the bottom of the sea was concerned.[29] Two months later the New York, Newfoundland, and London Telegraph Company was chartered. The immediate objective of the company was to throw a cable across the Gulf of St. Lawrence from Newfoundland to Cape Breton Island, but in the background was the far grander plan of a cable under the Atlantic from Newfoundland to Ireland. Cyrus Field, Peter Cooper, and three other New York capitalists were the original stockholders. Samuel Finley Breese Morse, the telegraph wizard, was soon drawn into the enterprise as a technical consultant. The information made available by the Brooke lead was what canny businessmen demanded before backing such a scheme. Since the 1840s the idea of a telegraph line under the sea had been occasionally discussed as a theoretical possibility, but the lack of knowledge of the ocean floor had restrained promoters from underwriting such a risky enterprise. Now, thanks to Brooke, the light showed green.[30]

Cong., 2d sess., p. 157; Professor W. P. Trowbridge to Alexander Dallas Bache, 16 Oct. 1858 (copy), Letters Received, Naval Observatory, RG 78, NA, microfilm copy, BP. See also Belknap, "Something about Deep-Sea Sounding," p. 166; Jewell, "Deep Sea Sounding," p. 44.

[29] See Lewis, *Maury*, pp. 76–78.

[30] When considering the possibility of laying an Atlantic cable, Cyrus Field in Feb. 1854 wrote to Maury on the hydrographic problems involved. On the strength of Berryman's soundings with the Brooke lead in 1853, Maury replied that from a hydrographic point of view an Atlantic cable was practicable.

As soon as he heard of the company's organization, Brooke displayed a lively interest in its operations. And on his return to Washington in 1856, the question of the Atlantic cable exerted a growing fascination upon him. In the summer of 1856 the navy appointed Lieutenant Berryman to run a series of soundings from St. John's, Newfoundland, to Valencia, Ireland, preparatory to the laying of a cable by private interests. Using the steamer *Arctic*, Berryman accomplished his mission and won warm praise from Secretary Dobbin. But Maury at the observatory did not share this enthusiasm and stormed that "Berrymans reported depths are not reliable." Brooke agreed with Maury. The trouble was that Berryman had not followed navy regulations, which were based on solid experience. Rather than using the Brooke lead with the standard sounding twine and spherical sinker, Berryman had modified the Brooke detacher, using a heavy, elongated sinker and a much thicker line than that prescribed. In the view of those at the observatory, the elongated sinker was suitable only for shoal water soundings. Berryman had also failed to note carefully "how long each 100 fathoms mark on the sounding line takes to go out"; instead, he employed a Massey indicator, although that instrument was designed for moderate depths rather than the deep sea.[31]

Brooke analyzed the difficulty of using the Massey indicator with an elongated sinker. He pointed out that the indicator depended upon the rotation of a propeller around a vertical axis, but this was not practical with the elongated lead because the axis of the lead itself revolved. Consequently, the rotations of the indicator and lead were combined. Brooke stated that Massey's indicator was not accurate at rates of descent slower than two nautical miles per hour; however, experiments demonstrated that a lead and line such as those used on the *Arctic* descended at a considerably slower rate. Only one general conclusion could be drawn from

[31] *Senate Executive Documents*, Report of Secretary of the Navy Dobbin, 1 Dec. 1856, 34th Cong., 3d sess., vol. 3, no. 5, p. 410; Maury to Frank Minor, 7 Dec. 1856, Matthew Fontaine Maury Papers, MSS Div., LC; "Justice" [John M. Brooke], "Deep-Sea Soundings—Lieut. Maury's and Lieut. Berryman's Systems Compared," New York *Herald*, 7 May 1857; Washington *National Intelligencer*, 19 May 1857; "Justice" [John M. Brooke], "Deep Sea Soundings," Washington *National Intelligencer*, 21 May, 1857; Lizzie Brooke's copy of Maury's reply to Berryman on the *Arctic*'s soundings, n.d., BP; Maury to Ingraham, 16 Jan. 1857, Letters Received Relating to Ordnance and Hydrography, RG 45, NA.

Berryman's soundings in Brooke's opinion, experience having shown that weights as heavy as Berryman's detacher with the indicator attached could not be recovered from depths greater than 2,500 fathoms. But Berryman had brought up samples from the bottom; therefore it appeared that the bottom where he sounded did not lie more than 2,500 fathoms under the surface.[32]

The superintendent of the observatory, not relying solely on his own opinions or those of Brooke, appointed a board consisting of two lieutenants and a professor to examine Berryman's report, charts, and abstract log. The board found "that many discrepancies exist between the charts and log, as well as the charts themselves, and also that in some places the report itself differs from both the chart, and the log." It concluded "that the work is unreliable; and that any results derived from such data would be of little value."[33]

Otway Berryman was not without his defenders. Secretary Dobbin in his annual report heaped praise upon that officer's work in the *Arctic*. True, the secretary did not overlook the contributions of Maury and Brooke, giving Maury full credit for his suggestion of a Telegraph Plateau between Newfoundland and Ireland.[34] The cabinet officer also acknowledged that Brooke's "most ingenious, yet simple contrivance" had paved the way for the verification of Maury's theory. But Berryman, fresh from his labors, was the real hero of the secretary's report. Others rallied to Berryman's defense, such as "H," who wrote a vigorous though rather illogical exposition published in the New York *Herald* on May 13, 1857.[35] Some of the newspaper articles in Berryman's defense were attributed to a New York lawyer.[36]

[32] "Justice" [John M. Brooke], "Deep Sea Soundings—Lieut. Maury's and Lieut. Berryman's Systems Compared," New York *Herald*, 7 May 1857.

[33] Lts. Reed Werden and Richmond Aulick and Professor Joseph S. Hubbard to Lt. M. F. Maury, 11 July 1857, Letters Received, Naval Observatory, RG 78, NA. Berryman was senior to both Werden and Aulick.

[34] *Senate Executive Documents*, Report of Secretary of the Navy Dobbin, 1 Dec. 1856, 34th Cong., 3d sess., vol. 3, no. 5, p. 409.

[35] This article was entitled "The Telegraphic Plateau—Lieut. Maury's and Lieut. Berryman's Systems of Taking Soundings Compared," and was in reply to Brooke's article of May 7; it was reprinted in the Washington *National Intelligencer* on May 19. "H" may have been Berryman, but judging from the errors of fact in the article it would appear to have been written by one of Berryman's defenders who had more enthusiasm than knowledge.

[36] Kate Corbin Brooke notes recording conversations with John M. Brooke, 1896, BP.

The real source of the Berryman controversy was the rivalry between Alexander Bache's Coast Survey and Maury's Naval Observatory. Berryman had served several years in the Coast Survey immediately before his assignment to the *Arctic* and become attached to its methods and equipment. The controversy generated bitter feelings on both sides. George Belknap recalled at a much later date that he had "heard Berryman talk about the matter at Aspinwall in 1859 and he was furious against Maury."[37] And Brooke remembered that he and Berryman had boarded at the same house in Washington and Berryman had "made himself very unpleasant."[38] One day at dinner, Berryman, who was considerably Brooke's senior, goaded Brooke to the point of rage and there might have been an explosion if Lizzie had not intervened. Brooke stated his position on Berryman's soundings in the Washington *National Intelligencer* and the New York *Herald*, sometimes under the nom de plume "Justice." Berryman's defenders, using pseudonyms, wrote principally in the New York *Herald* and the Washington *Union*.[39]

The rejection of the *Arctic*'s soundings induced the British admiralty to dispatch Lieutenant Joseph Dayman to rerun the line of soundings.[40] After a series of tests Dayman rejected the Massey indicator used by Berryman in favor of the Brooke deep-sea

[37] Belknap to Brooke, 26 Feb. 1879, BP. George Eugene Belknap (1832–1903), an officer of the United States Navy, won a reputation as commander of the *Tuscarora* in which he engaged in deep-sea soundings across the North Pacific in 1874 to test the suitability of the Pacific for a cable. His discoveries concerning the ocean floor, made with Brooke's lead, were widely acclaimed by scientists. In 1885 Belknap became superintendent of the Naval Observatory serving in that capacity for a year. He attained the rank of rear admiral in 1889 and retired five years later.

[38] Kate Corbin Brooke notes recording conversations with John M. Brooke, 1896, BP.

[39] See notes 32 and 36 above. A careful check failed to disclose any letters in the *National Intelligencer* bearing Berryman's name. Kate Corbin Brooke states that Berryman wrote for the New York *World*. She probably meant the *Herald*; the *World* was not in existence. In the Brooke Papers is the copy of a letter to the editor of the *Herald* signed "Veritas." This undated letter is in reply to the letter of 13 May signed "H" and may not have been published. Maury was, of course, Berryman's principal antagonist owing to his position, but Brooke was drawn in because his invention was involved. Maury wrote a bitter attack on Berryman, a copy of which is in the Brooke Papers. Maury stated his letter was in reply to one written by Berryman that had been published in the *Union*.

[40] Belknap stated that unless he had been misinformed the "discredit thrown upon Berryman's work was the prime cause of the detail by the British Admiralty of H.M.S. 'Cyclops,' Lieutenant Dayman, R.N. to make a supplementary survey" ("Something about Deep-Sea Sounding," p. 170).

sounding apparatus. By that time the Brooke lead had gained general acceptance as an essential tool for any cable-laying plans.

In 1857 Brooke designed an indicator or register for measuring the depth of the sea which he considered to be "free of errors arising from rotation of the sounding apparatus—two propellers turning in opposition with independent registering trains." The device was so constructed that the propellers were thrown out of gear when the sinker was detached. To insure that the indicator did not enter the mud, Brooke suggested that it be attached to the line about ten or fifteen feet above the detaching apparatus. It is apparent that Brooke's invention overcame some of the objections to the Massey indicator, designed for measuring moderate depths "by revolutions of a screw that went down with the lead." Brooke referred the matter to Maury and sent him a sketch of the indicator, but nothing was done about it.[41] Brooke did not apply for a patent at the time because he "had no model or money to get one made." When he left Washington in 1858 he secured a caveat and left with Mary Garnett, his cousin Dr. Yelverton Garnett's wife, the necessary papers to apply for a patent, should he later decide it worthwhile to do so.

The Berryman controversy was a disagreeable episode to Brooke, but he did not permit it to divert him from his profound interest in a transoceanic cable. Without surcease his active mind wrestled stubbornly with the practical problems to be encountered in laying a wire thousands of feet under the sea. In his free evenings he cogitated, wrote, and experimented. Ever alert to the main chance, he sent letters to men in a position to adopt or advertise his ideas. Among these were Cyrus Field, Peter Cooper, and Senator Stephen R. Mallory. In September 1857 Brooke wrote that he "had volunteered long ago to Mr Cyrus Field to lay it (the cable) across the Atlantic."[42]

In April 1857, before the first attempt to lay the cable was made, Brooke prepared a scientific paper entitled "The Ocean Telegraph."[43] In it he endeavored to show that the laying of an Atlantic cable was well "within the limits of probability" despite

[41] Brooke to Maury, 23 May 1857, Letters Received, Naval Observatory, RG 78, NA.

[42] Brooke's Washington Journal, 5 Sept. 1857, BP.

[43] This essay, dated 28 April 1857, was printed in leaflet form. There are several copies in the Brooke Papers.

the lack of experience in that specific field of engineering. Brooke asserted that the best cable was one which combined the lightness of twine with the strength of iron. Such a cable would sink slowly while the ship moved forward at maximum speed. The inventor suggested that the cable would "sink in the direction of its inclination." With a heavy cable, the force which Brooke called "back-set" would act as a drag on the vessel, whereas with a light line the back-set would be an asset because it would keep the cable taut.

Brooke foresaw back-set as the most difficult problem to be overcome in actually laying the cable. He was convinced that copper wire covered with gutta percha, advocated by some eminent men, was too susceptible to abrasion. Furthermore, he predicted that the iron-encased cable selected by Charles T. Bright, the English engineer of the Atlantic Telegraph Company, was vulnerable to the intense pressures of the ocean floor and might snap. It was essential, Brooke believed, that some means be devised to register the strain upon the wire as it unwound, so that the strain could be kept within limits. In May, Brooke's article appeared in the Washington *National Intelligencer* and the New York *Herald*, and in June it was published in the *U.S. Nautical Magazine*.[44] Twenty-two years later Brooke recalled that this article was in the hands of Bright and others before the first attempt to lay cable was made, "but its suggestion[s] with regard to increasing speed & veering rapidly to diminish rate of descent & tension were unheeded, with the result predicted."[45]

The failure of the first attempt to lay the cable in the summer of 1857 focused attention again upon Brooke's article. The *National Intelligencer* of August 31, 1857, contained "a notice and partial republication" of Brooke's views. In September the *U.S. Nautical Magazine* published an article entitled, "Failure to Lay the Atlantic Telegraph Cable." While scoring the management of the Atlantic Telegraph Company, the article praised Brooke in generous terms and recalled his predictions. Referring to Brooke's sci-

[44] J. M. Brooke, "The Atlantic Telegraph," New York *Herald*, 13 May 1857. The date of publication in the *National Intelligencer* is not known, but on 5 Sept. 1857 the editors stated that they had published the article early in the preceding May.

[45] Brooke to Belknap, 1 April 1879 (copy), BP.

entific paper, the magazine asserted "that in all respects, the theory there set forth, has been verified."[46] Declaring that American naval officers originated the project of uniting the hemispheres through their deep-sea soundings, the magazine asked: "Why then . . . have not some of the gifted men who originated, fostered and developed this idea been called to carry it into execution?" The answer, it said, was because the company was dominated by the English.[47] In high dudgeon the article thundered that the manufacture and laying of the cable "should have been left in the hands where it belonged," for "it is best to employ Americans to carry out American ideas." It pointed out that Brooke had predicted that the wire selected by the English company was too heavy and "afforded no protection in the line of strength." In conclusion it insisted that the cable had not broken through an accident, as the company claimed, for "the circumstances attending the operation of laying the cable, its back-set, the necessity and danger of checking it, the breaking of the continuity, and finally of the cable itself in a certain specified contingency, which actually happened, were clearly indicated" by Brooke in advance.[48]

Brooke was eager for a chance to lay the cable. Both he and Lizzie were prepared to go to England if necessary. By every means the young naval scientist endeavored to establish his qualifications. He continued to call on people and to write letters. Naturally, he explained his plan for "veering" the telegraph cable to John Rodgers. That officer, whose opinion meant so much to Brooke, "approved" the plan. Brooke called on the new secretary of the navy, Isaac Toucey, to discuss the cable and was pleased

[46] "Failure to Lay the Atlantic Telegraph Cable," *U.S. Nautical Magazine and Naval Journal* 6 (Sept. 1857): 464–71. The article blamed the failure on "incompetent management." The engineer was denounced as wanting in knowledge and capacity.

[47] It was true that the company was almost entirely English. Bright was engineer, and Whitehouse was the electrician. Sir William Thomson was on the board. Morse for a time was an honorary director of the Atlantic Telegraph Company, but he soon resigned. The only American active in the company was Cyrus Field.

[48] The customary view expressed in the American press that the cable snapped owing to the faulty application of the brakes at Bright's instruction was based in large part upon the explanation written on board the *Niagara* at the time by S. F. B. Morse. This view was shared by Morse and the New York *Herald* reporter (Carleton Mabee, *The American Leonardo: a Life of Samuel F. B. Morse* [New York, 1943], p. 334). For his part Bright blamed the accident on the *Niagara*.

when the secretary "approved the theory advanced in the essay." Brooke also wrote a letter to Peter Cooper offering his services. That venerable old man, in whose breast the light of hope burned brightly, answered promptly, urging Brooke to forward his plan with reference to laying the cable "to the President of the Telegraph Company (Atlantic) in England."[49] Brooke sent to Senator Mallory, chairman of the Senate Committee on Naval Affairs, who was then at Key West, a copy of his article with appropriate comments. In September, Brooke called on Orson Desaix Munn, editor of the *Scientific American*, the first popular scientific journal in the United States, and the two men "talked about the Telegraph." A lead story had just appeared in that journal which was clearly based upon Brooke's essay upon veering the wire, but it gave Brooke "no credit." Brooke lent Munn a block woodcut which illustrated his theory of the "cable-wave" induced by backset, and the editor offered Brooke the use of his columns. An examination of the magazine discloses, however, that no articles written by Brooke or alluding to him were published in it, nor was any drawing made from the woodcut printed.[50] In December 1857 Brooke took advantage of one of Cyrus Field's visits to Washington to explain his plan for laying the cable, and in January he rushed a written explanation to Field as the cable promoter was embarking for England on the *Persia*.[51]

On January 11, 1858, an article by Brooke on "Veering Telegraph Cable" appeared in the *National Intelligencer*. It developed the idea that Brooke had explained to Cyrus Field and demonstrated his unabated interest in the project as the time for a second attempt drew near. The article proposed a method for meeting the *"irregular strain*, arising from the motion of the vessel on the waves," which had "proved to be the most dangerous of those incidental occurrences which are sometimes considered accidents" in the "hazardous operation of laying telegraph cables in the deep sea." There had been several suggestions on how to meet the dif-

[49] Brooke's Washington Journal, 5 Sept., 3 Sept., 15 Sept. 1857, BP.

[50] Ibid., 8 Sept., 5 Sept. 1857; "The Failure of the Atlantic Cable," *Scientific American* 12 (Sept. 5, 1857): 413.

[51] Brooke's Washington Journal, 8 Jan. 1858, BP.

ficulty, but Brooke noted that they all required expensive machinery. His plan was very simple. He would utilize the inertia and pitching of the ship's ends by opposing to the line fed out from the stern of the ship a counterweight moving between guides attached to the foremast. The line would pass through a wheel attached to a span projecting from the stern of the vessel. The span would be secured to the counterweight by wires.

These ideas which Brooke had explained to Cyrus Field were laid before Charles Bright, the company engineer. Bright wrote a "very complimentary" letter to Brooke, thanking him "in his own name and that of the company for drawings and descriptions of a plan for laying the cable." Bright explained that the company had already adopted the counterpoise principle but had designed a movable sheave to shift horizontally rather than vertically as Brooke proposed. With the Greble and Berryman affairs fresh in his memory, Brooke was a little suspicious. "I am inclined to believe," he wrote, "that my proposition to place the counterpoise in the bows of the ship is new and perhaps they have adopted that part of *my* plan. We shall see."[52] As a matter of fact, the new cable-laying machine was equipped with self-releasing brakes which "could be adjusted to stand only a regulated strain before they released themselves." The brakes were designed by J. G. Appold, a Londoner "with a strong taste for mechanics." Brooke's contention that the machine used in 1857 had been too heavy and complicated was borne out. The new model adopted by William E. Everett, who had been delegated by Field, now general manager, to select a new machine for the 1858 trial, was much smaller and simpler than the earlier one. It took up only one-third as much space and weighed one-fourth as much.[53]

Brooke was on the West Coast preparing to sail for the Orient

[52] Ibid., 19 Feb. 1858.

[53] Philip B. McDonald, *A Saga of the Seas: The Story of Cyrus W. Field and the Laying of the First Atlantic Cable* (New York, 1937), p. 55; Henry M. Field, *The Story of the Atlantic Telegraph* (New York, 1892), pp. 147–48. Everett had been chief engineer of the *Niagara*, one of the two vessels employed in the abortive attempt in 1857, and had impressed Field by his knowledge. In 1858 when Field became general manager he installed Everett at a large machine works located at Southwark, where for 3 months Everett studied plans and models for the machine best adapted to laying an ocean cable.

when the Atlantic cable was completed between Newfoundland and Ireland. The success of the enterprise took him by surprise, but he took time to write his cousin Senator R. M. T. Hunter that "there has been some excitement about the telegraph cable. . . . The world is now satisfied that the thing is practicable. There will soon be cables enough. It is gratifying to know that Cyrus Field has succeeded despite the obstacles."[54]

Most people were less reserved. When the San Francisco papers learned the glorious news they made much of it and Brooke became something of a hero. He was requested by the president of the Mechanics Institute to exhibit at the institute's fair one of his deep-sea sounding leads, "as many of our most respected Citizens express a desire to see it." Brooke complied, and a few days later one of the San Francisco papers noted: "It is well worthy the inspection of the curious in such matters, and its simplicity is such that it cannot fail of being understood by everybody." The young inventor was extended a special invitation to attend a public celebration on September 27, 1858. But Brooke missed the affair, for the day before he sailed on the *Fenimore Cooper* into the Pacific. Brooke was not, however, forgotten. A poem read by William H. Rhodes recorded an imaginary conversation between John Bull and Brother Jonathan. While lauding generally the accomplishments of young America, Jonathan singled out for particular praise six American inventors or promoters, beginning with Benjamin Franklin and including Brooke. Of the naval officer the poem said: "Again, you scold me on the ground, / Of curiosity; / But Brooke paul-pryed, until he found / The bottom of the sea!"[55]

There is an ironic ending to the story. Some weeks before the extravagant celebration in San Francisco the magic wire, alarmingly weak and unpredictable from the beginning, had gone dead. But the happy people in California did not know it because in those days the San Francisco newspapers were still dependent

[54] Brooke to Hunter, 19 Sept. 1858, R. M. T. Hunter Papers, University of Virginia Library, Charlottesville (hereafter cited as UVa Lib.).

[55] "Poem Pronounced by Wm. H. Rhodes before the Citizens of California, Sept. 27, 1858, on the Occasion of Celebrating the Completion of the Ocean Telegraph," clipping from unidentified newspaper, BP.

upon the semimonthly steamers of the Pacific Mail; the New York newspapers were twenty-five days in transit.[56]

When Brooke returned to Washington in 1860, nature's challenge to man to link the continents by wire still had to be met. And now, after the sharp disappointment of 1858, there were many pessimists. But Brooke was not among them. True enough, when in Japan he had written that he had, at least for the time, lost interest in the enterprise. But now that he was back on the national scene he was fired up again and wrote a short note to Cyrus Field stating that he had been absent from the country for two years and was "desirous of learning something in relation to the Atlantic Telegraph project."[57] But Field, who had suffered grave reverses, had nothing to offer. Not for another six years would the cable be laid.

With the passage of time, Brooke's significant role in the laying of the Atlantic cable was almost entirely forgotten by the general public. A visitor to the Columbian Exposition in Chicago in 1893 was particularly interested in the Western Union Telegraph exhibit. But he noted that although a "relief map of the basin of the Atlantic Ocean" which revealed the Telegraph Plateau and a bust of Cyrus Field were prominently displayed, there was no indication that either Maury or Brooke had had the slightest connection with the great enterprise.[58]

Though the public forgot, those in a position to know of Brooke's work remembered the Brooke detacher. More than two years after the 1858 cable went dead, Maury wrote: "All we know about what is at the bottom of the *deep* sea, we owe to that instrument." Perhaps the finest tribute was paid by Daniel Coit Gilman, president of Johns Hopkins University, in a speech to the graduating class at Annapolis two decades after Cyrus Field finally conquered the Atlantic. He said: "There is at present an incessant call for naval officers to take places in pursuing the study of our coasts, the deep seas and electricity. It was not Morse,

[56] John Denton Carter, "Before the Telegraph: The News Service of the San Francisco *Bulletin*, 1855–1861," *Pacific Historical Review* 11 (Sept. 1942): 301–2, 306.

[57] Brooke to Field, 25 June 1860 (copy), BP.

[58] J. T. Murfee, Marion Military Institute, to the Editor, Montgomery (Ala.) *Daily Advertiser*, 23 Nov. 1893.

Edison or Sir William Thompson who gave us ocean telegraphy, but all we have came from the investigations of Lieut. Brooke, of the United States navy. Great improvements have been made, but they all depend upon Brooke's discoveries."[59]

The Atlantic cable was only the most dramatic attempt to span the seas with wire in the fifties. There were other cable-laying efforts then and later, and in all of them the depths had to be sounded as a preliminary measure. Brooke's detacher proved its worth many times over as a prerequisite to these operations. For example, in 1857 the commander of the Spanish naval forces in the West Indies requested from the observatory one of Brooke's leads "as a model for others to be used by him in effecting deep sea soundings, with the view of laying a telegraphic cable between Cuba and the United States."[60] The request was granted.

Brooke's activities must have interfered with his life at home, and perhaps Lizzie was neglected. They had only eight months in 1857–58 to enjoy the comforts of a shared house in Washington before Brooke left on a second cruise to the Orient.

[59] Maury to Brooke, 31 Jan. 1861, Letters Sent, Naval Observatory, RG 78, NA; Baltimore *Sun*, 11 June [1887].

[60] Maury to Captain Duncan N. Ingraham, 5 May 1857, Letters Received Relative to Hydrography from the Naval Observatory, 1856–58, RG 45, NA.

VI /

SURVEYING THE ROUTE

FROM SAN FRANCISCO TO

HONG KONG

THE North Pacific expedition had been recalled before it had completed the survey of the trade lanes to China. Yet, the need for the selection and survey of the best steamship route between San Francisco and China became more apparent every day. In 1857 the time was ripe to push the project through. John Rodgers was determined that the survey should be run and that John Brooke should run it. Brooke supported the plan vigorously. At the Naval Observatory, Maury was enthusiastic, and he offered Brooke the use of the *Fenimore Cooper*, one of the boats detailed to the observatory. Brooke, who had been impressed by the sailing qualities which the little schooner had demonstrated during the North Pacific expedition, was happy to accept the offer.

But the proposed expedition could not be undertaken without an appropriation from Congress. Brooke and Rodgers enlisted the help of Senator William Gwin of California, whose state stood to gain most by the survey. On December 15, the two officers and the senator called on Secretary of the Navy Toucey. In his journal

Brooke noted that the Connecticut Yankee "after listening to our explanation said that he would go for it." Brooke believed that a $10,000 appropriation would be adequate, and Gwin promised to secure congressional approval "as soon as possible." After a delay of two months, Toucey issued the necessary orders specifying that Brooke should use the *Fenimore Cooper*, then at San Francisco. Thus was thrust upon Brooke's waiting shoulders the largest responsibility he had yet assumed. Independent command was, of course, not a new experience to him, for he had had to rely on his own resources during the launch cruise and while in the strait of Senyavina. But in those cases the command had been for only a few weeks and the ultimate responsibility had rested upon the capable John Rodgers. In this new venture the responsibility was Brooke's from start to finish.[1]

Though Brooke ostensibly had a free hand, his freedom of action was narrowly circumscribed by the factors of time and money. It was desirable that he depart speedily, yet every expense was scrutinized by the economy-minded government. To make preliminary arrangements in the East for a scientific expedition to be organized physically in San Francisco was no easy matter. On the one hand, Brooke could not enlist all his personnel nor purchase all his supplies in the East and ship them to the West Coast by the isthmus; that would be a reckless extravagance. On the other hand, were he to expect to secure all his wants in San Francisco, he could be rudely awakened.

With dispatch he got his personal affairs in order. The hardest thing he had to do was to take Lizzie and Anna to Lexington where they would live with the Williamsons during his absence. Brooke postponed this unpleasant duty for two months until his official preparations were virtually complete. He was hardly out of sight of his family before he was plagued by remorse for things left undone which he ought to have done when they were together. Once more he resolved to read the New Testament—a chapter a day.

Secretary Toucey's detailed instructions informed Brooke that

[1] Brooke's Washington Journal, 19 Dec. 1857, BP; Toucey to Brooke, 9 April 1858, Appointments, Orders, and Resignations, Records of the Bureau of Naval Personnel, RG 24, NA.

the main purpose of the survey was to fix the exact positions of "islands, shoals and dangers" lying between California and China, so that the best commercial route could be determined. Among the islands south of Japan, Brooke was to make surveys sufficient to uncover dangers to navigation and to locate possible ports of refuge. The precise positions of prominent points on the Japanese coast were to be ascertained in order to verify the data gathered by the North Pacific expedition. Brooke was advised to keep a sharp lookout for guano islands and, should any be discovered, to examine them. Finally, the young commander was ordered to select the best places for coal depots along the route.[2] Under separate instructions Brooke was assigned the duties of acting purser, which meant the completion of myriads of forms—just the sort of paperwork Brooke detested.

As an experienced navigator and surveyor Brooke was eager to establish reference points to facilitate the computation of longitude. He was aware that the average chronometer varied one tenth of a second in its daily rate for each degree of temperature variation. In practical terms this meant that a daily temperature change of thirty degrees "would result generally in an accumulating error of three quarters of a mile each twenty four hours." Work on charts of the North Pacific expedition had shown that chains of reported shoals or islands extending along specific parallels of latitude were in fact often mere duplications of one object or one group of objects. It was a matter of prime significance to navigators that the false dangers be erased from the charts. Brooke was given no time limit, but it was estimated that the work would require three years.

The small size of the *Fenimore Cooper* limited the number of men who could be accommodated to twenty-one, so great care was required in selecting the crew. While still in Washington Brooke chose Lieutenant Charles E. Thorburn as the only other commissioned officer of the expedition, the appointment apparently being based upon the strong recommendation of Charles Welsh, chief clerk of the Navy Department. Thorburn, a citizen of Ohio, had entered the navy in 1847, six years after Brooke, and

[2] Toucey to Brooke, 24 May 1858, Confidential Letters Sent (Letter Book), RG 45, NA.

had spent most of his time at sea. He accepted the appointment "with great pleasure." Brooke's choice for draftsman and acting master was Edward Kern, the artist, his friend of the Bering Strait expedition. Joseph Heco, a young Japanese who had spent some years in the United States and was anxious to return to his homeland, was hired as clerk at the suggestion of Senator Gwin of California.[3] On the recommendation of Dr. William Whelan, chief of the Bureau of Medicine and Surgery, Brooke signed up Lucian H. Kendall as hospital steward, the nearest thing to a doctor aboard the *Cooper*. The position of ship's steward was given to Charles Rogier, who had served on the *Vincennes* and "whose services apart from the duties of his office would be important." Brooke also hired the armorer's mate, really an instrument maker, before he left Washington.

Brooke estimated "the whole incidental expenses of the survey for three years" to be $9,966, the largest item being $4,200 for the civilian draftsman's salary. Other items were: astronomical and surveying instruments, $900; shipment of instruments to California, $500; beads, axes, irons, etc., for barter, $300; equipment, tents for observatory, and whaleboat, $700. Brooke's requisition for equipment indicates detailed planning, the mere listing of the items requiring two and one-half long sheets.[4] The very large number of astronomical, hydrographic, and surveying instruments acquired underlined the basic scientific nature of the expedition. Most scientific items were obtained from the Naval Observatory or were transferred from the North Pacific expedition, but a few articles were secured in New York. In addition to scientific equipment, Brooke was responsible for stocking the *Cooper* with the multifarious supplies required for an extended cruise. Though most of the clerical supplies were procured in New York, several blank forms for scientific data, such as "time sight" and

[3] Heco to Brooke, 10 May 1858, BP.

[4] Expenses to be incurred in fitting out expedition to survey route from California to China computed by J. M. Brooke, BP; Toucey to Capt. D. M. Ingraham, Chief of the Bureau of Ordnance and Hydrography, 9 April 1858, Letters Received Relative to Hydrography from the Secretary of the Navy, 1856–62, RG 45, NA. Even more comprehensive is the list that states where Brooke obtained each item, in one of Brooke's miscellaneous notebooks in the Brooke Papers.

"time altitude," were prepared by the Government Printing Office under Brooke's supervision.

The expedition was adequately armed. Though his mission was peaceful, Brooke's travels in foreign lands had taught him the value of firearms when among strange peoples. His armament included handy little swivel howitzers, similar to the one he had used on the strait of Senyavina. There were other items to be considered. For reference and study the tiny *Cooper* carried numerous books, including twenty-two volumes on zoology and kindred subjects.[5] Brooke made arrangements to procure bulky items, including two tents to house the astronomical instruments and a whaleboat, in California. Looking ahead, he secured a letter from Rodgers instructing the naval storekeeper at Hong Kong to allow him to withdraw from the navy warehouse there any articles which had been left by the North Pacific expedition.

As the day of departure from Washington approached, last-minute duties converged upon the expedition commander, for there was much legwork in organizing such an undertaking. To give Lizzie "some notion of the hurry and trouble one has in managing the fitting out of such an expedition," Brooke outlined his itinerary for one day. It included visits to the office of the North Pacific expedition, the Naval Observatory, various bureaus of the Navy Department, the navy yard, the railroad depot, Senator Mallory's office, and conferences with Maury, Alexander Bache, and Joseph Henry.

On June 15, 1858, Brooke left Washington for New York where he had much to do before the scheduled departure of the *Star of the West* for Panama on June 21. The energetic young commander was almost overwhelmed by "the immense accumulation of articles" for which he was responsible during transit to California. But Brooke never sold himself short, confiding to Lizzie that though the organization of the expedition required more physical exertion than he had supposed, yet it seemed to him "a very easy thing."

Four weeks after his departure from New York, Brooke wrote

[5] Among these were Currier's *Animal Kingdom*, 5 vols., Swanson's *Natural History*, 9 vols., Pritchard's *Infusoria*, and Darwin's *Voyage of a Naturalist*.

Secretary Toucey from Mare Island that he had taken command of the *Fenimore Cooper*. To his annoyance, however, he found after careful examination of the schooner that she was "ready *for repairs*" only, despite the soothing report of the constructor that she was "sound as a nut."[6] The ninety-five-ton sailing vessel, which had begun her career as a New York pilot boat in 1852, had been fitted with a new bowsprit and mainmast, but the constructor had delayed internal improvements pending Brooke's arrival.

Brooke turned to advantage the extra time the unexpected delay provided by testing all the instruments thoroughly and conducting an exhaustive series of observations to determine the rates of the chronometers. In this work he was ably assisted by Kern. Special care was devoted to this problem, for in Brooke's words "the accuracy of a survey depends mainly upon the performance of the employed chronometers—delicate instruments affected by motion, changes of temperature, magnetism etc."[7] Brooke placed the chronometer case in the forward part of the cabin near the center of motion at the place least susceptible to the shock of the waves, to the air currents, and to the vibration of the after part of the vessel. Experiment demonstrated that five daily readings were sufficient.[8]

With the stores and equipment, as with the scientific instruments, the careful allocation of space was mandatory. Success was achieved without impairing the relative comfort of the crew of twenty-one. Somehow space was found for four and one-half months' provisions, though the schooner usually carried enough for only three and one-half months. Water for sixty-five days and wood for forty-five days were also stowed aboard. The shipping of the fourteen men not enlisted in the eastern states was en-

[6] Brooke to Sen. R. M. T. Hunter, 17 July 1858, R. M. T. Hunter Papers, UVa Lib.
[7] Note by J. M. Brooke on preparation of the *Fenimore Cooper* for sea, n.d., BP. In a letter to Secretary Toucey, Brooke dealt with the whole question of the effect of temperature upon rates in considerable detail; see Brooke to Toucey, 20 Sept. 1858, Officers Letters, RG 45, NA. Experience on the *Vincennes* had shown that chronometer rates determined in temperatures such as those of San Francisco in September were liable to an error of half a mile a day in the latitude of the Hawaiian Islands. Prudence dictated that such errors should be compensated for.
[8] The temperature within each compartment was observed at noon, 3 P.M., 8 P.M., 4 A.M., and 9 A.M. (*Rates of Chronometers of U.S. Schooner* Fenimore Cooper *from September 10, 1858 to August 8, 1859*, BP).

trusted to Kern, who was dispatched from Mare Island to San Francisco for that purpose. It was not until September 20, 1858, two months after his arrival at Mare Island, that Brooke was able to write Secretary Toucey that the *Fenimore Cooper* was "ready for sea."

Before noon on September 26, 1858, the *Cooper* slipped past the Golden Gate, just one day before the Atlantic Cable celebration. Almost at once the skipper noticed that the heavily loaded schooner was too deep in the water and that the mainsail did not set well. From the beginning it was apparent that the cruise would be both strenuous and wet, and that seasickness would be a common complaint. Brooke's journal relates that on the first day out the pilot had scarcely gone over the side when the schooner encountered a heavy head sea which "came on board frequently."[9] The next day heavy seas and a fresh wind made the schooner "exceedingly wet and uncomfortable" for everyone. In the afternoon all aboard were sick, and poor Heco had to seek out his bunk. Brooke averred that he himself suffered more from seasickness than ever before in his life. The cabin appeared upside down with everything within wet and disordered. Not until the third day was the table even set, for both the cook and steward suffered from nausea. After that conditions improved slightly, though the little craft was soaked topside much of the time and jumped about so much that it was necessary to keep the skylight covered to prevent the spray from going below. The *Cooper* was so deep in the water that half the time her lee beam was submerged. In such adverse conditions Brooke and Thorburn lived in their clothes for days on end, as they preferred to be ready to hit the deck at a moment's notice. It was frequently difficult if not impossible to

[9] The principal sources of information on the cruise of the *Fenimore Cooper* to be found in the Brooke Papers are: Brooke's *Fenimore Cooper* Journals, 22 Sept. 1858–22 Aug. 1859; personal letters from Brooke to his wife; Brooke's letter book as lieutenant commanding and acting purser; official letters received by Brooke as lieutenant commanding and as acting purser; miscellaneous letters received of a personal and semiofficial character. The Brooke Journals embrace the period from the departure of the launch from San Francisco to her wreck in the Bay of Yedo. The other sources begin with the inception of the enterprise in Washington. The log of the *Fenimore Cooper*, 14 Sept. 1858–6 Feb. 1860, is in RG 24, NA. That part of the cruise between San Francisco and Honolulu is covered also in Joseph Heco, *The Narrative of a Japanese: What He Has Seen and the People He Has Met in the Course of the Last Forty Years*, 2 vols. (Yokohama, 1892), 1:172–83.

get observations. As the schooner lurched and twisted her way to the south'west, she consumed daily about twenty-one gallons of water and sixty sticks of wood. At that rate the wood supply required that the *Cooper* make port in forty-five days.

During a period of calms beginning on October 2, Brooke sounded the deep sea. He made twelve casts over a twenty-six-day period, none of which was less than two thousand fathoms. Such soundings were not only important in helping to chart the bottom of the sea in broad outline but also served a useful purpose in survey work. By sounding in the position of alleged dangers Brooke could determine whether such dangers actually existed. As it turned out, in an area embracing several reported dangers, Brooke's soundings showed the ocean to be generally two or three miles deep, with no rocks or islands visible from the masthead.[10] These tests, by saving the government the expense of hunting for weeks for hidden shoals by observation and shallow soundings, gave further proof of the utility of Brooke's lead.

Brooke did not restrict his soundings to the period of calms. Several casts were made with a heavy sea running—seas as much as twelve feet high. It was possible to sound from the schooner in heavy weather because she lay to so well under short sail, but such soundings were difficult and often required three hours. In the trough of the sea the horizon could not be seen except from the masthead. Yet with skill, perseverance, and luck Brooke and his willing crew—to whom deep-sea sounding was a new experience—sounded successfully on several occasions. The one-armed apparatus worked admirably. Nine consecutive casts from 2,000 to 2,900 fathoms deep "were made with the same piece of twine and detaching apparatus, which last weighed less than one pound."[11] At times sharks or other large fish hovered near the sounding line in an annoying manner.

Ever alert to new techniques, Brooke experimented constantly.

[10] Brooke to Toucey, 15 Nov. 1858, Officers Letters, RG 45, NA; Brooke to Warren Winslow, 19 Dec. 1858 (copy), BP; Brooke to Maury, 23 Dec. 1858, Letters Received, Naval Observatory, RG 78, NA; also daily entries in Brooke's *Fenimore Cooper* Journals, BP.

[11] Brooke to Maury, 21 Feb. 1861, Letters Received, Naval Observatory, RG 78, NA.

Wanting a good sample of the water at the ocean's bottom for the purpose of testing its specific gravity, he substituted a glass tube one-half inch in diameter for the goose quills in the bottom of the sounding rod. The idea of the glass tube amused the crew, for the glass looked so fragile. Yet, on the first attempt, made with a sixty-two-pound shot, the glass tube worked perfectly and a specimen was recovered.

On occasion the ship's complement presented a romantic picture as they plumbed the depths by the light of the moon. In his journal on October 21 Brooke recorded one such occasion: "the evening presented us a very pleasing scene the moon ahead our masts and rigging in strong relief against the silver water the figures of the men grouped round the reel and illumined by the warm light of the lantern some of them costumed more romantically than is usual onboard a government vessel. They are seamen from California some have served with [William] Walker and altogether we might be taken in the schooner with our gun amidships for a pirate of the old style."

Not content with improvements in his conventional deep-sea sounding apparatus, Brooke experimented with echo sounding from one of the boats. For the experiments he used some glass tubes four or five feet long, a small gong, some steel bars, and a speaking trumpet.

As the schooner pushed through the zone known as the variables, just north of the trades, the patience, to say nothing of the stomachs, of all were tested. The ocean lay smooth as a sheet of glass one moment, only to become rough and stormy the next. The little schooner, sensitive to every whim of the sea, jumped and darted like a thing possessed, at times rising and falling as much as eighteen feet in twenty-five seconds. Brooke, who likened the maneuverings of the *Cooper* to a cricket, felt half seasick most of the time. As for Heco, he was seasick all of the time. Inevitably the *Cooper* fell farther behind schedule and Brooke worried about the need to rate the chronometers and the dwindling supply of wood. A constant source of annoyance to all was the lack of a suitable place for exercise. The only space available for walking was smaller than an ordinary dining room of that day, and seven-tenths of the time even that was covered with water. As tempers grew short, it is remarkable that Brooke had almost no need to resort to punishment.[12]

At two in the morning on November 9, eight days behind schedule, Diamond Head on the Hawaiian island of Oahu was made out in a northwestern direction. It was the first land descried since the *Cooper* had departed from San Francisco six weeks before. In that period not a sail had been seen on the vast emptiness of the Pacific. Not long after daybreak a steam tug pulled alongside, threw over a hawser, and towed the schooner into the inner harbor of Honolulu where the French frigate *Eurydice* and the English frigate *Calypso* lay at anchor. Fifty-two whalers were counted in the harbor of this mid-Pacific rendezvous.[13]

When the French made out the *Cooper*'s colors, they sent over an officer to offer assistance. The Frenchman expressed an intense interest in the scientific equipment aboard the schooner; instead of the usual ten minutes for calls of that nature, he remained on board for two hours. The English warship, however, ignored the *Cooper*. Brooke noted that the English frigate "is such a duty looking craft that we do not feel much annoyed." During the day Dr. Charles F. B. Guillou, who had served as assistant surgeon on the Wilkes expedition, visited the *Cooper*. A Philadelphian, he was consular physician at Honolulu. Guillou and Brooke became fast friends. The first day in port brought Brooke personal letters and papers up to the first part of September.

At Honolulu the *Cooper* stowed some much needed supplies. She was down to 475 gallons of water and had exhausted her wood supply. The crew overhauled the vessel, painting the schooner and boats and cleaning the tanks.[14] The first few days in port

---

[12] A study of the log reveals one instance when a seaman was placed in double irons for quarreling and drawing a knife.

[13] The whale business seemed to be flourishing, but the appearance was deceptive. The whale fishery in the North Pacific reached its peak in 1852 and thereafter began slowly to decline. During the period 1855–57 the average number of whalers to arrive in Hawaiian ports annually was 400. By the period 1870–72 the annual average had dropped to 71. The signs of decay were obvious to all by 1860, just a year after Brooke's visit. See Ralph S. Kuykendall and A. Grove Day, *Hawaii, a History: From Polynesian Kingdom to American Commonwealth* (New York, 1948), p. 117.

[14] Log of the *Fenimore Cooper*, 9 Nov. 1858, RG 24, N.A.

Brooke made the official calls incumbent upon him as the commander of a national vessel in a foreign port. He found Captain Pichou of the *Eurydice* "polite" and "kind," and the American schooner "received much attention and offers of service" from the French vessel. The English captain was of a different stamp. When Brooke chanced upon that worthy at official functions he found him "cool." There were many formal calls to be paid on shore, for as Brooke noted there was "more etiquette" in Honolulu than elsewhere. Brooke called on Abner Pratt, the American consul; James M. Borden, the American commissioner; a lady of the royal family and one of the princes; Robert C. Wyllie, the able Scot who had been minister of foreign relations since 1845; David L. Gregg, who as American commissioner had supported a reciprocity treaty; Elisha H. Allen, chancellor and chief justice, and former American consul; Mrs. Charles R. Bishop, prominent daughter of a native chief; and the French and English commissioners. King Kamehameha had gone to Hilo, so Brooke was not presented to him until later. Thorburn had once served as an aide in the Mediterranean Squadron and was able to give Brooke as much information on protocol as he needed. The French and British each kept a warship at Honolulu nearly all the time, and Brooke recorded that their officers "treat the government officials with great courtesy seeking to win their esteem."[15]

When the *Cooper* arrived at Honolulu the city was suffering from an interruption of the trade winds. In their absence the city lay under the blight of warm breezes from the south, called sick winds by the natives. These winds gave stimulus to the "boo hoo fever," an affliction supposedly introduced by an immigrant ship from Australia. The fever, though not dangerous, rendered its victims "very uncomfortable." Moreover, the excessively warm weather created by the sick winds turned the small cabin of the schooner into an oven; it was "impossible to work—write or think" in the cramped quarters. It took Brooke two weeks to rent a cottage on shore. But on November 22, the day that Brooke moved the instruments and equipment ashore, he became ill.[16] It was apparently the "boo hoo fever." Fortunately, Dr. Guillou

[15] Brooke's *Fenimore Cooper* Journals, 13 Nov. 1858, BP.
[16] Log of the *Fenimore Cooper*, 22 Nov. 1858, RG 24, NA.

took over his case personally and moved him to his own comfortable home, where the doctor and his good wife administered to Brooke's needs.

Up again in three weeks, Brooke worked doggedly to make up lost time. Before leaving San Francisco he had resolved to survey the chain of uninhabited islets pointing northwest from the Hawaiian Islands toward Midway and to return to Honolulu for provisions before heading for the China seas. Brooke adhered to this resolution even though delays required that he now undertake the survey to the northwest during the winter season. Too much valuable time had been lost already to wait for a more favorable season of the year.

The observations for rating the chronometers and for determining magnetic intensity being complete, the *Cooper* in the forenoon of December 29, 1858, stood out of the harbor. As the vessel ran north between Oahu and Kauai, the wind blew fresh from the east and the sea was "very rough." As usual under such conditions nearly the whole crew was seasick. Facing west the *Cooper* shaped a course to Bird Island and from there to Necker. The latitude and longitude of both islands were discovered to be out. Continuing west along the Tropic of Cancer, the schooner came up with French Frigate Shoal, "a very dangerous reef." Green and yellow rocks suddenly appeared under the vessel's bottom to the leeward of the reef, but in the nick of time the *Cooper* wore round.

French Frigate Shoal had been discovered by the comte de La Pérouse, the French explorer, on a passage from Monterey to Macao in 1786. Careful examination by the *Cooper* disclosed that this lurking danger really consisted of "an islet, sand banks above water and a reef." From the charts Brooke inferred that La Pérouse had seen only the southern part of the danger and had supposed erroneously that the islet was at the northwest extremity. As a matter of fact three or four days' investigation in the *Cooper* revealed that the reef and sandbanks extended eight miles to the northwest of the islet. The latitude of the islet given by the charts was "nearly right," but the longitude was "wrong some twenty miles." Brooke fixed its position at 23°45′ north, 166°25′ west.[17]

[17] Memorandum on French Frigate Shoal, 4 Jan. 1859, Brooke to U.S. Commissioner J. W. Borden, 8 Feb. 1859 (copy), and Contract entered into between Brooke, Kern, Thorburn and Benjamin F. Snow, 21 Feb. 1859, BP.

The reason for the unusual interest in this unoccupied and unclaimed speck of land lay in the discovery of guano. Thorburn and Kern found that the entire surface of the island was covered with guano—a quantity "sufficient to freight several large ships." That the suspected high quality of the guano might be confirmed, Brooke obtained samples from the surface and from a depth of four feet. There was no vegetation on this bleak islet which rose precipitously out of the sea on all sides but the south. Brooke was aware of the importance of a guano discovery to the agricultural and commercial interests of the country. Moreover, his instructions specifically enjoined him to be on the lookout for guano islands. Accordingly, he took possession of French Frigate Shoal in the name of the United States. The claim was asserted by a cross raised on the highest point of the islet with the following inscription: "Taken possession of on the 4th of January 1859, by Lieut. Commanding John M. Brooke, U S Schooner Fenimore Cooper, in accordance with Act of Congress passed August 18, 1856."[18] That the claim might not be overlooked, a rope was left onshore leading from the only landing place to the sign. The discovery of the guano, Brooke exulted to Lizzie, would "pay the United States forty times over the expense of the expedition."

While the islet offered guano and birds, the nearby sandbanks were alive with huge turtles, four feet in diameter, and hair seals. Thorburn and Kern returned from their first trip ashore with three turtles, an albatross, an echinus, and some eggs and shells. The next day Thorburn returned with half a dozen gigantic turtles which he had selected from a score he had turned over. The

[18] Brooke's *Fenimore Cooper* Journals, 4 Jan. 1859, and Memorandum on French Frigate Shoal, 4 Jan. 1859, BP. Brooke later explained to Lizzie why it was necessary to take the island in just this way: "I took possession of French F. Shoals to enable the president to protect the rights of an American citizen and thus secure it to the country. He could not have exercised sovereignty on any other ground than as protection of the rights of the discoverer and occupant. . . . It had then to be claimed by me or sacrificed to other nations" (Brooke to his wife, 6 June 1859, BP). The law stated: "That when any citizen or citizens of the United States may have discovered, or shall hereafter discover, a deposit of guano on any island, rock, or key, not within the lawful jurisdiction of any other government, and not occupied by the citizens of any other government and shall take peaceable possession thereof, and occupy the same, said island, rock or key may, at the discretion of the President of the United States, be considered as appertaining to the United States" (*An Act to Authorize Protection to Be Given to Citizens of the United States Who May Discover Deposits of Guano, August* 18, 1856, BP).

explorers reported that the hundreds of seals were "very fat" and "too tame to move." It was agreed that a large cargo of oil could be obtained easily.[19]

The waters surrounding French Frigate Shoal were infested with sharks, which Brooke described in his journal on January 5. "During the afternoon a turtle was killed, its blood attracted several large sharks one of which we hooked he struggled violently and I drove the harpoon through him. We then hooked a second large one about eleven feet long and harpooned him also. the other sharks began to gather and when the first we had taken was cut up they rushed in crowds to seise the offal there must have been at least twenty right under our counter, they struggled with each other lashing the sea until it boiled and foamed I never saw a more terrific sight it afforded an idea of what would occur if a man were to fall overboard. We managed to decoy several of them close to us, harpooning nine in all. I struck them as fast as the iron could be straightened. I saw one swim deliberately up and try to bite the shaft of the iron which held one of his companions. Numerous pilot fish accompanied the sharks but they differed from those I have seen before."

The cruise to the northwest of Oahu was exhilarating. It offered a rare combination of responsibility, achievement, and adventure which appealed to the schooner commander. The good weather held for several weeks, and despite its being the worst season of the year, much was accomplished. Aboard the *Cooper* informality prevailed, at no sacrifice of discipline, and the men became "Robinson Crusoeish" in their habits. A dog and cat picked up at Honolulu enlivened things on the schooner. As in the voyage from San Francisco, Brooke and Thorburn did not go to bed. They lay down on the lockers fully clothed ready to spring on deck at a moment's notice—a "perpetual watch," Brooke called it. In a rough sea when the vessel lurched they were often hurled to the deck without ceremony.

After surveying Maro Reef, an exceedingly dangerous reef, the schooner bore up for Laysan, sixty miles to the west. Kern and

[19] Brooke's *Fenimore Cooper* Journals, 5 Jan. 1859, and Brooke to Toucey, 7 Feb. 1859 (copy), BP.

Thorburn found it "a wonderful place, thousands and thousands of birds, albatrosses, petrel, frigatebirds, curlews, plovers, ducks and small land birds cover the surface of the ground, the albatrosses attacking them as they walked up." The island, of volcanic origin, was covered with a surface soil composed of guano and decayed vegetable matter which sustained a luxuriant growth of vines, small shrubs, grasses, and a few palms. Laysan was claimed by the kingdom of Hawaii.[20]

To this point the cruise had proceeded well—far better than Brooke had anticipated. Because the various reefs and islands had been discovered by different navigators, their positions in relation to each other were often in error on the charts. Between Honolulu and Laysan the *Cooper* erased twelve reported dangers.[21] It was Brooke's policy whenever possible to go ashore personally in order to examine the different islands as he was the only one on the *Cooper* who understood geology and related subjects.

At Lisianski, some nine hundred miles northwest of Honolulu, the *Cooper* ran into rough weather. For five days Brooke attempted to determine the position of that island, but swift, treacherous currents and continuous gales interfered. Twice, while the *Cooper* was on soundings searching for the island, a sudden gale sprang up and forced her to stand off for sea room. The schooner at times like this proved herself "a splendid sea boat." As dark, thick weather persisted, Brooke cut short his cruise and stood north for the prevailing westerlies. The delay at Lisianski forced him to abandon his original intention of surveying as far west as Pearl and Hermes Reef.

Before leaving Honolulu, Brooke had made some improvements in the *Cooper*'s rigging, and later, during the fair weather of the outward passage, he boasted that the vessel was "a good deal improved" and not as wet as formerly. Under all sail she now made ten knots against her former maximum of seven and one-half. But the return trip to Honolulu dampened his enthusiasm. Running north from Lisianski, the *Cooper* was struck in the thirtieth parallel by a terrific northeast gale which detained her for

[20] Brooke's *Fenimore Cooper* Journals, 14 Jan. 1859, BP.
[21] Brooke to his wife, 16 Jan. 1859, BP.

several days. From then on it was heavy going, as the rising sea laid siege to the fragile craft with towering waves as much as twenty-three feet high. Brooke began to complain again that the schooner was "very wet and uncomfortable." The deck was so "completely taken up by the sails and their sheets" that it was impossible to walk upon it. Spray penetrated every crack and cranny, and to add to the general confusion the turtles captured for the commissary swam about the deck. Some of the men were bothered by ugly sores that would not heal. Beginning as small scratches, the sores had become irritated by the constant dousing in saltwater. Two men were so badly incapacitated that they were unable to perform their assigned duties. The dog and cat seized with gusto any flying fish unfortunate enough to land on deck. Over the schooner, a tiny island of life on the endless surface of the sea, hovered the black albatrosses, haunting the ship by their presence.

On February 5, 1859, after an absence of thirty-eight days, the *Cooper* slipped again into Honolulu harbor. This time the British frigate *Calypso* promptly dispatched a boat to offer assistance. After calling on Captain Montresor, Brooke accepted an invitation from Dr. Guillou to stay at his house while the *Cooper* remained in port.

In Honolulu, Brooke acted promptly to reinforce the claim of the United States to French Frigate Shoal. He reported his discovery to Commissioner Borden and explained the steps he had taken to safeguard American interests. The commissioner promised to forward a report to the secretary of state. For his part Brooke submitted a detailed report to the secretary of the navy which he followed up with some samples of guano. News of the discovery caused considerable excitement in Honolulu, particularly when chemical analysis disclosed that the guano was of the best quality. Thorburn had estimated the quantity at not less than twenty-five thousand tons.[22] A substantial part of Brooke's time and effort during the month the *Cooper* remained in Honolulu was devoted to establishing the American claim to French Frigate Shoal to forestall appropriation by some foreign government.

[22] Brooke to Toucey, 7 Feb. 1859 (copy), BP.

Compliance with the act of 1856 on the discovery of guano was more complicated than a superficial glance would suggest. Brooke became increasingly irked by the red tape involved. The act did not fit exactly the circumstances of the discovery, but, as Brooke explained to his wife, it seemed that only by acting under its authority could he secure the guano for the United States. The act anticipated that the United States would benefit from an appeal to the profit motive of the private citizen. But Brooke was a naval officer commanding a national vessel. To Brooke it appeared imperative that he take positive steps to guarantee occupation of French Frigate Shoal before he left the Hawaiian Islands. So with Thorburn and Kern he entered into a contract with Benjamin F. Snow of Honolulu, whereby Snow in return for a quarter interest in the guano islet and sandbanks agreed to fit out and supply a vessel to visit the island within three months for the purpose of catching seals and securing guano specimens.[23]

Brooke also made adjustments in personnel and purchased substantial quantities of supplies. To his regret, Joseph Heco, the Japanese clerk, resigned; he had been seasick almost continuously on the tiny *Cooper*. Brooke wrote for him a fine letter of introduction to Flag Officer Josiah Tattnall, commanding the Far Eastern Squadron, to facilitate his return to Japan.[24]

Planning the *Cooper*'s itinerary to China called for careful consideration. Commissioner Borden specifically requested that the *Cooper* survey Johnston, an atoll situated in the Central Pacific.[25] This guano island to which the United States had a strong claim was occupied by the Pacific Guano Company, a California cor-

[23] Contract entered into between John M. Brooke, E. M. Kern, C. E. Thorburn, and B. F. Snow at Honolulu, pertaining to French Frigate Shaols, 21 Feb. 1859, BP. But in the end all Brooke's efforts to secure guano for the United States came to nothing. Later, he learned in Yokohama that the "Guano Island is a failure." The Brooke Papers do not indicate why. Brooke took the blow calmly, dismissing the subject with the comment to his wife that he was "*not* disappointed."

[24] Heco secured passage on the clipper ship *Sea Serpent*, which departed for Hong Kong on 12 March. He reached Kanagawa on 30 June, 2 months ahead of the *Cooper* (Heco, *Narrative of a Japanese* 1:181–84).

[25] Brooke explained to Secretary Toucey that Borden wanted the survey "in consequence of conflicting claims to right of possession and the importance of making such surveys as would enable vessels to approach the islands safely for the purpose of shipping Guano known to exist in large quantities" (Brooke to Toucey, 25 May 1859 [copy], BP).

poration. In addition to Johnston, Brooke resolved to visit the Marianas, but doubted that he would have time to touch the Carolines.

On March 9, the day of departure, the sun burned brightly and the tropical flowers were "prettier than ever." The schooner rode the trades to Johnston, making port in five days. But it was wet and "excessively uncomfortable" all the way, and the *Cooper* rolled violently. Brooke relieved the tedium by reading novels. At the anchorage at Johnston, Captain A. D. Piper, superintendent of the Pacific Guano Company, climbed aboard the *Cooper* and "offered every facility in his power." Johnston consisted of two small islands and a reef, twelve miles in circumference.[26] The enterprising captain, deeply bronzed by the sun, had placed beacons, buoys, and signals on many rocks and points and had discovered the anchorage in which the *Cooper* was moored. He was even building a sloop to aid in loading guano.

At Johnston, which was almost devoid of vegetation, Thorburn surveyed while Kern made sketches, stuffed birds, and preserved fish. Brooke dined with the remarkable Captain Piper in the latter's "gunny bag house" and carried out his scientific duties. During the *Cooper*'s four days at the island "a base line was measured on shore, a triangulation made, the anchorage, and approaches examined, the latitude, the magnetic intensity, dip, and declination determined, and equal altitudes of the sun observed for the longitude by fifteen chronometers running well together."[27] Lucian Kendall, the hospital steward, relieved Brooke of some of the meteorological work. Thorburn, on the other hand, was not much help in scientific work. Though he made routine observations at sea, he was careless and inclined to do only enough to get by. Moreover, while his knowledge was sketchy, he resisted constructive criticism.

Leaving Johnston, the *Cooper* steered to the southward until she reached the parallel of 15°40' north latitude. Along that line the schooner skimmed west at ten knots searching for half a dozen

[26] Johnston, also known as the Cornwallis Islands, was discovered by a British sea captain named Johnston on the *Cornwallis* in 1807. Today Johnston is under the administrative control of the United States Air Force.

[27] Brooke to Toucey, 25 May 1859 (copy), BP

reported dangers laid down on Rodgers's chart. Wilkes had been over much the same ground on a course slightly south of that followed by the *Cooper*. Brooke found that none of the reported dangers existed, at least in the locations assigned them. At this time Brooke definitely abandoned the idea of visiting the Carolines. He was in haste to get to the islands just south of Japan, for the early summer months following the change in monsoons was the only season suitable for surveying there.[28]

The voyage to Guam was monotonous, and Brooke's journal is replete with references to the excessive motion of the schooner, the smoke in the galley, and the unremitting heat and dampness. Heavy seas and strong currents were encountered most of the way. Though the *Cooper* was a good sea boat, it was clear that she was entirely too small for the extensive survey operations demanded of her. Not only was there no room for exercise, but the schooner was so loaded with scientific equipment that even normal observations were difficult. For example, the iron in the sounding reels prevented the accurate determination of magnetic variation.

Three weeks after leaving Honolulu the *Cooper* beat up for the reported position of Smyth's Islands, or Gaspar Rico. This supposed group of islands was found to be a coral reef. The reef was examined and soundings were made, but Brooke did not land to make magnetic observations for fear the schooner would drift off during the night. The *Cooper* then stood west for Guam, which Brooke described later as having "the only harbor in the [Marianas] chain suitable for a coal depot" for steamers running between California and south China.[29]

Sighting Apra Harbor on the west coast of Guam on the evening of April 12, the schooner laid off till sunrise under mainsail and jib. A Russian whaler and Hawaiian schooner were made out in the harbor. Learning that the Spanish governor of the Marianas, Don Felipe de la Corte, was at Agana, eight miles north of the harbor, Brooke and Kern proceeded there to pay their respects to him. Though only about thirty-five years old, the governor impressed Brooke as a man of self-control and "much in-

[28] Ibid.
[29] Ibid.

telligence" and was a person of versatile attainments, being also a colonel of engineers and a judge. Don Felipe was very polite and offered to assist Brooke in any way that he could. As an engineer he took a genuine interest in the *Cooper*'s scientific operations. Guam offered the first opportunity to grant the men shore leave since leaving the Hawaiian Islands.

Rough notes jotted down by Brooke to serve as the basis for his journal indicate that he asked many questions while in Guam on a wide range of subjects. For example, he inquired about earthquakes, morality, prices, the rice harvest, land tenure, the rights of foreigners, the extent of cultivation, epidemics, crops, storms, and general weather conditions. He learned some interesting things. From March to October 1856, for instance, 3,469 people had died of smallpox. Brooke learned also that Guam experienced fifty or sixty earthquakes a year.[30]

One day while Brooke was ashore a terrific storm struck Guam. Despite the fact that both anchors were down, the *Cooper* was shoved stern foremost toward a reef. The boats capsized in the breakers off the reef, and the oars and thwarts disappeared before they could be saved. The spray was so thick that one could not see the length of the schooner. At the crucial moment, just as Thorburn in desperation was ready to cut away the masts, the wind hauled. An excerpt from the ship's log reveals the fury of the storm more than seven hours after it began: "At 9.15 the wind blew so hard that a man could not stand on deck. raining in torrents, spray covering the schooner fore and aft, so that [one] could not see end of main boom from the main hatch." The Hawaiian schooner in the harbor was thrown on the reef.

Brooke gave the governor and others seeds of thirty-seven different varieties of vegetables.[31] As Brooke wrote Secretary Toucey, the gift was useful to the inhabitants and to visiting American whalemen, for in the Marianas, as in other tropical countries, "many vegetables native of the temperate zone gradually

[30] Rough notes to be used in preparing Brooke's *Fenimore Cooper* Journals, c. 12 April 1859, BP.

[31] The list, dated May 1859, BP, included Palatine lettuce, early curled Silesia lettuce, large orange carrots, watercress, summer crookneck squash, early York cabbage, green curled kale, early China beans, large red onions, and spinach.

degenerate." In return the governor gave Brooke specimens of cotton, maize, tobacco, and rice, all of which flourished in the Marianas.[32]

The work at Guam completed, the *Cooper* on May 3 set a course for the South China Sea, which she entered through the Balintang Channel eleven days later. Between Apra and Hong Kong soundings of 3,000, 3,300, and 900 fathoms were made, and in each case a specimen from the bottom was secured. In the zone of the trades sounding was difficult and time-consuming; Brooke believed that only from a steamer could soundings "be well made and at proper intervals to afford a complete profile of the bottom." These soundings from the *Cooper* were of considerable significance. George Belknap, an expert in the field, wrote Brooke in 1879 that for more than a decade "no deep-sea work surpassed yours in accuracy—or, in my belief, equalled it."[33] The area of the western Pacific in which the soundings were made was denoted as the Brooke Deep.

The long voyage across the Pacific molded the *Cooper*'s crew into a highly efficient unit. As the ship neared the China coast, Brooke wrote his wife that five men aboard were "certainly among the best" he had ever known. The worst characters had left the expedition in Honolulu.

On May 19, 1859, nearly eight months after leaving San Francisco, the *Cooper* dropped anchor at Hong Kong. The accomplishments of the expedition to that point were reviewed by the Washington *National Intelligencer*. Quoting from the Hong Kong *Mail*, the paper stated that "from a variety of sources" 496 dangers had been reported to exist on the track between California and Hong Kong, but the investigations of the *Cooper* disclosed that only about one-fifth of them actually existed. Moreover, the *Cooper*'s survey indicated that many of the actual dangers had "been marked down where they are not and not marked where they are." The article praised Brooke generously and emphasized the importance of the Brooke lead in cable laying. Readers were reminded that Brooke's invention was used by the Royal Navy in the Red Sea and elsewhere to facilitate the laying of cables. The

[32] Brooke to Toucey, 25 May 1859 (copy), BP.
[33] Ibid.; Belknap to Brooke, 26 Feb. 1879, BP.

original article appearing in the Hong Kong *Mail* doubtless was based on an interview Brooke had granted a representative of that paper.[34]

During the month he was in Hong Kong, Brooke wrote several letters to Lizzie in which he expressed his views on various controversial subjects, such as slavery, war, and the perennial question of religion. The letters reveal that Brooke had grown in tolerance and understanding and had learned to curb his temper. He even displayed flashes of good humor. In short, Brooke, while learning to adjust himself to long separations, had grown up. He admitted that he was conceited, but at least he had enough sense to know it.

It was while calling upon some German missionaries that Brooke was needled into defending the Southern position on slavery. The missionaries were caring for homeless Chinese children. Brooke was impressed, noting that the happy, well-dressed children sang all day long. But for Brooke, at least, this pleasant setting was spoiled by an Irish woman, a Mrs. McGrath. Well-off at home, she had come to China to do good works. As Brooke reported to his wife, "She seems to rely implicitly upon Mrs. Stowe's cabin [*Uncle Tom's Cabin*] and pitched into me unmercifully about darkies. I fear that I offended her as she bit her lip and colored once or twice. I hope she will not consider me rude. But the fact is I am bored by these English notions about slaves. I did not wish to argue only made a few remarks and laughed at some of her notions that was all. The only remark approaching a want of proper tenderness, *in talking to a lady*, which I made was that I had read that when a committee was appointed by Parliament to investigate the condition of the miners in England that they found underground people twelve years of age that did not know what the word God or Creator meant. The English have most extraordinary notions about slavery."[35]

Brooke condemned war. While the *Cooper* lay at Hong Kong there was a widespread fear that Europe would soon be engulfed

[34] Washington *National Intelligencer*, 9 Sept. 1859. The paper reprinted an article of the Hong Kong *Mail* dated 16 June 1859. A concise summary of the accomplishments of the *Fenimore Cooper* between San Francisco and Hong Kong is included in Secretary of the Navy Toucey's annual report to the president submitted on 2 Dec. 1859 (*Senate Executive Documents*, 36th Cong., 1st sess., vol. 3, no. 2, pp. 1150–51).

[35] Brooke to his wife, 7 June 1859, BP.

in a general war. It seemed that France and Austria would come to blows and that England might be drawn in. The people in Hong Kong hung nervously on the news from Europe. Considering war futile and brutal, Brooke regarded with disgust the glee with which some American merchants looked at war as a means to swell their profits. He wrote Lizzie: "As men generally are selfish many Americans are delighted with the idea that their ships will do all the carrying for Europe. They forget the orphans and widows and the vast amount of misery throughout the world which war entails. For my part I pray there may be no wars in the world, but that all the nations may be at peace. As I get older and see more of the world I think less of military glory and although if our country were at war I would try to distinguish myself still I am not anxious for it. . . . If there is anything calculated to prove the innate wickedness of man it is the love of military glory which pervades the world. . . . The best men speak of war as something fine something glorious. Now when a nation is struggling for its liberties tis well enough, but this wishing for war to obtain personal distinction is certainly criminal in the highest degree. . . . I would prefer to be a farmer ready to resist invasion but not to enter upon a war of foreign conquest or aggression. Perhaps I have not the right kind of feeling to be a naval officer."[36]

As for formal religion, Brooke, despite good intentions and an obviously humane disposition, was still unconverted. He confessed to Lizzie that he knew what he ought to do, but he had not the courage to do it. "I ought to be a Christian," he wrote, "I ought to *try* to be a Christian but I lack the force of purpose. And yet often I do pray very earnestly for a new heart."

While at Hong Kong, Brooke was exceedingly busy: the purchase of supplies, keeping purser's accounts, making observations, and exchanging formal calls competed relentlessly for the limited time at his disposal. The expenditure of the physical and mental effort required was rendered more exasperating than usual by the enervating climate of Hong Kong and the pleasant social distractions. With no recent instructions from the department, Brooke was very much on his own. He determined to leave with the southwest monsoon in order to reach Japan before the autumn gales.

[36] Ibid., 20 June 1859.

VII /

SOJOURN IN JAPAN
AND RETURN TO THE
UNITED STATES IN
THE KANRIN MARU

T HE southwest monsoon had steadied by June 23, when the *Cooper* under a bright sun got underway for Loochoo. As the schooner emerged from the picturesque Lyeemoon Pass into the South China Sea, many fishing junks came into view. Because Chinese pirates were active in those waters—three junks recently had attacked a British steam gunboat—the *Cooper* "made all the preparations necessary to give them a warm reception should they favor us with a visit during the night."[1] Running north for the next two days, Brooke avoided cruising too close to land, for were the schooner becalmed she would offer a tempting prize for lurking pirate craft.

[1] Brooke's *Fenimore Cooper* Journals, 23 June 1859, BP.

Sojourn in Japan and Return to the United States

Brooke was anxious to reach Kanagawa in order to consult with the American minister, Townsend Harris, about surveying during the autumn the new treaty ports opened by Harris under the Treaty of Yedo. One of the new ports, Kanagawa (now a suburb of Yokohama), had been opened in place of Shimoda. Brooke wanted particularly to survey Osaka, just north of the Inland Sea.[2] In December he intended to return to Hong Kong.

The immediate destination of the *Cooper* was Loochoo, or Okinawa, which was reached in ten days. When the governor of Loochoo sent greetings, friendly salutations were exchanged in the cabin and then the cherry cordial was produced. After a polite interval Brooke presented the governor's messengers with a list of supplies needed by the *Cooper*, which they promised to procure. Early the next morning, the Fourth of July, the governor sent aboard a present consisting of a pig, a goat, some chickens, eggs, and vegetables.[3]

Old acquaintance was renewed when the official Naghador came aboard. He immediately recognized Brooke and Kern and seemed delighted as he shook hands and laughed again and again. Naghador and another native, quickly making themselves at home, "walked into the cabin and took some cherry cordial but the motion of the vessel made them both seasick so they hurried off to terra firma." About the same time two French Catholic priests visited the schooner. They were eager for the letters from their associates in Hong Kong that Brooke had brought.[4]

That his visit might not be misunderstood, Brooke explained to the governor in simple terms the significance of the scientific work in which the *Cooper* was engaged. Then tactfully but firmly he stated: "I have therefore only to request that your excellency will direct that the necessary facilities for making observations

[2] Article III of the treaty opened Kanagawa and Nagasaki from 4 July 1859, Niigata from 1 Jan. 1860, and Hyogo (Kobe) from 1 Jan. 1863. Article XIV of the treaty stated that it should go into effect on 4 July 1859. At that very time the *Cooper* was enroute to Japan (Payson Jackson Treat, *The Early Diplomatic Relations between the United States and Japan, 1853–1865* (Baltimore, 1917), pp. 71–95. The Treaty of Yedo stipulated that Americans might reside in Yedo, present-day Tokyo, after 1 Jan. 1862 and in Osaka after 1 Jan. 1863.

[3] Brooke's *Fenimore Cooper* Journals, 4 July 1859, BP.

[4] Ibid.

may be afforded at Tumai or other suitable place, and that your Excellency will cause to be delivered, on board, such fresh provisions and refreshments as we may require, for which proper payment will be made."[5]

Brooke found that Loochoo had changed little since his visit in the *Vincennes*. Yet, by 1859 some of the novelty of such visits had worn off. Brooke was able to be more informal than Rodgers or Perry had been in his dealings with the governor. For instance, at an audience the American informed the governor that "the provisions supplied were not of good quality and that such as were sent arrived too late in the day." The supply problem improved.[6]

The enjoyment of the sojourn in Naha was augmented by the two Catholic priests, who were comfortably situated in a house built at the direction of the French admiral in those seas. The priests were observant and intelligent men and transmitted to Brooke valuable information on several subjects. Particularly interesting were the diary entries one had made of the series of heavy earthquakes that had shaken the island late in 1858. They assured Brooke that there were Japanese soldiers on the islands even though the Americans never encountered any. The French priests were respected in Loochoo, but like their predecessors, they had made no converts. Brooke observed that French influence was as strong as the American on Okinawa, and he deemed it the proper policy of the American government "to respect foreigners of all nations abroad [and] to treat them as well as we expect and wish them to treat us."[7]

At Loochoo, Brooke's main object was to make observations. The declinometer was erected at Tumai on the site of Perry's old coal depot, only a few paces from a small temple or shrine. Next to the temple was a house occupied by native priests which Brooke soon decided was the coolest spot in the vicinity. Between observations Brooke and Kern sometimes retired there "to take a cup of tea and enjoy the shade." In addition to experiments in declination and vibration, Brooke ran a series of celestial observations which required that he sleep on shore. For a week of perse-

[5] Brooke to His Excellency the Governor of Napa [Naha], 4 July 1859 (copy), BP.
[6] Brooke's *Fenimore Cooper* Journals, 7 July 1859, BP.
[7] Ibid., 9 July, 11 July 1859.

verance and effort Brooke was rewarded by a complete and "most satisfactory" set of observations.[8]

The work at Okinawa complete, the *Cooper* set sail on July 12 for Tanega-shima, the largest of the Osumi Islands. As the landing party from the *Cooper* approached Tanega-shima, the air was rent with the warning sound of horns, but at the landing the Americans were courteously received. On such occasions Tim, a Japanese who had been taken aboard in Honolulu, was of great assistance as interpreter. The *Cooper* remained at Tanega-shima three days; on the second day, Brooke was courteously received at the temple by the young governor and some fifty soldiers. The officials displayed a friendly curiosity about the observations, which Brooke satisfied by permitting the governor and his suite to examine the sextant. The effectiveness of Brooke's gentle and forthright approach was evidenced by the scene when the shore party left the island for the last time. "As the boat shoved off," Brooke recorded, "the people gathered on the pier thick as bees the Governor at their head, they waved to us and made signals of friendship and kind feeling as long as we could see them."[9]

As the *Cooper* worked her way up the east coast of Japan, the good weather held. Scientific data were accumulated steadily. On several occasions Brooke went ashore for observations, and often a boat was dropped over the side to sound and survey. The elevations of mountain peaks were measured regularly. It was possible to tie into an integrated whole the astronomical observations between Tanega-shima and Kanagawa because each day the *Cooper* could sight upon objects that had been observed the day before.[10]

Along the coast of Japan the relations with both the officials and people were uniformly good. Finding the officials who visited the schooner particularly fond of champagne and cherry cordial, Brooke dispensed these beverages quite freely in the cabin. Perhaps this explains why supplies were furnished the *Cooper* on the coast without quibble. In some ports the natives came alongside the *Cooper* in large numbers, and frequently they were permitted on board. Exhibiting an insatiable curiosity, they invariably mani-

[8] Ibid.
[9] Ibid., 19 July 1859.
[10] Ibid., 31 July 1859.

fested a spirit of friendliness and good humor. The people often brought little presents, usually fruits and vegetables. In his journal Brooke described such a meeting: "At an early hour numerous large boats loaded with people came alongside. It was difficult to keep them out of the vessel until the decks were put in order but partly through the exertions of Tim and the presence of a quartermaster and sentinel armed with cutlasses they were kept off until half past seven when we permitted them to come onboard men women and children. the young girls were dressed in all their finery, heads ornamented with artificial flowers and knots of crape or gauze, tastefully arranged. Mothers carried their children on their backs." The people were well disciplined and there was no trouble in getting them to leave the vessel, except for a few of the women. The women of southern Japan were especially sociable and "perhaps not as modest as they should be in the presence of strangers."[11] The visiting Japanese were always delighted at Tim's recitation of his adventures.

The arrival of the *Cooper* at Kanagawa was a milestone. Brooke notified Senator Mallory that in the passage from Hong Kong the *Cooper* had "made some valuable surveys on the East Coast of Southern Japan and rectified several errors of the charts." In a letter to Secretary Toucey the expedition commander reviewed briefly the *Cooper*'s work between Hong Kong and Kanagawa.[12] A Russian squadron was much in evidence in the harbor and promptly dispatched a boat to the *Cooper* to offer services; throughout Brooke's sojourn in Japan his relations with the Russians would be excellent. At Kanagawa, Kern and Brooke called at the American Consulate where Joseph Heco had been engaged as official interpreter by the new American consul, E. M. Dorr. Heco described the consul as "a big well-made, handsome man standing over 6 ft. 2 in., with a heavy grey beard."[13] Dorr received his American visitors "very kindly in the temple of Kanagawa," which he had selected as the American Consulate in preference to the residence the Japanese had built for him at nearby

[11] Ibid., 25 July, 26 July 1859.
[12] Brooke to Mallory, 12 Sept. 1859 (copy), BP; Brooke to Toucey, 5 Sept. 1859, Officers Letters, RG 45, NA.
[13] Heco, *Narrative of a Japanese*, 1:211.

Yokohama. To celebrate the arrival of the *Cooper* at Kanagawa, Brooke distributed eight bottles of champagne among the thirsty crew.

In Japan the maintenance of discipline became difficult. Long confinement on the small schooner had acerbated the dispositions of some crew members. The second afternoon off Kanagawa Brooke and Thorburn had to discipline two seamen from the schooner who had gone ashore in the morning and proceeded to get roaring drunk. As soon as it could be arranged, the crew were granted shore leave in shifts but this did not end the problem. A few days later it was necessary to place Robert Weir in irons "for being drunk on duty, quarreling, and striking his superior officer in the execution of his duty."[14]

At Kanagawa, Brooke made the never-ending observations for chronometer rates. After the first series was completed, Brooke, Kern, and some attendants set out on August 16 for Yedo (Tokyo) on horseback to consult with Townsend Harris on how best to utilize the *Cooper* during the fall and winter months. The Americans were amazed to find the road lined with houses almost the entire twelve miles between Kanagawa and Yedo. Most of the houses were really inns built for the refreshment of the multitude of travelers crowding the road. As they rode along, the Americans, though closely observed by the natives, were treated with great respect. They saw only two beggars on the busy thoroughfare. When hungry, Brooke's party stopped at an inn of "very respectable appearance."[15]

At the temple where Townsend Harris resided, Brooke and Kern found the American minister dining with the Russian consul from Hakodate and a Russian naval officer.[16] After the Russians had taken their leave, Harris and Brooke sat up quite late talking. Brooke explained that his instructions directed him "to avoid the

[14] Log of the *Fenimore Cooper*, 18 Aug. 1859, RG 24, NA.

[15] Brooke's *Fenimore Cooper* Journals, 18 Aug. 1859, BP.

[16] Harris saw much of the Russians and liked them. He wrote not long after his arrival in Japan: "The more I see of the Russian officers the more I am pleased with them. They are polished in manner and are exceedingly well informed. There is scarcely one of them that does not speak two or more languages" ("Townsend Harris's Journals in Japan, 1856–1858" [typewritten copy, transcript from the original journal], 14 Nov. 1856, MSS Div., LC).

China Seas and western Pacific" during the typhoon season, but he promised to survey the west coast of Japan in the spring, if possible. Brooke proposed that in the meantime he survey the new treaty port Hyogo (Kobe) and the eastern end of the Inland Sea, if the Japanese did not object.

Plans were laid for the *Cooper* to leave for Hyogo on September 1 to commence survey operations. Delayed in Yedo two days and on the road one day by heavy rains, Brooke and Kern then returned to Kanagawa, reaching Consul Dorr's home in the afternoon of August 22. Hardly had the travelers caught their breath when they were startled by an emergency message from Thorburn delivered by two Japanese officials. The message was laconic: "We are on shore I have saved what I could. You had better come quickly."[17]

The Japanese officials confirmed that the *Cooper* had been beached at Yokohama, the small fishing village that was cornering the trade Harris had expected to accrue to Kanagawa under the Treaty of Yedo. Despite assurances that the *Cooper*'s crew were ashore and that "houses had been appropriated for them and the stores of the vessel," Brooke with Kern at his side hurried to the ship. They "found her hard on the beach listing inshore to starboard and nearly full of water." Little could be done until low tide the next morning. Ashore Japanese policemen stood guard.[18]

Lieutenant Thorburn, giving Brooke a detailed account of the disaster, explained that during the gale the lead had shown but two fathoms of water, and the carpenter had stated that the vessel "could not stand many more such thumps as she worked as though injured below." In that predicament Thorburn had consulted the petty officers and old seamen who advised "that the most probable means of saving the largest amount of Government property, and lives of the crew, would be to beach the Schooner, bow first." Thorburn thereupon slipped his cables and ran the *Cooper* on shore. Brooke then secured detailed information from George Morison, master of the merchant ship *Lochlomond* which had ridden out the gale at Yokohama. Morison confirmed that

[17] Brooke to Toucey, 5 Sept. 1859, Officers Letters, RG 45, NA; Thorburn to Brooke, 22 Aug. 1859, BP.
[18] Brooke's notes, Yokohama, Japan, 23 Aug. 1859, BP.

during "the whole of the forenoon, the squalls were as violent as they could possibly blow." He believed that had the gale continued an hour longer, every vessel in the harbor would have been thrown upon the beach. The fury of the storm is attested by the terse entries in the *Cooper*'s log. Brooke absolved Thorburn of any blame, reporting to Secretary Toucey that he believed Thorburn had done all that anyone could have done under the circumstances.[19]

At the time of the wreck, Thorburn had been able to land all but one of the chronometers and all articles on the port side of the schooner. The next day, when the ebbing tide left the schooner high and dry on the stony beach, the surveying records, purser's accounts, and some valuable property were salvaged. Brooke's private library, however, was almost totally destroyed. For the salvage operations the Japanese governor, who extended every courtesy, furnished twenty men to assist the crew.

Three days after the wreck the *Cooper*'s crew were "busily employed overhauling instruments books etc." Except for damage to two thermometers and two barometers, and the loss of one theodolite, the precious instruments were intact. As for the wrecked vessel, though Brooke was impatient to begin repairs, he did not wish to act until a thorough examination by skilled carpenters revealed the full extent of the damage. At this juncture, Commodore A. A. Popoff of the Russian navy, commanding a squadron of seven steamers, "offered every assistance" in repairing the *Cooper* and fitting her for sea. Though the true purpose of the Russian squadron in Japanese waters was to give support to the imperialistic designs of the Russian diplomats, relations were good between the Americans and the Russians. The Russian com-

[19] Thorburn to Brooke, 24 Aug. 1859, Officers Letters, RG 45, NA. Thorburn's detailed report was 4 pages long. Morison to Brooke, 7 Sept. 1859 (copy), BP; Brooke to Toucey, 5 Sept. 1859, Officers Letters, RG 45, NA. The schooner's log for 23 Aug. describes the frantic efforts of those aboard to save the vessel: "7.45 Heavy sea, wind increasing. Schooner pitching heavily, heel took to the mud, let go 120 lbs anchor backed by the 95 lbs kedge, bent on seven 70 lbs sounding shot to the starboard chain & veered 15 fms. (that being the length of light chain) on all the anchors, which brought her up. Comd. throwing over board the sounding shot, empty shell & canister, started the water. From 8 to 12. Wind & sea increasing at 8.00 schooner struck heavily aft & started the anchors home. At 10.00 schooner ashore, sea breaking half way to the mast head over the vessel. Crew employed saving Government property."

modore, who was a naval constructor and had built five vessels for the Russian navy, accompanied by his chief carpenter, a "practical mechanic," made a personal examination of the *Cooper*. Popoff estimated that the vessel could be repaired by his large force of mechanics in a week or ten days, for though the false and main keels were split off from amidships aft, the keelson appeared undamaged.[20]

Later, however, discovery of three or four rotten floor timbers caused some misgiving. Then, in ripping up the ceiling or structural lining of the ship to remove the ballast stowed between it and the outer planking, it was found that forty-one timbers of the floor and futtock were rotten. Only seven timbers were sound. The keelson turned out to be "rotten at the step of the foremast, the timbers gone on both sides." The plain truth was that the *Cooper* was a floating coffin and it was a miracle she had not long since been destroyed by the elements. So great was the damage that repairs seemed useless. Clearly the *Cooper*'s days as a surveying vessel were over.[21]

Before taking such a drastic step as condemnation of his vessel, Brooke again called in Commodore Popoff. The Russian still believed that the *Cooper* might be repaired with the means at his disposal, but, owing to the rottenness of her timbers, he did not think it "expedient to attempt repairing her," nor did he believe "that she could be taken to any other port for that purpose, as her frame is so rotten that she would probably founder at sea."[22] The extensive repairs required would amount to rebuilding the vessel. Brooke decided reluctantly to make no attempt to repair the *Cooper*.

The loss of the schooner deprived Brooke of his freedom of action. The ultimate destiny of the tiny surveying expedition now hinged on Flag Officer Tattnall, commanding the East Indian

[20] Brooke to Toucey, 5 Sept. 1859, Officers Letters, RG 45, NA. Early in August 1859 Count Nicolai Muraviev-Amurski, governor-general of Eastern Siberia, had arrived off Yokohama with a squadron of 7 vessels carrying 105 guns. In Japan, Muraviev's goal was to obtain the cession of the island of Sakhalin (Treat, *Early Diplomatic Relations*, p. 137).

[21] Brooke to Mallory, 12 Sept. 1859 (copy), BP. See also Brooke to Toucey, 5 Sept. 1859, Officers Letters, RG 45, NA.

[22] Brooke to Toucey, 5 Sept. 1859, and Popoff to Brooke, 2 Sept. 1859, Officers Letters, RG 45, NA.

Squadron, whose flagship, the *Powhatan*, was expected daily from Shanghai. While awaiting the *Powhatan*'s arrival at Yokohama, the *Cooper*'s crew, with the aid of the Russian sailors and some Japanese laborers, removed the masts from the *Cooper* and housed ashore everything that could be transported. In these operations the Americans were treated in a "very kindly" fashion by the Japanese authorities; and the American consul was "unremitting in his attentions." [23]

By coincidence Brooke at this time learned why the *Cooper*, a comparatively new vessel inspected at Mare Island only a year before, had proved to be rotten. At Yokohama, Captain King of the *Wanderer* called on Brooke and told an amazing story. King, the nephew of Josiah Johnson who had sold the *Cooper* to the navy, related how and why the schooner had been built. Aaron Westerveldt, who had reassured Brooke about the soundness of the schooner when they had met earlier in Hong Kong, had built several pilot boats, none of which was a fast sailer. Determined to build a fast boat, Westerveldt had offered to construct for Johnson a small vessel from the refuse timber of the clippers *Golden Gate* and *Sweepstakes* for $7,200, and Johnson had accepted the offer. The *Cooper* was, therefore, constructed from large timber "cut down to the *heart* wood." This wood was of an inferior grade; the grain was coarse, the rot running with the fiber. A pilot boat built of good lumber would have cost $10,000. Westerveldt's new boat proved not to have enough speed to satisfy Johnson; he then sold it to the navy as a tender for the Ringgold expedition. Visiting the *Cooper*'s hulk with Brooke, King "pointed out the large flue of the wood of the timbers in corroboration of his statement that she was built of pieces reduced from the size necessary in vessels of larger size." Bitterly, Brooke disposed of the matter by describing the *Cooper* "as one of Ringgold's purchases, cheap and bad." [24]

[23] Brooke to Harris, 3 Sept. 1859 (copy), BP.

[24] Brooke's Yokohama Journal, 18 Sept. 1859, BP. With the arrival of the *Powhatan*, Brooke requested Tattnall to order a survey of the *Cooper* and her stores. A board was appointed and it found the schooner "unfit for any further service at sea." It recommended that the vessel and her equipment be sold at public auction. This was done. Dr. George K. Hall, who had arrived from Shanghai 2 months before, was the largest purchaser. In December, Dr. Hall informed Brooke "that he had contracted with the Japanese to repair and launch the Fenimore Cooper in 20 days for the sum of 1700 Itsibos, one half paid in

The months during which Brooke was stranded in Yokohama witnessed a growing tension between the forces favoring the opening of Japan to foreigners and those opposing it. The various treaties negotiated between the shogun and the Western powers had not been ratified by the emperor, or mikado. At this period, after two and one-half centuries of rule, the power of the Tokugawa Shogunate was slipping. Many rivals of the Tokugawa among the feudal lords sought to weaken the prestige of that family by resurrecting the dormant political powers of the mikado. Thus the whole antiforeign question became inextricably mixed with the growing tension between the courts of the shogun and the mikado. The shogun, under pressure from the west, was on dangerous ground, for most of the great feudal lords were antiforeign in their sentiments. This xenophobia manifested itself in assassinations committed usually by bands of unattached samurai known as ronins; in fact, they were outlaws. In August 1859 the French and British legations complained that their personnel were being stoned by ronins, and on August 25, two days after the *Cooper* was beached, the first assassination occurred.[25] Brooke was on hand to play a prominent role.

The circumstances surrounding the outrage are described in Brooke's report of the affair to Consul Dorr. He wrote that being informed that some Russians were "severely wounded," he rushed to the spot with Kern and found a lieutenant "weltering in his blood, wounded in several places" and a seaman who had been "killed outright." Though everything possible was done to save the lieutenant, he died in a few hours. Brooke noted that the Japanese authorities had "behaved very well" but did nothing to aid the wounded men until he arrived.[26]

Brooke's "humane and friendly action" in aiding the Russians

advance" (ibid., 5 Dec. 1859). The contract was approved by the Japanese government and apparently was fulfilled. The Japanese itsibo (ichibu) had one-third the gold content of the dollar.

[25] Treat, *Early Diplomatic Relations*, *pp.* 137–39. See also Tyler Dennet, *Americans in Eastern Asia: A Critical Study of the United States with Reference to China, Japan, and Korea in the 19th Century* (rept. New York, 1941); Inazo Nitobe, *The Intercourse between the United States and Japan* (Baltimore, 1891); Kenneth Scott Latourette, *The History of Japan* (New York, 1947); Edwin A. Falk, *From Perry to Pearl Harbor: The Struggle for Supremacy in the Pacific* (New York, 1943).

[26] Brooke to Dorr, 26 Aug. 1859 (copy), BP.

earned Townsend Harris's warmest praise. "Spontaneous acts of this kind," wrote Harris, "do more to create and confirm a good understanding between Nations, than scores of Diplomatic letters, and you are to be as much envied for the opportunity, which you had for the exhibition of the kindly feelings of your heart, as you are to be commended for your action on that occasion."[27] The close bond Brooke established with the Russians at this time was partially responsible for Commodore Popoff's wholehearted cooperation in examining the *Cooper*.

In November 1859 Brooke observed in his journal that he was surprised that the Japanese were able to meet such large demands for their products. A month later in a letter to Lizzie he predicted that Yokohama would supplant Kanagawa as a trading center, though it was the latter which had been opened by treaty, because "the Japanese have thrown all the trade on this [Yokohama] side of the bay." He noted that though silk had doubled in price since his arrival, a large profit could still be made. As the price of silk rose, it would become too expensive for many Japanese and they would turn to cotton for clothing. Though Brooke could have borrowed money and made a fortune in the silk trade, he asserted that he did not think "an officer has any business entering into such work as that."[28]

Brooke continued to find disciplining his crew necessary. The sudden burgeoning of trade and a lack of restraint by consuls affected the crews of all the visiting ships; rowdy conduct by drunken sailors was common. The *Cooper*'s crew were infected by these dangerous attitudes because the two buildings allocated for them were "in the most dissolute part of the town" with sake shops only "a few steps from our door." At Brooke's request Consul Dorr secured an order from the Japanese governor to have offenders "placed in the Prison at Kanagawa for safe keeping," because Brooke could not spare any men to guard prisoners.[29]

[27] Harris to Brooke, 31 Aug. 1859, BP. The Russian murder ushered in a wave of antiforeign sentiment marked by 6 assassinations over a period of 7 months. Most of these terroristic acts occurred during Brooke's sojourn in Yokohama. But it was not until the murder of Lord Ii, the principal minister, in March 1860, that foreigners realized that the antiforeign feeling was merely one facet of the titanic power struggle against the shogun.

[28] Brooke to his wife, 15 Dec. 1859, BP.

[29] Brooke to Dorr, 4 Sept. 1859 (copy), BP; Log of the *Fenimore Cooper*, 5 Sept. 1859, RG 24, NA.

The seriousness of the disciplinary problem was emphasized by a tragedy which occurred on September 4, 1859. While Brooke was at home conversing with some Japanese interpreters, Thorburn burst into the room exclaiming that there was a row among the men. Fearing trouble with the Japanese, Brooke buckled on his sword, thrust two pistols into his belt, and dashed out hard on Thorburn's heels. The fracas was in the house next door, which had been reserved for the crew. Brooke discerned the fight was a family affair with no Japanese involved. "Entering," Brooke wrote, "I saw [Robert] Weir and [William] Medkiff struggling together[.] I stepped up to them caught hold of them by the arms and separated them immediately drawing a revolver from my belt intending simply to threaten when to my surprise it went off in my hand and I immediately saw that I had shot Weir in the breast (right breast)." Brooke attributed the misfire to the fact that the pistol had been soaked by seawater at the time of the wreck. Though he had cleaned and loaded it a few days later, Brooke deemed it likely that there had been "some derangement of the lock."[30]

Dr. George K. Hall examined Weir and pronounced his wound serious but not fatal. Weir was quite comfortable for ten days; then he suddenly developed a difficulty in breathing, and on September 19 he died. Brooke immediately notified Flag Officer Tattnall of Weir's death and requested that an investigation be conducted. Upon the arrival of the *Powhatan*, Tattnall appointed a naval court of inquiry. The court was "expressly required after a statement of the facts, to express an opinion on the merits of the case." As witnesses the court called Dr. Hall, Thorburn, Kern, Rogier, Kendall, and Frank Cole. The testimony of all exculpated Brooke.[31]

The problem of discipline was solved in October when Brooke transferred to the *Powhatan* "the riotous portion" of the *Cooper*'s crew. To assist in his work ashore Brooke retained, in addition to Thorburn and Kern, Charles Rogier, ship's steward; Lucian Kendall, hospital steward; Charles Falk, instrument maker; Charles

[30] Memorandum written by Brooke immediately after the wounding of Weir, 5:15 P.M., 4 Sept. 1859, BP.
[31] There is a summary of the testimony in the Brooke Papers, dated 1 Nov. 1859.

Smith, boatswain's mate; Frank Cole, seaman; and James Burke, cook. Tim also lingered in Yokohama with the expedition, although in September Brooke had received written assurance from the governor of Yokohama that Tim would be permitted to return to his family on the Inland Sea and to retain the money paid him for his services on the *Cooper*.[32] With some peace and quiet Brooke now expected to advance his survey and astronomical work during the four months before the *Powhatan* was scheduled to sail with the *Cooper*'s entire crew.

A particular worry to Brooke was the danger of fire. The foreign quarter of Yokohama, located in the southeast portion of the town, was vulnerable, because the frame houses and godowns, or warehouses, were packed closely together. From the beginning Brooke was alert to the danger and as a precaution moved his ammunition to the *Powhatan*. In January 1860 a big fire ravaged the foreign quarter and Brooke had "*a great time*" for twenty-four hours. The huge godown next to Brooke's house went up in flames, and at once Brooke began to move his equipment. The governor of Yokohama took charge of the delicate instruments, while Tim directed a Japanese crew carrying the rest of the equipment to a safe location in the country. Luckily for Brooke the wind veered and his house was saved. When the excitement was over, Japanese whom Brooke did not even know brought presents of oranges, eggs, bread, and other commodities. When Brooke's property was returned the next day, he found only two things missing—his pocket knife and the top of a teapot—even though sixty-five people had helped to move the property into the country and back. If the Japanese "had been disposed they could have taken half." Even more remarkable is that nothing was broken. These friendly acts by officials and people took place at the height of the antiforeign agitation; the whole affair speaks well for Brooke's relations with the Japanese.[33]

[32] Midsoeno Tsicoogono Cami and Kato Tkino Cami to Jhon [*sic*] M. Brook[e], Lieutenant Commander [*sic*] of the U.S. Navy, Sept. 1859, BP. Not until Brooke was ready to return to the United States did Tim consent to leave for his own home. At that time Brooke gave Tim his discharge and his pay amounting to 477 ichibus 6 tempos and obtained assurance from the governor at Yokohama a second time that Tim should not be molested (Brooke's Yokohama Journal, 6 Feb. 1860, BP).

[33] Brooke to his wife, 4 Jan. 1860, and Brooke's Yokohama Journal, 4 Jan. 1860, BP.

Once the *Cooper* had been disposed of and the recalcitrant members of the crew transferred to the *Powhatan*, Brooke resumed his scientific duties. He carried out an extensive series of astronomical and magnetic observations and also ran a careful survey of Kanagawa Bay. Japanese boats were used frequently in running the sounding lines. The work often attracted crowds of curious but amiable Japanese. The Japanese authorities cooperated, the governor, for example, promising to identify the survey markers in such a way that the natives would not disturb them. The support of the central government did not, however, clear away all the barriers created by the country's feudalism. Such a problem developed when Brooke and Kern, accompanied by officials detailed by the governor of Yokohama, climbed a bluff near Kanagawa to erect a signal tower. As they were putting up the tower, some strange officials appeared on the scene and in "great trepidation" informed Brooke that the ground on which he stood belonged not to the emperor but to a feudal prince from whom permission must be secured. Brooke replied that he had climbed the hill with some difficulty and did not propose to do so again for the same purpose. He explained to the officials the purpose of the tower and secured their permission to leave it with the understanding that if the prince did not like it he could take it down.[34] By the middle of December, Brooke had secured all the data necessary except some soundings for the chart.

Brooke's survey of Kanagawa Bay was of great commercial importance, but while in Japan, Brooke performed another service of perhaps greater significance. Over a period of four months he gave advice to Japanese officials who were making ready their first mission to the West. For long periods, while the *Powhatan* was in China, Brooke and Thorburn were the only American naval officers in Yokohama. Thorburn was engrossed in speculative ventures, so the Japanese could turn to Brooke alone for answers to their questions on geography, navigation, and finance. The relationship began in October when Brooke conferred with the new governor of Yokohama regarding Tim. The governor, Shimmei Buzen no Kami, had been appointed by the shogunate as first am-

[34] Brooke to his wife, 3 Dec. 1859, and Brooke's Yokohama Journal, 5 Dec. 1859, BP.

bassador of the Japanese mission preparing to visit America. To the conference Brooke carried a small atlas and a map of the world so that the various routes to the United States could be discussed. At this session, Brooke answered such questions as how much water could be carried on the *Powhatan*, whether rice could be procured in Honolulu, and how hot it was at Panama. At subsequent consultations Brooke gave the Japanese officials a school atlas, a geography, a set of four charts "comprising the world," and a small piece of the Atlantic telegraph cable. When the Japanese stated "that Mr Harris had told them that there was some prospect of Americans soon making a passage to the moon," Brooke replied that that was a mistake.[35]

It had been tentatively arranged that the Japanese mission should sail for the United States in the *Powhatan* about February 22, 1860.[36] At the first instructional session Brooke explained that the Japanese could go to America by sailing either east or west. They "replied that Mr Harris had said they would go by the East touching at the Sandwich Islands and not at San Francisco." When the *Powhatan* arrived from Shanghai on October 31, it was learned that Tattnall wanted to return to the United States west-

[35] Brooke's Yokohama Journal, 17 Nov. 1859, BP.

[36] At the suggestion of the Japanese, Article XIV of the Treaty of Yedo provided that the treaty should be ratified in the United States. Townsend Harris was most agreeable, for this meant that the Japanese would dispatch their first Western mission to the United States instead of to Europe. In August 1858 the Japanese minister of foreign affairs applied to Harris for an American warship to carry the mission to and from Washington. Harris and Tattnall proposed to the secretary of state and the secretary of the navy respectively that a national vessel be directed to meet the Japanese mission at the Isthmus of Panama, it being their intention to furnish transportation for the mission as far as the isthmus in one of the vessels of the East India Squadron. At Harris's request Tattnall dispatched the steamer *Mississippi* to Shimoda on 15 Feb. 1859, with instructions to prepare for the voyage to Panama. By that time, however, some of the Japanese officials were urging postponement because powerful interests complained that such a mission would defy the Japanese prohibition on foreign travel. Harris feared that delay would play into the hands of the British, and so, when the *Mississippi* arrived, he offered its use to the Japanese. After negotiations it was arranged that the departure should be postponed for a year, 22 Feb. 1860 being designated the tentative date of departure. That no other country might steal a march on the United States, it was stipulated that Japan should send no similar embassy to another country until the one destined for the United States had reached Washington (Allan B. Cole, "Japan's First Embassy to the United States, 1860," *Pacific Northwest Quarterly* 32 [April 1941]: 135–37). Subsequently, Tattnall was authorized upon his relief to return to the United States on the *Powhatan*, picking up the Japanese mission on his way to China.

ward by the Cape of Good Hope and to leave on January 1.[37] Tattnall asked Harris's help in securing these changes. Harris, at an interview with the Japanese commissioners, found they were resolved to go by Panama, but he thought they might be persuaded to push up the date of departure to February 1. That settled the matter, though Brooke noted it was likely that the *Powhatan* would "put into San Francisco for a spare crank pin prior to attempting the Horn or Straits of Magellan."[38]

Before Tattnall's arrival, the Japanese had decided to dispatch a vessel of their own across the Pacific as an advance agent or escort of the *Powhatan*. Though they had been in seclusion, the Japanese were not entirely ignorant of Western inventions and ideas. In the naval field they had purchased steamers from the Dutch and organized the nucleus of a navy.[39] The idea of sending a vessel of their own was good, but Brooke could see flaws. Could the Japanese, who were so pitifully short on experience, actually navigate the Pacific? There was much room for doubt. That opened the door to Brooke. If he were to sail on the Japanese warship as an adviser, and some of the *Cooper*'s crew were to accompany him to reinforce the Japanese, the possibility of a successful crossing would be immeasurably increased. At Brooke's request Dorr suggested to Harris that Brooke go in the Japanese steamer. Harris, "much pleased with the idea," spoke to the Japanese about it but explained the matter of appointment rested with Commodore Tattnall.[40]

If Brooke went, he wrote his wife, he "would go to direct the course etc., and would have American seamen on board in addition to the crew of the Japanese." Should the responsibility of navigating the ship be given to him, he intended to request that

[37] Tattnall and his officers did not deem it wise to take the *Powhatan* around Cape Horn in the winter "because her rigging is not good and some of the heavy timber of her guards is rotten" (Brooke's Yokohama Journal, 6 Nov. 1859, BP).

[38] Ibid., 11 Nov. 1859.

[39] There is no doubt that the idea originated with the Japanese. A memorandum in the Brooke Papers states: "The sending of the Candinmarro originated with the Japanese themselves and may be regarded as evidence of friendly feeling frankly shown" (Memorandum of John M. Brooke, n.d.; from internal evidence it is probable that this is a copy of a press release prepared by Brooke when the *Kanrin Maru* arrived in San Francisco).

[40] Dorr to Brooke, 3 Jan. 1860, BP.

Tattnall should see that the Japanese vessel was properly fitted out for the voyage. When the *Powhatan* arrived, the Japanese government asked that Brooke be assigned to assist in the navigation of their steamer the *Kanrin Maru*.[41] Tattnall promptly agreed and ordered Brooke to ready himself for the voyage. Kern at Brooke's request was ordered to accompany him, and Brooke was authorized to select a boat's crew of men from the old complement of the *Cooper*. In addition to Kern, Brooke picked nine of the most capable members of the *Cooper*'s crew. Lieutenant Thorburn was ordered to report for duty on board the *Powhatan*.

As the time of departure for San Francisco drew near, the governor of Yokohama presented Brooke a sword, five pieces of damask, fifteen pieces of checked silk, a lacquered box, ten ducks, and some vegetables. The Japanese embassy gave Brooke a cabinet and a model house.[42]

Of the one hundred Japanese aboard the *Kanrin Maru*, the ranking Japanese officer was Kimura Settsuno-kami, whose position was defined by a Japanese as secretary of naval affairs but to whom Brooke usually referred as "Commodore," and sometimes as "Admiral."[43] Brooke described him as "very quiet" and "tena-

[41] Brooke to his wife, 8 Jan., 19 Jan. 1860, BP. A memorandum in the Brooke Papers states that "some two months prior to the embarkation of the Embassy the Japanese government informed Mr Harris and Flag Officer Tattnall of their intention and requested that an American officer might take passage in her to aid in navigating the vessel as although the Candinmarruh had made several trips between Nagasaki and Yedo under steam the Japanese required experience in making such a lengthy passage as that to San Francisco and during the stormy season of the year."

[42] In accepting the gifts Brooke stated that he would carry them to the United States and keep them if authorized to do so by the government.

[43] Masakiyo Kanesaburo Yanagawa, *The First Japanese Mission to America (1860), Being a Diary Kept by a Member of the Embassy*, ed. Masatoshi Gensen Mori, trans. Junichi Fukuyama and Roderick K. Jackson (Kobe, Japan, 1937, p. 84. The exact number of Japanese aboard is not clear. Yanagawa, who traveled on the *Powhatan*, gives the names of the 21 most important Japanese and states that there were 93 other Japanese and 11 Americans, making a grand total of 125. Fukuzawa Yukichi lists 17 important Japanese and states that there were 96 Japanese in all—"a larger number than usual for the ship"; he also states there were 4 or 5 Americans on board, making a total of 101 (*The Autobiography of Fukuzawa Yukichi*, trans. Eiichi Kiyooka, 3d ed. rev. [Tokyo, 1947]). Yanagawa's figures appear the more likely to be correct even though he did not travel on the *Kanrin Maru*, for his figures are given in his journal kept at the time. This journal is regarded as the most complete of the 5 extant of the first Japanese mission. Fukuzawa's autobiography was written many years later. Moreover, Fukuzawa had a very subordinate position as a personal servant on the voyage.

cious of position and old custom." The Japanese commander of the vessel was Captain Katsu Rintaro, who, Brooke heard, was "the very best man in the Japanese service." Later, upon his return to Japan, Katsu held high government office. Perhaps the most important Japanese on the ship from a practical viewpoint was Manjiro Nakahama, the interpreter. He was a remarkable person and would prove to be invaluable on the voyage.[44]

The *Kanrin Maru*, which had been purchased from the Dutch, was a bark-rigged screw steamer of 292 tons, less than three years old. She had been used between Nagasaki and Yedo, but usually under steam; consequently the crew was "not accustomed to handling sails in heavy weather."[45] A few of the Japanese seamen had served on Dutch warships and were competent, but as a whole the engineers were far more experienced than the seamen. The ship was primarily a sailing vessel, however, with an auxiliary engine of only one hundred horsepower. She carried but six days' supply of coal.

On February 7, 1860, the Americans assigned to the *Kanrin Maru* loaded their equipment in small boats and carried it out to the steamer. The vessel then moved down the Bay of Yedo and just before dusk dropped her anchor off Uraga. As the corvette worked into the anchorage, Brooke was given his first opportunity to observe Captain Katsu's skill as a navigator. There were several junks in the way, but the captain acquitted himself creditably.

The *Kanrin Maru* spent two days off Uraga making final preparations for sea: the ship was watered, the anchor scraped, and many leaks on the decks were caulked. When the Americans had stowed their equipment, Brooke divided them into two watches, excusing the cook. There was much for the Americans to do, for it was soon apparent that the instruction the Japanese had received from the Dutch had been incomplete. The Americans taught their friends how to use small arms and secured one of the long guns which the latter could not handle. Brooke liked the Japanese and predicted his men would get along with them "very admirably in-

[44] Yanagawa speaks of him as Nakamura Manjiro and lists him as an instructor. Allan Cole gives his name as Nakahama Manjiro, as does Chitoshi Yanaga, "The First Japanese Embassy to the United States," *Pacific Historical Review* 9 (June 1940): 113–38.
[45] Brooke to Toucey, 25 March 1860 (copy), BP.

deed." The prospects for cooperation with the commodore and captain were promising, though the captain was "somewhat unwell." At this stage of the voyage both officers impressed Brooke as being "very agreeable."

The cooking arrangements on the steamer were novel. The original galley was replaced by two huge kettles for boiling rice. The Americans used braziers to cook their food when the weather permitted. When it did not, they were forced to subsist on a Japanese diet. Until proper arrangements could be made, Kern and Brooke ate raw seaweed and fish with the commodore and captain. As unusual as the cookery were the clothes. The Japanese wore no uniforms, but rather a conglomeration of Japanese and European clothing. The executive officer, perhaps as an emblem of office, did wear a breastplate.

At Uraga, Brooke worked closely with Manjiro, who was unusually communicative, and formed a high opinion of him. Brooke was amazed at the rapidity with which the interpreter absorbed instruction. For example, Manjiro almost immediately understood the principle of compensation as applied to chronometers. "I am astonished at the intelligence of these people," wrote Brooke. Manjiro also quickly comprehended "the object of making observations of wet and dry thermometers." After two days on the steamship Brooke was convinced that Manjiro "had more to do with the opening of Japan than any other man living." [46]

Early in the afternoon of February 10, 1860, the *Kanrin Maru* weighed anchor and, winding through the junks, passed into Uraga Strait headed for the open sea. [47] She was getting away two days ahead of the *Powhatan*, although Brooke had wished for a week's headstart to be sure of beating the frigate to San Francisco.

[46] Brooke's Yokohama Journal, 8 Feb., 9 Feb. 1860, BP.

[47] The chief sources of information on the preliminaries to this voyage and the voyage itself are the journals Brooke kept in Yokohama and on the *Kanrin Maru* and Brooke's correspondence with Lizzie, Secretary of the Navy Toucey, and others. Of value are Yanagawa, *The First Japanese Mission*, and "Journal of Muragaki Awaji-no-Kanei [Kami], during his journey to and stay in the U.S.A., 1860" (translation), Roland S. Morris Papers, MSS Div., LC. See also Cole, "Japan's First Embassy to the United States"; Yanaga, "The First Japanese Embassy"; and Patterson DuBois, "The Great Japanese Embassy of 1860: A Forgotten Chapter in the History of International Amity and Commerce," *Proceedings of the American Philosophical Society* 49 (July 1910): 243–66.

Figuring the distance by the great circle from Cape Nojima to San Francisco to be 4,476 miles, Brooke decided to project the great circle on the chart and follow that course as closely as possible unless cold weather intervened. He calculated the passage would require a minimum of thirty days.[48]

Three days out, the *Kanrin Maru* encountered winds of gale force and heavy seas. So it would be much of the way! With only three days' supply of coal left, it was necessary to depend on the sails. The commodore and captain had been sick since leaving port, and the responsibility of running the vessel devolved on Brooke.

On February 14 Brooke noted: "the Japanese have broken the Cabin sky light all to pieces by putting their feet on the glass so we are dependent on the light of a bulls eye. . . . At 10 heading course E. N. E. I can not put sail on the vessel as the Japanese are not competent to manage it. The officers are very ignorant indeed having had probably no experience in heavy weather. All the orders are given in dutch I think it absolutely necessary that the Japanese should have a marine language of their own. The helmsmen do not know how to steer by the wind. Weather braces & bowline the[y] dont attend to. The weather is excessively disagreeable. No chance of an observation. I had a fall. the decks are very slippery, no sand onboard. This is a rough beginning. The Japanese have good oiled coats and mittens, they are improving as seamen. Very heavy weather Clewed up maintopsail buntline parted, the Japanese could not furl the sail sent our men aloft, they furled it lightning but no thunder." In the same general area the *Powhatan*, a far larger ship, was also finding the going rough. In fact, Tattnall told the Japanese that "never in all his twenty-eight years' experience of the sea, had he ever encountered such a tempest."[49]

As the *Kanrin Maru* fought her way across the North Pacific in the dead of winter, the unexpected was the rule. Early in the

[48] The *Powhatan*, which had been to Japan with Perry, was a far larger ship than the *Kanrin Maru*. She was a first-class steam frigate of 2,415 tons, carrying a crew of 400. Launched at the Gosport Navy Yard in 1855 and mounting 11 guns, the *Powhatan* was considered one of the best ships in the navy.

[49] "Journal of Muragaki-Awaji-no-Kami," 14 Feb. 1860, Morris Papers, MSS Div., LC.

cruise Kern complained of a heavy Japanese box that was banging around the cabin. "We supposed it contained Japanese mess stores," wrote Brooke, but "to our surprise [we] found it full of percussion caps enough to have blown the cabin up. about 40,000." Brooke and Manjiro stowed the caps in a proper place. About the same time the galley caught fire. To add to the confusion, the Japanese sailors threatened to hang Manjiro from the yardarm when he urged them to go aloft. Brooke was equal to this crisis. "I told him that in case of any attempt to put that threat into execution to call upon me. that in case of mutiny upon the part of the Japanese sailors if the Capt. would give authority I would hang them immediately." Brooke commented that the Japanese could not really be said to keep a watch for "with the exception of 3 or 4 all go below and require fifteen or 20 minutes to get on deck." This was true even when scudding before a high sea.[50]

The rough weather of the western Pacific did not moderate. The seas rose higher and higher as frequent and violent squalls lashed the ship with hail and driving rain. The Japanese, whose sailing had been limited to coastal waters, got quite a scare. One of them, Fukuzawa Yukichi, later described his impressions: "Storm followed storm. Waves broke over the decks continually. I remember that whenever the ship keeled over on her side, I could look up through the skylight from below, and see the tops of great waves in the distance. A list of thirty-seven or thirty-eight degrees was not uncommon; we were told that if she went over forty-five degrees, she would founder to the bottom. Still, she kept her course, and fortunately had no serious mishaps. For a whole month we saw nothing but the waves and the clouds."[51]

Brooke and his Americans continued to steer and handle the ship, the enlisted men in effect serving as officers of the watch. "The Japanese seem to rely entirely upon us," recorded Brooke. "It would be amusing if it were not such a serious matter to see how completely they abandon the ship to our two or three men of the watch."[52] A case in point was the night the Americans furled

[50] Brooke's *Kanrin Maru* Journal, 15 Feb. 1860, and Brooke to Toucey, 25 March 1860 (copy), BP.
[51] *Autobiography of Fukuzawa Yukichi*, pp. 116–17.
[52] Brooke's *Kanrin Maru* Journal, 16 Feb. 1860, BP.

John M. Brooke, apparently early in the Civil War

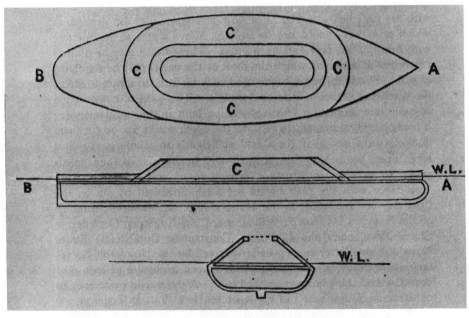

Brooke's design for the ironclad *Virginia*, showing the submerged ends. Drawn for his pamphlet *The Virginia, or Merrimac; Her Real Projector* (Richmond, 1891)

Drawing of John L. Porter's model for the *Virginia*, without submerged ends. From Brooke's 1891 pamphlet on *The Virginia*

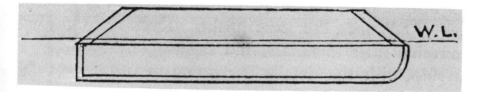

ef of Ordnance John M. Brooke, late in the Civil War

John M. Brooke, apparently shortly after the Civil War

Catesby ap Roger Jones, after the Civil War

Kate Corbin Brooke

Rosa Johnston Brooke and George
Mercer Brooke, Brooke's children
by his second marriage

Rear Admiral John Rodgers in the 1870s

John M. Brooke as a professor at VMI

the main topsail when not a Japanese could be induced to go aloft. The Japanese could not set sails alone, and when they tried to steer, they did such a poor job that Brooke could not take advantage of the currents. But there was one thing the Japanese could do at all hours; that was eat. They cooked rice continuously and ate day and night. The officers enjoyed particularly their midnight meal when they hauled their mats and braziers on deck and ate various delicacies—fish, radishes, rice, and confectionaries—which they washed down with gulps of hot tea.

Ashore the Japanese people were noted for their courtesy, obedience to orders, and good discipline. These qualities deserted them when they put out over blue water. To Brooke the metamorphosis was a revelation. In his journal he described it: "There does not appear to be any such thing as order or discipline on board. In fact the habits of the [Japanese] do not admit of such discipline and order as we have on our men of war. the Japanese sailors must have their little charcoal fires below their hot tea and pipes of tobacco. the Saki is not very carefully kept from them. Add to this that the orders are all given in dutch and that very few of the seamen understand that language and one may form some idea of the manner in which duty is carried on The Capt is still confined to his bed the Commo. also the officers leave the doors open which slam about leave their cups dishes & kettles on the deck to roll and slide about so that there is nothing but confusion. . . . Manjiro is the only Japanese onboard who has any idea of what reforms the Japanese Navy requires."[53] But Brooke was quick to explain, if not to justify, the incompetence of the Japanese. This was their first sailing cruise; the weather was unusually severe; and the Japanese had been taught by the Dutch.[54] It was Brooke's belief that when undisciplined men of any country are placed in unusual and dangerous circumstances, artificial distinctions break down and the abilities of the individual come to the fore. Storms and privation were "great levellers." The Japanese showed innate ability, and Brooke hoped with Manjiro's help to make passable sailors of them before the voyage was over.

[53] Ibid.
[54] Brooke noted in an undated memorandum included in the Brooke Papers that it did not seem that the Dutch had impressed upon the Japanese the importance of order and discipline.

The Japanese officers, like the common sailors, were woefully ignorant of seamanship, but they did display skill in navigation. They had rated the chronometers before leaving Yedo and at sea demonstrated a familiarity with lunar observations. Manjiro continued to show a real facility with the instruments and largely took over the simple observations. Ono Tomogoro, one of the officers, won Brooke's praise as an excellent navigator. All things considered, it was "a high old cruise" and the novelty was exhilarating to say the least.

Nine days after leaving port the Japanese were finally divided into watches.[55] But even this organization turned out to be but a partial solution. Commented Brooke: "But an unexpected difficulty occurred, of 6 officers of the grade of Lieutenant some are totally ignorant of their profession. the Commo: is unwilling to give those who are competent watches as they are not of as high shore rank as some who are incompetent the consequence is that he prefers to leave things as they are, no stations no watches etc. The Commo: knows nothing whatever of seamanship, the old fellow knows that I can take care of the vessel and so the matter rests. I shall urge the point however and shall succeed in making some improvements before we leave. Manjiro is intensely disgusted he is forced to yield to the Commo: But he has convinced the officers of the propriety of putting them in watches."[56] More and more Brooke was compelled to work on the Japanese through Manjiro. And the interpreter had to watch his step—living between two worlds as it were. Clearly, until the Japanese gained experience it behooved Brooke to move cautiously through the stormy seas and to "make as little sail as possible." Much time was lost owing to the inability of the Japanese to make or reduce sail.

After fifteen days at sea Captain Katsu was still sick though improving. He was able to sit up, and Brooke tried to restore his

---

[55] Brooke's *Kanrin Maru* Journal, 19 Feb. 1860, BP. Brooke had thought that the Japanese were divided into watches from the beginning and had merely failed to come on deck. He discovered later, however, that they had neglected the essential duty of organizing watches. This indicates both a gross ignorance on the part of the Japanese and a blind faith in the Americans.

[56] Ibid., 20 Feb. 1860.

strength with a diet of raw eggs, soup, and wine. "He is the most quiet man I ever saw," Brooke remarked. "I never hear his voice, the officers seldom go near him although he is very highly esteemed by them." As for Commodore Kimura, he kept to his own room except for an occasional stroll on deck. And so it went. Day after day Brooke's journal mentions briefly that the commodore and captain were confined to their rooms. Fukuzawa recalled that "Katsu proved a very poor sailor—he did not leave his cabin during the whole journey across."[57]

At the end of three weeks, Brooke forced the inevitable showdown, as he explained in his journal. "On the 1st [of March] I had an understanding with officers & Capt. It has been necessary heretofore to keep a constant lookout myself and to have our men on watch as the Japanese are totally incompetent, the wind being ahead I proposed to show the officers how to tack ship, they were too lazy to come on deck made various excuses etc. I therefore called all my men and sent them below with orders to do nothing without my consent. I then informed the Capt that I should not continue to take care of the vessel unless his officers would assist. He gave them a lecture put them under my orders and I sent my watch on deck."[58] With this arrangement the Japanese did improve, and by the time the voyage was over Brooke was willing to predict they would make "excellent sea officers," fully competent to manage their own vessel. Certainly Brooke and his small crew of Americans spared no effort to give the Japanese a much needed practical course in seamanship and navigation. At one point Brooke deliberately guided the *Kanrin Maru* into a circular storm and out again in order to demonstrate that such storms were understood by scientists and could be successfully overcome by vessels at sea.[59] Brooke did not exaggerate when he noted in his journal after the cruise was over that he had navigated the Japanese steamer to San Francisco with the aid of nine men from the *Cooper.*

Weeks at sea disclosed certain defects in the construction and rigging of the *Kanrin Maru*. When the vessel was under sail, the

[57] Ibid., 25 Feb. 1860; *Autobiography of Fukuzawa Yukichi*, p. 119.
[58] Brooke's *Kanrin Maru* Journal, 3 March 1860, BP.
[59] Kate Corbin Brooke Diary, 9 Sept. 1874, BP.

propeller could not be hoisted high enough to clear the water. By trailing in the water, it cut down the speed by a knot and a half and interfered with the rudder. The sails were too small for their yards and the blocks too small for the rigging. Also, the vessel needed new boats and a new battery. But in some respects Brooke still thought her "a very fine vessel."

As the *Kanrin Maru* approached the United States, spirits rose and the Japanese became exhilarated. Even the commodore began to show signs of life. The vessel arrived in San Francisco on March 17, thirty-seven days from Uraga, having traveled all but the first three days under sail. The Japanese ship had made a lonely crossing of the North Pacific; she had met but one vessel, the *Flora* of New York, carrying a load of coolies from Hong Kong to San Francisco. And yet, much to Brooke's amazement and the delight of the Japanese, the *Kanrin Maru* had beaten the *Powhatan*, which was supposed to have left Japan on the same day. Brooke had been sure that the lack of skill on the part of the Japanese would cause his vessel to trail Tattnall's by eight or nine days. He did not know, of course, that the American vessel had been delayed and that a little more than half way across the Pacific she had left the direct route to San Francisco and, taking advantage of a good breeze, had run south to the Hawaiian Islands for some coal.[60]

On March 19 Brooke reported the arrival of the *Kanrin Maru* to Captain Robert B. Cunningham, commandant of the navy yard at Mare Island. At the request of Admiral Kimura, he stated that the Japanese desired to have the steamer refitted at Mare Island before their return to Japan, for the little vessel had been battered by high winds and heavy seas and had sustained considerable damage. It was calculated that it would take several weeks to prepare the ship for another transoceanic crossing. Brooke advised Cunningham that he would remain with the Japanese "until the

[60] "Journal of Muragaki-Awaji-no-Kami," 28 Feb. 1860, Morris Papers, MSS Div., LC. The *Powhatan* had left Yedo 10 Feb. on schedule, but was delayed at Yokohama 3 days. Finally on 13 Feb. the *Powhatan* departed from Yokohama and steamed past Uraga into the open sea. The *Kanrin Maru* had left 3 days earlier. The American vessel spent nearly 2 weeks in the Hawaiian Islands, arriving 5 March and leaving 18 March. The frigate had used steam much of the way, and unexpected headwinds made her coal supply run low.

arrangements necessary to the fulfillment of the Admiral's desires are completed." The commandant promptly opened the facilities of the navy yard to the visitors. Along with an official dispatch Cunningham sent Brooke a warm personal note in which he expressed pleasure that it had fallen to Brooke "to receive the distinguished honor of navigating the first 'Japanese man of war' into our waters, at the particular request of his Imperial Majesty, the Emperor of Japan."[61]

The arrival of the Japanese warship aroused great interest; Brooke and Kern were plied with questions by curious Americans. For their part, the Japanese were astounded at the strange Western customs. Brooke and Kern did their best to explain Western ways and took the Japanese on a tour of the city, visiting a shipyard, an ironworks, a sugar refinery, and the government mint. Festivities were concluded with an official reception ashore and a series of toasts.[62]

The Japanese deeply appreciated the assistance of Brooke and the other Americans in taking the *Kanrin Maru* across the Pacific. Captain Katsu wrote Brooke that the voyage marked the first time the Japanese had "ever clossed, 3 thousand miles, because for you on board." The Japanese officials offered Brooke a large sum of money which, as a naval officer, he did not feel free to accept.[63] But they were determined that Brooke should accept something, and when he left the *Kanrin Maru* to return to Washington, the

[61] Cunningham to Brooke, 20 March 1860, BP. Cunningham, like other Americans, had confused the emperor with the shogun. It was the shogun who supported the policy of foreign intercourse.

[62] Hine, *Edward Kern*, pp. 144–45.

[63] Captain Katslintaro to J. M. Brooke (translation), n.d., and Brooke to Adm. Thornton Jenkins, 15 Sept. 1881 (copy), BP. Brooke told his second wife 14 years after the event that when the *Kanrin Maru* reached San Francisco, Manjiro "opened the large chest of gold and told Capt. B. to help himself, to take what he wanted as a remuneration for his services." Brooke, of course, declined (Kate Corbin Brooke Diary, 9 Sept. 1874, BP). In a speech before the America-Japan Society in Tokyo on 7 May 1935, Prince Iyesato Tokugawa, president of the society, stated that "as an evidence of their appreciation of this kind and efficient service, the Japanese admiral requested him [Brooke] to help himself to any amount he chose to take out of an iron chest which he was informed contained $80,000, an invitation which he was, of course, compelled to decline but the sincerity of the admiral's offer was beyond question" (*Japan Advertiser*, 9 May 1935). This information Tokugawa acknowledged he had obtained from an article written by Lt. James Johnston, U.S.N., in 1861.

officers of the warship gave him "many souvenirs, chiefly their uniforms, if the old style embroidered silk garments could be so called, with other articles of dress." After the Japanese embassy reached Washington in May, the chief ambassador said, when presented to the secretary of state, that as his first move he wanted to express his thanks for Brooke's services and to request that that fact be recorded in the archives of the United States.[64]

In view of the importance of the early publication of charts based on his surveys, Brooke wanted to return to Washington from San Francisco with the records and chronometers as soon as the Japanese could dispense with his services. Consequently, on April 5, seven days after the arrival of the *Powhatan*, Brooke, Kern, Rogier, and Kendall took passage on the mail steamer *Golden Age* for Panama. The rest of the *Cooper*'s crew were discharged in San Francisco. Flag Officer Tattnall and Captain A. S. Taylor of the marines left the *Powhatan* at San Francisco and proceeded on the mail steamer with Brooke. Tattnall planned "to go straight to Washington to consult the Government regarding the reception of the Ambassadors," while Captain Taylor expected to meet the embassy at the isthmus and from there escort it to Washington.[65] Brooke's trip was made particularly enjoyable by the company of a Mrs. Hitchcock, the wife of a doctor, and her daughter Lillie, who were traveling under his protection. Other acquaintances in the army and navy added to the pleasure of the trip east. At Aspinwall (Colón), Brooke saw several old friends, including George P. Welsh.

After nine days at San Francisco, the old side-wheel steamer *Powhatan*, carrying the first Japanese embassy to the West, steamed out of the harbor and shaped a course for Panama. The *Kanrin Maru*, still in the dock undergoing repairs, did not sail for another month on her return voyage to Japan by way of the Ha-

---

[64] Brooke to Joseph Heco, 20 Jan. 1896 (copy), and Brooke to Adm. Thornton Jenkins, 15 Sept. 1881 (copy), BP.

[65] "Journal of Muragaki-Awaji-no-Kami," 4 April 1860, Morris Papers, MSS Div., LC. The embassy was carried across the isthmus by the Panama Railroad on a special train. At Aspinwall the diplomats were received aboard the steam frigate *Roanoke*, flagship of the Home Squadron, which carried them to Hampton Roads. There they transferred to the chartered steamer *Philadelphia*, which transported them up the Chesapeake to Washington, where they arrived on 14 May.

waiian Islands.[66] Brooke did his part to assure a pleasant reception of the Japanese at Honolulu. On the day he left San Francisco, he wrote a letter to Robert Wyllie, Hawaiian minister of foreign relations, advising him "of the rank and character" of the Japanese officers soon to arrive.[67] The *Kanrin Maru* finally reached Yedo on July 1.

On Friday, April 27, 1860, Brooke arrived in New York, where he spent the weekend. Monday morning Brooke left for Washington. Bad news awaited him there; Lizzie had been "very ill." At once Brooke requested an emergency leave. Secretary Toucey in granting him leave for three months directed that he discharge Kern, Rogier, and Kendall, because the special duty for which they had been engaged had terminated.[68]

When Brooke reached Lexington early in May, he found Lizzie still seriously ill. While watching anxiously over her, his restless mind looked ahead to the work awaiting him in Washington. There was much to be done that only he could do, and he was anxious to be about it—leave or no leave—as soon as Lizzie was well. One of the first things Brooke did in Lexington was to dash off a note to Maury, whom he had missed in Washington, with the news that he had "some specimens of bottom from the Pacific & some water from the depth of 3300 faths." A week later, on May 11, Brooke dispatched a preliminary report to Secretary Toucey. To emphasize the importance of speedily publishing the results of his survey Brooke cited the recent wreck upon French Frigate Shoal of an American clipper ship valued with her cargo at $150,000. Fortunately for the wrecked ship, an expedition sent out from Honolulu as a result of Brooke's guano discovery was at French Frigate Shoal at the time and rescued the stranded crew. Brooke recalled that he had reported from Honolulu that the shoal

[66] At the Mare Island Navy Yard the *Kanrin Maru* was put in "fine order" (Charles Wolcott Brooks to Brooke, 19 May 1860, BP).

[67] Wyllie to Brooke, 15 Nov. 1860, BP. In this letter Wyllie thanked Brooke, stating that "the King and His Ministers looked upon it, as an act of great and very considerate kindness in you, to anticipate to us that useful information. It was a guide to us in our reception of those officers, whom we found, collectively and severally, to be worthy of all that you wrote in their favour."

[68] Brooke to Toucey, 1 May 1860, Officers Letters, RG 45, NA; Toucey to Brooke, 3 May 1860 (copy), Letters to Officers, RG 45, NA.

extended several miles northwest of the position assigned on existing charts, which were in error by twenty-five minutes of longitude. Informing the secretary that several wrecks had occurred recently near Shimoda from a want of adequate charts, he requested an appropriation of $5,000 for the hiring of competent draftsmen and the rental of drafting rooms. Secretary Toucey acted promptly, instructing his assistant to send a copy of Brooke's letter to the naval affairs committees of the House and Senate with the recommendation that the appropriation be made.[69]

When Lizzie showed improvement, Brooke hastened back to Washington. Meanwhile, the Japanese embassy had arrived from Aspinwall. A commission consisting of Captain Samuel F. Du Pont, Commander Sidney Smith Lee, and Lieutenant David Dixon Porter had been "appointed to take charge of the Embassy." Captain Du Pont told Brooke that he had reserved a place on the commission for him, but with Brooke's indefinite absence in Lexington he had been compelled to fill it.[70] Two days after their arrival in Washington, the Japanese were introduced to Secretary of State Lewis Cass, and the Japanese first ambassador expressed to Cass his verbal thanks "for the services of Lieutenant Brooke and the repairs of the *Kanrin Maru*."[71]

The visit of the Japanese embassy engendered tremendous interest in the Eastern trade. From both the Atlantic and Pacific coasts demands came that the charts based on the surveys of the North Pacific expedition and the late cruise of the *Fenimore Cooper* be published without delay. The preparation of the *Cooper* charts fell to Brooke, but it was hard for him to concentrate. Not only did he have many annoying details to harass him, as at the end of any protracted absence, but he was also frequently called in as a

[69] Brooke to Maury, 4 May 1860, Letters Received, Naval Observatory, RG 78, NA; Brooke to Toucey, 11 May 1860, Officers Letters, RG 45, NA, and endorsement on the back of this letter, at the end of which is written: "Done May 15, 60."

[70] Brooke Journal, 3 June 1860, BP. In Lexington on 3 June Brooke began to keep a regular journal again, having discontinued the practice when he left San Francisco. Information on the embassy's visit can be found in Miscellaneous Letters of the Department of State, 1789–1895, M-179, NA.

[71] Cole, "Japan's First Embassy to the United States," p. 146.

consultant.[72] "I have not only my own business to attend to," he wrote, "but am called upon to give information etc to Senators and others in reference to Eastern Russia and the Amour [Amur] and Japan so my time is much occupied."[73] Soon the illness of his wife forced him to return to Lexington.

Leisure time in Lexington gave Brooke a chance to reflect. His thoughts revealed a pronounced distrust of Russian and British imperialism and a respect for the Japanese people. He believed strongly that the United States should do everything within its power to promote friendship with Japan and to bolster that country's strength. Despite his friendly relations with the Russians in Yokohama, Brooke was suspicious of their designs and fearful of an attempt by them to seize Hokkaido. Further, he was certain that the British wanted Nagasaki, which guarded the Korea Strait, the southern gateway to the Sea of Japan. In his judgment, the Japanese realized their independence depended upon friendship with the United States and the adoption of Western techniques. Envisioning Japan as a tremendous potential market for American cotton, Brooke advocated vigorously the establishment of a steamship line between "California China Japan and the Amoor or other Russian ports." As to personal relations, he observed that the Japanese customs officials at Yokohama in the performance of their duties were bullied and insulted by foreigners. Consequently, he was not surprised that there should be antiforeign sentiment.[74]

Meantime, Lizzie's health improved sufficiently for her to move to Washington with her husband in June. Again the Brookes established themselves at Mrs. Bryant's on G Street, between 13th and 14th. It was a comfort to Brooke to have Lizzie with him

---

[72] For example, Charles Welsh, chief clerk at the Navy Department, stated that Brooke's action in bringing Rogier, Kendall, and Kern to New York was irregular, that Brooke should have waited for specific authorization from the department though obviously that would have taken weeks. But Brooke was anxious to begin the charts and planned to use Kern and Rogier in this work. By assuming the responsibility Brooke demonstrated his aversion to red tape. Brooke's direct action was approved by the secretary of the navy (Toucey to Brooke, 12 June 1860, Letters to Officers, RG 45, NA).

[73] Brooke to his wife, 22 May 1860, BP.

[74] Brooke to Sen. William M. Gwin, 4 June 1860 (copy), BP.

as he resumed his duties, although with good reason he continued to worry about her delicate health.

Brooke continued his work on deep-sea soundings. Corresponding with people in the United States and abroad, he kept up with the latest scientific developments. Experiments on the *Cooper* had reinforced his belief that casts made in the ocean where the currents were moderate could be relied upon within one hundred fathoms when corrected by comparison with standard casts made in water having little or no current. In areas where the ocean currents were swift, it was more difficult to obtain accurate results. On August 7, 1860, Brooke obtained a patent on a deep-sea sounding meter to be used with his lead; this apparently was the indicator he had designed before leaving on the *Cooper* cruise. For its manufacture, Brooke made arrangements with William Würdemann, a capable instrument maker in Washington. The agreement provided that Brooke and Würdemann should share the profits from any of the sounding meters sold.[75] Two were sold to the army for survey work on the Great Lakes before the Civil War.

To assist Maury's scientific endeavors Brooke gave him, for the use of the Literary and Philosophical Society of Manchester, England, specimens of the deep-sea bottom he had obtained during his cruises in the *Vincennes* and *Cooper* and specimens from shoal waters off the coast of Japan.[76] Through Baron F. von Gerolt, Prussian minister to the United States, Brooke forwarded to the eminent German authority on infusoria, Professor Christian Ehrenberg, reports and specimens of his deep-sea soundings that enabled Ehrenberg to prove the existence of organic life at the bottom of the deep sea. In recognition of his contributions through invention and research in the field of deep-sea sounding, Brooke

[75] Patent no. 29,454, Patent Index, 1790–1873, Records of the Patent Office, RG 241, NA; Brooke to Würdemann, 19 Dec. 1866 (copy), BP. In the Brooke Papers is the copy of a letter, dated 10 Oct. 1860, to an unidentified correspondent, in which Brooke mentioned that he had "prepared" a sounding meter to be used with his lead and that Würdemann would make them.

[76] Brooke to Maury, 21 Feb. 1861, Letters Received, Naval Observatory, RG 78, NA. The Microscopical Section of the Manchester Society was appreciative. On behalf of the society one of the officers wrote Maury: "You say most truly Lt. Brooke has shown us 'how the egg can be made to stand on end' with a piece of twine, and his simple method does honour to his ingenuity" (Gloys. Mosely to Maury, 15 March 1861 [copy], BP).

was awarded the Prussian Gold Medal of Science by the king of Prussia.[77]

Officers in Washington frequently had their routine work disrupted by special duty. Brooke was no exception. Late in June he received orders to report at the Boston Navy Yard as a witness at the court martial of Lieutenant Charles E. Thorburn, from whom Brooke had parted company in Japan when Thorburn was assigned to the *Powhatan*. Thorburn had not relished the return to New York around Cape Horn as a watch officer. At Panama he had left the *Powhatan* without authority on the eve of sailing, and the vessel had been forced to sail without him. Captain George F. Pearson, commanding the *Powhatan*, suspected that Thorburn's action was intentional and brought charges against him for deserting his station. At the ensuing court-martial Thorburn requested that Brooke be summoned as a character witness.[78]

Brooke arrived in Boston three days before the defense rested its case. Conferring informally with Brooke, Thorburn said that he believed he had "a good chance of getting off" as the government had no proof.[79] But Thorburn was unduly optimistic; the court found him "guilty of absence without leave from his station" and sentenced him to dismissal. The finding of the court was approved by Secretary Toucey and President Buchanan, although the president "remitted the sentence to permit Thorburn to resign from the service."[80] Brooke was never called as a witness, and it is probable that when the defense learned of his poor opinion of Thorburn it decided his testimony would do more harm than good. Brooke had thought Thorburn's financial manipulations in Japan were improper for a naval officer.

[77] The award was delayed by the Civil War, so that Brooke did not actually receive the medal until 1867 (Brooke to Gerolt, 14 April 1867 [copy], BP). The Prussian government had intended to present Brooke with a decoration in 1861 for his "scientific contributions and inventions" but deferred the plan when Brooke resigned from the U.S. Navy (Gerolt to Brooke, 30 April 1861, BP).

[78] Toucey to Brooke, 28 June 1860, BP; Nelson M. Blake, Chief, Naval Section, War Records Branch, National Archives, to the author, 4 Feb. 1952. Blake obtained the information from Records of Proceedings of General Courts-Martial, Case No. 3044, 25 June–3 July 1861, Lt. Charles E. Thorburn, Records of the Office of the Judge Advocate General (Navy), RG 125, NA.

[79] Brooke to his wife, 1 July 1860, BP.

[80] Blake to the author, 4 Feb. 1952.

From his return from Japan until the outbreak of the Civil War, Brooke's principal duties were connected with the preparation of charts based on his surveys. For this purpose he was placed on special duty responsible directly to the secretary of the navy. Brooke pursued his work persistently with the assistance of Edward Kern and Charles Rogier, who were hired as draftsman and clerk. Initially he had counted on Thorburn's help in reducing the observations, but Thorburn's resignation from the navy cut off any help from that direction.[81]

Brooke calculated carefully the cost of preparing "a report of the survey of the Route between California & China" for the fiscal year beginning July 1, 1860, and arrived at a figure of $4,640 which he submitted to Secretary Toucey. Rent was not included because Commander John Rodgers had offered Brooke the use of the offices assigned to the North Pacific expedition at 19th and F streets. The department approved the estimate, and the work was begun.[82]

In October, Brooke submitted his first progress report. He stated that "the meridian differences between San Francisco, Honolulu, Guam, Hong Kong, Loo Choo and Kanagawa, primary stations in the survey of the route between California and China," had been determined after a comparison of the chronometer rates of the *Cooper* with those of the *Vincennes*. The results were excellent. In hydrography, the specimens obtained in deep-sea soundings ranging from 12,000 to 19,800 feet were, Brooke stated, being examined by "eminent microscopists."[83] After seven months' work, Brooke notified Secretary Toucey that an additional $3,000 would be needed to complete the report and charts. By this time the states of the Lower South had seceded from the Union.

On the subject of chronometers Brooke had become an authority as a result of experiments on board the *Vincennes* embracing fourteen months and those on board the *Cooper* lasting ten months. Despite his inability in the cramped quarters of the schooner to regulate temperature through lamps, he had obtained comparable

[81] Brooke to Toucey, 11 May 1860, Officers Letters, RG 45, NA.
[82] Brooke to Toucey, 28 June 1860 (copy), BP.
[83] Brooke to Toucey, 3 Oct. 1860, Officers Letters, RG 45, NA.

results by his method of using a closed case and of determining a daily mean temperature. Brooke found the correspondence of rates and temperatures on the *Cooper* nearly as consistent as on the *Vincennes*. This close correlation led Brooke to conclude "that although individual chronometers may differ considerably . . . when taken in sets of from ten to fifteen the mean ratios [nearly] agree."[84] Brooke revealed his active interest in the subject by his correspondence with T. S. Negus and Company, Eggert and Son, and other chronometer makers. He compared rates with these men and, drawing on his practical experience, offered opinions on such technical matters as the influence of temperature on rates and properties desired in chronometer lubricants.

Finding that the subject of the West Coast Indian was of considerable interest among ethnologists and other scientists, Brooke offered evidence that the forebears of at least one of the tribes had come from Japan. When in California, Brooke, Commodore Kimura, Captain Katsu, Manjiro, and other Japanese had visited the plantation of Captain J. B. Frisbie, where the Japanese had noticed that an Indian boy bore a striking physical resemblance to people of their own race. Brief inquiry disclosed further that at least half a dozen words in the language of the tribe from which the boy had come were either identical with or similar to Japanese words. To Brooke the obvious explanation was that a Japanese junk had drifted across the ocean in some bygone day, and in a letter to Secretary Toucey he wrote persuasively along this line. As he was thoroughly familiar with the winds and currents off Japan and in the North Pacific and was acquainted with the stories of men like Joseph Heco, Manjiro, and Tim, who had been shipwrecked, he could speak with some authority. Speculations along these or similar lines has continued to our own day.[85]

As always Brooke's restless mind was teeming with new ideas. In January 1861 he noted in his journal that several inventions or improvements had occurred to him "within a short period." Five

---

[84] Placing the chronometers in the *Fenimore Cooper*, undated notes, BP.

[85] Brooke to Toucey, 24 Sept. 1860 (copy), BP. The New York *Times* of 21 March 1932 reported that Shujiro Watanabe, a Tokyo publicist, had concluded "that the evidences of a far-advanced civilization, antedating the Indian, found in certain Western States, is due to the descendants of Japanese whose ships had been wrecked on the California shore."

inventions were mentioned, and although there is no evidence that any of the five was completed it is, nonetheless, of interest to note their variety: (1) a winged war rocket "so arranged as to rebound from a ship's side on striking and to dart beneath her and explode"; (2) a boat designed to carry troops safely within artillery range; (3) an improved anchor; (4) a transit stand column; and (5) a posthole cutter. The rocket was based upon the principle of a time fuse. The boat design was intended to reduce the size of the target drastically by carrying the troops below the waterline.

Ordnance and shipbuilding also attracted Brooke's attention. He studied the problem of water resistance to a flat-nosed or square hull and concluded that the resistance was not so great as commonly supposed. As the vessel moved forward it formed what he termed a "water bow" which cut through the surrounding water. And, Brooke asserted, as the sharpness of the water bow increased with the speed of the boat, it followed that the greater the boat's speed the less the resistance of the water. As an example he took the whale, which despite its huge size and flat head could move very fast. Yet, by turning its head, the whale lost headway almost at once, for the turning of the whale's head replaced the water bow with a new mass of water possessing tremendous inertia. A flat-nosed vessel with a sharp water bow might at high speeds be retarded less on a straight course, in theory at least, than a vessel with the conventional sharp hull.[86] Brooke applied this principle to elongated projectiles for rifled cannon, suggesting that at high velocities the flat-nosed projectile might be slowed down less by air resistance than the pointed projectile. Within just a few months Brooke, to his surprise, would be in a position to test his theories.

During his year in Washington, Lizzie's failing health was a constant source of anxiety to Brooke. Life itself seemed to be slowly draining out of her. Consequently when Secretary Toucey proposed that Brooke survey Chiriqui, on the Caribbean coast of Panama (then part of the Grenadine Confederation), and Golfito, Costa Rica, on the Pacific side of the isthmus, Brooke begged off.[87] About this time he settled the purser's accounts of the *Feni-*

[86] Brooke's Washington Journal, 3 Feb. 1861, BP.
[87] Ibid., 18 July 1860.

more Cooper and found there was a balance due him of $191.41. Drawing the money from the Treasury, he took a month's leave with Lizzie and four-year-old Anna. They spent part of the time on the peninsula between the York and the James, apparently visiting relatives. It could not have been a very gay time for Lizzie seems to have been preoccupied with thoughts of death. While in Hampton she wrote letters for John and Anna that were not to be opened until after her death. To John she pleaded: "Above all bring Anna up a Christian never let her be subjected to Roman Catholic influence and have her as much with you as possible & not in the way of Boarding Schools." Somehow, Lizzie cheated death at this time, but after her death John respected her wishes.[88]

[88] An inscription in Anna M. Brooke's Bible states that she and her father were confirmed in the Episcopal church at Lexington, Va., on 12 June 1870. Anna was 13 at the time. Anna lived with Brooke at Lexington until her death.

VIII /

EARLY SERVICE IN

THE CONFEDERACY

WHATEVER John Brooke's personal problems may have been on his return to Washington, he could not insulate himself from the din of sectional controversy. The papers were full of it and Brooke in letters from friends and relatives was bombarded with opinions. In September 1860 John Van McCollum, who had resigned from the navy in 1859, wrote from Erie, Pennsylvania, where he was in the mill business, lauding the Democratic party. "Although somewhat scared I do not think 'honest old Abe' will be elected," he wrote. McCollum was a Douglas supporter.[1]

In December, before South Carolina's secession, Brooke heard from his brother William, who was still living in New York. "I cannot see any way out of our present political troubles except secession," William groaned. "The Republican party will not concede what the South demands and ought to have and the South cannot yield without giving up at once and forever her just share of power and influence in this union and consenting to the inevitable ultimate abolition of slavery, not directly in so many words, but indirectly and surely."[2]

By the time Brooke wrote his cousin Colonel Charles Garnett

[1] McCollum to Brooke, 16 Sept. 1860, BP.
[2] Brooke to Brooke, 5 Dec. 1860, BP.

of Hanover County, Virginia, two days after the firing on the *Star of the West* off Charleston, he was beginning to feel the anxiety of conflicting loyalties. "Since our conversation on the subject of a system of defence for the Coast of the United States against foreign aggression," he announced, "affairs have taken such a course that it would not be proper for me whilst holding a commission under the General Government to pursue the subject further."[3]

The disintegration of the Union depressed Brooke, and it was seldom that he felt in the mood to record the day's happenings. As a naval officer and scientist he had little interest in politics. At the end of January, while Virginia sought to pour oil on the troubled waters, Brooke was in a quandary. By the middle of February he could see little but disaster ahead and expressed his views in a gloomy letter to R. C. Wyllie in Honolulu. "You are I presume in possession of late dates from the United States. The unsettled condition of the country has in fact led me to defer writing in the hope of having at least some pleasant information to convey in relation to the disposition of the agitating questions which are now convulsing the country. But whilst I have great faith in the good sense of my countrymen I can not but apprehend disastrous consequences from the violent and aggressive disposition of party heads in and out of power."[4]

Two months later came Sumter and Lincoln's call for seventy-five thousand volunteers. Branding Lincoln's call a signal for the invasion of the South, Virginia seceded on April 17. Two days later Lincoln proclaimed a naval blockade of the Lower South. The hour of decision had arrived for all naval officers—should it be union or native state? Twenty years later Brooke would recall that "when the State of Virginia seceded, in accordance with my convictions, I laid down my pencil on the chart of 'French Frigate Shoals' which I was drawing, went to the Navy Department and handed in my resignation." In fact, Brooke's action was not quite that dramatic, for he waited until April 20, 1861, to submit a terse letter to Secretary of the Navy Gideon Welles: "I hereby resign my Commission as a Lieutenant in the Navy of the United

[3] Brooke to Garnett, 11 Jan. 1861 (copy), BP.
[4] Brooke to Wyllie, 14 Feb. 1861 (copy), BP.

States."[5] To Brooke the violence that had flared in Baltimore when the Sixth Massachusetts Regiment passed through the city may well have been the final straw.[6] Brooke was in good company, for Robert E. Lee and Matthew Fontaine Maury resigned from the federal service on the same day as he did.

But why did Brooke resign at all? His mother was from New England, he had been reared in the Northwest, and he had gone to school in the North. Moreover, he had joined the navy when fourteen. Most of his twenty years of service had been spent overseas, though there had been four different tours of duty in Washington. The answer seems to be that blood ties were very strong. Both William Brooke and Colonel William Garnett favored the Southern cause. So did Brooke's close friend John McCollum. After the war, Admiral S. P. Lee stated that Brooke was influenced to resign by his prominent relatives, R. M. T. Hunter and Muscoe Garnett.[7] This was no doubt true, but it does not follow that their influence was decisive. The person closest of all to John Brooke, was, of course, his wife. There was no doubt where Lizzie's sentiments lay; she was Southern to the core. One thing is certain: John Brooke thought the matter through for himself and acted on his own convictions.

After Brooke resigned, he immediately left for Lexington. However, the secretary of the navy refused to accept the resignation and ordered that Brooke's name be "stricken from the rolls" at

[5] Brooke to Adm. Thornton Jenkins, 15 Sept. 1881 (copy), BP; Brooke to Welles, 20 April 1861, photostatic reproduction in the Brooke Papers, original in Letters from Officers Tendering Their Resignations but Dismissed Instead, Nov. 1860–Dec. 1861 (Letter No. 29), RG 45, NA. By his resignation Brooke terminated the report and charts of the *Cooper's* cruise. His assistants were discharged at the end of the month. But even had Brooke remained with the union, it is doubtful that he would have been allowed to finish his work. John Rodgers stayed with the Union, but his labors on the North Pacific expedition report were soon interrupted. After the war the reports of both expeditions were forgotten. J. E. Nourse in *American Expeditions in the Ice Zones* (Boston, 1884), p. 131, states that all the records were preserved except for those of the naturalist, which were destroyed by fire in Chicago.

[6] An indication that the incident may have affected Brooke's decision is the fact that included in the Brooke Papers is a long account of the fracas clipped from the Baltimore *Sun* of 24 and 25 July 1901. Almost all other clippings in the Brooke Papers relate to Brooke, his friends, or his work.

[7] Adm. Lee to Elisha Riggs, 29 Sept. 1866, as quoted in a letter from Lee to Brooke, 2 Oct. 1866, BP.

the direction of the president.[8] Thus was Brooke rewarded for twenty years of service at low pay. Separation from so many close friends was a sad affair and Brooke hardly received consolation from statements such as that attributed to David Dixon Porter, the future admiral, that he only regretted the loss of two men from the United States Navy: Catesby Jones and Brooke.[9] Certainly more personal was John Rodgers's warm expression of friendship. "No political diference between us," he wrote, "shall ever interrupt the kind feeling, the affection which I entertain for you and however politics may go, I hope you will not suffer them to put a division between our private sentiments." Rodgers promised to protect Brooke's interests in Washington until the bloody strife was ended.[10]

To head the Confederate Navy Department, President Jefferson Davis appointed Stephen Russell Mallory, who for seven years had headed the Senate Committee on Naval Affairs. At the start Mallory had no ships. Of the ninety ships in the United States Navy at President Abraham Lincoln's inauguration, only one, the *Fulton* at Pensacola, had been seized by Southerners. Not a vessel had been brought South. Moreover, the agricultural South had a pitifully puny merchant marine to fall back on. The Confederacy suffered from a lack of developed resources, machine shops, and dockyards. And throughout the war the navy lacked trained mechanics. Until the secession of Virginia the Confederacy was without a first-class navy yard, as Pensacola was suitable only for repair work. But the ill-considered evacuation of Norfolk by the Federals on April 20, 1861, gave the South a thousand pieces of heavy ordnance with bores ranging from 6.4 inches to 11 inches, a first-class dry dock, two thousand barrels of powder, and thousands of shells. Further, there were four scuttled ships of some potential value, including the screw frigate *Merrimack* which had been burned to the waterline. The adherence of

[8] Welles to Brooke, Late Lieutenant U.S.N., Lexington, Va., 14 May 1861, Appointments, Orders, and Resignations, Records of the Bureau of Naval Personnel, RG 24, NA. *The United States Naval Academy Graduates Association Register for Graduates* was a little kinder. Concerning Brooke, and many of those who followed the same course, the register states: "Dismissed." But a footnote explains why—"Resignation not accepted; went South."

[9] Kate Corbin Brooke Diary, 11 Sept. 1874, BP.

[10] Rodgers to Brooke, 4 May 1861, BP.

Virginia to the Confederacy brought still another priceless boon in the form of the Tredegar Iron Works, the only establishment south of the Potomac capable of producing heavy ordnance.

Southern officers in the United States Navy had divided almost evenly on the question of state loyalty. Of the 671 officers in the navy who, at the beginning of 1861, were thought to have some Southern affinity, 321 resigned and went South. Of the officers as a whole the South got about one in five. In addition to serving aboard vessels of war, Confederate naval officers supervised port and river defenses, built ships, superintended foundries and powder plants, and procured ships and supplies abroad. Of the noncommissioned officers, such as boatswains, gunners, carpenters, and sailmakers, only a handful went South. One of the gravest problems facing the Confederate navy was enlistments.

At Lexington, Brooke left Lizzie and Anna with Colonel Williamson of the Virginia Military Institute faculty. Lizzie was in no condition to contend with the bustle of Richmond, for she was expecting a baby in July. From Lexington, Brooke hurried to Richmond, soon to be the Confederate capital, and offered his services to the Commonwealth.[11] Commissioned a lieutenant in the Virginia navy on April 23, 1861, he was ordered by Captain Samuel Barron of the Office of Naval Detail and Equipment to report to General Robert E. Lee, commanding the Virginia forces, "for such duty as he may assign you."[12] As it developed, this meant duty as naval aide to the general, then stationed in Richmond. It was stimulating to be at the hub of activity, especially as Brooke's cousin Colonel Robert Selden Garnett was Lee's adjutant general. From the beginning Brooke was tremendously impressed by General Lee, writing Lizzie the first day he was at the general's headquarters that "Genl Lee is a Second Washington if there ever was one."

At the headquarters of the Virginia forces, though there was no news of fighting, there was a terrific press of business. Brooke

[11] Brooke's Richmond Journal, 23 June 1861, BP. On this day Brooke began to keep a journal again. In the first entry he traced his activities subsequent to his resignation from the U.S. Navy on 20 April 1861.

[12] Barron to Brooke, 26 April 1861, BP. The order was issued at General Lee's command.

was immediately directed to assist in reading letters and reports and in answering them, so he was kept "busy enough." After a stint of paperwork he was given the task of finding some manufacturers for percussion caps, because, he recorded, "great fears were entertained as we were without a sufficient number of caps for one good fight." From his seat on the governor's Advisory Council, Matthew Fontaine Maury reported that late in April there had been "percussion caps enough, for a ½ doz. rounds & no machine to make them with." The shortage of flints was equally serious. Brooke noted in his journal that "the State had a few rifles about 1000 revolvers 2500 sabres and 46000 old flintlock muskets of inferior make. 37 new brass six pdrs. without carriages, twelve parrot [Parrott] rifle cannon mounted." Every effort was made to accumulate a supply of ammunition, though for a month the situation was critical. It annoyed Brooke that with the state in such a plight the ignorant newspaper editors should demand that an attack be launched against Washington.[13]

On May 15 Brooke was appointed to a board to examine and report on the position and construction of the fortifications at Fort Powhatan and on Jamestown Island. Serving with him were Colonel Andrew Talcott of the State Engineer Service and Captain Archibald Fairfax, ordnance officer at the Norfolk Navy Yard. The board recommended that the battery at Fort Powhatan be moved to Kennon's six miles down the James on the left bank.[14]

At the end of May, General Lee grew fearful lest the enemy land at Burwell's Bay, Isle of Wight County, and cut the Norfolk and Petersburg Railroad. Consequently, he dispatched Brooke to Zuni on the Blackwater River to secure the line of communication to Norfolk. Brooke was instructed to station troops sent from Fort Powhatan at suitable positions to safeguard the bridges spanning the Blackwater. From Zuni, which he described as "a real sleepy place," Brooke forwarded to his headquarters a detailed report on the roads and bridges in the area, and then hurried to Norfolk to

---

[13] Maury to Frank Minor, 16 May 1861, Matthew Fontaine Maury Papers, MSS Div., LC; Brooke's Richmond Journal, 23 June 1861, BP. In his journal Brooke does not give the exact date when this shortage existed, but from internal evidence it would appear it was around the end of April.

[14] [Talcott, Fairfax, and Brooke to Lee], 17 May 1861 (copy), BP.

arrange with General Benjamin Huger for the dispatch of rein-
forcements from Suffolk to Zuni should the need arise.[15]

When it was clear that Virginia's destiny was indissolubly
linked with the cotton states, Brooke applied to Secretary Mallory, still in Montgomery, for a "commission in the permanent
Navy of the Southern Confederacy when such navy shall be
organised." On May 2 Mallory wrote him that he had been appointed a lieutenant in the navy of the Confederate States. The
law provided that former officers of the United States Navy accepted into the Confederate service should hold the same relative
rank they had held in the old service. This provision insured that
officers from states which seceded late should not find themselves
at the foot of the list.[16]

For a few weeks, until the Confederate Navy Department was
established in Richmond, Brooke continued on General Lee's
staff. With Lizzie in Lexington, he wrote that at least he preferred
living alone in Richmond to being on the African station or the
coast of Asia. Brooke was cheered by the presence of relatives and
old friends. Brother William had left his job in New York and
come to Richmond at the outbreak of war. As William was not
physically fit for military service, John took steps to find him a civilian position. Yelverton Garnett had left Washington and was
busy establishing a medical practice in Richmond. Word had
come that Lizzie's brother Dick Garnett, stationed at a western
post, had resigned his commission in the United States Army and
was heading east to offer his services to the Confederacy. Anton
Schönborn, who had worked with Brooke on the *Vincennes*, appeared in Richmond and reported that Edward Kern was "coming
on soon."[17]

During these early weeks of the war Brooke expressed in letters to his wife a growing hatred of the North. Speaking of General Henry Alexander Wise's expedition to northwest Virginia, he
stated that the general would have "ample force and full powers to

[15] Lee to Brooke, 27 May 1861, and Brooke's Richmond Journal, 23 June 1861, BP.

[16] Brooke to Mallory, 27 April 1861 (copy), BP; Act of 16 March 1861, supplementary to
"an act to organize the Navy," *Laws for the Army and Navy of the Confederate States.*

[17] Brooke to his wife, 4 June 1861, BP. Kern actually stayed with the Union, serving
for a time in the topographical engineers. He died at his home in Philadelphia in November
1863 (Hine, *Edward Kern*, pp. 146–52).

wind up the traitors in that section." As for the Yankees generally, Brooke averred that there was "much arrant cowardice amongst them." Early in June he wrote Lizzie "that we have at last a homogeneous country. I never wish to have anything to do with the late U S or rather the Northern people." Brooke was a man of deep feeling, and once he made a difficult decision he could be expected to become emotionally involved.

While still in Richmond on General Lee's staff Brooke gave thought to the naval needs of the whole South. Significantly, he considered the purchase of ironclads and munitions abroad. On May 6, 1861, four days after his appointment to the Confederate service, Brooke wrote to Secretary Mallory, noting that the proposed Union blockade "will render the importation of arms very difficult, and the process of manufacture is too slow to provide a sufficient number even if we had the best machinery." Brooke thought that if Napoleon III were favorably disposed, "an iron plated ship might be purchased in France loaded with arms and brought into port in spite of the wooden blockade."[18]

Secretary Mallory was considering the same problems. He had already canvassed the possibility of building ironclads in the Confederacy, with discouraging results, and on May 10 he submitted a detailed report on ironclads to Charles M. Conrad, chairman of the Committee on Naval Affairs of the Confederate Congress. Emphasizing French primacy in the field, Mallory stated his belief that the South must utilize ironclads to offset the tremendous preponderance in wooden vessels enjoyed by the North and smash the blockade.[19] On the same day Congress appropriated $2 million for the acquisition "with the least possible delay, in France or England, [of] one or two war steamers of the most modern and

[18] Brooke to Mallory, 6 May 1861 (copy), BP.

[19] William N. Still, Jr., *Iron Afloat: The Story of Confederate Armorclads* (Nashville, 1971), pp. 12–13; Mallory to Conrad, 10 May 1861, *Official Records of the Union and Confederate Navies in the War of the Rebellion*, ser. 2, 2:67–69 (hereafter cited as *Official Records, Navy*). This same letter is given with the date 8 May 1861 in *Official Records, Navy*, ser. 2, 1:740–43. It is probable that Mallory commenced the lengthy report on 8 May, after receipt of Brooke's letter, but did not submit it to Conrad until 10 May. An evaluation of Mallory's message is given in Joseph T. Durkin, *Stephen R. Mallory, Confederate Navy Chief* (Chapel Hill, N.C., 1954), pp. 152–53, and in James Phinney Baxter, *The Introduction of the Ironclad Warship* (Cambridge, Mass., 1933), pp. 224–25.

improved description." Promptly Secretary Mallory issued orders to Lieutenant James H. North directing him to make arrangements if possible with the French government for the purchase of an armored frigate.[20] This was the secretary's first effort to obtain armored vessels, and Brooke's letter of eleven days earlier at least had reinforced Mallory's thinking and demonstrated his own interest in the subject. In the end, attempts to purchase ironclads abroad failed. The South would have to make its own.

On June 3 when Secretary Mallory arrived in Richmond, Brooke had "some conversation with him," which apparently included the subject of ironclads, and prepared to transfer from General Lee's staff to the Confederate navy. He did not like the thought of leaving Lee, but as a naval officer with an inventive turn of mind he felt an urge "to do something in the ordnance line." At least it was comforting to know that General Lee spoke of him "with great regard." And there was no doubt Mallory could use to full advantage a man of Brooke's peculiar talents.[21]

As a matter of fact the secretary of the navy did not wait for Brooke's formal transfer to the naval ordnance office before utilizing him. On June 7 Brooke wrote Lizzie that "Mallory wants me to make some calculations in regard to floating batteries which I shall do today." He did not specify "ironclad" batteries for the matter was one of great secrecy, and Brooke was never one to divulge military secrets. On occasion Lizzie chided her husband for his reticence. Mallory's request for calculations was the genesis of the *Virginia* (*Merrimack*). According to Mallory, when Brooke was asked to assist in designing an armored vessel, "he entered upon his duty at once."[22] Considerable reflection and research were necessary, for though ironclads were already making their appearance in the navies of Europe, the United States Navy had never owned such a vessel.

[20] *An Act to authorize the purchase or construction of certain vessels of war*, approved 10 May 1861, *Official Records, Navy*, ser. 2, 2:66–67; Mallory to North, 17 May 1861, ibid., 2:70.

[21] Brooke to his wife, 4 June 1861, BP; Testimony of Brooke before Joint Committee of Congress, 26 Feb. 1863, *Official Records, Navy*, ser. 2, 1:783.

[22] Report of Secretary of the Navy Stephen R. Mallory, 29 March 1862, *Official Records, Navy*, ser. 2, 2:174.

Brooke's ideas for an ironclad warship gradually took practical form, and on June 19 he wrote Lizzie that he had been working all day on plans. In the next day or so he submitted outline drawings for an ironclad vessel to the secretary of the navy, who approved the design.[23] The plan called for a casemated vessel with a shield of wood plated with laminated iron, inclined from the horizontal at "the least angle that would permit working the guns." Tentatively Brooke suggested that the wooden backing be two feet thick and the iron armor, three inches. The shield, or casemate, was to be placed upon a hull with sharp ends projecting beyond the shield to insure "fineness of line." The plan specified that the eaves of the casemate and the extended ends of the vessel be submerged two feet in order to obtain greater buoyancy and speed without exposing the hull or increasing the draft. Brooke envisioned a false superstructure of tank or boiler iron to divide the water and prevent it from banking up on the submerged ends. The superstructure, corresponding in form to the hull, could be decked, but no higher than would permit free use of the pivot guns.[24] Brooke contemplated application of his plan to a new ship, though, as we shall see, it was because of necessity first used to convert the old wooden *Merrimack* into the ironclad *Virginia*.

The novel and unique feature of the *Virginia* was, as James Phinney Baxter has written, "the extension of the bow and stern beyond the shield under water." Secretary Mallory, in reporting to the House of Representatives on the plan and construction of the *Virginia*, stated: "The novel plan of submerging the ends of the ship and the eaves of the casemate, however, is the peculiar

[23] The Brooke Papers do not give the exact date though certainly it was between 19 June and 23 June.

[24] For descriptions of Brooke's original plan, see Brooke's Richmond Journal, 23 June 1861, BP; John M. Brooke, "The Plan and Construction of the 'Merrimac,' " in R. U. Johnson and C. C. Buel, eds., *Battles and Leaders of the Civil War*, 4 vols. (New York, [1887–88]), 1:715–16; John M. Brooke, *The Virginia, or Merrimac; Her Real Projector: A Statement of the Facts Connected with Her Conversion into an Iron-clad* (Richmond, 1891), p. 4; Testimony of Brooke before Joint Committee of Congress, 26 Feb. 1863, *Official Records, Navy*, ser. 2, 1:783–84; letters from Lt. Catesby ap R. Jones to Brooke, 25 Nov. 1861–5 March 1862, and Brooke to [J. William] Jones [secretary, Southern Historical Society], 10 July 1874 (copy), BP; Report of Secretary of the Navy Mallory, 29 March 1862, *Official Records, Navy*, ser. 2, 2:174.

and distinctive feature of the *Virginia*. It was never before adopted." The extended submerged ends was the only feature of the design Brooke claimed to be original; he never held that there was anything new about the casemate.[25]

Certainly the idea of inclining the armor of the shield to increase resistance through deflection of projectiles was not new; it was almost as old as armor itself. Inclined armor had been proposed in Spain in 1727, in England in 1805, and in America during the War of 1812 and periodically thereafter. The Stevens battery for which Congress made an appropriation in 1842 had armor set at an angle of forty-five degrees. Though the French and British had investigated the relative merits of vertical and inclined armor and had chosen the former for their ironclads, the details of these experiments were not known in the South. There were arguments on both sides of the question. To Brooke, the ability of sloping sides to deflect projectiles more than outweighed the inconvenience and physical discomfort resulting. Contrary to popular belief, the *Virginia* was not even the first vessel in the South to use this technique. In Charleston Harbor early in the war South Carolina constructed a floating battery and a shore battery of railroad iron placed at an angle.[26] In each instance the technique demonstrated its worth.

Brooke adopted laminated iron plates from necessity. Experiments abroad had demonstrated that a solid plate of armor offered more resistance to high-powered ordnance than laminated armor of the same total thickness. Therefore, the less one resorted to lamination in the construction of armored vessels the better. Brooke would have preferred solid three-inch iron plates to the laminated one-inch iron plates he first used, but the South was not equipped to produce iron plates as thick as those made abroad. Moreover, it was believed that the Tredegar Iron Works, which would have to roll the plates, could not punch bolt holes in iron plates more than one inch in thickness. After Secretary Mallory had approved his plan, Brooke made working drawings and requested that Engineer William P. Williamson and Naval Con-

[25] Baxter, *Introduction of the Ironclad Warship*, p. 228; Report of Secretary of the Navy Mallory, 29 March 1862, *Official Records, Navy*, ser. 2, 2:175.
[26] Baxter, *Introduction of the Ironclad Warship*, pp. 221–23.

structor John Luke Porter be summoned to Richmond from the Norfolk Navy Yard to carry the plan into execution.[27] Williamson and Porter arrived on June 22 and immediately conferred with Brooke and Secretary Mallory.[28] Porter had brought a model for a casemated vessel with inclined iron-plated sides. Porter's model resembled Brooke's plan in that the casemate was of similar shape and had eaves submerged beneath the surface, but it did not have the submerged ends extending beyond the casemate that augmented speed and flotation.[29]

After Porter's model had been examined, the secretary introduced Brooke's novel design, explaining the unique features. After discussion, Williamson and Porter accepted the principle of extended submerged ends "and by unanimous consent" adopted Brooke's plan.[30] In his journal Brooke expressed relief and some surprise. He wrote, "I was afraid that Mr. P—— would, having an idea of his own make objection to my plan but he did not[,] regarding it as an improvement."[31]

Inquiry established that there were no suitable engines available for a new ironclad. Williamson then suggested that the screw frigate *Merrimack* be used. Though considerably damaged by fire and immersion, her engines and boilers were not irreparably ruined and the engineer believed he could restore them to working

[27] Testimony of Brooke before Joint Committee of Congress, 26 Feb. 1863, *Official Records, Navy*, ser. 2, 1:783. Porter had been appointed a constructor in the U.S. Navy in 1857.

[28] Brooke's Richmond Journal, 23 June 1861, BP.

[29] For Porter's description of his model, see John Luke Porter to the Editor, Richmond *Examiner*, 11 April 1862; John L. Porter, "The Plan and Construction of the 'Merrimac,'" *Battles and Leaders of the Civil War*, 1:716–17. Descriptions by Brooke can be found in Brooke's Richmond Journal, 23 June 1861, BP; Testimony of Brooke before Joint Committee of Congress, 26 Feb. 1863, *Official Records, Navy*, ser. 2, 1:783–84; Brooke, *The Virginia, or Merrimac; Her Real Projector*, p. 4.

[30] Brooke's Richmond Journal, 23 June 1861, BP. See also Testimony of Brooke before Joint Committee of Congress, 26 Feb. 1863, *Official Records, Navy*, ser. 2, 1:783–84; Brooke, *The Virginia, or Merrimac; Her Real Projector*, p. 4; Report of Secretary of the Navy Mallory, 29 March 1862, *Official Records, Navy*, ser. 2, 2:174. A letter from Brooke to his wife, 24 June 1861, BP, corroborates the statement in Brooke's Journal.

[31] It was apparently the discussion of the relative merits of the Brooke and Porter plans by Brooke, Porter, Williamson, and Mallory on 22 June that prompted Brooke to resume keeping a journal for the first time since he had left Washington. Brooke wanted the record to be straight. In his journal Brooke described the two plans, noted their differences, and made sketches of his own.

order.[32] This 3,200-ton vessel, completed in 1856, had been one of the largest vessels in the United States Navy. Scuttled by the Federals when they evacuated Norfolk, the vessel had been raised by the Confederates and placed in dry dock at Norfolk. The vessels of the *Merrimack* class had been conceived of as essentially sailing vessels with small auxiliary engines. In 1860 Secretary of the Navy Toucey had recommended that "the engines of the Merrimac should be renewed"; these engines were not much, but they were better than nothing.

Though the *Merrimack* had been burned to the waterline, her hull had not been seriously damaged. Her draft of over twenty feet was considerably more than was desirable, but there was no choice. Williamson declared that the engines "could not be used well in any other vessel unless she had equal draft of water [to the *Merrimack*], or nearly so."[33] There was some consolation in the fact that using the hull, engines, and boilers of the scuttled ship would not only save much time but would reduce the cost by roughly two-thirds. The defective engines and deep draft, however, would render the craft unsuitable for ocean service, although Brooke had been thinking in terms of a seagoing vessel when he drew up his plan.

On June 25 Williamson, Porter, and Brooke submitted a formal report to Secretary Mallory stating that the *Merrimack* could be converted into an effective ironclad mounting ten guns. They estimated the cost of conversion at roughly $110,000, the greater part being allocated for labor. Mallory, accepting the report without waiting for congressional approval, moved swiftly. "Porter was directed to proceed with the constructor's duties. Mr. Williamson was charged with the engineer's department, and to Mr. Brooke were assigned the duties of attending to preparing the iron and forwarding it from the Tredegar Works, the experiments necessary to test the plates and to determine their thickness, and devising heavy rifled ordnance for the ship, with other details per-

[32] Testimony by Brooke before Joint Committee of Congress, 26 Feb. 1863, *Official Records, Navy*, ser. 2, 1:784. A sketch of the problems encountered in preparing the *Virginia* for sea is given in Brooke's letter to [J. W.] Jones, 10 July 1874 (copy), BP.

[33] Testimony of Brooke before Joint Committee of Congress, 26 Feb. 1863, *Official Records, Navy*, ser. 2, 1:784.

taining to ordnance."[34] In his journal Brooke noted laconically: "My plan for a floating battery will be applied to the Merrimac now at Norfolk."

On July 11 Commodore French Forrest, commandant of Gosport Navy Yard, was ordered to begin the conversion of the wooden frigate to armor. Forrest's duties, however, were entirely in the administrative sphere. Before the month was out a contract had been signed by Mallory with the Tredegar Company to supply the armor plates at a rate of 6½ cents per pound. Much of the iron came from railroad tracks that were rolled to the desired thickness; particularly important were the rails General Thomas J. Jackson obtained from stripping the Baltimore and Ohio.[35] Since June 24 Brooke had been attached to the Ordnance Office, though on special service directly under the secretary of the navy. He now obtained a room in the Navy Department "for our secret work" and got busy. On the basis of later estimates Mallory asked Congress for $172,523 for construction of the ironclad, and the sum was appropriated on August 24.

During the long hot summer of 1861, while his official duties crowded upon him, John Brooke had his share of personal problems. First there was Lizzie. John worried about her and wished that she could be with him. He wrote frequently and, whenever he could arrange his work, slipped off to Lexington for a few days to be by Lizzie's side, as when Lucy was born early in July. In Richmond, while searching futilely for a house for his enlarged family, John worried not only about Lizzie but about the new baby as well. The gentle tone of Brooke's letters to his wife during these troublesome days showed that he had come of age emotionally; he had learned to adjust himself to the perplexities of married life and to accept separations philosophically. By now he had lost much of his earlier conceit and impatience, and he would have been among the first to admit his shortcomings. Lizzie, on the other hand, seems to have moved in the opposite direction.

[34] Williamson, Brooke, and Porter to the Secretary of the Navy, 25 June 1861, quoted in Brooke, *The Virginia, or Merrimac; Her Real Projector*, p. 12; Report of Secretary of the Navy Mallory, 29 March 1862, *Official Records, Navy*, ser. 2, 1:175.

[35] Charles B. Dew, *Ironmaker to the Confederacy: Joseph R. Anderson and the Tredegar Iron Works* (New Haven, 1966), pp. 115–16.

Though her health appeared better than it had been a year earlier, her spirits sagged; she had lost the exuberance and good cheer of her early married life. Lizzie now looked at the gloomy side of things and was inclined to be critical. Long separations and poor health had worn her down, and now there was the war. How she hated it! To cheer her up, her husband urged her not to be "uneasy about the war," and he painted the contemporary picture in rosier colors than the situation perhaps warranted. Devotedly he tried to add to his wife's comfort and enjoyment by sending her tea, linen for sheets, peaches, candy, and an occasional book. He was afraid to send her novels for, he reminded her, she had read them all. Religion was still a stumbling block. Though Brooke had not yet been able to develop faith enough to accept the Christian religion in many of its ramifications, he was still trying and on occasion wrote Lizzie that he had been reading "the book."

Brooke's official duties seemed to require that he be everywhere at once: Tredegar in Richmond to push preparation of the iron plates for the *Merrimack;* Jamestown Island to conduct gun tests; Norfolk to consult with Porter and Williamson. In addition, Brooke was appointed to numerous boards and was requested to assist in such ordnance matters as the arrangement of signal books and the invention of projectiles and fuses. The demands whirled in from all sides. In June 1861, for example, Brooke invented for General Lee a shell for smooth bores which he hoped would "go as far and as straight as the best rifle cannon projectiles."[36] Throughout the day and well into the night the inventor worked, week after week, though he tried to avoid working on Sundays. His eyes began to give him trouble and his health so good when he left Washington, was impaired; his weight dropped to 133 pounds, 14 pounds less than when he had returned from Japan and the lowest point in many years.

The variety of Brooke's activities during the summer of 1861, and for that matter during the entire war, is indicated by his journal entries. One day he was arguing with Commander Maury concerning the tactical use of torpedoes, and a few days later he was devising with Secretary Mallory, Captains Hollins and Ingra-

---

[36] Brooke to his wife, 28 June, 23 July 1861, BP.

ham, and a naval constructor "plans to meet the enemy's gun boats on the Mississippi." At the latter conference Brooke proposed the use of ironclads in addition to the "tugs and armed vessels in tow or lashed alongside" suggested by the others. Brooke drew up a plan.[37] Captain Hollins soon left for New Orleans, and within two months contracts were awarded in that city for the construction of the *Louisiana* and the *Mississippi* and at Memphis for the *Arkansas* and the *Tennessee*. Brooke believed the prudent course for the Confederacy was to "build proper vessels superior to those of the enemy," which was in line with Mallory's thinking. He believed that the South enjoyed one advantage: while the North must design vessels for possible sea service, the Confederacy, because of the blockade, needed only to build vessels capable of navigating the rivers and bays of the South. In part this meant reliance in the long run on harbor defense ironclads of light draft that were admittedly unseaworthy.

In the summer and fall of 1861 Brooke performed duties in an entirely unrelated field, when he was appointed to a board to select a uniform for the navy. President Davis designated the color as gray, a color "universally disliked in the navy." "We have made something that certainly will not be objectionable on the ground of display," Brooke wrote of the uniform chosen. The button, which Brooke designed, was much admired. It depicted "a ship under sail seen from the bow, surrounded by stars in arch over sea." In November, Brooke drew up regulations pertaining to the uniform at Mallory's request.[38]

As the *Merrimack*, soon to be the *Virginia*, was being readied for her iron sheathing, matters relating to that vessel took more and more of Brooke's time. On August 12 he was ordered by the secretary "to test the iron plates now being prepared at the Tredegar Works, in the best manner to determine what their powers of resistance to shot and shell will be when placed on the Merrimac according to the plans adopted."[39] Brooke was instructed to report the results as early as practicable. He decided to conduct

---

[37] Brooke's Richmond Journal, 30 July 1861, BP.

[38] Ibid., 27 Nov., 17 Aug., 20 Dec. 1861.

[39] Mallory to Brooke, 12 Aug. 1861, BP.

the tests on isolated Jamestown Island rather than in Richmond where "there would be publicity."

Brooke's fear of premature publicity was justified, for only by a considerable headstart could the South hope to offset the far greater industrial plant of the enemy. As a matter of fact, on August 3, 1861, the United States Congress passed an act directing Secretary of the Navy Welles to appoint a board of officers to study plans for armored warships. The board was appointed on August 8 but did not meet until September 5. It was from just such leisurely action by its opponent that the Confederate navy hoped to gain. After two weeks' deliberation the board, with many plans to choose from, recommended construction of the *Monitor*, the *Galena* and the *New Ironsides* as a start. Union action was not influenced specifically by the Confederacy's frantic efforts to convert the *Merrimack* into an ironclad, but from the belief that every avenue should be explored in fighting what could be a long war.[40]

Another aspect of the press question worried Brooke. Notices in the newspapers led the uninformed to expect more of the *Virginia* than they should, especially after the brilliant victory achieved by the Southern ironclad in its first day of fighting. Such empty hopes could boomerang. Brooke began to question whether the South could tolerate a free press during the emergency.

The first day's experiment at Jamestown, consisting of three shots fired from an eight-inch Columbiad at three hundred yards, was witnessed by half a dozen naval officers, Captain John R. Tucker, commanding the James River Squadron, and Lieutenants Catesby ap Roger Jones, commanding at Jamestown Island, William P. Powell, David McCorkle, James H. Rochelle, Robert D. Minor, and Brooke. Also present was Nelson Tift, a Georgia merchant and friend of Secretary Mallory. Nelson Tift and his brother Asa had just agreed to supervise the construction at New Orleans of the ironclad *Mississippi*. Tests over a three-day period "proved that at three hundred yards a solid 8 inch shot could do

---

[40] Howard P. Nash, Jr., "A Civil War Legend Examined," *American Neptune* 23 (1963): 197–203.

no more than break three one inch wrought iron plates and bruise the wood to the depth of five or six inches—pine."[41] Shell, of course, was even less effective.

Greater strength was nonetheless desirable, for the firing might be at close range and the enemy might employ heavier ordnance than eight-inch Columbiads. So an attempt was made to procure thicker plates. Naturally, Brooke was delighted when the foreman of the rolling mill at Tredegar succeeded in punching bolt holes in two-inch wrought iron plates. Piercing the additional metal, however, required additional ·time and money.[42] Rolling 732 tons of iron plates for the *Virginia* consumed almost the entire attention of the Tredegar rolling mills for six months; the last deliveries were not made until February 12, 1862.[43]

Problems arose frequently that required Brooke's presence in Norfolk. In addition to the substitution of two-inch iron plates for one-inch ones, Brooke recommended five other changes to the constructor, including piercing the shield for bow and quarter ports and increasing the number of hatches from two to four. In November, Brooke began to fear that Porter had placed the center of gravity too high. But when Brooke suggested that the constructor "put six inches of iron on bow and stern," Porter asserted the ship could not carry the additional weight.[44]

The acrimony between Brooke and Porter increased as pressure for completion of the ironclad mounted. The casemate necessitated use of cannon with long barrels, yet, owing to the lack of faith in breechloaders, only muzzle-loaders could be used. Such guns had to be pulled inside the casemate for sponging, which

[41] Brooke's Richmond Journal, 2 Nov. 1861, BP. The results were not noted in Brooke's Journal until two months after they occurred, because Brooke had been too busy to keep up his journal.

[42] Brooke stated that the foreman made the attempt at the risk of breaking the punching machine. Kathleen Bruce in *Virginia Iron Manufacture in the Slave Era* (New York, 1931), p. 355, has asserted, however, that the 2-inch plates were not punched but drilled, and this is the position of Still in *Iron Afloat*, p. 20, and Dew, *Ironmaker to the Confederacy*, pp. 116–17. The answer to this contradiction is probably that in the initial experiment Brooke saw the holes punched, but, subsequently, drilling was resorted to in order to save the machinery.

[43] Dew, *Ironmaker to the Confederacy*, p. 118.

[44] Brooke to Porter, 3 April 1862, in Brooke, *The Virginia, or Merrimac; Her Real Projector*, pp. 14–15.

placed a heavy premium on space. But in construction Porter did not coordinate his plans with the ordnance bureau, with the result that ship and guns did not form an integrated system. It has been suggested that Secretary Mallory made a cardinal error in dividing responsibility between these two proud men instead of giving one of them responsibility for the whole project.[45]

The armor plate was only one of Brooke's problems in regard to the *Virginia*. An ironclad must be able to deliver blows as well as receive them. By order of the secretary of the navy Brooke prepared two 7-inch rifled cannon, the first of the powerful Brooke rifles that became the mainspring of Confederate naval ordnance. Six of these monsters were ordered initially from the Tredegar Iron Works, two for the *Virginia* and the rest "for the Mississippi river boats." Brooke also designed a 6.4-inch rifled cannon (32-pounder), and twelve were ordered from Tredegar, which had made more than twelve hundred cannon before the war. Between September 1861 and March 1862 Tredegar cast fourteen Brooke guns.[46]

In the fall of 1861 Brooke gave more and more thought to ordnance matters. Besides designing guns, he experimented continually with different types of fuses and projectiles. He developed a wrought iron elongated shot to be fired red hot from rifled cannon. Cupped at the base, the projectile had a groove an inch from the rear end to take the rifling in the same manner as lead. This no doubt was an attempt to adjust to the short supply of lead that handicapped the Confederacy. For use against ironclads Brooke designed a flat-headed wrought iron bolt. Such a projectile could literally punch a hole through armor plate. Neither incendiary shells nor flat-headed bolts were original with Brooke. Filling shells with molten iron was a natural outgrowth from the introduction of shells two decades earlier. As for flat-headed bolts, Joseph Whitworth had demonstrated their armor-piercing powers in England in 1858. But the use of unusual types of projectiles and the zest for experiment indicate that Brooke used imagination. In

[45] Wells, *The Confederate Navy: A Study in Organization* (University, Ala., 1971), p. viii; Still, *Iron Afloat*, pp. 18–19.
[46] Dew, *Ironmaker to the Confederacy*, p. 119.

ordnance matters, as with iron plating for the *Virginia*, Brooke received the solid cooperation of Uri Haskins, a British subject, who was foreman of the Tredegar rolling mill.

Gradually Brooke became the clearinghouse for all new ideas pertaining to naval ordnance. As Mallory leaned ever more heavily on his judgment in these matters, the two were in frequent consultation. In his journal on November 3, 1861, Brooke noted that Mallory "proposes to establish an experimental Dept of Ordnance." Such work, clearly differentiated from routine administrative tasks, needed an energetic, guiding hand. Brooke was the secretary's choice. Promptly, Secretary Mallory issued the following sweeping order: "Lieut John M. Brooke detailed for duty under the officer in charge of Ordnance in this Department is required to take special Charge of the examination of all propositions for the improvements of Ordnance, Ordnance stores, submarine batteries, hydrographic information, and all matters in the armament and equipment of vessels."[47] The order meant that Brooke, while continuing to design ordnance material himself, would evaluate all proposals suggested by others. It was quite a display of confidence in the thirty-four-year-old officer, who before the outbreak of the war had never had any particular experience in ordnance work. The order formalized a condition which had evolved in the crucible of war. The chief of the Bureau of Ordnance and Hydrography at this time was Commander George Minor, and, of course, Brooke's correspondence technically passed over his desk.

That Brooke's power had not been circumscribed was soon apparent. On November 5 Brooke sent to the secretary, through Minor, a suggestion that uniformity be established in the forms and dimensions of shells and in the rifling of cannon. He proposed that this change be effected by issuing a circular directed to all parties engaged in the manufacture of naval ordnance. As Brooke noted in his journal, "Capt. Minor forwarded it [Brooke's recommendation] with a letter of his own suggesting that the present plan which is no plan at all should be adhered to. I stated verbally to the Secretary that there was no plan but that each contractor

[47] Order of Secretary of the Navy Mallory, 4 Nov. 1861 (copy), and Brooke's Richmond Journal, 4 Nov. 1861, BP.

was following his own notions and he then wrote a circular letter as I desired."[48]

On November 6 Brooke recommended to Secretary Mallory that a complete record and register be kept of all guns cast or procured for the navy. He also began to assemble data when any gun burst, so that the cause could be analyzed and proper safeguards be enforced.

On Brooke's recommendation Mallory appointed Catesby Jones first lieutenant and executive officer of the *Virginia* and ordered him to ready the ironclad's armament. The first 7-inch Brooke rifle cast at the Tredegar Works was started for Norfolk by railroad on November 12, but there were aggravating delays.[49]

While Jones made preliminary arrangements for a crew, Mallory gave thought to the other officers for the warship. Brooke requested that a place be saved for him. When Mallory commented that it would be difficult to spare Brooke from the department, the latter answered that "one who remained out of the field went to leeward." Brooke yearned for a crack at the Yankees and feared, moreover, that if he did not go, some people might think that he lacked confidence in the ship he had done so much to build. Finally, Mallory agreed that when Brooke had made arrangements at the office he could join the ship, but he expressed the opinion that the officers and men should "be thrown together and be exercised at the guns preparatory to going in the ship." This was reasonable. But as the ship was not expected to be ready for three months, Brooke was put on the spot. Could he afford to drop his ordnance work in midstream and spend several weeks or months training on the *Virginia?* "Now this will interfere with the prosecution of my ordnance work very materially," he wrote. "I propose to perfect as rapidly as possible our ordnance for the whole navy and I do not now see clearly how I am to manage."[50] It seemed that Mallory, quite properly was giving Brooke a choice—solid service in the Ordnance Office or a chance at glory

[48] Brooke's Richmond Journal, 5 Nov. 1861, BP.

[49] Ibid., 6 Nov., 20 Nov. 1861. The failures to deliver the goods were frequent and Jones expressed his dissatisfaction to Brooke; see Jones to Brooke, 25 Nov., 23 Dec., 29 Dec. 1861, BP.

[50] Brooke's Richmond Journal, 20 Nov. 1861, BP.

in the *Virginia*. But Brooke wanted both assignments, not one at the cost of the other. He played for time, hoping that by feverish activity he could get far enough ahead in his work to justify going on the ship.

In 1861 many officers in the navy had little faith in ironclads and chose to rely on small, shallow-draft, wooden steamers carrying one or two guns. Matthew Fontaine Maury urged that a hundred such vessels be built to drive away the blockading ships. To rally support he asked Brooke to attend a meeting of the Virginia Convention and express his views on the subject. Brooke complied and gave his opinion "that such a force would be the only one to effect the object."[51] For protection against heavy guns it was desirable to have three inches of iron, but the amount of armor that could be carried depended upon the size of the vessel. Beneath a certain point, the utility of iron diminished. Besides, with the difficulty Brooke had encountered in getting iron plate, it appeared that a fleet of small wooden gunboats could be constructed much more rapidly than could a fleet of ironclads.

Mallory soon called a meeting of the department to select the model and armament for the small wooden gunboats. Present, besides Mallory, were Maury, whom Brooke called the "originator of the gun boat on a large scale," Captain Franklin Buchanan, Commander George Minor, Lieutenant Joseph N. Barney, Engineer Thomas A. Jackson, Constructor Porter, and Brooke. The model adopted was a propeller-driven gunboat 106 feet long with a draft of six feet. The armament consisted of one 9-inch Dahlgren smoothbore and one 6.4 rifle. The 9-inch gun was included only at Brooke's insistence; most of the other officers would have been content with an 8-inch weapon. At all times Brooke demanded for the Confederate navy the maximum fire power feasible. To speed the program Congress, to whom the Virginia Convention had referred the matter, appropriated $2,000,000. Maury offered Brooke the command of a gunboat division, but the latter declined on the ground that he hoped to ship in the *Virginia*.[52]

From the time Catesby Jones was appointed first lieutenant

[51] Ibid., 21 Nov. 1861.
[52] Ibid., 14 Dec., 21 Dec. 1861.

and ordnance officer of the *Virginia* in November 1861, he corresponded regularly with Brooke. At the Norfolk Navy Yard, Jones fought vigorously, in the face of many exasperations, to get the ironclad ready for combat with the least possible delay. By Christmas 1861 only a small part of the starboard side of the casemate was sheathed and none of the stern. With good reason Jones was disturbed, for, according to his information, the North expected "to have their iron clad ships in January." Brooke, in Richmond, did all he could to expedite the iron plates and ordnance on their way.

Jones, who had assisted with gun experiments at the Washington Navy Yard in the fifties, conducted extensive tests for the new gun and trained the crew. His gun tests at Craney Island and elsewhere with the rifled guns and shells for the *Virginia* were particularly important because, owing to the shortage of powder, the Ordnance Office had been able to conduct "no experiments of value" with rifled cannon. The experiments with the *Virginia*'s guns also supplied Brooke with information of a more general nature. Brooke was adding to his knowledge of ballistics by requiring naval officers to complete blank forms for all practice rounds fired from rifled cannon under their command. With the information thus gathered, Brooke projected graphically the times of flight and ranges for solid shot and shells. The original plan was soon expanded to include guns of many calibers—smoothbores as well as rifles—for Brooke discovered that J. A. B. Dahlgren's highly regarded range tables did not include elevations greater than six degrees, " a great omission." Jones helped here, too, writing Brooke detailed reports of his experiments with the 9-inch smoothbores as well as with the 6.4-inch and 7-inch rifles.[53]

On December 20, 1861, Brooke noted that Captain Franklin Buchanan, a Marylander, had "gone to Norfolk to see the Merrimac which vessel he is to command." Brooke, who had attended Annapolis while Buchanan was superintendent, had as much confidence in him as "in any of the older officers." Jones, however, was disappointed that he had not obtained the command himself.

[53] Ibid., 27 Nov., 25 Dec. 1861.

"Old Buch" was given a free hand in the selection of his officers and chose able men.

On January 5, 1862, Jones informed Brooke that the first enlisted men had arrived for the *Virginia*. They were army men from General John Bankhead Magruder's command. Jones had hoped to procure fifty or sixty seamen from the Peninsula, but he had been able to get only nine. The delays continued, and indeed, time was running out even faster than Jones knew. Six days after the armor on the *Virginia* was completed, the *Monitor* was launched at the shipyard of Thomas Rowland on Long Island. Still the work dragged on in Norfolk. Jones wrote on February 5, 1862, a full week after the *Monitor* was launched, that "the want of interest and energy in completing the Merrimac is disheartening."[54] Northern ironclads were expected at Hampton Roads any day.

The work of preparing the *Virginia* for sea devolved upon Jones. Buchanan had made a brief appearance and then gone away for a protracted period. "Her Captain should be here and so I wrote him a month ago," Jones exclaimed. "Until he was ordered [to the command] I was listened to, but of course that cannot be now."[55] There was another matter of concern. Word was spreading that the constructor had made a mistake in calculating the center of gravity of the vessel. It was apparently a confirmation of Brooke's earlier suspicion. There was, however, one bright ray in the sky. After considerable difficulty the 7-inch Brooke rifle was mounted on a temporary carriage and in February 1862 was tested with shells run in through the blockade. Using a maximum charge of twelve pounds, the big gun had thrown, according to estimates, a one-hundred-pound shell four and one-half miles. All observers "were much pleased" at the gun's performance.[56] Though the shells made at Tredegar had not arrived, Jones was able to test

[54] Jones to Brooke, 5 Feb. 1862, BP.

[55] Ibid. Buchanan was not absent from Norfolk through choice; he "was detained in Richmond in charge of an important bureau, from which he was relieved a few days before the fight" (Catesby ap R. Jones, "Services of the 'Virginia' (Merrimac)," *Southern Historical Society Papers* 11 [1883]: 67).

[56] Fred Volck, Navy Department, to Brooke, 10 Feb. 1862, BP.

some shells manufactured at the Norfolk Navy Yard. Transportation was so undependable that the executive officer suggested sending the Tredegar shells as soon as they were ready—say fifty at a time.

Brooke noted in his journal on February 13, 1862, that the *Virginia* when floated in dock drew less water than anticipated. In order to lower the eaves of the casemate and the ends of the vessel to two feet below the surface according to Brooke's plan, the draft would have to be correspondingly increased, a serious handicap. This condition was all the more surprising because four inches rather than three inches of iron had been put on the shield. With the supposedly submerged ends awash, Jones wanted more than one inch of iron on the vulnerable hull.

In the end sickness in Brooke's family kept him from joining the *Virginia*. On February 16 he noted in his journal: "Yesterday Mr. Mallory sent for me and after asking me as to the condition of my family who are all sick, said he thought I could not go in the Merrimac that he wished to send her out in a day or two. . . . I said I wished to go if possible he said he knew that but that under the circumstances he did not see how I could go. I told him if he thought it right I would stay. He said he did think so most decidedly."

The C.S.S. *Virginia* was put in commission on February 17, 1862. Out of the dock the ironclad, even with most of her stores and ordnance aboard, still floated too high in the water; the eaves of the casemate were a foot above the surface instead of well below as the plan specified. It was obvious that Porter had blundered; he either should have cut away more of the old wooden hull at the beginning or should have added more iron to the ends as Brooke had recommended. Even with the addition of stores and a large quantity of ballast, Jones anticipated trouble in lowering the ship the amount necessary to meet the specifications—a full three feet. At this late date Buchanan was still not present and Jones had great difficulty in getting anything out of the ordinary done. The *Virginia* needed fifty men to complete her crew.

When Captain Buchanan finally took command of the ship on February 25, 1862, he "found the ship by no means ready for service." Jones complained bitterly to Brooke that "the water is now just above the eaves, we have yet to take [on] our powder, and most of the shell, and 150 tons of coal which it is thought will bring it down a foot more—I should feel much better satisfied if the hull had six inches of iron where it now has now but one, tis our most vulnerable part, and unfortunately for us, where a shell can easily penetrate."[57] Jones referred to the one-inch belt of iron extending three feet below the eaves and stretching from stem to stern. At this late date the ironclad lacked 18,200 pounds of powder for her battery. Moreover, the small howitzers suggested by Brooke to repel boats and boarders had not been mounted on the upper deck and none of the port shutters had been fitted on the ship.[58] When the powder finally arrived, Buchanan laid plans to challenge the Federals around March 7. Once the iron plate and guns had been received in Norfolk there was not a great deal Brooke could do to speed the *Virginia* on her way, except to rush the port shutters, powder, and shells for the 7-inch Brooke rifles. While retaining, of course, a keen interest in everything that concerned the vessel, his active mind turned to other things.

Aware that the James River could serve as an avenue of approach to Richmond, Brooke suggested that the army keep a battery of field artillery stationed at the lower end of Jamestown Island to prevent the enemy from landing there.[59] Once more he urged that a strong battery of four heavy guns be posted at Kennon's on the James, as he had been suggesting since the state board had reported to General Lee the preceding spring. And to guard against ironclads, Brooke recommended that heavy rifled cannon be used.

Meanwhile Franklin Buchanan had been promoted to flag officer and placed in command of the naval defenses of James River.[60] In addition to the *Virginia* and the gunboats *Beaufort* and *Raleigh* at Norfolk, Buchanan could count on the assistance of the James River Squadron, consisting of the *Patrick Henry*, the *James-*

[57] Jones to Brooke, 25 Feb. 1862, BP.

[58] Buchanan to Gen. John B. Magruder, 2 March 1862, Franklin Buchanan Letter Book, 1862–63, Southern Historical Collection, University of North Carolina, Chapel Hill (hereafter cited as UNC).

[59] Brooke's Richmond Journal, 27 Feb. 1862, BP.

[60] No one was appointed captain of the *Virginia* when Buchanan was elevated to flag officer, so he doubled as captain with Jones, the executive officer, second in command.

town, and the *Teazer*. Writing to General Magruder on Sunday, March 2, he stated his intentions to be off Newport News at the end of the week. Buchanan planned to strike first at the great wooden sailing ships anchored there and then to turn on the shore batteries.

When the big Confederate ironclad moved down the Elizabeth River on the morning of March 8, 1862, to give battle, she was a strange-looking vessel. On her, the product of the labor of fifteen hundred men over a period of six months, rode the hopes of the South. Formidable in appearance, she was withal a huge question mark. The submerged hull was 275 feet long. Astride its central portion was the great shield, or casemate, 160 feet in length, with the sides placed at an angle of thirty-six degrees from the horizontal. These sides were constructed of twenty-four inches of pine and oak backing to which were bolted four inches of iron. The ends of the casemate were rounded, the more readily to deflect projectiles; the top of the casemate was about eight feet wide and was protected by iron grating. Time had prevented the construction of a superstructure on the ends of the vessel, so that in still water nothing was visible to the eye except the casemate. The *Virginia* was armed with a submerged cast-iron ram or beak of wedge shape which was poorly secured. This ram was about three feet in length and weighed fifteen hundred pounds. In view of the shortage of ammunition, Mallory hoped particularly that Buchanan would use it. Neither the rudder nor propeller of the ironclad was adequately protected.

The vessel's excessive draft of over twenty-two feet and her weak, cranky engines made her difficult to maneuver. The *Virginia* could make but five knots, and it took from thirty to forty minutes to turn her around. The ten-gun battery consisted of two single-banded 7-inch Brooke rifles, two single-banded 6.4-inch Brooke rifles, and six 9-inch Dahlgren smoothbores; the 7-inch rifles were placed at the bow and stern ports, the others in broadside. The ship was supplied with shells for all of the guns, but, owing to delays in manufacture and transportation, she carried solid shot for the smoothbores only. The crew, numbering 320, was "very green"; hence Jones based hopes for success on the "intelligence of the officers." A lieutenant or midshipman was placed at each gun, for the crew had had but little drill at them. Strong and ugly as the *Virginia* was, she was extremely vulnerable between wind and water as a result of the constructor's serious mistake in calculating the center of gravity.[61]

Shortly before noon on March 8, 1862, the *Virginia*, attended by the gunboats *Raleigh* and *Beaufort*, moved in on the enemy. The *Virginia* and her consorts destroyed the *Cumberland* and the *Congress* that day; then came the dramatic arrival of the *Monitor* and the first battle of ironclads the next day, ending in a draw.[62] There were many "ifs" in the second encounter. For one thing, there is no doubt, in light of what happened later in the war, that if the *Virginia* had been supplied with wrought iron bolts for her 7-inch rifles she could have pierced the eight-inch turret of the *Monitor*. That the bolts were not ready on time was owing to the tremendous pressure on the Ordnance Office to supply all parts of the Confederacy with ammunition.

[61] The best description of the *Virginia* as she went forth to battle is Catesby ap R. Jones, "The First Confederate Iron-clad 'the Virginia,' formerly the United States Steam Frigate 'Merrimac,' " *Southern Magazine* 15 (Dec. 1874): 200–202. The account is clear and concise; and though written 12 years after the battles of Hampton Roads it is accurate in so far as statements can be checked against contemporary documents. Jones corresponded with Brooke while preparing the article. Accounts written more than 26 years after the battles that ignore or misrepresent errors in construction are Porter, "Plan and Construction of the 'Merrimac,' " pp. 716–17, and John W. H. Porter, *A Record of Events in Norfolk County, Virginia, from April 19th, 1861, to May 10th, 1862* (Portsmouth, Va., 1892), pp. 327–57. The Porter articles do not agree in many places with the Brooke Papers. They are undocumented and appear to be based on memory or, in the case of the younger Porter, on secondhand information.

[62] The official Southern version of the battles is given in the account rendered by Flag Officer Buchanan to Secretary Mallory on 27 March 1862, from the naval hospital (Adm. Franklin Buchanan Papers, Southern Hist. Coll., UNC). Wounded in the first day's battle, Buchanan was not present for the battle against the *Monitor* and so depended upon the report of Acting Commander Catesby Jones. A personal account of the first day's fighting by the flag lieutenant of the squadron is Robert D. Minor to Brooke, 11 March 1862, BP. Like Buchanan, Minor was wounded the first day and missed the battle with the *Monitor*. Catesby Jones, executive officer of the *Virginia*, who fought her against the *Monitor*, wrote an account 12 years after the event, "Services of the 'Virginia' (Merrimac)," pp. 65–75. Another account written by a participant 20 years afterward is William Harwar Parker, *Recollections of a Naval Officer* (New York, 1883), pp. 251–72. An eyewitness account by a spectator on shore is James B. Jones, Camp Arrington, Va., to Mrs. Bettie Hayes, 10 March 1862, Mrs. T. Boyd Massenburg Papers, 1862–70, Southern Hist. Coll., UNC. A clear and concise analysis is given in Baxter, *Introduction of the Ironclad Warship*, pp. 285–301.

Something good came to the Confederacy out of this apparent misfortune. The North, jumping to the conclusion that the *Monitor* could resist the Confederacy's heaviest blows, accelerated production of an ironclad that was already out of date; maneuvers after the war would show "the monitors' low freeboard, light draft, and lack of power reduced to zero their efficiency at sea."[63] On the other hand, it was sheer good fortune that the enemy did not strike the *Virginia* in her vital zone near the waterline. The South was lucky, too, that the 11-inch Dahlgrens on the *Monitor* were fired with a fifteen-pound charge, the maximum charge deemed to be safe by Federal ordnance experts. Later it was found that a charge of thirty pounds could be used with some safety. The apparent superiority of armor over ordnance was, therefore, misleading.

The battles in Hampton Roads did not revolutionize naval warfare as many have proclaimed. At the time of this duel of ironclads, England had sixteen ironclads built, building, or authorized. The French were even further along and did not build a wooden ship of the line after 1855. But the battle between the *Virginia* and the *Monitor* was the first battle between ironclads and one of the first between steam warships. As such, it focused attention on the giant strides that had been made in naval architecture over the past few years, and with a rush brought the man in the street up-to-date. To both the Confederacy and the Union the fight revealed the imperative necessity of building armored warships, and it made clear how outmoded such weapons as Maury's wooden gunboats really were. An officer writing to Brooke on March 11, two days after the battle with the *Monitor*, analyzed the situation clearly: "As to the wooden gun boats we are building, they are not worth a cent."[64]

In a long letter to Brooke in which he described the first day's action, the wounded Bob Minor, the flag lieutenant, wrote: "You richly deserve the gratitude and thanks of the Confederacy for the plan, of the now celebrated 'Virginia', and I only wish that you

[63] Walter R. Herrick, Jr., *The American Naval Revolution* (Baton Rouge, La., 1966), p. 9. See Brooke's Report on his system of rifled guns, 8 Jan. 1863, Civil War Ordnance, Records of the Bureau of Ordnance, RG 74, NA.

[64] George T. Sinclair to Brooke, 11 March 1862, BP.

could have been with us to have witnessed the successful operations of this new engine of Naval warfare, fostered by your care and watched over by your inventive mind."[65] With prescience, Minor went on to warn that "there will doubtless be an attempt made to transfer the great credit of *planning* the 'Virginia' to other hands than your own, so look out for to you it belongs, and the secty should say so in communicating his report of the victory to Congress." Minor's premonition was right. On March 20, several newspapers published articles giving credit to John L. Porter.[66] When Secretary Mallory gave full credit to Brooke in his report to the House of Representatives and the report was published in the Richmond *Examiner* on March 29, Brooke hoped the matter was settled. But five days later Porter published a letter in the *Examiner* claiming credit. Brooke's response was to apply for a patent on his design for ironclad warships based upon the unique feature of his plan that had been applied to the *Virginia:* the submerged ends of the vessel, extending beyond the forward and after ends of the shield. Patent 100 was granted to Brooke by the Confederate Patent Office on July 29, 1862.[67] This should have ended the matter. But in 1887 the question was resurrected when Thomas Scharf published a book on the Confederate navy awarding the honor to Porter.[68] Brooke would fight back.

After the battle with the *Monitor*, the *Virginia* lay at the Norfolk Navy Yard undergoing repairs, though she had emerged from her battles with comparatively little damage. The damaged parts were repaired and iron port shutters were added for further protection. The original cast-iron ram had been too long and was replaced by a new one of steel and wrought iron two feet in length. The new ram was made square rather than pointed at Brooke's suggestion. The Brooke rifles were supplied with chilled wrought iron bolts designed for piercing armor. The vulnerable waterline

[65] Minor to Brooke, 11 March 1862, BP.

[66] An early letter of Porter's was published in the Charleston *Mercury* on 19 March 1862. It was Brooke's belief that Porter "first wrote a friend making a most extravagant claim in regard to what he had done" in designing the *Virginia* and the friend had had the letter published (Brooke to Joseph A. Yates, 1 Aug. 1887 [copy], BP).

[67] The original patent is in the possession of the author.

[68] J. Thomas Scharf, *History of the Confederate States Navy from Its Organization to the Surrender of Its Last Vessel* (New York, 1887), pp. 145–51.

of the *Virginia* was reinforced by increasing the armor below the eaves of the casemate from one inch in thickness to three. This additional iron lowered the vessel another foot so that her draft was increased to twenty-three feet. Brooke, as earlier, played a vital role. He pushed through the preparation of iron plates at Tredegar, and he tested his wrought iron bolts for 6.4- and 7-inch rifles, got them into production, and shipped them to Norfolk. He had other duties as well, for at this time the threat to New Orleans was growing and Brooke was pressed to send 7-inch rifles for the ironclads *Mississippi* and *Louisiana*, which were being constructed at the Louisiana city under private contract.[69]

[69] Catesby ap R. Jones, "The First Confederate Iron-clad 'the Virginia,' " p. 206; Brooke's Richmond Journal, 11 March, 13 March, 14 March, 15 March, 21 March, 28 March 1862, BP.

IX /

PRACTICAL AND

THEORETICAL

CONTRIBUTIONS TO

CONFEDERATE ORDNANCE

THE Battle of Hampton Roads led to a reconsideration of Maury's plan for wooden gunboats. In January when Maury had informed Brooke that he had asked Mallory to reconsider "the gunboat model adopted" and to substitute 8-inch guns for 9-inch guns, Brooke's attitude had hardened. A few days before the battle, Brooke queried his cousin Muscoe Garnett of the Ways and Means Committee about an appropriation for armor-plated gunboats to be used in river and harbor defense, and he urged upon Mallory the importance of such light-draft vessels. Though small ironclad gunboats could not resist heavy shot, they could repel shell to which wooden vessels were vulnerable. No action was taken until after the great battle. Then Mallory asked Brooke "to make the computations of weight etc. for small gun boats iron clad." The same day the House of Representatives urged the navy to build with minimum delay as many small ironclad rams as possible, and it authorized President Davis to suspend construction of the wooden gunboats. Brooke and Mallory promptly "devised a plan of iron clad gun boats to substitute for the wooden gun boats." Having lost the fight, Maury soon left for England on a quasi-diplomatic mission. By May 1 steps had been taken to add "at least twelve new ironclads" to the fleet, and beginning in the spring of 1862 four out of every five warships built in the Confederacy were armored.[1]

During March and April 1862 the *Virginia*, now commanded by Flag Officer Josiah Tattnall, held the center of the stage. The intense fear and excitement aroused in the North by the initial appearance of the ironclad is well known; Gideon Welles, secretary of the navy, pictured it well in his diary. Secretary of War Edwin M. Stanton and other excitable Northern leaders gave free rein to the most absurd fears, believing that the Confederate ironclad would lay waste to New York, Washington, and other cities. They resolved, therefore, to contain the *Virginia* in Hampton Roads by strongly reinforcing the Federal squadron off Fort Monroe. Under no circumstances did the authorities in Washington wish the *Monitor* to accept the gage of battle from the *Virginia* for single-handed combat in deep water where the *Virginia* could navigate. But Northern fears were not well founded. The improvised Confederate warship had been considered unseaworthy by her builders from the beginning. She was made and fit for harbor defense only. The *Virginia* could not even be taken up Chesapeake Bay without so lightening her that she would be hopelessly exposed below the waterline. It may be doubted, therefore, that the Union fleet actually neutralized the *Virginia* as many have stated. It is on the basis of this assumption that some claim the North really won at Hampton Roads. As a matter of fact, the reinforcement of the squadron in Hampton Roads deprived the Union navy of vessels that could have been used elsewhere.

Meanwhile, General George B. McClellan, inching up the peninsula between the James and the York, besieged Yorktown on

[1] Brooke's Richmond Journal, 17 March, 20 March 1862, BP; Still, *Iron Afloat*, pp. 84, 144.

April 5. During the next five weeks, the Federal army was embarrassed by the *Virginia* and the small ships of the James River Squadron, for they denied to the Federals naval support on James River. This in turn precluded the use of troop transportation on that river. The mere presence of the *Virginia* impelled McClellan to modify his plan of simultaneous advances up the York and the James. Moreover, Commodore L. M. Goldsborough, commanding the blockading squadron, advised McClellan on April 2 that he could not give naval aid in the attack on Yorktown—he had to defend Fort Monroe. Thus by pinning down the Federal warships, the *Virginia* quite effectively disrupted McClellan's carefully laid plans.

On April 7 a vastly more powerful *Virginia* was released from the repair dock and readied for combat. It was Brooke's hope that the strengthened ironclad would destroy McClellan's transports and supplies being marshaled for the push up the peninsula. On April 11, and later, the *Virginia* and her wooden consorts challenged the reinforced Federal fleet huddled beneath the guns of Fort Monroe, but the Federals declined the challenge.

The capture of Fort Monroe was a matter of supreme importance in checkmating Federal gains on the peninsula, and Brooke prepared a comprehensive plan for the attack of that fort by ironclads to be built at Norfolk and along the James. This plan he "made known" to the defense board on April 8. Secretary Mallory, impressed with it, by May 1 had initiated construction of the proposed iron-plated vessels. Brooke also kept in touch with Acting Master W. G. Cheeney at Norfolk, who planned to destroy the *Monitor* with a submarine built at Tredegar. Unfavorable weather delayed the attack, and it was never made.[2]

On May 4 Brooke heard "with astonishment" that orders had been given to evacuate Norfolk. Eight days later he was dumbfounded to hear that the *Virginia* had been scuttled by her crew. He observed sourly that if the Confederacy were in danger it resulted from "execrable management not on the part of execu-

[2] Brooke's Richmond Journal, 8 April 1862, and Cheeney to Brooke, 2 May 1862, BP. Over a 2-week period Cheeney had made "several trials" with his little cast-iron cigar-shaped boat but "an easterly wind constantly prevailing" which made the water rough interfered with his plans.

tives but on the part of directors who act without concern." The loss of the *Virginia* was felt keenly throughout the South. Even Secretary Mallory confided to his diary that the destruction of the ship was "premature." Nonetheless, Flag Officer Tattnall, the commander of the scuttled ship, was acquitted by the court martial that he requested. Before the court finished its deliberations Brooke had heard enough to convince him that his friend had "acted properly under the circumstances." Tattnall had followed the only sensible course open to him. As it was, he saved his men, who were used at once by Catesby Jones to man the naval guns at Drewry's Bluff. There, the *Virginia*'s sailors helped significantly to repel the Federal fleet threatening Richmond.

No more ships with submerged ends were constructed by the Confederacy, because of the emphasis on smaller ironclads for harbor defense. But Brooke's principle was adopted by the British navy for the powerful battleship *Inflexible*, completed in 1881. That same year, Admiral David Dixon Porter called the monitors, still used by the United States Navy, as "simply useless" for naval operations in the open sea.[3]

With the destruction of the *Virginia*, the *Monitor* and other ships off Fort Monroe were ordered up James River to reinforce the small Federal squadron that had slipped into that river a few days earlier. The Confederate navy worked feverishly to complete the defenses. But as late as May 10 Brooke groaned that there were but three batteries guarding the river and the channel obstructions were incomplete. From Richmond he sent out shot and shell and iron shields for the battery at Drewry's Bluff, eight miles below the city, and for other batteries. Such efforts saved the day, for Brooke's old friend John Rodgers, in command of the attacking squadron, found it impossible to pass the bluff without strong support from the army and fell back on City Point after a four-hour battle. At City Point, Rodgers contented himself with keeping the upper James and Chickahominy under observation until the beginning of the Seven Days Battles. By May 27 the number of heavy guns on the James had grown from four to fourteen.

[3] Sprout, *Rise of American Naval Power*, p. 172. The *Monitor* went down in a heavy sea off Cape Hatteras in December 1862.

The successful defense of Richmond in the spring of 1862, however, laid bare antagonisms between the Confederate army and the navy. Morale in the latter service was at a low ebb. Brooke observed that "the officers of the navy are very much dissatisfied, the army steps in to take all the batteries etc. after the Naval Officers get them into condition."[4] But there were examples of cooperation, such as when General Robert E. Lee on June 5, 1862, wrote Commander George Minor, naval chief of ordnance, asking the navy's help in constructing a railroad battery. The job was given to Brooke, and he designed a battery consisting of a rifled and banded 32-pounder mounted on a flatcar with two-inch iron plates covering its sloping sides and roof, to be hauled by a locomotive. This railroad battery, which appears to have been the first in history, was tested in battle at Savages Station on June 29 and was judged by Lieutenant Samuel E. Barry who commanded it to be a complete success.[5]

For Brooke the spring and summer of 1862, following the destruction of the *Virginia*, were months of discouragement. And for a time in the summer of 1862 he began to doubt that he had followed a sensible course in resigning from the old service; he complained to Lizzie that he had "sacrificed everything and gained nothing by the change." A basic gripe among ambitious young officers was the preponderant influence seemingly exerted by the older officers. Linked with this complaint was the absence of promotion as a reward for even the most conspicuous service. It has been said that the surplus officers in the senior grades were a "most annoying problem" for Secretary Mallory. Coupled with it was the system of tying promotion to seniority. In May 1862 Brooke confided to his journal that "the Navy is being ruined by the Seniority System. The officers—effective ones—are all very much dissatisfied, but keep quiet in consequence of the approach

---

[4] Brooke's Richmond Journal, 21 May 1862, BP.

[5] Dew, *Ironmaker to the Confederacy*, p. 183; Barry to Brooke, 7 July 1862, BP. On 4 Oct. 1883, Lt. Cmdr. Charles M. Thomas, secretary of the U.S. Naval Institute, wrote Brooke: "I believe your armored train was the first known to history and I want it to be seen that the English attempt in Egypt was a copy of an American idea." Thomas had asked Brooke to prepare a description of his railroad battery which Thomas proposed to use in an article he hoped to publish in the *United States Naval Institute Proceedings*. See also Dew, *Ironmaker to the Confederacy*, p. 183.

of the enemy."[6] Some weeks later, in July, Brooke remarked that the Confederate navy was more cluttered with deadwood in the upper echelons than the old navy had been before the retiring board acted in 1855. Despite Mallory's personal acts of kindness Brooke was disgusted with the "system of making no promotions and filling all the positions which require information and activity with men according to their age, leaving to the younger officers the task of mending bad work."

In the spring of 1862 Brooke transferred his principal interest from ironclads to ordnance. From the time he designed his 7-inch rifled cannon he had been keenly aware of the value of solid shot against ironclads, and his journal contains several references to that fact. A month before the battle with the *Monitor* Brooke wrote: "I shall try in a day or two solid wrought iron shot red hot from rifled gun. I propose it to meet the enemys iron clad vessels." But it had been physically impossible to supply solid shot in time. As Brooke explained in a comprehensive report to Secretary Mallory, it had been believed initially "that wooden vessels only, would be encountered by the 'Virginia,' and the various foundries and workshops were so fully occupied in meeting other pressing demands, that shells and round shot alone, the latter for her smooth bores, were supplied."[7] Against wooden vessels shells were far more destructive than solid shot. The futile battle with the *Monitor*, however, put emphasis upon solid shot. On March 10, 1862, Brooke noted that he was having wrought iron solid shot made for the *Virginia*'s rifles "to be used on the Erickson" in Hampton Roads. On March 11 he conducted experiments at Tredegar with an elongated punch headed projectile fired from a rifled gun at an oak target eighteen inches thick faced with four inches of iron. The projectile, or bolt, pierced the iron and lodged in the oak backing.[8] Brooke also experimented with his red-hot shot. In spite of all efforts, however, work was slow, and by March 28 only about twenty bolts had been shipped to Norfolk.

In concentrating upon ordnance problems Brooke was making

[6] Wells, *Confederate Navy*, p. 28; Brooke's Richmond Journal, 21 May 1862, BP.

[7] Brooke's Report on his system of rifled guns, 8 Jan. 1863, Civil War Ordnance, Records of the Bureau of Ordnance, RG 74, NA.

[8] Brooke's Richmond Journal, 11 March 1862, BP.

his own a field in which revolutionary changes were occurring. Though the Confederate Office of Ordnance and Hydrography utilized standard smoothbores and shell against the numerous wooden vessels in the Union navy, Brooke when designing weapons to meet ironclads placed principal emphasis upon new techniques such as rifling, reinforcement of the barrel, and armor-piercing projectiles. Because the South had to improvise, it of course did not rely entirely upon ordnance it could produce itself. Every effort was made to import Blakelys, Armstrongs, and Whitworths from England, and to capture Federal cannon. The multiplication of ordnance types complicated distribution of ammunition and dissemination of detailed information. Furthermore, because the South was on the defensive as a result of the Federal blockade, the lines of responsibility between the army and navy were not always clearly defined. Brooke guns, therefore, although designed for naval combat, were used of necessity by both services to protect rivers and harbors.

On January 8, 1863, Brooke submitted to the secretary of the navy a detailed report describing what the Confederacy had done in the field of naval ordnance, with particular emphasis upon rifled cannon.[9] The report demonstrates with clarity that ordnance experiments were not conducted on a random or haphazard basis. Brooke had studied thoroughly all the available literature on the subject in English and some in French, gathered for him by Confederate agents in Europe. Further, Brooke revealed that he had a comprehensive knowledge of the work done before the war by American ordnance experts and some information about developments in the North during the course of the conflict.

During the first two years of the war the Naval Ordnance Office had to rely upon the Tredegar Iron Works for the fabrication of heavy guns. It was Brooke's good fortune that the company was headed by Joseph Reid Anderson, a West Point graduate with whom he worked easily. The relationship with Tredegar was a happy one, and Brooke noted that he "always found the directors and employees of the Tredegar Works apparently anxious to obtain the best results; they impart such information as can only be

[9] Brooke's Report on his system of rifled guns, 8 Jan. 1863, Records of the Bureau of Ordnance, RG 74, NA.

obtained from the practical mechanic. I have not hesitated to avail myself of their experience."[10] Though a few other companies tried to manufacture guns, they failed to meet Brooke's stringent specifications. Late in 1863, however, the ordnance plant at Selma, Alabama, administered by the able Catesby Jones, began to produce naval guns that supplemented those made at Tredegar, thereby lessening the dependence upon a single firm close to enemy lines. Jones and Brooke shared mutual respect and cooperated closely.

For the Confederacy, Brooke designed 6.4-inch, 7-inch, and 8-inch rifles, and also 10-inch and 11-inch smoothbores. The 6.4-inch rifle, weighing 9,000 pounds and envisioned for broadside use, was designed in October 1861. The same month Brooke invented the larger 7-inch rifle, weighing 15,000 pounds, which was intended for the pivots.[11] The North was busy, too, although before the war the emphasis in the United States army and navy had been on smoothbores. By December 1860 John Dahlgren had completed designs for three calibers of rifled cannon. Also, Robert Parker Parrott had experimented with rifled cannon and at the time of the secession crisis he began to produce 20-pounders and 30-pounders that were bought by various state governments. Soon Parrott was casting 8- and 10-inch rifled guns.[12]

Like most guns of that day Brooke's guns were made of cast iron, but they were strengthened by a layer of wrought iron bands shrunk on the barrel between the trunnions and the breech. This technique permitted the use of heavier charges, thereby augmenting range and muzzle velocity. The bands were expanded by heating so they could slip over the breech, but when cooled they shrank, reinforcing the gun where it was weakest. The first Brooke guns, smoothbores as well as rifles, had a single series of bands shrunk on. Later, to give added strength, guns were made with a second or even a third series of bands shrunk upon the first.[13] The treble-banded 7-inch rifle was designed in March 1862

[10] Ibid.

[11] Ibid. The 6.4-inch rifle could throw shells of 65 pounds and bolts of 80. The 7-inch rifle fired shells of 110 pounds and bolts of 120.

[12] Warren Ripley, *Artillery and Ammunition of the Civil War* (New York, 1970), pp. 109–10.

[13] Brooke produced his first double-banded and treble-banded guns in 1862. On 13 March 1862, in his Richmond Journal, BP, he first referred to a double-banded gun: "I

but was not completed until the following November because of "the want of facilities in the foundry."[14] Even then, the pressure of time precluded experiments to determine the effectiveness of the weapon against armor. Adding bands necessitated changes in design. For example, the addition of a second band to the 6.4-inch rifle required that the form be altered, adding 2,000 pounds to the gun's weight. It was necessary to make the 6.4-inch rifle in two patterns; the 7-inch, in three patterns; and the 8-inch, in one. The 10-inch smoothbore was double banded, and the 11-inch, treble banded. In the North guns were being banded also, but whereas Parrott's bands consisted of a single piece of metal, Brooke's included several rings pushed together.[15] Banding was not original with Brooke, for the Englishman Alexander T. Blakely had pioneered in this field, and it was standard practice in England at this time to strengthen cast-iron guns with bands.

In this work of shrinking on bands or hoops to reinforce the barrel, the Navy Ordnance Office stood alone. Brooke observed that "the Army Ordnance Department is still opposed to banding guns." Of course, the army's problem was different from that of the navy. Built-up guns were designed for special targets such as ironclads, where tremendous penetrating power was needed. Normally, the army did not meet such targets except in harbor defense.

Brooke fully appreciated the American Thomas Jackson Rodman's method of casting guns hollow and cooling the interior of the barrel first to lessen the chance of cracking and admitted that this technique might eliminate the need for bands. But the Confederacy had neither the time nor facilities to introduce such a system, and Brooke was not convinced that the Rodman system was in all ways superior to his own system of banding.[16]

Like all heavy guns made, both South and North, Brooke's

shall make a very strong double banded gun strapped trunnions to throw heavy bolts very long." On 28 March he noted: "Gave the plan of 7 In gun to Mr. Delaney at Tredegar works for pattern maker[.] It will be treble banded and 13 ft 3 in in length from cascable to muzzle face."

[14] Brooke's Report on his system of rifled guns, 8 Jan. 1863, Records of the Bureau of Ordnance, RG 74, NA.

[15] Ripley, *Artillery and Ammunition*, p. 128.

[16] Brooke's Report on his system of rifled guns, 8 Jan. 1863, Records of the Bureau of Ordnance, RG 74, NA.

guns were muzzle-loaders, it being the prevailing belief that breechloading dangerously weakened heavy guns. In Europe, however, some breechloaders were produced at this time. The overall length of Brooke 6.4-inch guns varied from 141 to 144 inches and that of the 7-inch from 143 to 147.5 inches. Brooke's rifles were characterized by seven lands and grooves in the bore to give twist in what is called a "hook-slant fashion," similar to those found in the English Blakely and perhaps adopted from it.[17] In any case, Brooke believed, as he reported to Mallory, "that for a cast iron gun the rifle twist should be as slow as possible, so as to establish only such an amount of rotation of the projectile as would insure its travelling point foremost throughout its flight."

By January 8, 1863, according to Brooke, fourteen 6.4-inch guns had been produced and sixteen 7-inch ones. Records of the Tredegar Iron Works indicate that after May 25, 1862, the company turned out thirteen 6.4-inch Brooke rifles, thirty-nine 7-inch ones, and one 8-inch one. Using Brooke patterns the company also cast during the same period ten 32-pounders (6.4 inch), four 10-inch, and two 11-inch, all smoothbores. Guns made from Brooke patterns were only a fraction of the 1,048 cannon produced at Tredegar between January 1, 1861, and April 1, 1865. Work at Selma remained slow. With the utmost effort only one gun could be manufactured in a week, although Jones had hoped to cast one a day. Nonetheless, from January 1864 to March 1865, fifteen 6.4-inch and thirty-nine 7-inch Brooke rifles and eighteen smoothbores were shipped from Selma. Of the total, fifty-three were sent to Mobile. Like other Brooke guns, those made at Selma were used afloat on vessels such as the *Tennessee* and for coastal and river defense. Also, Brooke rifles were occasionally reamed to make smoothbores of a larger caliber, i.e., a 6.4-inch rifle into an 8-inch smoothbore, and an 8-inch into 10-inch.[18]

[17] Ripley, *Artillery and Ammunition*, p. 128.

[18] Brooke's Report on his system of rifled guns, 8 Jan. 1863, Records of the Bureau of Ordnance, RG 74, NA; E. R. Archer, Tredegar Company, to Brooke, 29 Oct. 1887, BP; Bruce, *Virginia Iron Manufacture*, p. 461; Walter W. Stephen, "The Brooke Guns from Selma," *Alabama Historical Quarterly* 20 (Fall 1958), pp. 464–65; Ripley, *Artillery and Ammunition*, p. 131. William N. Still, Jr., in "Selma and the Confederate States Navy," *Alabama Review* 14 (Jan. 1962), p. 24, says that most of the more than 100 large naval guns cast at

When designing the Brooke gun Brooke was working under pressure to produce, within the South's limited means, the best possible cannon with the least possible delay. He had neither the time nor facilities for exhaustive experiments. What he sought to do was to devise from information available in the Confederacy a sound gun that could be put in production quickly and modified as actual experience dictated.

Brooke was more interested in the practical than in the theoretical aspects of ordnance, but he did not hesitate to question supposedly established principles. Such an attitude led to his discovery of the utility of the air space. When a gun is fired, the greatest strain occurs at that place where the propelling charge is ignited, and for that reason it is necessary that the barrel behind the trunnions be the strongest part of the gun. In an attempt to lessen the strain on the gun without decreasing its power, various techniques have been resorted to, including the use of large-grained, slow-burning powder. Another technique dogmatically prescribed by the ordnance manuals of the Civil War period was that the cartridge should always be rammed home, because if it was not, there was a pronounced tendency of the gun to burst. The belief that it was dangerous to have any appreciable space between the charge and the bottom of the bore, or between the projectile and the charge, was accepted without question on both sides of the Atlantic.

Though restricted to the use of cast iron in the construction of gun barrels, Brooke tried in every way to increase the power of his guns without increasing proportionately the hazard of bursting. For example, in March 1863 he mentioned to a naval engineer his intention of "using slow and quick powder in the same cartridge to reduce initial strain and yet preserve velocity of shot." Subsequently, Brooke began to design cartridges with some air space. Hence, when he received a report, dated July 31, 1863, stating that in a Brooke rifle which had burst, the cartridge had been "well rammed down," he wrote on the letter: "This was precisely what ought not to have been done, for the cartridge was

Selma were Brookes. He also points out that the Brooke guns cast between July 1863 and January 1864 were "used for testing purposes."

designed to leave air space. It was in contact when pushed home to the bottom of the vent."[19] It must have occurred to him that an air space would give the gas more room in which to expand before coming in contact with the stationary projectile. This would seem to lessen the strain on the gun rather than increase it as the experts maintained. And there was a logical explanation why guns burst so often when the cartridge was not rammed home: "the great strain which occurs in starting the shot is thrown upon a part of the gun which is not so strong as that part immediately around the charge when in its proper place."[20]

While these novel ideas were circulating in Brooke's mind, an accident occurred which enabled him to explain his views dramatically. In August 1863 two huge Blakely rifled guns were run into Wilmington through the blockade from England; with a bore of 12.75 inches and a length of 194 inches they were the largest rifles in the Confederacy. General P. G. T. Beauregard had them assigned to Charleston for protection of the inner harbor.

Soon Brooke received an official communication from Charleston that one of the Blakely guns had burst "at the fourth discharge, the breech cracked in three places." Brooke immediately told Mallory that he was convinced from a study of a drawing of the Blakely rifle that the chamber of the gun "was to be used as an air chamber to diminish the pressure." Brooke urged that his theory be tested by firing the second Blakely rifle with the cartridge placed "wholly in front of the chamber."[21] After President Davis and Colonel Josiah Gorgas, army chief of ordnance, had been consulted, the experiment was authorized. The tests of the second Blakely rifle with charges as high as fifty-five pounds were a complete success, the gun showing no signs of strain. By the tests Brooke demonstrated that an air space, instead of endangering the barrel as had been previously believed, actually lessened the strain on it.

[19] Brooke's Richmond Journal, 28 March 1863, and notation by Brooke on letter from Capt. John C. Mitchell, Fort Johnson, S.C., to Capt. W. J. Nance, Charleston, S.C., 31 July 1863 (copy), BP.

[20] Brooke to Lt. N. H. Van Zandt, Naval Ordnance Officer, Charleston, S.C., 14 Sept. 1863 (copy), BP.

[21] Lt. J. H. Rochelle to Brooke, 11 Sept. 1863, Brooke to Mallory, [c. 14] Sept. 1863 (copy), BP.

The real significance of Brooke's discovery was that it greatly augmented man's mastery over gunpowder. Thus, at the very time that experiments in England with the Armstrong 600-pounder seemed to indicate that the limits of material strength had been reached, Brooke, by overturning an established principle, made it possible to relieve the strain on the gun without diminishing the power of propulsion. Conversely, the air space principle made it possible to increase the powder charge beyond what had previously been deemed safe limits without straining the gun. This, of course, meant greater muzzle velocity, range, and power of penetration. It has been authoritatively stated that Brooke's "improvement over all former devices for rifling large guns, and his developing of the principle of the air chamber enabled the Confederacy to convert a large number of smoothbore guns into effective rifled guns."[22]

Though Brooke's interest was shifting to ordnance, he was not completely through with ironclads. At Mallory's request he submitted in July 1862 a written report giving his views on the construction of seagoing ironclads in the South with the limited means at hand. For such vessels Brooke recommended inclined sides like the *Virginia*'s in preference to the vertical sides used by the French and English. Moreover, he rejected turrets of either the Coles type, advocated in England, or the type used by John Ericsson in the *Monitor*. Brooke thought that the plan of the *Virginia*, with a few small changes, could be used for seagoing ironclads of comparatively light draft. Among the improvements he suggested were raising the ports so they would be six and one-half feet out of water and preparing a horizontal shield for the rudder and propeller.[23] On the basis of this report Mallory instructed Brooke to draft plans for a seagoing ironclad to be built in England for the Confederacy. Brooke's plans were taken to England in August or September 1862 by a Captain Lawson. "The lines & detail" were executed by Constructor W. A. Graves.

As a reward for his hard work and initiative, Brooke was

[22] Charles W. Stewart, Superintendent, Library and Naval War Records, to Matthew Page Andrews, 4 Dec. 1913, Heavy Rifled Guns, Development by Lt. John M. Brooke, C.S.N., 1863–64, Guns and Gunnery–BG, RG 45, NA.

[23] Brooke to Mallory, 16 July 1862 (copy), BP.

promoted "commander for the war," effective September 13, 1862. This promotion in no way affected Brooke's relative rank on the regular list, for it was intended that after the war officers should revert to their permanent grade. Even these temporary wartime promotions, however, were made by the president with the advice and consent of the Senate. Only one other lieutenant was similarly recognized at the time and only two others had been previously. But the promotion was not an unalloyed blessing. When it was announced, a fellow officer refused to shake Brooke's hand. Brooke asked for an explanation, and the officer replied that it was because Brooke accepted promotion over his seniors. Catesby Jones, however, congratulated Brooke on his promotion and expressed the view that advancement for meritorious service would serve a good purpose.[24]

During the fall and winter of 1862 Brooke accomplished much. He served on various boards and tested many inventions and improvements, including a gun to shoot underwater, a magnetic mine for the destruction of ironclads, and an inflammable liquid to engulf ironclads in flame. Brooke also gave advice on placing torpedoes or mines in the James, and he supervised the arrangement of naval guns on the banks of that river. But he was far more than a consultant; he also supervised diverse operations and tested various ideas of his own relating to ordnance. He prepared the ordnance for the new ironclad *Richmond;* developed new types of fuses and projectiles; and designed instruments for experimental purposes, including a gunner's quadrant. Among projectiles, Brooke invented both shells and bolts. Rifle projectiles were made in many shapes and sizes, and in the Confederacy many were produced in small shops and not always too carefully. But they were generally given the name of the inventor. The large number marked "Brooke" indicate his activity in the field. Brooke preferred the ratchet base in his projectiles. His design for percussion caps for small arms enabled the Confederacy "to supply the requirements of its armies."[25]

[24] Mallory to Brooke, 17 Sept. 1862, BP. On promotions Brooke wrote Catesby Jones: "Com Forrest, Arthur Sinclair [,] Tucker and others are opposed to the introduction of the merit element. Most of them always opposed it. Now they go for the repeal of the law and petition Congress to that effect" (21 Sept. 1862, BP).

[25] Stewart to Andrews, 4 Dec. 1913, Heavy Rifled Guns, Development by Lt. John M. Brooke, C.S.N., 1863–64, Guns and Gunnery–BG, RG 45, NA.

Brooke also pushed the fabrication of his 7-inch treble-banded rifle and the 10-inch double-banded smoothbore and conducted experiments to ascertain the range, accuracy, and penetrating power of different types of guns. During these days Brooke seemed to be the general handyman in the Naval Ordnance Office, for he also developed an improved method of sighting cannon and prepared a code of signals for the navy. In these multifarious activities Brooke worked closely with the privately owned Tredegar Iron Works and with the Naval Ordnance Works in Richmond. For example, he conducted experiments to determine the density and tensile strength of the iron from the Cloverdale and Grove furnaces in Botetourt County, Virginia, used by the Tredegar Works in the fabrication of guns.[26] Such experiments he regarded as of the "first importance."

Despite the supply of pig iron, however, the production of heavy guns at Tredegar was slow because of the lack of skilled mechanics. Brooke grew impatient, but the treble-banded 7-inch Brooke rifle was finally finished and placed on board the *Richmond* as a bow gun on November 26, 1862. Tests of this gun, known as the "Big Brooke," aboard the ship were highly satisfactory.[27]

The tremendous power of the Brooke rifles was demonstrated at Charleston, South Carolina, on April 7, 1863, when a major Federal attack was repulsed. The attack was made by nine armored vessels, seven of which were monitors. Commodore Dudley Knox has written that without adequate military support "Admiral [Samuel Francis] Du Pont was averse to attacking the undoubtedly very strong Charleston defenses, but after the *Monitor-Virginia* action in Hampton Roads, Secretary of the Navy Gideon Welles became convinced that monitors were capable of running past the Charleston batteries without military support, and then compelling surrender of the city."[28] Welles proved to be mistaken.

[26] Brooke's Richmond Journal, 28 Oct., 30 Oct. 1862, 6 Feb., 14 Feb., 16 Feb., 26 Feb. 1863, BP.

[27] A 140-pound wrought iron bolt propelled by 25 pounds of powder was tried at a target consisting of 4 2-inch plates bolted to a backing of wood 22 inches thick at a range of 260 yards. The bolt "passed through the outer plating broke the next two layers of plates so that pieces could be taken out and broke also the fourth so that the wood could be seen in the crack" (Brooke's Richmond Journal, 25 Feb. 1863, BP).

[28] Dudley W. Knox, *A History of the United States Navy*, rev. ed. (New York, 1948), pp. 268–69, 264.

During a period of about two hours the Confederates fired an estimated 2,300 rounds at the Federal fleet at ranges between 550 and 800 yards. In the engagement, the turrets of the *Nantucket* and the *Nahant* were jammed, heavy guns on the *Patapsco* and the *Nantucket* were disabled, and the "Keokuk was hit ninety times, the turrets being penetrated in many places and the water-line pierced nineteen times, putting the ship in a sinking condition as she left the scene." After the battle Colonel Gorgas showed Brooke a telegram from General Beauregard which stated that the Brooke rifles had been "invaluable" in the defense. The general, noting that the ironclad *Keokuk* had been sunk by a Brooke gun, asked that more such guns be sent to Charleston. Brooke, anticipating the need, had sent a double-banded 6.4-inch gun and a single-banded 7-inch gun, plus 525 bolts and 50 shells.

Only a few of the guns at Charleston were Brooke rifles. By common consent, however, the Brooke rifle was the most powerful and accurate gun used in the Confederacy; its wrought iron bolt was specifically designed for use against ironclads. The performance of these guns corroborated what qualified observers had already noted. Brooke received much praise for his guns, particularly his rifled cannon, from many contemporaries of the army and navy who had experience with them. Catesby Jones wrote him that "there can be no doubt that your gun is the best in the Confederacy." Lieutenant Colonel Joseph A. Yates, who had practical experience with Brooke rifles at Charleston, stated that he considered "the Brooke gun decidedly the most efficient gun in use for operating against Iron-clad vessels." Commander James W. Cooke, who commanded the ironclad *Albemarle* during operations in the North Carolina sounds, wrote Brooke he thought the Brooke gun "superior to all others." In 1913, a half century after the gunfire had died away, the superintendent of the Library and Naval War Records wrote: "The 'Brooke rifled gun' is conceded to have been the best weapon of its kind used by either side in the Civil War; it has a record of more than 2,000 rounds without suffering deterioration. The life of the modern naval gun is about 200 rounds before having to be relined."[29]

[29] Jones to Brooke, 20 April 1863, Statement of Col. Joseph Yates, Artillery Headquarters 4th Military District, in reply to questions asked by [Naval Bureau of Ordnance], 21

On March 31, 1863, one week before Du Pont's attack at Charleston, Commander John M. Brooke succeeded Commander George Minor as chief of the Office of Ordnance and Hydrography. It was a question of the old making way for the new, because Minor had entered the naval service only four months after Brooke was born. There seems to have been no undue friction between Minor and Brooke, for in August 1862 Minor referred to Brooke as "this meritorious officer [who] has rendered valuable service to the department in perfecting improvements in rifled cannon and projectiles." As chief of ordnance Brooke assumed the added responsibility of maintaining administrative records and of setting production goals, as well as arranging domestic and foreign contracts. To assist him in the latter duty, he appointed William Murdaugh, a Virginia classmate at the Naval Academy and an ordnance expert, to make purchases abroad. To help him with his multifarious responsibilities at the office, Brooke had an assistant chief, an ordnance inspector, and a few clerks.[30]

The Confederate navy was dwarfed by the army, the greatest number of officers on duty in the navy at any one time being only 727. Jefferson Davis took a personal interest in military affairs, for he was a West Point graduate and was not close to Mallory. The navy came out second best in the Confederacy. One defect in the navy's organization was the failure to assign responsibility for ship construction; this had led to the confusion and friction between Brooke and Porter in converting the *Merrimack*. Not until July 1863 was the matter alleviated by assigning responsiblity to the chief constructor, who reported directly to the secretary of the navy.[31]

There were weaknesses in the naval ordnance office when Brooke took control, but in most respects it was a healthy organization and since the end of 1862 had been able to arm its vessels adequately. George Minor had done his work well. A year before

April 1863 (copy), and Cooke to Brooke, 16 May 1864, BP; Stewart to Andrews, 4 Dec. 1913, Heavy Rifled Guns, Development by Lt. John M. Brooke, C.S.N., 1863–64, Guns and Gunnery–BG, RG 45, NA.

[30] Minor to Secretary of the Navy Mallory, 15 Aug. 1862, *Official Records, Navy*, ser. 2, 2:251; Wells, *Confederate Navy*, pp. 49, 52.

[31] Wells, *Confederate Navy*, pp. 19, 3–4, 95.

Brooke became chief, a major rearrangement of the location of naval facilities had been instituted, after the fall in rapid succession between February and June 1862 of Nashville, Jacksonville, New Orleans, Pensacola, Norfolk, and Memphis.[32] These changes eased the transition for Brooke when he added time-consuming administrative chores to his scientific and technical functions.

When Brooke assumed his new duties there were ordnance workshops at Charlotte, Atlanta, Richmond, and Selma, "and in addition, private shops were employed in the manufacture . . . of ordnance, gun carriages, projectiles, etc." Shells, which were particularly effective against wooden ships, were produced in Norfolk, New Orleans, Atlanta, Charleston, Charlotte, and Richmond, but the Naval Ordnance Works at Charlotte was the only installation where the navy could produce the wrought iron bolts used against ironclads.[33] It was Brooke's aim from the beginning in so far as possible to produce all major equipment and most minor items pertaining to naval ordnance at establishments run by the navy in order to insure "uniformity of construction and excellence of workmanship." This was in contrast to the ship construction program where the policy was to encourage shipbuilding under private contract. Of course, Tredegar, a private firm, was the great producer of cannon, but a harmonious relationship with that firm dated from the beginning of the war. Selma, which took some of the load off Tredegar in the latter part of the war, was a government facility.

It was an advantage that the existing establishments were "all within convenient distance of each other and of points to be supplied," so that the resources of the country could be used equally and transportation be "divided among the various railroads."[34] The rearrangement, which followed the loss of key cities in 1862, called for a withdrawal into the interior and decentralization. Although greater security was obtained thereby, it was at a sacrifice

[32] Still, *Iron Afloat*, p. 8; William N. Still, Jr., "Facilities for the Construction of War Vessels in the Confederacy," *Journal of Southern History* 31 (Aug. 1965): 291.

[33] Report of Brooke to Secretary of the Navy Mallory, 25 Nov. 1863, *Official Records, Navy*, ser. 2, 2:547. This 6-page report traces in detail the activities of the Ordnance Bureau between Jan. and Nov. 1863. Wells, *Confederate Navy*, p. 55.

[34] Report of Brooke to Mallory, 25 Nov. 1863, *Official Records, Navy*, ser. 2, 2:547.

of the efficiency that would have come with a more integrated structure. With shipyards, ordnance shops, foundries, ironworks, and other vital establishments spread over such a wide area, there was a crucial dependence on transportation, which generally meant railroads. But the Southern railroads were poor at the beginning of the war, and with overuse, lack of maintenance, and enemy action, they became steadily worse.[35] Yet, while Brooke was chief of ordnance, his office managed to furnish guns and ordnance equipment for warships built and building from the James River to the Mississippi and for the defense of rivers and harbors throughout the South. The shore batteries supplied and manned by the navy were of considerable assistance to the army in the dispersal of enemy ship concentrations. In some instances the navy transferred heavy ordnance directly to the army.

Brooke endeavored "to make guns as rapidly as possible [and] to employ every means to that end." In April 1863 there were about fifty Brooke rifles "in service."[36] After three months at his new post, Brooke hoped he would soon be producing for the navy all of the munitions required "and of the best quality." During the summer of 1863 he hurried production of the 10-inch and 11-inch double-banded smoothbores of his own design. Brooke had not in the least lost faith in the superiority of rifled guns against armor. But many of the enemy's ships were wooden and were, therefore, especially vulnerable to powerful smoothbore shell guns. Moreover, smoothbores could be produced more readily than rifles and were easier for the untrained artillerymen to master.

A scant three months after Brooke took over the Ordnance Office there came the twin disasters at Gettysburg and Vicksburg. Brooke, now in a position of considerable authority and influence, looked resolutely for a silver lining. His faith in Lee, who he thought had been selected by providence, was undimmed. In his journal on July 8, 1863, Brooke wrote: "Today Richmond has suffered quite a revulsion, first we have news of glorious victories by Lee. Now it is said that he falls back heavily pressed by the enemy to Hagerstown from Gettysburg where tremendous battles

[35] Still, "Facilities for the Construction of War Vessels in the Confederacy," p. 291; Still, *Iron Afloat*, pp. 89–96.

[36] Brooke's Richmond Journal, 11 April 1863, BP.

were fought, that the Potomac is unfordable, that his pontoon bridge has been destroyed etc. then it is reported that Vicksburg has fallen. The Secretary of War thinks our affairs in disastrous condition. Well I dont. Lee was necessarily obliged to fall back and I suppose he anticipated it. It is not to be supposed that his army could permanently occupy Pennsylvania." Further news from the front brought sorrow to the Brooke family. It was learned that Brigadier General Richard Brooke Garnett, General Brooke's aide in the old days and Lizzie's only remaining brother, had been killed leading the center brigade in Pickett's charge at Gettysburg.

In November 1863, after eight months as chief of ordnance, Brooke reported that the ordnance works at Charlotte, under the direction of Commander T. J. Page, had "been improved by the addition of machinery . . . adapted to the construction of marine engines and other heavy work." The Atlanta ordnance plant, under the command of Brooke's old shipmate of the *Vincennes*, Lieutenant David P. McCorkle, was "actively engaged in the manufacture of projectiles and various articles of equipment required for the vessels at Mobile and other points." The Atlanta plant also furnished "a large number of projectiles" to the Army of the West. The Richmond Ordnance Works, which had been organized by Brooke's good friend Lieutenant Robert D. Minor, a younger brother of George Minor, had developed rapidly. Of particular significance was its aid to the Tredegar Iron Works in the banding and rifling of guns cast and bored at the Tredegar. Moreover, the Richmond plant produced "a large number of gun carriages, projectiles, and ordnance stores of all kinds." At Charleston, under the careful supervison of Lieutenant N. H. Van Zandt, gun carriages and projectiles were manufactured. Van Zandt, furthermore, was of tremendous assistance to Brooke in conducting experiments with various types of guns that the overworked staff in Richmond did not have time to oversee.[37]

The foundry and rolling mill at Selma, which had been purchased jointly by the army and the navy, was by November 1863

---

[37] Report of J. M. Brooke, Chief of Ordnance, 25 Nov. 1863, *Official Records, Navy*, ser. 2, 2:547–48.

under the exclusive jurisdiction of the navy. Under the driving leadership of Commander Catesby Jones, "very considerable progress had been made toward the completion of these works." A lack of skilled labor was, however, a serious drawback. Brooke was exceedingly anxious to complete the Selma works, because a "deficiency of heavy ordnance" had been felt from the beginning of the conflict. A particularly hopeful condition existed at Columbia, South Carolina, where the powder mills, under the superintendence of P. B. Garesché, were producing an ever-increasing volume of good-grade powder.[38]

A special responsibility of the chief of ordnance was the Confederate States Naval Academy. Under the direct supervision of Lieutenant William H. Parker, the steamer *Patrick Henry* had been fitted up as a school ship, without in any way "diminishing her efficiency as a vessel of war." Brooke reported in November 1863 that fifty-two midshipmen were aboard the ship. Though the naval academy was under Brooke's general supervision, he wisely left the details to Parker, the superintendent. Parker had stood first in Brooke's class at Annapolis and had served as an instructor there just before the Civil War.

As chief of ordnance, Brooke continued to be concerned by the bursting of guns. Such accidents caused loss of life and had a crippling effect upon morale. Brooke always sought to determine the cause, and after each accident he insisted that a comprehensive report detailing all the circumstances be filed with the Office of Ordnance. Investigation disclosed that accidents were usually the result of careless handling of the guns out of ignorance or improper supervision. A common fault was that of overloading the gun.[39] Cast-iron guns even when banded were admittedly weak. But they were all the South could produce. The heavy guns were supposed to be loaded with maximum charges only when used against ironclads at short ranges; consequently, they were not expected to endure many firings when so loaded. But if used wisely,

---

[38] Ibid., pp. 548–49.

[39] Brooke made references to overloading in his journal and correspondence; for example, see Brooke to his wife, 29 July 1862, and Brooke's Richmond Journal, 31 July 1863, BP.

there was a good chance that built-up guns would outlast the ironclads against which their murderous fire was directed. The standing rule was that the smallest effective charge be used against all targets.[40] This rule, however, was often disregarded, and guns were fired repeatedly with maximum charges against ordinary targets or in siege operations conducted at long range. In 1863 Brooke noted in his journal there was "a want of knowledge and skill on the part of our artillerists" in conducting long-range firing. Undoubtedly, this was one reason Brooke hurried production of 10-inch and 11-inch smoothbores. Such guns were less susceptible to abuse. With proper care the Confederate rifled guns were strong enough. Reports show that at least one was still rendering effective service after seventeen hundred or eighteen hundred rounds.[41] But abuse drastically shortened the life of the best guns.

Accidents occurred most frequently when navy guns were transferred to the army. For example, Brooke attributed the bursting of a 6.4-inch Brooke rifle at James Island, South Carolina, to the failure of the gun crew to follow his instructions. The naval ordnance officer at Charleston grumbled that the navy's rifled guns were "damned by ignorant [army] ordn officers who know not how to use them." In his view, the army was "as jealous as they are ignorant of ordn subjects." This officer asserted that he was the only officer in Charleston who knew how the naval guns were constructed. And a naval officer wrote from Mobile that he had not believed "that a regiment called heavy Artillerists would be as ignorant as I find them."[42]

Not all ruptures, however, were caused by careless handling. There were some that could be explained only by an inherent weakness of the gun. It was a proud boast of the Tredegar people

---

[40] Brooke to Gen. P. G. T. Beauregard, Commanding at Charleston, S.C., 3 Aug. 1863 (copy), and Brooke to [all officers commanding batteries], 17 Oct. 1864 (copy), BP. The second letter is a general letter of instructions specifying maximum changes permitted for various types of projectiles with the Brooke 7-inch and 6.4-inch double-banded rifles. Such instructions were issued periodically for all types of guns in accordance with Brooke's report to Secretary Mallory of 5 Nov. 1863.

[41] Lt. Col. Joseph Yates, Commanding Artillery, Fort Johnson, S.C., to Brooke, 21 March 1864, BP.

[42] Lt. N. H. Van Zandt to Brooke, 18 Sept. 1863, Capt. R. L. Page to Brooke, 18 April 1864, BP.

before the Civil War that none of their guns had ever burst. But the exigencies of the war changed that. It was not always possible in wartime to obtain either the best pig iron or craftsmanship. In an effort to maintain a continuous supply of good iron, the Tredegar Iron Works by the middle of 1863 had found it necessary to buy or lease twelve iron furnaces in the Valley of Virginia. These blast furnaces greatly extended the operations of the Richmond firm but did not solve the problem, for eager recruiting officers conscripted into the army the workers of the mountain furnaces. Later the furnace operations were stopped or curtailed by marauding Federal cavalrymen. Another unforeseen catastrophe was the fire at the Tredegar Works in May 1863. Two triple-banded 7-inch Brooke rifles being finished in the machine shop were affected by the heat, and one of them burst later at Charleston, putatively from this cause. This destructive fire also burned the patterns of a 7-inch rifle and a double-banded 10-inch smoothbore that Brooke lamented "would have been placed in the foundry the next day."[43]

To supplement his knowledge Brooke kept up a correspondence with Southern naval agents abroad and diligently scanned foreign newspapers for ordnance news. Aware of the rapid changes in ordnance and ironclads being made in England and France, Brooke expressed the need for "a supply of standard works" on the construction of guns, projectiles, fuses, and powder and asked that a naval officer be appointed to collect such information.[44]

The most baffling and persistent problem which confronted Brooke as chief of ordnance was that of an insufficient number of skilled workers to operate his ordnance plants. Civilian manpower for the navy was critically affected by the drafting of workers for the army and the calling up of militia companies. Under the conscription act, the army swept into its ranks skilled and unskilled workers alike, without distinction; it looked upon them all as potential soldiers. As few men as possible were exempted from military service. When a naval ordnance worker was conscripted into

---

[43] Brooke's Richmond Journal, n.d. [c. 25 May 1863], BP.
[44] Brooke to Commodore Samuel Barron, England, 11 Jan. 1864, *Official Records, Navy*, ser. 2, 2:572. See also M. F. Maury, England, to Brooke, 3 Feb. 1864, BP.

the army, he was usually lost to the Naval Ordnance Office permanently, for it took months of effort in cutting red tape to recover the services of a conscripted worker, if he ever was recovered. Even when the navy was able to restore a worker to his old position in an ordnance plant, the arrangement was unsatisfactory because the worker remained in the army and was only detailed to the navy. In other words, the navy could borrow the skilled worker until the army decided it needed another soldier in the field. As the army was confronted with an ever-dwindling supply of manpower, it became steadily more reluctant to detail new men to the navy and more eager to reclaim those it had detailed previously.

The problem was never solved, though Brooke and his associates hammered at it continuously. Secretary of the Navy Mallory was well aware of the problem and sent along letters to the secretary of war and even the president but accomplished little. The conscription problem had an important corollary, too, especially in the early years of the war. Many of the skilled workers were foreigners; rather than be drafted, they left the country. Some were frustrated working in a country under siege and others were criticized by natives because of their higher pay scales. Negro slaves were used as skilled workers and made a vital contribution, but they could not fill all the gaps.[45]

In his report of November 1863 to the secretary of the navy, Brooke did not expound the need for skilled workers, but he did show that at Selma the deficiency of the labor force had prevented the completion of the important foundry and rolling mill. In order to stabilize his labor supply in the future, Brooke offered some sound recommendations. He urged that the government build low-cost housing units for the ordnance workers to be rented at nominal rates and subsidize the workers further in their battle against the growing inflation by supplying them with necessities at below the market price. With an eye to the more distant future, Brooke advocated the establishment of a system of apprenticeship for young government workers.[46]

The shortage of skilled mechanics became so critical in April

[45] Wells, *Confederate Navy*, pp. 8, 33, 37; Dew, *Ironmaker to the Confederacy*, p. 287.
[46] Report of J. M. Brooke, Chief of Ordnance, 25 Nov. 1863, *Official Records, Navy*, ser. 2, 2:548–51.

1864 that Brooke devoted nearly an entire report to that subject. At Selma, which Brooke called the "most important" of all the navy establishments, the casting of 6.4-inch and 7-inch rifles for combat had begun the preceding December, but the want of skilled workers was still "a serious drawback." Only "by suspending all other work and concentrating his force upon the manufacture of guns" had Jones been able to supply Mobile with eight or nine double-banded rifles. At Atlanta, Richmond, and Charlotte new tools and machinery had increased capacity "so that the wants of the service could be fully supplied" provided an adequate number of mechanics was obtained.[47] The lack of skilled mechanics also had handicapped the Richmond Ordnance Works in aiding the Tredegar in banding and rifling guns.

Brooke had little patience for a problem which he thought need not exist. He informed Mallory that "there are in the Southern States more than a sufficient number of mechanics to work these establishments to the full capacity and to supply all the heavy ordnance required to arm the ironclads and other vessels completed and building, and to furnish guns for the defense of our ports against which the ironclads of the enemy can not stand. But these men have been swept into the Army en masse and their services can only be obtained by special and individual detail." The chief of ordnance complained that, despite the most strenuous exertions by his bureau, "the services of not more than one in ten are secured." It was exasperating, because the Ordnance Office needed two hundred mechanics, and Brooke knew the army could supply his needs for he had the names and addresses of more than one hundred mechanics serving in the field with the army.[48]

The lack of skilled workers was not the only problem. At the Tredegar the shortage of critical materials such as pig iron had an even more immediate impact than the lack of workers. A lack of pig iron prevented the great foundry from working at more than

[47] Report of J. M. Brooke, Chief of Ordnance, 30 April 1864, *Official Records, Navy*, ser. 2, 2:641. A lucid description of the manpower problems Jones faced at the Selma Naval Works after he took charge in June 1863 is given in Still, "Selma and the Confederate States Navy," pp. 27–29.

[48] Report of J. M. Brooke, Chief of Ordnance, 30 April 1864, *Official Records, Navy*, ser. 2, 2:642.

one-third of capacity during the four years of war.[49] As a naval officer Brooke had more leverage in securing the transfer of labor from the army to the naval ordnance establishments than in protecting the small private furnaces that supplied the pig iron from the hungry recruiters. And with the furnaces the lack of production often boiled down to a shortage of labor.

In 1864 the Selma Foundry, still under Catesby Jones, moved ahead despite exasperating delays caused by a lack of machine tools, skilled labor, and money to pay wages. This establishment continued to concentrate on heavy guns designed for use against ironclads and during 1864 shipped fifty-nine of them to Mobile, Charleston, and Wilmington. Even though the number of mechanics needed at Selma was "comparatively small," an adequate number could not be secured. "Repeated applications for details of mechanics from the army have been made," wrote Brooke, "but as the services of the men were generally considered more important in the field than in the workshop, and the details were therefore disapproved by the commanding generals, very few have been granted." The shortage of workers compelled the Selma works to suspend production of projectiles for several months. This failure was serious, since, for various reasons, the supply of ammunition at other establishments was curtailed at the same time. Jones became so disgruntled that only by assuring him that his services were "more important to the country than any which you could otherwise perform in the Navy" could Secretary Mallory induce him to remain at Selma.[50]

The Naval Ordnance Works at Charlotte produced in 1864 gun carriages and ordnance equipment of nearly every description. Under the superintendence of Engineer Ashton Ramsay, it was the only establishment in the Confederacy that could do heavy forging. Shafting for steamers and wrought iron projectiles were forged and finished at Charlotte, which from its central posi-

[49] Dew, *Ironmaker to the Confederacy*, p. 287. A similar situation obtained at Selma, despite its proximity to iron deposits (Still, "Selma and the Confederate States Navy," p. 26).

[50] Report of Brooke, Chief of Ordnance, 5 Nov. 1864, *Official Records, Navy*, ser. 2, 2:756; Mallory to Jones, 10 Sept. 1864, Papers of the Jones Family of Northumberland County, Virginia, MSS Div., LC. A letter from Jones to Brooke, 4 Sept. 1864, BP, shows Jones's discontent.

tion suffered "less interruption from the movement of the enemy" than did any other naval ordnance establishment. Brooke was aware of the superiority of steel projectiles over wrought iron but was unable to undertake manufacture of the former even at Charlotte owing to "the limited amount of skilled labor at hand, insufficient to supply the current demands for the ordinary munitions of war."[51]

Nearly all of the carriages and ammunition needed by vessels on the James River and at Wilmington, and ordnance equipment for some navy shore batteries, were supplied in 1864 by the Naval Ordnance Works at Richmond, still under Lieutenant Minor. The Richmond Works also took over in large part the making of gun patterns. Unfortunately, the military situation around Richmond in 1864 required most of the workers enrolled in the naval battalion to spend "the greater part of the summer" in the field.[52]

The production of ordnance equipment at the Atlanta Ordnance Works, under Lieutenant McCorkle, was threatened in June 1864 by enemy activity. At the suggestion of the military authorities, McCorkle began moving stores and machinery to Augusta, Georgia, on the Savannah River. He was successful in saving the machinery, engines, boilers, and most of the stores before the Federals moved into Atlanta. The chaotic situation in Georgia growing out of General William T. Sherman's defeat of General John B. Hood delayed the development of the works at Augusta. The Columbia Powder Mills in 1864 continued to operate under Gareché and to supply a sufficient quantity of powder of excellent quality to meet the demands of the navy.[53]

Though the Confederacy had passed its zenith, Brooke continued his experiments. He introduced his banded 10- and 11-inch smoothbores into naval service. The treble-banded 11-inch gun was a monster, weighing 28,000 pounds. The gun worked as rapidly as the 11-inch Dahlgren but was more massive. This Brooke smoothbore fired spherical shot of 190 pounds weight, manufactured abroad, with a maximum powder charge of forty pounds.

[51] Report of Brooke, Chief of Ordnance, 5 Nov. 1864, *Official Records, Navy,* ser. 2, 2:757.

[52] Ibid.

[53] Ibid., pp. 755–57.

The gun was designed for close action. At this period Brooke also perfected a device for adjusting gunsights through the use of mirrors. This device was commended by Colonel Gorgas, the army ordnance chief, and Lieutenant Colonel Yates, an army ordnance expert.[54]

Another sphere of activity for Brooke was that of torpedoes, including what are now called mines. The Confederacy utilized these weapons to obstruct rivers and harbors, and they destroyed a larger number of Northern ships than did gunfire.[55] In fact, forty-three Union ships, including four armored vessels, were sunk by mines or torpedoes, most toward the end of the conflict.[56] Although these weapons did not change the outcome of any major battle, they did on occasion enable the beleaguered Southerners to shift to offensive tactics. At other times they gave the Confederates the opportunity to regroup or escape. The South's experiments would have a profound influence on future naval warfare. The leading student in the field has concluded that "the mines, submarines, torpedo boats, destroyers, and mine-sweepers in modern navies are results of the crude weapons developed by the Confederates." The Union did not neglect the field, but because it was on the offensive and enjoyed immense naval superiority, it did not have as strong an incentive to experiment. Conversely, the Confederacy made most effective use of mines and torpedoes as defensive weapons when Union ships moved into "the smooth shallow waters of upper rivers and inner harbors."[57]

Several types of mines were used, including stationary, drifting, and spar. The drifting and spar torpedoes have been called offensive, and the stationary, whether electrical or mechanical, defensive. To overcome this new menace, the Union navy placed nets and booms around its ships and anchorages. Also, as the

[54] Brooke to Gen. Henry L. Abbot, 7 May 1868 (copy), Gorgas to Brooke, 24 March 1864, Yates to Brooke, 23 June 1864, BP.

[55] Durkin, *Stephen R. Mallory*, p. 264.

[56] Milton F. Perry, *Infernal Machines: The Story of Confederate Submarine and Mine Warfare* (Baton Rouge, La., 1965), pp. 4, 196; a list of the vessels is given on pp. 199–201. R. B. Bradford gives the figure as 22 vessels destroyed and 12 damaged (*A History of Torpedo Warfare* [Newport, R.I., 1882], p. 46).

[57] Perry, *Infernal Machines*, p. 197.

herald of today's minesweeper, small boats were sent out to take up or destroy mines.

Both the Confederate army and navy were active in torpedo work. Matthew Fontaine Maury, Hunter Davidson, and Beverley Kennon were leading figures in the navy, while Brigadier General Gabriel J. Rains was the most active army officer in this field. Maury was the navy pioneer. When Maury left for England in 1862, Davidson was put in charge of the navy program. Neither the army nor the navy depended exclusively upon its own personnel. For example, Captain Ambrose McEvoy of the Confederate army, who had a flair for invention, was called to Charleston in 1863 to help destroy torpedoes. Early in the war he had developed an artillery fuse which was submitted to General Robert E. Lee for consideration. Lee referred the matter to Brooke. The latter accepted the fuse, and it proved to be of great value to the armed forces.[58]

By late October 1864 a stalemate had developed on the James with powerful fleets facing one another. As time favored the Federals, Flag Officer J. K. Mitchell, commanding the Confederate squadron, was eager to break the Federal cordon and take the enemy's pressure off General Lee at Petersburg. Accordingly, he placed an open-ended log barrier across the James, and to protect the approaches beyond the boom from Federal patrol boats, he posted rowboats armed with small spar torpedoes. At his request, Brooke designed these spar torpedoes.[59] Another naval weapon for which Brooke claimed credit was the stationary mine known as "the turtle." Shaped like a hemisphere, it was placed on the bottom beneath a floating torpedo, and when the latter was removed it would explode. The turtle's smooth, curved surface offered nothing for grapnels to grab.[60]

In retrospect the Confederacy could claim to have pioneered in

[58] Ibid., p. 58.

[59] Ibid., pp. 140–41.

[60] Draft of article prepared by Brooke, n.d., BP. This article was apparently written in 1866 but never published and is probably the same as that which Brooke sent Lt. Cmdr. R. B. Bradford at the Naval Torpedo Station at Newport, R.I., 29 March 1882. A copy of the covering letter, which relates to torpedoes, is in the Brooke Papers. See also Perry, *Infernal Machines*, p. 179.

the use of torpedoes and submarine mines. In 1876 Hunter Davidson wrote that since the Civil War he had been constantly engaged in torpedo work in the United States and abroad, and that he had seen no "material improvement" in the electrical torpedo system he had developed in the Confederacy. Brooke, as chief of ordnance and hydrography, had given ready assistance.[61] Such support was not universal, for Davidson, using a new weapon that was branded by some naval and military leaders as inhumane, was subject to sneers and ridicule.

John Brooke was so busy as chief of naval ordnance that he had little time for personal affairs. But they haunted him, for Lizzie's health continued to decline. On June 1, 1863, she returned to Lexington for the summer with Anna. On the twenty-third another daughter was born, but in a few months the infant died. Of the four children born to Lizzie and John—all daughters—only Anna survived infancy. The greatest blow of all came on June 14, 1864, when Lizzie, worn out by her long battle with consumption, died at the age of thirty-seven. The bereaved husband was deeply shaken; only the pressure of war work seems to have sustained him. For a protracted period he kept no journal. With the new year he once again began a journal, opening it with this statement: "For the past six months I have led a life at variance with my natural inclinations in the belief and hope that I would thus avoid certain reflections and moods of unhappiness that unchecked would be unsupportable. I believe the necessity of it existed[,] is now past and I may direct my thoughts and actions with the divine aid which I now implore to the accomplishment of noble ends."[62]

Late in the war, Brooke performed an unusual service in connection with the Confederate cruiser *Shenandoah*. The Confederate navy was eager to send a raider into the Pacific to destroy United States commerce in those waters and for this purpose purchased in England in October 1864 the *Sea King*, a full-rigged sailing ship of 790 tons with auxiliary steam power of 220 horsepower. Meanwhile, Brooke had prepared a plan for a projected cruise into the

[61] Hunter Davidson, "Electrical Torpedoes as a System of Defense," *Southern Historical Society Papers* 2 (July 1876): 3–4, 6.
[62] Brooke's Richmond Journal, 2 Jan. 1865, BP.

whaling grounds of the North Pacific, based upon his personal knowledge of the activities of the whaling fleet in that area. This plan was approved by Mallory and transmitted as a memorandum to James D. Bulloch, a Confederate agent in Europe, who, just at this time, was considering how best to utilize the *Sea King*.[63] Bulloch turned Brooke's plan over to Lieutenant James I. Waddell, who had been selected to command the raider, soon to be rechristened the *Shenandoah*, and ordered him to proceed against the whalers in the Pacific.[64] The raider sailed from London in October 1864 and, after capturing a few prizes in the Atlantic, shaped a course for the whaling grounds of the North Pacific where she appeared in April 1865. Before she was through, the *Shenandoah* had captured or destroyed twenty-nine vessels in the Pacific and had virtually wiped out the whaling fleet in those waters.[65]

As General Sherman's army rampaged through the Carolinas, affairs in the Naval Ordnance Office disintegrated rapidly. On February 17, 1865, Columbia was burned and the powder works were lost, and the same month the ordnance works recently set up in Fayetteville were destroyed. The fall of Charleston and Wilmington ended the war in so far as the navy was concerned. But Mallory fought on. As the evacuation of Richmond grew imminent, he urged that the Tredegar and other important establishments be destroyed to prevent their falling into the hands of the enemy. This was not done, and with the evacuation of Richmond on April 2 the Confederate navy lost both the Tredegar and the Richmond Ordnance Works. The next day Selma was captured. The end was at hand.

[63] Mallory to Bulloch, 19 Aug. 1864, *Official Records, Navy*, ser. 2, 2:708; Brooke to J. R. Soley, [Feb. 1883], BP.

[64] Bulloch to Mallory, 29 Sept. 1864, *Official Records, Navy*, ser. 2, 2:729. Cf. James D. Bulloch, *The Secret Service of the Confederate States in Europe, or How the Confederate Cruisers Were Equipped*, 2 vols. (London, 1883), 2:130. According to Stanley F. Horn in *Gallant Rebel, the Fabulous Cruise of the CSS*. Shenandoah (New Brunswick, N.J., 1947), pp. 17–19, the idea originated with Lt. Robert R. Carter, who had served on the North Pacific expedition and was a friend of Brooke's. When Mallory hesitated, Carter enlisted Brooke's help and the two officers convinced Mallory of the soundness of the proposal.

[65] Brainerd Dyer, "Confederate Naval and Privateering Activities in the Pacific," *Pacific Historical Review* 3 (Dec. 1934): 443; Carroll Storrs Alden and Allan Westcott, *The United States Navy, a History*, 2d ed. rev. (Philadelphia, 1945), p. 254.

During its short life the Confederate navy had produced hundreds of smoothbores and rifles, converted many smoothbores into rifles, and manufactured tremendous quantities of ammunition and equipment. In the end the navy did not fail from a lack of guns or ammunition. In July 1863 Brooke had declared that the navy was "deficient in guns." But in the next few months with the opening of the Selma Foundry, the expansion of the Tredegar after the fire of May 1863, the acquisition by the Tredegar of its own blast furnaces in the Shenandoah Valley, and the assistance of the Richmond Ordnance Works through the banding and rifling of guns, the situation improved markedly. It is true, however, that the pinch of iron at times was critical. The inadequate number of mechanics was throughout the conflict the most serious internal problem confronting the Naval Ordnance Office. But the real cause of collapse was external. When the Union armies engulfed vital areas of the South, further resistance was futile.

During the last two years of the war Brooke had filled the post of chief of ordnance and hydrography capably. A modern student has concluded that "Brooke was one of the few men in the Confederate States Navy who showed genius during the Civil War." Brooke had been "open to suggestion, eager to improve old ways or to admit error when it occurred." It had been Mallory's practice to give his subordinates free rein; consequently, his orders were often so general "as to be no orders at all."[66] But because Brooke was a prodigious worker, had initiative, and welcomed responsibility, the relationship had worked to his advantage.

As chief of ordnance Brooke proved to be an able administrator. After the Civil War, General Joseph Reid Anderson, "Master of the Tredegar" and no mean administrator himself, wrote with reference to Brooke: "I was personally cognizant of his administration of the affairs of the Confederate Bureau of Ordnance, and am of opinion that he is a man of administrative ability of a high order." The secretary of the navy, Brooke's immediate superior, was no less enthusiastic. To Brooke, Mallory once wrote: "whatever success attended the efforts of the Confederate Navy was, in no small degree due to your skill and ability." One modern stu-

---

[66] Wells, *Confederate Navy*, p. 12.

dent has called the work of the bureau "impressive," while another has written that the bureau "admirably fulfilled its mission."[67]

John Brooke, Robert Minor, and two companions left Richmond at 1:00 P.M. on April 2, 1865, the day of the evacuation, with an ambulance and two horses; Brooke had left Anna at Yelverton Garnett's house for safekeeping. The records of the Office of Ordnance had been packed and shipped to Greensboro. At sunset on April 4 the small party reached Powhatan Court House where Brooke slept on the counter of Farris's store. The next day, amidst a swirl of rumors and a swelling number of refugees, the party set out for Cumberland Court House. Many stragglers from the army were in evidence. On April 6 Brooke and his companions reached Appomattox Court House, and on the tenth, Danville. President Davis, Secretary Mallory, and other high officials of the crumbling government had left Danville by railroad just the day before for Greensboro.

The day after his arrival at Danville, Brooke took the train to Greensboro, where he arrived on April 11. He remained at Greensboro until May 1, when he was paroled under the terms of the military convention entered into between Sherman and General Joseph E. Johnston on April 26.[68] These were days of despair. All that Brooke had fought for was gone. The South was desolate, and Brooke's naval career of twenty-four years was finished.

Armed with his parole, Brooke returned to Richmond to rejoin Anna and, as he wrote John Rodgers, to await "information as to the proper course to be pursued in giving up a hopeless contest."[69] The former chief of ordnance was without funds, the Confederate government having failed to provide specie even for the return trip to Richmond. Brooke found the Confederate capi-

[67] Anderson to Rep. John Randolph Tucker, 18 Aug. 1885, BP. This was a letter of recommendation prepared at the time Brooke was seeking the position of superintendent of the Coast Survey. Mallory to Brooke, 20 Jan. 1867, BP; Still, *Iron Afloat*, p. 8; Wells, *Confederate Navy*, p. 57.

[68] Permit for John M. Brooke, 1 May 1865, signed by Flag Officer French Forrest, C.S. Navy, Commanding, Greensboro, N.C., BP.

[69] Brooke to Rodgers, 9 May 1865, Rodgers Family Papers, Naval Hist. Foundation, MSS Div., LC.

tal paralyzed. In need of money, he was unable to sell his few personal belongings "which usually serve to bridge over such chasms." It was still too early to make plans for the future, but on May 9 Brooke determined "to take advantage of the first opening." He did not relish the prospect of seeking employment abroad, because of Anna, although he thought he might be forced to do so.

X /

EARLY POSTWAR YEARS

T HOUGH Brooke was romantic and sentimental as a young man, with age and experience he learned to be practical. But as always his attitudes were genuine and his feelings ran deep. One of the strongest threads in the postwar life of the former Confederate was his renewed friendship with old shipmates who had fought for the Union. In the war he had given all he had and lost, but that was in the past. To Commodore John Rodgers, who had fought with dash and valor for the Federals, he wrote only two weeks after General Johnston's surrender: "As the war is over and we are no longer political enemies I write to assure you that my personal regard for you has not changed."[1]

Brooke was warmed by the commodore's prompt and cordial response, but the letter found him confused as to his status. His position was soon clarified by the president's proclamation of amnesty on May 29, which excluded him on three counts: he had resigned his commission when Virginia seceded; he had graduated from the Naval Academy; and he had held higher rank in the Confederate navy than lieutenant.[2] Only by personal application to the president could the thirty-eight-year-old former Confeder-

[1] Brooke to Rodgers, 9 May 1865, Rodgers Family Papers, Naval Hist. Foundation, MSS Div., LC.

[2] Johnson's proclamation was similar to Lincoln's of 1863 except it was more restrictive. There were 14 categories or "classes of persons" who were denied pardon. The eighth category barred "all military and naval officers in the rebel service who were educated by the Government in the Military Academy at West Point or the United States Naval Academy."

ate officer, hope to obtain amnesty. And this could be a rocky road. After all, Admiral David Dixon Porter, one of the North's leading naval heroes, once told Baron Gerolt, the Prussian minister, that Brooke had done the North "more harm than any other man in the South."[3] In any case, action on an individual application promised to be slow, for, as Brooke lamented to Rodgers, "There will be an immense number of applications for pardon more than the president can possibly attend to personally." Yet he must make the effort, because he considered it his "duty to take the oath of allegiance to the present government and to do all that I can for the welfare of the whole country." Moreover, he was eager to go to work with no legal limitations. As E. Merton Coulter points out, to a business or professional man a pardon was extremely important. Without it a person could not buy or sell property, apply for a patent or copyright, vote, or recover property that had been confiscated.[4]

Brooke was determined that should he find it necessary to leave the country it would be on a temporary basis to secure subsistence. He took the required oath of allegiance promptly and on June 3 applied to President Andrew Johnson for pardon.[5] He asked Rodgers to help him in the matter and, if possible, to enlist the support of Admirals Charles Davis and Samuel Phillips Lee, among others.

That Rodgers's kind feelings toward Brooke did not represent a universal sentiment was soon made clear. Admiral Davis at the Naval Observatory informed Rodgers that his first effort to intercede on Brooke's behalf at the Navy Department "failed entirely." Davis noted that the views of those officers "who joined the rebellion" were "quite different" from those who had not, and to pardon the former Confederates would be to condemn those Southern officers who had remained with the Union. But at least, Davis said, he had not lost his "kind feelings for Brooke" and would try to help him. It would appear that the more distin-

---

[3] Kate Corbin Brooke Diary, 10 June 1874, BP.

[4] Brooke to Rodgers, 1–2 June 1865, Rodgers Family Papers, Naval Hist. Foundation, MSS Div., LC; E. Merton Coulter, *A History of the South*, vol. 8, *The South during Reconstruction, 1865–1877* (Baton Rouge, La., 1947), pp. 32–33.

[5] Brooke to Pres. Andrew Johnson, 3 June 1865 (copy), BP.

guished a Southern officer's career had been, the more animosity his name aroused. As matters stood, Brooke felt that there was much mistrust on both sides and the sooner the president extended the hand of reconciliation the better it would be.[6]

In the long run the person who did the most to secure Brooke's pardon was Admiral S. P. Lee, Brooke's old commander on the Coast Survey and a relative of the influential Blair family. During the Civil War, Lee had commanded the blockading squadron off Virginia and North Carolina. In June 1865 he "wrote urgently" on Brooke's behalf "to our great and good President," and in October he personally withdrew Brooke's files from the adjutant general's records and presented them at the White House "for early action." Lee assured his fellow Virginian that he would "follow the matter up with careful attention." Finally, in August 1866, Lee sent Brooke his pardon with the comment that "it is for you to determine after so much delay what its value may be to you." Brooke's close friend Robert D. Minor, former first lieutenant of the *Virginia*, wrote from Richmond that "all your friends here are rejoiced to hear of your pardon."[7]

In the first dark days after the war when he had no money at all, John Brooke's relatives and friends, North and South, rallied around him. Cousin Robert Tunstall of Norfolk, shortly after the surrender, sent Brooke fifty dollars and lamented that his "limited means" would not permit him to send a larger sum. Tunstall was hard-pressed himself. He had "a pretty full house" with some twenty people under his roof. "You can judge of the expense of supporting such a family at the present prices," he wrote. William Brooke wrote from Caroline County that he had been happy to learn that his brother was back in Richmond, for "after diligent inquiry I had been unable to hear a word of your whereabouts." A lack of greenbacks prevented William from coming to Richmond "at once."[8]

In a continuing correspondence Commodore Rodgers showed that he was willing to back his kind feelings with hard cash. From

[6] Davis to Rodgers, 13 June 1865, Brooke to Rodgers, 23 June 1865, Rodgers Family Papers, Naval Hist. Foundation, MSS Div., LC.

[7] Lee to Brooke, 27 Oct. 1865, 20 Aug. 1866, Minor to Brooke, 2 Nov. 1866, BP.

[8] Tunstall to Brooke, 16 May 1865, Brooke to Brooke, 20 May 1865, BP.

the *Dictator* at New York, he wrote: "It occurs to me that you might find it convenient to have some small sums of ready money . . . I have $200 in my hands entirely at your service—frankly— as old shipmates: So if so small a sum would be of any service to you, take it as frankly as it is offered—You can repay me when you like—or never." Brooke, though deeply appreciative, replied: "fortunately my Japanese traps have carried me over the bridge and I think it highly probable that before I get to the bottom of the locker I shall have work."[9]

After pursuing many job possibilities without result, Brooke must have felt profound relief when he was notified in October 1865 by General Francis Henney Smith, the superintendent of the Virginia Military Institute in Lexington, that he had been appointed to a newly created chair to teach practical astronomy, geodesy, meteorology, and physical geography at that state college. At the same meeting the Board of Visitors had resolved that the superintendent and Brooke "take such steps as may be necessary to obtain such books instruments and apparatus as may be required to organize the chair of Practical Astronomy, etc."[10] Although Brooke was commissioned a colonel in the Virginia militia, which was the rank assigned at the Institute to full professors, he preferred his naval title of captain and that was often used except in official correspondence. Little did Brooke realize at the time that the appointment would begin a relationship that would last until he retired.

When Brooke accepted the position he was not yet forty, but the strain and sorrows of the war were reflected in his gaunt appearance. A stern visage indicated his serious temperament. Brooke's beard was becoming longer and soon would be full, even bushy. This in part offset his growing baldness. In time, perhaps as a concession to vanity or to keep his head warm, he would begin to wear a black velvet cap with a high flat crown and no brim. At VMI it was the custom to wear a uniform, but after the war, owing to the pervading poverty, there was no standard for a number of years. Brooke apparently wore his Confederate naval

[9] Rodgers to Brooke, 14 June 1865, BP; Brooke to Rodgers, 23 June 1865, Rodgers Family Papers, Naval Hist. Foundation, MSS Div., LC.

[10] Board of Visitors Minutes, Virginia Military Institute, 9 Oct. 1865.

uniform. In the seventies a standard dark blue uniform would be prescribed.

Captain Brooke was no stranger to Lexington. Lizzie and her parents had moved to the small college town in the Shenandoah Valley in 1853 when Brooke was on the North Pacific expedition. At that time Lizzie's sister Louisa was married to Colonel Williamson, who had been at the Institute since 1841. In the future, whenever Brooke was on a cruise, Lizzie had joined her father in the valley town, even though her mother died in 1854 and her sister Louisa five years later.

Brooke's appointment aroused enthusiasm among his friends and relatives. "I rejoice to hear of your prospect of a chair in the Military Institute," wrote Rodgers. Expressing the view that perhaps teaching was his friend's forte, Rodgers wrote, "You have naturally the gift of talking, and your varied experience in the world will aid you in giving interest to your labors." Brother William was delighted to hear of the appointment, but with some qualification. With prescience, he observed, it "would suit you first rate for a time at least, particularly if you can find a wife to suit too." General Robert Patterson in Philadelphia was "greatly gratified to learn that you are elected to a professorship in the Virginia Military Institute one of the first schools in the Union."[11]

The Virginia Military Institute was a state-owned college of engineering and science which had been founded on the site of a state arsenal in 1839. Francis H. Smith, who had graduated from West Point in 1833 and taught there for two years, was at the time of his appointment as the VMI superintendent a professor of mathematics at Hampden-Sydney College. Starting with Smith, who doubled as professor of mathematics, and John Thomas Lewis Preston, professor of French, the school had enjoyed a steady growth until the Civil War. The concept of the citizen soldier was strong, and certainly the school owed much in its conception to L'Ecole Polytechnique, for the president of the VMI Board of Visitors from the school's inception until 1845 was the well-known engineer Claudius Crozet, a graduate of the French

[11] Rodgers to Brooke, 17 Oct. 1865, Brooke to Brooke, 22 Nov. 1865, Patterson to Brooke, 14 Feb. 1866, BP.

school. But the institution that had the most profound influence on the Virginia Military Institute was the United States Military Academy, which all of the professors in the early days with the exception of Preston had attended. In time the junior positions in the faculty were filled with outstanding graduates of VMI who grew up with the school. During Brooke's long service, most of his colleagues were graduates of the Institute.

No one did more to mold the Institute than its venerable superintendent, who held that position for fifty years. Smith believed that the Institute, as a school where practical subjects were taught, held a special place in the educational system of the state. It could supply the state with engineers to construct the internal improvements so urgently needed and teachers who could instill discipline in the schools. Moreover, in an age when warfare was not so complicated as it is today and state sovereignty meant far more, it was important to have young men who as citizen soldiers could rally to the Commonwealth's defense in time of peril. Until 1858 only Virginians were admitted.[12] Undergirding Smith's ideas was the concept that poor boys should be enabled to attend the Institute by means of state cadetships, which would pay board and tuition and obligate the recipient to teach within the state for two years after graduation.

General Smith's goals were achieved to a remarkable degree. During the first twenty years of the Institute's history it provided Virginia with 160 teachers, some of whom adopted teaching as a career, and 52 civil engineers. And on the battlefields of the Civil War, 259 VMI men sacrificed their lives as citizen soldiers.[13] But in 1864 the physical plant was almost totally destroyed when Union General David Hunter burned the Institute. Given the physical destruction, the financial distress, and the sagging morale after Appomattox, only an act of great faith and determination could raise the Institute from the ashes. The indomitable Francis Smith turned to the task with vigor, proposing to start immediately on the physical rehabilitation of the Institute so that a full corps could be enrolled. It was his conviction that a restored physical plant would attract some cadets who could pay their own way

[12] William Couper, *One Hundred Years at V.M.I.*, 4 vols. (Richmond, 1939), 1:335.
[13] Ibid., 1:353, 3:100.

and thus help underwrite capital expenditures and operating costs. In addition, by acting quickly the Institute not only could supply the state with highly trained practical men to aid in the urgent work of restoration but could move into the forefront of southern education. Smith contemplated borrowing the money for capital expenditures, and to facilitate this he asked for an act of faith by the faculty: that they agree to forgo one-third of their salaries. Such a gesture, he felt, would make it easier to sell the bonds needed to restore the physical plant. The faculty agreed, and the action was promptly approved by the Board of Visitors.

With high hopes the Institute resumed its academic work on October 16, 1865, with eighteen cadets reporting for duty the first day. By the end of the academic year, fifty-five had been enrolled. The superintendent reported that "without any facilities for messing or quartering the cadets, provision was made for boarding them in Lexington, while the various offices of the Superintendent's quarters were used for lecture rooms."[14] Not wishing to compromise his goals, Smith listed eleven departments, though in fact not all of the courses were offered. It was his intention to establish the schools of applied science in agriculture, engineering, and the fine arts approved by the Board of Visitors shortly before the war. In addition to retaining those faculty officers who had survived the war, General Smith hired two other officers in addition to Brooke. They were General George Washington Custis Lee, a son of General Robert E. Lee, who was appointed professor of civil and military engineering and applied mechanics, and Colonel William B. Blair, a graduate of West Point, who taught natural and experimental philosophy. Despite the big plans, it was a year of sacrifice; a full professor, for example, drew only $900 in salary.[15]

One of the most serious problems facing the Institute was the lack of a library and scientific equipment. Consequently, immediate steps were taken to correct this deficiency. By purchase with funds from private donations and by the recovery of some books taken by the invaders, the superintendent had collected "about 1000 volumes" by June 1866. Strenuous efforts were made to

[14] Annual Report of the Superintendent, VMI, 27 June 1866.
[15] Ibid., 4 July 1867.

acquire necessary laboratory equipment, which General Smith estimated would cost $15,000.[16] At the time of his appointment Brooke was directed to obtain the necessary books, instruments, and apparatus for his courses. But until he obtained his pardon he did not deem it proper to request help from such people as the head of the Naval Observatory or the Coast Survey.[17] Meanwhile, he did what he could on a private basis, while the governor was relied upon to get instruments from the federal bureaus.

William Stimpson, the naturalist of the North Pacific expedition who worked for the Chicago Academy of Science, urged Brooke to start collections of "shells, birds & other 'grumpies' " in order to excite the interest of his students and offered to identify any specimens. Joseph Henry at the Smithsonian Institution offered a shell collection "properly labelled,"[18] and Captain Andrew W. Johnson, who had remained with the Union, gave Brooke many charts and other publications from the observatory. Also, Johnson persuaded Captain Thomas Scott Fillebrown, Brooke's old shipmate, to obtain a barometer, and he himself sent a list of instrument makers whose prices were reasonable and who bore no antipathy toward the South.

After the Civil War two matters of significance for VMI's future were thoroughly debated. The first was whether the Institute should be moved to Richmond; the second concerned the attempt to transform the school into a land-grant college under the Morrill Act. The problem of moving was a matter for immediate consideration, for there would be no point in restoring the buildings in Lexington if the Institute were to move to Richmond. At the time of his appointment Brooke was in Richmond, and General Smith asked him to sound out board members there. He wrote Smith: "such members of the Board as I have seen consider the change to Richmond indispensable."[19] Brooke strongly supported the move to Richmond and associated it with the conversion of VMI into a land-grant college, an idea he also supported. To no one did the Institute mean more than to General Smith, and understandably

[16] Ibid., 27 June 1866.
[17] Brooke to Smith, 11 Oct. 1865, Brooke File, VMI Records.
[18] Henry to Brooke, 17 April 1866, BP.
[19] Brooke to Smith, 11 Oct. 1865, Brooke File, VMI Records.

he felt strongly that VMI should remain in Lexington. In the end he prevailed. John Letcher, the president of the Board of Visitors, recorded that "when the idea was almost universally derided and ridiculed," the superintendent determined to rebuild on the original site.[20] By insisting on the Lexington location, Smith prevented VMI from being designated a land-grant school, because the two matters were interrelated politically.

Eager to resume the work envisioned for the Institute's special schools before the war, General Smith directed Brooke; Colonel Marshall McDonald, professor of geology; and General Custis Lee, professor of applied mechanics and engineering, to cooperate in the preparation of a geographical and geological map of Virginia and a physical history. This project was an expansion of an earlier request General Smith had made that Brooke prepare a geographical map of the state "upon the model of the great Geo. Map of France or Borden's Geog. Map of Massachusetts." In the new project each officer was given certain specific duties. Brooke, for example, was directed to conduct primary triangulations and was made responsible for the work in physical geography and meteorology. The Board of Visitors accepted the superintendent's recommendations but stipulated that expenses must be met independently of Institute funds.[21]

As was his nature, Captain Brooke entered upon his new duties with vigor, and in September 1866 he wrote Matthew Fontaine Maury that he had erected a small laboratory and mounted a transit like the one he had used on the North Pacific expedition. He hoped soon to have other instruments and expected to make meteorological observations. Because of the lack of "astronomical and other instruments" he taught only physical geography at first, but he had high hopes.[22] To General Patterson he described the Institute as "an educational establishment which before the war was nearly equal to West Point in imparting practical and scientific knowledge particularly adapted to preparation of young men for such professions as lead . . . to the development of material

[20] Letcher to Gov. Gilbert Walker, 5 Jan. 1871, Annual Report of Board of Visitors, VMI.

[21] Board of Visitors' Minutes, VMI, 3 July 1867.

[22] Brooke to Maury, 28 Sept. 1866 (copy), BP.

resources of the country." The new professor believed firmly in the South's future and the importance of educating its young men in such a way as to develop the region economically. This was the position of "all sensible people in the South," he wrote Patterson. Brooke deemed it equally important that the North demonstrate a "kindly nature" so that people in the South could believe there was a real desire on the part of the northern people for the South to share in the prosperity of the whole country. The Virginia Military Institute had a special responsibility in this development, particularly as it related to the state of Virginia. Brooke informed Commodore Rodgers that the Institute would be of "vast importance" as a school of applied science in furthering the state's *material progress.*" In the spring of 1866, when Brooke was teaching only physical geography, he informed Baron Gerolt that his duties were "very light," but when maps were procured that particular course would "be considered of more importance than it has been in Virginia heretofore."[23]

After a time the lack of activity and any real challenge in his teaching duties at VMI combined with the uncertain conditions in the country to produce in Brooke a spirit of restlessness. Having Anna with him was "the great consolation." She had chickens to take care of, and occasionally she and her father went walking and looked for wildflowers. Politically, the situation was quiet in Lexington, and Brooke was convinced that the only thing which prevented the restoration of the Union was the persistence of a few fanatics and demagogues. He had a high regard for Andrew Johnson and thought him a statesman.[24] To the Confederate secretary of the navy, Stephen R. Mallory, for whom he had great admiration, Brooke confided in December 1866 that his new occupation was "pleasant enough," but as the only sailor in the area he was like a fish out of water. Commenting on the people of Lexington, Brooke observed that they were "kind and good Scotch Irish Presbyterians, a people who never carry too much sail for

[23] Brooke to Patterson, 9 Feb. 1866 (copy), BP; Brooke to Rodgers, 11 Oct. 1865, Rodgers Family Papers, Naval Hist. Foundation, MSS Div., LC; Brooke to Gerolt, n.d. [c. Feb. 1866] (copy), BP.

[24] Brooke to Rodgers, 6 May 1866, Rodgers Family Papers, Naval Hist. Foundation, MSS Div., LC.

their ballast." He asserted that VMI was "Episcopalian in tone" and the church records bear him out.[25] No doubt Brooke's religious legacy from Lizzie bore heavily upon him, but not for several more years would he be confirmed. Brooke found all of the professors "excellent men and without exception the best group I have ever been associated with." Catesby Jones, writing from New York, believed Brooke "fortunate to have the position you now hold at *this* time." There were, he noted, many former Confederates who could not find jobs.[26]

Financially, however, the prospect was black in the years immediately following the war. The hand-to-mouth existence that his low salary forced him to lead worried Brooke, and he indicated to Mallory and others that he must augment his pay in some way or obtain different employment. He complained that he was "continually hard up." During the latter part of 1866 he gave serious thought to getting command of a vessel on a proposed steamship line between California and Japan. Admiral Lee, who had just secured Brooke's pardon, again rallied to his support and wrote to one of the large stockholders in the company "showing him how fortunate he is in the opportunity to secure your services for his company." But in the end nothing came of this effort. Nonetheless, it was clear that the restless professor was giving much thought to his future. A letter from his old naval companion and close friend Bob Minor was not calculated to soothe him, even though Minor wrote he did "not wish in any way to cause any dissatisfaction with your present very pleasant duty." It was Minor's opinion that Brooke could "do *far far* better in a pecuniary vein than you can possibly be now doing at Lexington."[27]

"Shut up in this valley," as he phrased it, Brooke by October 1866 had evolved an idea which in his early correspondence was called the "ordnance and hydrography plan." What he proposed was that he, Bob Minor, and Catesby Jones form a company to

[25] Brooke to Mallory, 15 Dec. 1866 (copy), BP. Throughout the nineteenth century the vestry of the local Episcopal church was dominated by VMI professors, and almost all of the senior professors were Episcopalian. In addition, every superintendent from 1839 to 1970 was an Episcopalian and a large percentage of the cadets were of that faith.

[26] Jones to Brooke, 29 June 1866, BP.

[27] Lee to Brooke, 14 June, 29 Sept. 1866, Brooke to Lee, 7 Sept. 1866 (copy), Minor to Brooke, 25 Oct. 1866, BP.

supply foreign governments with naval matériel. The firm, acting as agents, would furnish the matériel desired from American ordnance works and shipyards on a commission basis or through contract. Brooke's initial intent was to emphasize the guns, projectiles, fuses, and torpedoes developed by the Confederate Naval Ordnance Office, many of which he had designed. The former ordnance chief had learned that to produce the Brooke gun would infringe on no patents.[28] He also contemplated furnishing the useful Brooke deep-sea sounding lead on order. Certainly no country in the recent past had experimented more in naval ordnance than the late Confederate States. This work could be resumed. Brooke thought of the proposed company as a "Civil Bureau of Supply," a successor in a sense of the Confederate Office of Ordnance and Hydrography which, but for the fortunes of war, would still have been functioning as a government bureau.

To the frustrated professor who was not reconciled to an academic career, the project had much to commend it. If successful, it could augment Brooke's meager salary and yet enable him to remain in Lexington, which was a good place to rear Anna. Of tremendous appeal was the prospect of working again in ordnance and hydrography, fields that continued to fascinate him and in which he had demonstrated a high degree of professional skill. And Brooke was not without contacts. Since the war Rodgers, S. P. Lee, and other Union officers had been not only friendly but extremely helpful. And before the war Brooke had certainly been closer to the shogun's government in Japan than had any other American naval officer. When in Washington he had enjoyed a pleasant relationship with Baron Gerolt, who was still the Prussian minister. The Russian government had thanked him for the help he had rendered Commodore Popoff in Japan. Also, there were former Confederates scattered abroad who could put in a good word.

It was natural that Brooke should turn to Jones and Minor, for during the Civil War these three officers had worked closely together on a basis of mutual respect. Catesby Jones, a Virginian, had entered the United States Navy five years earlier than Brooke

---

[28] Brooke to Jones, 3 Dec. 1866 (copy), BP.

and had developed a broad experience in the ordnance field. In the Confederate navy, when serving as executive officer of the *Virginia*, he had been in almost daily contact with Brooke as they struggled to ready the converted ironclad for battle. Later he had been in charge of the vast Selma ordnance works. At the time Brooke broached his plan, Jones was in New York as a consultant for various South American states.

Robert D. Minor, a younger man than Jones, had entered the United States Navy the same year as Brooke. Joining the Confederacy, he had been wounded in the Battle of Hampton Roads while first lieutenant of the *Virginia*. Later he became chief of the Richmond Ordnance Works and had been in constant touch with Brooke. After the war Minor held a succession of jobs in New York, Richmond, and rural Virginia. A kind and lovable person, he was perhaps closer to Brooke than any other Confederate comrade.

When the Confederate government evacuated Richmond in April 1865, Captain George Minor had taken some of the Confederate ordnance records with him, including those for the construction of guns, and later he had left them in Greensboro at the residence of Colonel John Sloan. After the war Sloan had given many of the official records to the United States government, but at Brooke's request had returned the latter's private papers to him.[29] Though the recovered papers did not include some reports and drawings on rifled guns, Brooke learned that Jones had many "photographic drawings" of the Brooke gun in his possession.[30] Furthermore, Robert Minor had recovered many of the drawings from the Richmond Ordnance Works. Of particular value were the drawings of torpedoes and mines.

The idea for the company had its genesis in a request to Jones for information on mines by E. G. Read, a former Confederate naval officer who was working for Peru and Chile. Jones passed

[29] Brooke to Sloan, 24 Aug. 1865 (copy), Sloan to Brooke, 5 Sept. 1865, BP.

[30] Jones to Brooke, 29 June 1865, BP. Original reports on the Brooke gun can be found in the National Archives. See Brooke's Report on his system of rifled guns, 8 Jan. 1863, Civil War Ordnance, Records of the Bureau of Ordnance, RG 74, NA; Charles Stewart, superintendent, Library and Naval War Records, to Matthew Page Andrews, 4 Dec. 1913, Heavy Rifled Guns, Development by Lt. John M. Brooke, C.S.N., 1863–64, Guns and Gunnery–BG, RG 45, NA.

on Read's request to Minor, who was then in New York, and Minor turned it over to Brooke. The professor compiled information and made drawings of torpedoes he had designed for the Confederacy and sold the material to Read for $600, thereby considerably easing his desperate economic plight. He gave Minor, who acted initially as middleman, a generous commission. From this modest beginning Brooke developed the plan for an agency to supply the munitions and ordnance needs of foreign governments. In fact, after arrangements were made with Read, Brooke wrote Minor that he thought they "could work together on such matters very advantageously," and he suggested that Jones and Read might be interested.

Before writing Minor and Jones, Brooke explored the possibility that the Tredegar Company in Richmond might do the kind of work he had in mind. It was to be expected that he should turn there, because the Tredegar had been the largest ordnance manufacturer in the Confederacy and Brooke knew the establishment and its personnel intimately.[31]

From the beginning Brooke adhered to the principle that the firm must not aid a "wrong cause." Minor fully concurred. Jones believed that the necessary contracts could be made without violating any law, and he did not anticipate any interference from the United States government.[32]

The immediate response to Brooke's proposal was good. Minor believed it advisable "to get underway quietly" with an order that would occupy them for "two or three months." Jones was slower to commit himself, but after consideration he wrote Minor that the proposition was "very agreeable." Taking a broad view, he emphasized that the firm should not restrict itself to naval ordnance of Confederate design. The partners should undertake to supply heavy ordnance, small arms and ammunition manufactured in the North as well as in the South for both land and sea

[31] During the war the Tredegar had taken over a number of furnaces in the Shenandoah Valley. Fired by charcoal, they could not compete after the war with northern furnaces that used anthracite coal. Thus Tredegar lost out in the ordnance field and produced no cannon after the Civil War except for a brass howitzer for the Maryland Oyster Patrol (Dew, *Ironmaker to the Confederacy*, p. 316).

[32] Jones to Minor, 14 Oct. 1866, Minor Papers, Virginia Historical Society, Richmond (hereafter cited as VHS).

warfare, and naval vessels of all types. The scheme depended upon making arrangements with manufacturers both north and south of the Potomac. Brooke had envisioned the firm as a vehicle to utilize his inventive genius as well as a way to make money. Jones, with more practical business experience, was intent upon building up a large volume of business to satisfy current needs by making use of whatever was available. The older officer urged that letters of recommendation be obtained from prominent United States naval officers in order to assure "the confidence of Foreign Governments."[33]

It was obvious that for the firm to succeed someone must give much time to it. Initially, no one could do this, but the partners hoped to compensate by coordinating their fragmented efforts. Such a policy would require frequent consultation, and with Jones in Selma or New York, Minor in New York or Richmond, and Brooke in Lexington, meetings were difficult to arrange and expensive. Yet they made the effort. To advertise the firm, a brief statement was prepared describing the services offered. To persuade prospective purchasers, glowing recommendations were obtained from Stephen Mallory and Franklin Buchanan. The documents were combined in a circular and printed in English, French, and German. Moreover, assurances were received that Commodore Rodgers and Henry Augustus Wise, chief of the Bureau of Ordnance, would work quietly in the firm's behalf.[34]

To supplement Brooke's earlier contact with the Tredegar Company, Jones visited foundries in Pittsburgh and Reading. He found the Pittsburgh proprietor closefisted and unwilling to pay even a 5 percent commission for a contract based on government prices. The Reading firm was "much more liberal." Minor got in touch with a company in Norfolk and found it willing to pay "quite a handsome percentage."

Brooke was confined by his teaching duties, but he wrote to Baron Gerolt and his cousins Yelverton Garnett in Washington and Louis Garnett in San Francisco. Yelverton had a wide acquaintanceship in diplomatic circles, while Louis was in a position

[33] Minor to Brooke, 2 Nov. 1866, BP; Jones to Minor, 10 Nov. 1866, Minor Papers, VHS; Jones to Brooke, 11 Nov. 1866, BP.
[34] Jones to Minor, 25 Dec. 1866, Minor Papers, VHS.

to explore the Japanese connection. Minor and Jones felt it important that someone go to Washington. As Brooke was the only one
of the three with a pardon and had more contacts than the others,
he was urged to go. In March 1867 he slipped away for a few days
and had encouraging talks with the Prussian and Austrian ministers. The only tangible result of the trip, however, was a prospective arrangement with the Danish vice-consul for the firm to inspect 25,000 muskets. Because Minor was the only partner who
could give up the forty days needed for the inspection, he agreed
to act for the firm.

From no country did Brooke expect as much as from Japan.
This expectation derived not only from his exceptional contacts
with the Japanese that had climaxed with the *Kanrin Maru* adventure but because responsible leaders in Japan from all factions had
come to see the necessity of modernizing that country's armed
forces if Japan was to avoid the humiliations heaped upon China.
Brooke's sympathy for the Japanese was genuine, and he wanted
Japan to become strong and remain independent. He seemed to
believe that in 1866 he could pick up where he had left off in
1860. Consequently, no sooner had Minor and Jones accepted his
ideas on establishing an agency to supply foreign governments
than he began to push on the Japanese front. Looking ahead,
Brooke talked to John Allmand, an American who had just obtained a gunboat for the Japanese in the United States and was returning to Japan in December 1866. Endeavoring to make Allmand the company's agent in Japan, Brooke wrote him a letter to
be presented to the governor of Yokohama and explained that the
letter concerned "the increase of the naval power of Japan, the introduction of heavy ordnance, for ships & land services, and *of torpedoes* a most important means of defence as well as attack."[35]

Several things had happened since 1860, however, which
changed the situation in Japan markedly. In the first place, the
Perry mission had brought to the surface an intestine struggle between the Tokugawa Shogunate that had ruled Japan since 1600
and the powerful western clans that coalesced in the name of the
emperor, or mikado. From the Perry Treaty of 1854 to the Meiji

[35] Brooke to Allmand, 25 Nov. 1866 (copy), BP.

Restoration in 1868 Japan was in ferment, and after 1860—when Brooke had last been in Japan—the shogun's cause went steadily downhill. The people Brooke knew were supporters of the shogun. Many of them would soon lose out when the shogunate was overthrown. Moreover, while America had been distracted by its own civil war, the great European powers had filled the void. In fact, America was under a cloud as the result of a contract. In 1863 the Japanese government had contracted for the purchase of three war steamers in the United States, the details to be handled by Robert Hewson Pruyn, the United States minister to Japan. By 1867, however, although the Japanese had paid $6 million in advance, only one of the three vessels had been delivered and the Japanese were not satisfied with it.[36]

Early in April 1867 Brooke's hopes were boosted temporarily by a telegram from Louis Garnett in San Francisco stating that a Japanese commission headed by Ono Tomogoro had left California for Washington. Tomogoro had been astronomer in the *Kanrin Maru,* and Brooke knew him well and respected his abilities. Brooke jumped to the conclusion that the Japanese were coming to confer with him. The professor made hasty preparations to go to Washington, but before leaving he finally heard from Allmand in Japan. "The French have the upper hand here now," Allmand declared, "and do nearly all the Government business." Furthermore, Allmand believed that the poor performance on the Pruyn contract had injured Americans substantially. The purpose of the Tomogoro mission, he explained, was to make a settlement on the Pruyn contract as well as to purchase some warships.[37]

In Washington, Brooke learned that the Japanese commission's principal object was to purchase an ironclad vessel from the American government. To Commodore Rodgers, commandant of the Boston Navy Yard, Brooke wrote: "My old friends the Japs are here and as [they] have great confidence in me they have asked my advice in matters of some importance. It is my desire to protect their interests."[38] He feared that the American government

[36] Allmand to Brooke, 26 Feb. 1867, BP.

[37] Brooke to Minor, 11 April 1867, Minor Papers, VHS; Allmand to Brooke, 26 Feb. 1867, BP.

[38] Brooke to Rodgers, 4 May 1867 (copy), BP.

would be willing to dispose only of a vessel "not considered serviceable."

In the meantime, the Japanese began to show interest in the ironclad ram *Stonewall*, built at Bordeaux, France, for the Confederacy in 1864. Not arriving until after Lee's surrender, the ironclad had been placed eventually at the Washington Navy Yard. It took the prudent Japanese commissioners two weeks to make up their minds, but finally they decided to purchase the vessel,[39] apparently having been influenced by recommendations from Brooke and Minor.

Brooke nourished the belief that he could be of assistance to the Japanese in equipping and inspecting the *Stonewall*, and perhaps even in taking the vessel to Japan. Tomogoro made it clear, however, that the Japanese would depend upon the United States government to equip and inspect the vessel despite his personal preference to give the work to Brooke and Minor. This would have ended the chapter on the *Stonewall* but for Brooke's friends. From the beginning Secretary of the Navy Gideon Welles had asserted that the navy could not "undertake to deliver the Stonewall in Japan." He informed the State Department that though "the Navy Department would prefer not to detail officers or select a crew to take the 'Stonewall' to Japan, it will assist in securing them if desired."[40] While Welles was writing to Secretary of State Seward, Admiral Thornton Jenkins, chief of navigation; Captain Fillebrown in the Hydrographic Office; and, of course, Admiral Lee were pushing Brooke's cause zealously. Though Brooke in the end was not appointed, he could not blame the navy or Reconstruction. His friends in the United States Navy had done their best for him. The Japanese had insisted tenaciously that an officer on active duty in the United States Navy be appointed.[41] Welles

[39] Memoranda concerning the Iron-Clad Ram "Stonewall," Miscellaneous Letters of the Department of State, 1789–1895, M-179, NA; Secretary of State Seward to Secretary of the Navy Welles, 25 May, 30 May 1867, Domestic Letters of the Department of State, 1784–1906, M-40, NA.

[40] Welles to Seward, 15 May, 23 May 1867, Misc. Letters of the Department of State, M-179, NA.

[41] Fillebrown to Brooke, 30 May 1867, BP; F. W. Seward, Asst. Secy. of State, to Welles, 1 June 1867, Domestic Letters of the Department of State, 1784–1904, M-40, NA.

retreated from his original position at Secretary Seward's request, and the chief of ordnance at the Washington Navy Yard was entrusted with the mission. The assistant secretary of the navy explained to Admiral Lee that on a previous occasion the Japanese "had fallen into the hands of thieves, & had been cheated badly about a vessel he built for them; that the N. Dept. determined that this transaction shd. be a respectable one between the two nations."[42]

The Japanese venture marked the highest hopes of the Minor, Jones, and Brooke company. With its failure, discouragement set in. Even before the arrival of the Tomogoro mission the weaknesses of the existing relationship were evident. Business could be secured best in Washington; therefore it was essential that one or more members of the firm reside there. Such an arrangement required some outside source of income until the firm was self-sustaining. After discussing their predicament at length with an officer of Reaney and Son and Archbold Company of Chester, Pennsylvania, Minor offered a solution—that Brooke, Jones, and Minor obtain temporary appointments as agents of separate companies. Reaney offered to hire Minor at $1,800 per year plus office and traveling expenses, if Brooke secured a similar employment contract at Tredegar. Jones, it was felt, would be offered a place with McManus and Company, gun founders, or the Parrott Company of Cold Spring, New York, which produced the cannon of that name. The plan was for Brooke and Jones to concentrate on ordnance, while Minor gave his attention to machinery. Minor emphasized that the arrangement was for the purpose of enabling their own firm to get underway and would be temporary in nature. The former Confederates would secure work for the companies "to be done at the same price as other constructors would do it, or if they could not take it at the 'lowest bid' price, we would be free to give it where the interest of the parties ordering the work would be best served." Brooke was noncommittal, saying that the proposition should be carefully considered and Jones's views obtained. But, he confided, he had "been very *unhappy*" at

[42] Jenkins to Brooke, 7 June 1867, Lee to Brooke, 7 June 1867, BP.

the Institute and did not regard his employment there "as permanent."[43]

On his own initiative Minor wrote General Anderson at Tredegar, and that official made Brooke a handsome offer. It was an indication of Anderson's high regard for Brooke, with whom he had worked closely during the war. Brooke appreciated the offer but reserved judgment until he could ascertain Jones's opinion. Jones was cool to the proposition and insisted on a conference so the matter could be thoroughly discussed. His initial impression was that the proposed arrangement would impair their freedom of action and should only be consummated out of necessity. Nonetheless, Minor, the eternal optimist, gave up his insurance agency so that he would be prepared for what he felt sure would be better days. It was necessary in his judgment that the plan be put in operation by early August with an office established in Washington. Jones remained cautious. "It is a matter to be well considered," he wrote Minor, "and in your own case I should very much doubt the propriety of giving [up] a certain position for an uncertain one, particularly if there is not a necessity for it." Moreover, Jones was in the process of making some arrangements concerning his farm in Alabama, and if successful he believed he could establish an office in Washington and handle the business so long as the firm *"had no business."* [44]

Soon after the Japanese departed in June, Jones and Minor met and Jones strongly advised against the agency arrangement, maintaining that so long as they were paid by separate firms their position as agents could be misconstrued by others. Brooke concurred in Jones's opinion and the proposition was dropped.[45] Brooke, Minor and Jones, however, was not dissolved; each of the principals in his own way sought to procure business. At one time or another they held hopes of securing orders from Denmark, Switzerland, Spain, Great Britain, the North German Confederation, Austria, Greece, Italy, Turkey, and Brazil. And the partners re-

[43] Minor to Brooke, 9 May, 11 May, 10 June 1867, Brooke to Minor, 13 May 1867 (copy), BP.

[44] Anderson to Minor, 18 May 1867, BP; Jones to Minor, 11 June, 25 June 1867, Minor Papers, VHS.

[45] Minor to Brooke, 1 July 1867, BP; Jones to Minor, 25 June 1867, Brooke to Minor, 5 July 1867, Minor Papers, VHS.

newed their hopes of getting business from Japan when their friend E. G. Read went to the island empire. But something always seemed to interfere and dash their expectations. Only a few trivial orders were received. The first brought a modest payment of $25 from the state of Virginia for "furnishing specifications and lists of equipment for three small steam vessels." Brooke's share was one-third. Receipt of the "first fee" was "a very agreeable surprise" to the professor, and he shared Minor's trust that the fee would be followed by others.[46] A few weeks later the firm earned a profit of $23.50 for some fuses Minor made for Read before he left for Japan. From these modest heights the trail led to a dead end.

During this period Brooke seems not to have exerted himself as strenuously as his associates. Both Minor and Jones remarked on the long intervals between some of his letters. By the summer of 1868 Jones was quite dejected and in a letter to Minor asked: "Have you or Brooke any jobs in view or have any efforts been made to get them? Where is B. now?" Again, "What has become of Brooke. What has he been doing? anything for the firm?"[47] Not only was Brooke confined by his academic duties, but he was very much in love. Unfortunately his feelings were not fully shared by the object of his affection. Sensitive as always, he went through an emotional wringer. At one point, for example, he wrote Minor that he was "depressed by *associations*." He had been assiduously wooing Kate Corbin Pendleton, a widow. Brooke met Jones in Alexandria shortly thereafter, and when he left, Jones gave Minor his impressions: "He [Brooke] is much troubled about the widow, so much so that he declares himself incapacitated from attending to our business—'the course of true love never did run smooth'—He expects to go to Fredericksburg to see the lady again—Can you not aid him, t'would be aiding the firm."[48]

The firm continued on a desultory basis for a few more months, but the correspondence slacked as interests were developed elsewhere. By 1869 Brooke was becoming accustomed to

[46] Minor to Brooke, 10 June 1867, BP; Brooke to Minor, 19 June 1867, Minor Papers, VHS.

[47] Jones to Minor, 21 Aug., 12 Oct. 1868, Minor Papers, VHS.

[48] Brooke to Minor, 5 July 1867, Jones to Minor, 21 July 1867, ibid.

academic life. Discussing his position at the Institute with Minor, he admitted that his situation was "good in many respects." But he craved work in a field "in which there might be excitement and consequently more interest." Yet, he was still unwilling to give up a certain job for an uncertain one, despite the potential benefits.[49] Finally, in August 1869, Jones, who had been seeking business for the firm in New York at his own expense, decided that prospects were hopeless. Minor reluctantly concurred in Jones's decision.[50] Thus, it seems clear that Brooke, who conceived the idea of forming the firm in the first place, was from a lack of activity most responsible for its demise.

The formal dissolution of the firm ended the business correspondence between Jones and Brooke but not their friendship. With Minor the relationship changed but did not end. While Brooke remained at VMI and Minor worked, first for the Tredegar Company and then as an engineer with the James River Improvement Company, they continued to correspond, but not as frequently as in the past. They still talked of getting contracts to supply ordnance matériel for foreign governments and in the period of the Franco-Prussian War regained for a short while their earlier ebullience.

In April 1870 Brooke, Minor, and General Custis Lee were offered employment by the Egyptian government, Lee to be a brigadier general of engineers and Minor and Brooke to be colonels of ordnance. The contracts were for five years at salaries of about $3,500 plus forage and quarters. This seemingly attractive offer was "respectfully declined."[51] Before the year was out Custis Lee became president of Washington College in Lexington following the death of his illustrious father.

[49] Brooke to Minor, 15 March 1869, ibid.
[50] Minor to Brooke, 20 Aug. 1869, BP.
[51] Offer from Egyptian Government, April 1870, Minor Papers, VHS.

XI /

FRUSTRATION IN SCIENCE,

FULFILLMENT IN LOVE

FOR some fifteen years after the Civil War, Brooke was an active inventor. After that, as the years crept up and he became more involved in family responsibilities and Institute routine, he lost his zest for such work. When active, he was motivated not only by a desire to augment his professor's salary by selling patents and collecting royalties but by a compulsion to explore the questions raised by his restless mind. His inventions fall into two general categories: first, those of a mechanical nature applicable to general use; second, those relating to naval warfare. As in the case of the joint company with Minor and Jones, Brooke enjoyed little success. There were various reasons for failure, but as a whole it is fair to say he was a victim of the times in which he lived.

Following his return to civilian life, Brooke endeavored to find a market for his improved cat hook and a derivative of it, a boat hook. In May 1861, it will be recalled, he had obtained a patent on his cat hook for seventeen years, but after the war he was uncertain as to its status. In May 1866, however, he learned that his patent was "still respected."[1] Though he did not yet have a pardon, he kept in touch with the Tredegar Company and was as-

---

[1] E. R. Archer to Brooke, 31 May 1866, BP.

sured by its officials that the company would be happy to make a model for him so that he could bring the invention to the notice of the navy. But the matter hung fire until Brooke got his pardon in August.

Bob Minor described Brooke's device as "admirable in its simplicity." From his retreat in the Shenandoah Valley, Brooke depended initially on such friends as Minor and Catesby Jones either to sell the invention or make arrangements for its manufacture with royalties accruing to him. He offered his friends a generous commission of one-third, but they refused to accept more than one-fifth. Brooke hoped that the United States Navy or some individual would buy the patent right for $10,000.[2] As an alternative to sale, he was willing to authorize a person to produce his improved cat hook provided he got a royalty of three-fifths. Minor, writing from New York City, suggested William N. Webb or Francis Skiddy as possible manufacturers and first approached Skiddy, who was a capitalist and shipowner. Meanwhile, Brooke sent Baron Gerolt in Washington a description and drawings of the hook "to be forwarded to the Navy Dept of Prussia where if it be deemed worthy of a trial some experiments may be made with a view to its adoption."[3]

In November 1866 Brooke wrote his patent lawyer in Washington that he had "modified the arrangement of the hook when used for lowering boats" and asked if the modification was covered by his 1861 patent.[4] A model of this improvement, called a boat hook, was made by the Tredegar Company, and Bob Minor who was in Richmond commented that it was "very neatly made and works to a charm." Nonetheless, Minor preferred the original cat hook arrangement because of its "simple form" and thought that it would be "more readily adopted."[5] In New York, Minor was delighted to find a "very favorable reception" of the cat hook by a number of men, and he was optimistic about selling the patent right or licensing its use. Despite his optimism, Minor was dubious about getting $10,000 for the invention. As a result of conver-

---

[2] Brooke to Minor, 5 Nov. 1866 (copy), BP.

[3] Minor to Brooke, 15 Sept. 1866, Brooke to Gerolt, 3 Oct. 1866 (copy), BP.

[4] Brooke to Mason, Fenwick & Lawrence, 6 Nov. 1866 (copy), BP.

[5] Minor to Brooke, 19 Nov. 1866, BP.

sations in New York, Minor recommended that the new boat hook device not be combined with the cat hook in one apparatus. Brooke agreed. The levelheaded Catesby Jones thought Minor was "too sanguine" and wrote that "all speak well of the invention, but it is of limited demand, and in the present depressed state of the shipping interest, few are disposed to incur any expenses that can be possibly prevented. All fight shy of purchasing it."[6]

Minor left the Tredegar model with Jones in New York for interested businessmen to examine, and as a hedge against possible failure in New York he made a tentative arrangement with Reaney and Son and Archbold of Chester, Pennsylvania, whereby that company agreed to manufacture a hundred or so cat hooks and place them in ship chandlery stores for sale. Brooke would get a percentage on each hook sold. Hearing from Jones in New York that it was doubtful whether the cat hook could be disposed of there, the inventor decided to deal with Reaney, "leaving royalties to be determined hereafter." Minor agreed that the sooner the arrangement was made the better. Brooke sent Reaney and Son a description and drawings for a cat hook designed to hold five tons and hoped that the information would suffice for all sizes. "In an inland place like Lexington," he wrote, "there are no means of comparison such as are afforded by inspection of the anchors and cathooks of various sizes now in use, and I think you will therefore probably suggest some modification, of the proportions at least, of the design which I sent." Brooke believed that *"small hooks for general purpose* discharging cargo[,] ware house work &c would be popular."[7]

After a vexing delay by his patent lawyer Brooke finally obtained a patent for a "Boat detaching tackle" in September 1867. With a patent Brooke was sanguine, because a federal law required in many situations that ships carry some such apparatus. In 1867 alone twenty-seven patents for boat-detaching devices were issued, only two of them to southerners. Reaney had made iron cat hooks of five different sizes for distribution at ship chandleries and now agreed to produce Brooke's boat hook as well. But

[6] Minor to Brooke, 28 Nov. 1866, Jones to Brooke, 3 Dec. 1866, BP.

[7] Brooke to Minor, 12 Feb. 1867 (copy), [Brooke to Reaney], 26 April 1867 (copy), Brooke to Minor, 13 May 1867 (copy), BP.

progress was slow. With reference to both inventions Reaney wrote in the spring of 1868 that "the shipping and building interest has been so extremely dull that there has been no chance of introducing anything."[8]

Eventually taking matters into his own hands again, Brooke wrote to T. S. Negus, the New York instrument maker, to see if he could dispose of the boat hook. After a long delay Negus replied in an apologetic manner that he had "not been able to do anything with it." Six months after writing Negus, Brooke was still trying to sell the two inventions in New York. "It was my intention to offer both inventions to the Govt," he wrote a businessman, "but you will readily perceive that however friendly the officers of the Govt may be to me personally, and they are generally, very favorably disposed, political influences would interfere."[9] He still hoped northern capitalists might buy the inventions and dispose of them to the government. By this time Brooke had dropped his price to the $3,000–$5,000 range. As the months passed and no offer to purchase the patent right came in, Brooke grew despondent and contemplated reducing the price further. As late as August 1870, no sale had been consummated and the royalty payments from Reaney had been insignificant. In the long run Brooke profited from neither the cat hook nor the boat hook.

Over the years Brooke impressed his friends with his analytical turn of mind. In 1870, however, he pursued a will-o'-the-wisp. By theoretical analysis he developed what he thought was a self-tightening nut. The nut and its washer were to be so constructed that in a condition of vibration they would tighten rather than loosen. The potential market was enormous. In a flush of excitement Brooke wrote to General Anderson at the Tredegar Company about his invention. "But before incurring the expense of a patent which I cannot very well afford," he explained, "I wish to have the opinion of those who are familiar with such subjects and if possible some practical test as my invention which promises well is liable to be pirated."[10] Robert Archer at Tredegar was

---

[8] Records of the Patent Office, Patent Index, 1790–1873, RG 24, NA; Reaney and Sons to Brooke, 4 March 1868, BP.

[9] Negus to Brooke, 29 Jan. 1869, Brooke to E. E. Roberts & Co., New York, 14 Feb. 1870 (copy), BP.

[10] Brooke to Anderson, 1870 (copy), BP.

skeptical, but Brooke was persuasive and Archer made two bolts and nuts "fitted up in handsome style" for submission to the Patent Office. Meanwhile, Brooke had secured the services of a new patent agent in Washington recommended by Archer. But at the very last minute the inventor saw a flaw in his supposed invention. The lingering doubts of the capable Archer doubtless caused Brooke to check his suppositions carefully, and he found he was in error. Writing to his patent agent, he said: "There appears to be a fatality attending this nut business. For although when I mailed the papers to you this morning I was perfectly satisfied as to the correctness of the theory and experiment seemed to confirm it, I found on inspection of the models after the mail was closed, that the theory was incorrect and the supposed invention worthless." [11]

The Christmas season in 1872 found Brooke making drawings and preparing a detailed description of a pneumatic and hydraulic pump for raising water which he had invented a month earlier. Except for Christmas Day there was no holiday at the Institute in those days, and Brooke found his Institute duties "pressing," so he had to avail himself "of odds and ends of time." From the beginning the pump seems to have been a joint project with Thomas T. Munford of Lynchburg. Munford, a brigadier general in the Confederate army, had graduated from the Virginia Military Institute in 1852 and throughout his life took a deep interest in that institution. With regard to the pump, Brooke supplied the theoretical knowledge and Munford, who was proprietor of the Lynchburg Iron Works, supplied the capital. Brooke secured a patent in June 1873, assigning to General Munford a half interest in the invention. [12] After disappointing experiences with two business firms that he hoped could manufacture the pump, General Munford turned to his able mechanic, C. P. Leavitt, to perfect the design. By January 1875 Munford had orders for about two dozen pumps and was talking about organizing a company. But perfecting the pump proved to be slow work because of many interruptions, and not until more than three years after Brooke had invented it was Munford able to write: "I am now satisfied that Mr. Levitt has gotten in a position to perfect the pump and to do something with

[11] Brooke to William Baldwin, 23 May 1870 (copy), BP.
[12] Specifications for Letters Patent no. 139,538, dated 3 June 1873, BP.

it." By this time Leavitt had constructed one pump and had ten more under way. In 1876 Leavitt, who had been compelled to make his own tools, felt there was "a very active demand for pumps," but production was hampered by a lack of proper castings. Later the same year Leavitt left General Munford's employ, and the pump business seems to have languished. Certainly Brooke never made much from his pump invention.[13]

In 1870 Brooke designed what he called an "oscillating seat for row boats," but he did not apply for a patent. Brooke's improvement in his view made it possible to shave a few seconds off a boat's time in a close race. The new seat enabled the sculler to use his power more effectively than he could with the fixed seats then used. In return for half the profits, he offered the invention to a boat-building firm in Troy, New York; but after considering a description and drawing of the seat, the firm seems to have rejected the proposition.[14]

Meteorology was a subject of continuing interest to Brooke. Not only did he teach it at VMI, but he kept records and conducted experiments. In 1871 he devised what he called a "meteorama" to aid meteorologists in forecasting weather and submitted the invention to General Albert J. Myer, chief signal officer of the army, who had just established the Weather Service as part of his office the year before. With this "simple contrivance" barometric readings for a wide area could be more effectively given than by graphic representation.[15] As Brooke wrote to Baron Gerolt, the meteorama would "present the condition of the atmosphere, when adjusted in accordance with the meteorological reports from the various stations to the eye in such a way as to enable the operator to see at a glance what changes are to be anticipated." Brooke in a confident mood informed Bob Minor that he believed "no other means can give equally valuable results in the hands of competent persons." After examining the meteorama, General Myer replied that he was favorably impressed. "I have much faith in your skill and ingenuity to perfect your plans," he wrote.[16]

[13] Munford to Brooke, 10 Jan. 1876, Leavitt to Brooke, 16 Jan. 1876, BP.
[14] Brooke to Walter Balch and Co., Troy, N.Y., 24 March, 18 April 1870 (copy), BP.
[15] Brooke to General Myer, 20 Dec. 1871 (copy), BP.
[16] Brooke to Gerolt, 9 Jan. 1871 (copy), BP; Brooke to Minor, 6 Feb. 1871, Minor Papers, VHS; Myer to Brooke, 28 Feb. 1871, BP.

Brooke saw Myer in Washington, and a model of the meteorama was made. It is presumed that this useful instrument was put to good use.

The question of mine safety aroused Brooke's interest, and in 1878 he wrote Marsden Manson, a former assistant in the Physics Department at VMI who was a geologist and consulting engineer in San Francisco, for information about mines "in which extraordinarily high temperatures prevail." Brooke had devised a means to reduce temperatures economically, and a few days later he submitted his plan for improved ventilation to a New York company for consideration. "The advantages of this improvement," he wrote, "consist chiefly in the simplicity, facility of application and automatic action." Though the improvement might well have had these attributes, nothing seems to have come of the venture.[17]

But what continued to fascinate Brooke was naval ordnance. During the war he had devoted much of his personal energy to producing cannon and ammunition. Afterwards, he concentrated on sea mines. Perhaps he felt that with the development of the Brooke gun and the discovery of the utility of the air space he had done all he could with cannon. Certainly the limited facilities in Lexington prevented much practical experimentation with guns. But with mines, or torpedoes as they were called, the situation was different. This was a relatively undeveloped field which since the Civil War had been attracting widespread interest in the United States and abroad. Although Brooke had had overall responsibility for experimental work in the Confederate navy, much of the practical work in mines had been handled at first by Matthew Fontaine Maury and later by the specialized Confederate States Submarine Battery Service under Hunter Davidson. Brooke had also worked with the army Torpedo Bureau and Secret Service Corps through Gabriel J. Rains, Charles A. McEvoy, and Francis D. Lee. As was noted earlier, the primitive mines of the Civil War were utilized mainly as defensive weapons, both army and navy being concerned primarily with river and harbor defense.

After the war Brooke had more time to experiment with underwater weapons, and in the period 1870–74 he was particularly

[17] Brooke to Manson, 19 Oct. 1878 (copy), Brooke to Munn and Co., 23 Oct. 1878 (copy), BP.

active, as his fertile mind teemed with untried ideas. He worked on a stationary mine, which was apparently an improvement of his Civil War "turtle"; conferred with and wrote to the officers in charge of the Naval Torpedo Station at Newport, Rhode Island; and corresponded with the army engineer in charge at Willet's Point, New York. Also, the former chief of ordnance kept in touch with his former Confederate comrades, C. A. McEvoy in England and Davidson, who worked in Europe and South America. Both McEvoy and Davidson were actively engaged in mine work. On the other hand, Maury, Rains, Francis Lee, and Beverley Kennon turned to other work after the war. Maury, who had pioneered in Confederate mine work before going to England in 1862, had when abroad completed a comprehensive mine system, but in 1865 while in Mexico, he had released his patent rights to an Englishman.[18]

When the American government seemed indifferent, Brooke attempted to sell his ideas to the British and Germans. In 1866 Baron Gerolt at the request of the Prussian Ministry of the Navy began to gather information on the use of mines by the Confederacy. Turning to Brooke, he asked for drawings and descriptions of the best torpedoes developed in the Confederate States. Brooke responded that he would be glad to furnish "all the information I possess in regard to torpedoes."[19] In return, the baron sent Brooke a sextant for his VMI classes.

International events in the summer of 1870 accelerated Brooke's torpedo activity. Three days after Napoleon III declared war on the North German Confederation, Brooke received a telegram from Baron Gerolt urging a conference in Washington. In response Brooke left for the national capital where he and the Prussian minister discussed mines, torpedo boats, and submarines. From Washington, Brooke went to Newport, Rhode Island, to consult Vice Admiral David Dixon Porter and ascertain his "views in regard to the system of marine torpedoes adopted by the U.S."[20] The admiral authorized Brooke to obtain any information on torpedoes not inconsistent with the best interests of the United

[18] Perry, *Infernal Machines*, p. 191.

[19] Brooke to Gerolt, n.d. (copy), BP.

[20] Brooke kept a timetable and an expense account for his peregrinations; they are in the Brooke Papers.

States and gave him a card of introduction to Commander Edward Orville Matthews, head of the Torpedo Corps stationed at Newport. Brooke had a comprehensive conversation with Matthews on the latest techniques in torpedo warfare, including an improvement of Brooke's design for a mine "designed to maintain a constant depth below the surface of the water at all stages of the tide."[21] Brooke then proceeded to New York where he conferred with Hunter Davidson about torpedo warfare. Davidson would soon leave for Berlin.

Back in Lexington after an absence of six weeks, Brooke made a working drawing of the harbor defense mine that he had described to Commander Matthews and sent it to Newport. He then prepared with Bob Minor a formal proposal, including drawings and a description of the mine, which he valued at $10,000. This proposal was forwarded to Davidson, now in Wilhelmshaven, for submission to the Prussian government. Davidson was offered a fifth of whatever he could get for the invention.

For a time Minor and Brooke were buoyed by a letter from Davidson saying "that the Prussians think favorably of the sea torpedo proposition and want the estimates." But frustration again supplanted hope. Government red tape and the shortness of the war closed the promising road to riches. By the end of the year the German armies had established their complete superiority over the French. Davidson returned to the United States and once again Brooke lost out in his bid for ordnance work for reasons beyond his control. Writing from Cambridge, Maryland, Davidson explained that the documents on Brooke's invention had not arrived until after he had left Wilhelmshaven. Davidson expressed regret and observed that he was "quite sure that something could have been realized on it." It was not much consolation for Davidson to suggest that if Brooke had gone to Prussia "at once" he "would have been worth *$100,000* easy." Though treated with courtesy Davidson had been outmaneuvered by agents from other countries. In passing, Davidson observed that Baron Gerolt did not carry much weight in Berlin and was retained in Washington because of George Bancroft's influence.[22]

[21] Brooke to [Matthews], 7 Sept. 1870 (copy), BP.
[22] Brooke to Minor, [c. 13 Oct. 1870], Minor Papers, VHS; Davidson to Brooke, 22 Dec. 1870, BP.

Although the former Confederates lost out, torpedoes did play a significant part in the Franco-Prussian War. As Prussia had only a small navy, France was denied the effective use of torpedoes, offensively or defensively. With Prussia it was different. At the outbreak of the war, Prussian newspapers announced that Prussia had strewn its harbors and river approaches with mines. Taken up by the French press, these reports had a paralyzing effect upon the French, and their armored fleets "were rendered practically useless so far as inflicting damage on the enemy was concerned." As a matter of fact, however, there was some bluff involved. Prussia actually did not have enough mines and those it had were of a primitive nature, but it filled the gap by using dummies. Both mechanical and electrical mines were used. By the end of the war the Prussians were using small boats with spar torpedoes that frightened French blockading vessels.[23] Use of such torpedo boats was what Brooke had advocated with his emphasis on offensive warfare, and through Baron Gerolt, he had transmitted to Berlin estimates for seagoing torpedo boats.

Brooke had been considering an offensive torpedo system even before the Franco-Prussian War. Writing to Captain Fillebrown in 1869, Brooke had quoted the chief of ordnance as having said: "The interests of the country demand that every new improvement in ordnance or war materials should be carefully investigated and when shown to be valuable speedily adopted." On the strength of this statement, Brooke described a plan he had conceived for torpedo boats "by which torpedoes may be replaced as soon as exploded by others[,] changed without exposing the operations of the apparatus." The concept could be applied to either surface or submarine vessels. Brooke likened an engagement between such a torpedo boat and an ironclad to that between a "sword fish and the whale." Fillebrown was asked to inquire discreetly whether the navy wanted such a weapon. Although Brooke had "had enough of patents," he was willing to make an arrangement with the navy for his torpedo boat, which he felt overcame problems presented by earlier inventions. There is no evidence that the government accepted his offer.[24]

[23] Bradford, *History of Torpedo Warfare*, pp. 84–85.
[24] Brooke to Fillebrown, 14 Dec. 1869 (copy), BP.

By the time he answered Baron Gerolt's request for information a year later, Brooke had perfected his torpedo boat system. He noted that in the past torpedo attacks had been made by small boats that depended upon secret or underwater approach. Such boats were complicated in construction and were utilized as auxiliaries to ordinary warships. Their record had not been good. Brooke's system called for the construction of numerous very fast, seagoing iron steamers with twin screws. They would be so constructed that in a running engagement with a ponderous opponent, such as an ironclad, they could not easily be sunk. This relative invulnerability would be obtained by placing the engines and boilers protected by coal bunkers below the waterline and through numerous vertical and horizontal partitions dividing the hull into watertight compartments. The vessel would have telescopic stacks and would protrude only far enough out of the water to remain seaworthy. Because the torpedo boat was designed to attack its slower adversary quickly, in most cases the lighter vessel would not be sunk or incapacitated before accomplishing its mission.

To meet different situations Brooke advised that the torpedo boat carry various types of torpedoes, including those of the spar and towed variety. Such specialized vessels would only require a small crew. To the Prussian minister Brooke stated: "It is now generally admitted that the torpedo is destined to be the most effective of all weapons in marine warfare. the state which first applies upon such a scale as is here indicated will be the first to reap its advantages in full." Such vessels could be constructed quickly and cheaply, and Brooke volunteered to supervise their construction for the Prussian government in the United States. But there was confusion in forwarding the estimates, and before this could be done the short war was over.[25]

Although Brooke preferred torpedo boats to submarines, he was not unfamiliar with the latter. In fact, during the Franco-Prussian War at the request of the Prussians he made a general inspection of a highly publicized submarine called the "Intelligent Whale" with its designer, General O. S. Halstead. It was Brooke's opinion that this submersible, in which the American government

[25] [Brooke] to Gerolt, n.d. (copy), BP.

had shown an interest as far back as 1864, was "safe and efficient" and could operate at far greater depths than required in offensive torpedo operations. Yet, he was convinced that the United States, despite its interest in the "Whale," had not given sufficient attention to the submarine as a weapon. During the course of the Franco-Prussian War, Brooke offered to build a submarine for the Prussian government. Not until the war was over did he learn that the Germans had not used his plan, because the French had not given them "any trouble in that way."[26]

From 1871 to 1873 Brooke continued to hope for favorable action by the American government on his constant-depth torpedo. Commander Matthews at the Torpedo School even mentioned visiting Lexington so that he and Brooke could discuss such weapons as mines and torpedoes, and Brooke sent Matthews drawings of the mine he had designed. But as time passed the old Confederate's hopes dimmed. The letters Matthews wrote to Commodore Augustus Ludlow Case, chief of the Bureau of Ordnance, and to Case's successor, Admiral William Jeffers, refer to how busy he was. Increasingly Matthews gave his time to matters concerning the appointment of faculty, student standards, and building construction at the Torpedo School.[27]

In 1873 Matthews was succeeded by Captain Edward Simpson, who had served with Brooke on the Coast Survey. The frustrated Brooke unburdened himself to Simpson: "I wish to call to your attention, an invention which I submitted confidentially to him [Matthews] some three years ago, and which he commenced experimenting upon. etc. . . . [He] seemed to be much interested in his results which were favorable, wrote to me that effect. He also proposed to visit me after some business which he had to transact at the Dept. should have been completed. But this intention he did not carry out, and after his visit to Washington, he seemed to take no interest in the matter." Admiral Jeffers in letters to Captain Simpson criticized Matthews's regime in strong

[26] Brooke to Gerolt, 19 Aug. 1870 (copy), Memo, n.d. [c. Aug. 1870], Brooke to A. W. Johnson, 22 Feb. 1887 (copy), Gerolt to Brooke, 18 Oct. 1870, 10 Feb. 1871, BP.

[27] Matthews to Case, 19 Feb., 21 March, 25 March, 9 May, 18 May, 24 May, 17 June, 9 Sept., 25 Sept. 1872, 12 April, 23 April 1873, Correspondence and Reports, Letters Received from Commander Matthews, 1871–73, RG 74, NA.

terms. "Matthews began on a very quiet scale, but was afterwards siezed with a mania for building, and latterly did nothing else [at Newport]," complained Jeffers. "The practical work was a farce, and nothing has been accomplished beyond the application of torpedoes to launches."[28] The effect of all this on Brooke was that valuable time was lost and there was the growing possibility that someone might preempt his invention. He was disturbed by the work being done in England. To Simpson, Brooke confided that he would have sent his "invention across the water long ago" except he felt obligated to give Matthews ample time. Impatient, in 1872 he had even written to his friend General Henry Larcom Abbot of the army engineers at Willet's Point about the invention, but he never mailed the letter.[29]

The appointment of Simpson seemed to augur well when that officer wrote Brooke: "I always had faith in your inventive genius, and I am prejudiced in favor of your proposed system. I will look into it when I get settled, and will do all I can for it if I approve it." But Simpson did not follow through, either. A year later Jeffers, now chief of ordnance and interested in practical results, remarked that Simpson had given too much time to theoretical matters and the only torpedo he had developed at Newport was the pole torpedo. Jeffers, deciding to take matters into his own hands, complained that "there is no doubt but that we are at present entirely 'at sea' on the Torpedo question." He asserted that he was going to New York to discuss the Ericsson torpedo with its inventor, but he made no mention of John Brooke. To get results Jeffers hoped to coordinate efforts with the army rather than have the services demonstrate "how very little either of us know on the subject."[30]

Though Brooke focused his attention on torpedoes after the war, he did a little work with ordnance. One aspect of ordnance that attracted his attention was the accuracy of guns. Even the

[28] Brooke to Simpson, 8 June 1873 (copy), BP; Jeffers to Simpson, 22 July 1873, Semiofficial private letters to Capt. Edward Simpson, Torpedo Section, 1873–75, RG 74, NA (see also letters of 12 June, 8 July, 19 July, 22 July, 5 Sept., 6 Sept. 1873).

[29] Brooke to Simpson, 8 June 1873 (copy), BP.

[30] Simpson to Brooke, 22 June 1873, BP; Jeffers to Col. W. C. Church, 7 March 1874, Semiofficial private letters to Capt. Edward Simpson, Torpedo Station, 1873–75, RG 74, NA.

best guns were not accurate if sighted improperly. In 1869 Brooke
devised a simpler means of sighting guns by the use of a mirror to
line up the gunsights. To Captain Simpson he remarked that "the
cumbrous apparatus now in use can not be conveniently transported." Brooke's apparatus could be packed in a small box. For
some reason consideration of the merits of the invention was delayed for ten years; not until 1880 was a report rendered by the
inspector of ordnance at the Washington Navy Yard. The inspector reported that Brooke's instrument for sighting guns had two
advantages over the existing system, but he also listed several
disadvantages. For the instrument to be used properly, great care
had to be exercised. Moreover, some of the parts of the instrument were susceptible to damage. No specific recommendation was made, but the disadvantages appear to have outweighed the advantages. There is no evidence that any further
action was taken by the Navy Department.[31]

While working in physics at VMI in 1870 Brooke devised an
instrument he named the "electric pointer" which by plotting a
hostile vessel's changing course on a chart enabled the shore defenders to destroy the vessel with torpedoes. Brooke submitted
the invention to his old shipmate Captain Fillebrown in Washington and asked him to refer it to Commodore Case, chief of ordnance, for evaluation. Should it prove useful, Brooke was willing
to sell it to the government for a price "deemed sufficient by
officers familiar with the subject." The European countries were
making rapid progress in perfecting a system of torpedo defense;
consequently, Brooke felt it his duty to offer the electric pointer to
his own government, "despite the old saying, a prophet is not
without honor save in his own country."[32] As Brooke felt harbor
defense was more a responsibility of the army than the navy, he
also prepared a letter for General Andrew A. Humphreys, chief
of engineers, describing the invention, which he asked Captain
Simpson to transmit. Just when everything seemed to be falling in
place, Brooke learned that his invention had been anticipated in

[31] Brooke to Simpson, 5 April 1870, BP; Cmdr. H. L. Howison, Inspector of Ordnance, to Commodore Jno. C. Febiger, Commandant, Washington Navy Yard, 10 Jan.
1870, Correspondence regarding the Examination of Inventions, RG 74, NA.
[32] Brooke to Lee, 16 April 1870 (copy), BP.

Austria. To the surprise of everyone, Admiral Jeffers had by chance come across a report of the United States commissioner to the Paris Exposition of 1867 in which an invention similar to Brooke's was described.[33] Brooke conceded that the invention of Captain Kocziczka of the Austrian imperial engineers precluded his claim. But no one could understand why such an important invention had been so generally overlooked by both the army and the navy for three years.

Brooke's last ordnance invention was that of a gun which could be fired under water. When guns were fired at high velocity under water, the walls of the muzzle, constrained by the surrounding water, were placed under an abnormal strain by the expansion of the powder gases. Brooke devised a method providing for the escape of the gases by a lateral tube at the instant the projectile entered the water. The idea was submitted to Admiral Thornton Jenkins for his consideration. There was no immediate response, but it can be surmised that Jenkins referred the matter to examiners for tests. In any case, on a sketch drawn and signed by John M. Brooke, Admiral Jeffers noted, "Filed Bd. of Ordnance."[34]

Brooke's numerous disappointments with his inventions were offset by renewed family ties and a second marriage which brought a quiet happiness. Throughout his life he was a person to whom family in the personal sense meant much. While indifferent to genealogy, he maintained a warm interest in his blood relations which he refreshed by visits and correspondence. Naturally, then, with the return of peace in 1865 Brooke's thoughts had turned to his mother's relatives in Duxbury, Massachusetts, with whom he had had no contact since before the war. He wrote to his uncle Briggs Thomas and must have been gratified by the reply. Thomas expressed much pleasure at receiving John's letter and said that the whole family rejoiced that John and William were "among the living." "You may rest assured," he wrote, "that all your nere relatives here especialy your Uncles & Aunts retain the same affectionate feelings and sympathy for our Sister Lucy['s] Children that we ever have and trust ever shall have." Thomas

[33] Fillebrown to Brooke, 20 April 1870, BP.
[34] Brooke to Jenkins, 22 Nov. 1878 (copy), BP.

was concerned about Brooke's health and employment prospects and hoped his nephew could visit Duxbury. The Thomas relatives had heard of some of Brooke's Civil War accomplishments and took a family pride in them.[35] For the next thirty years Brooke conducted a correspondence with three generations of his mother's family. In 1867 and again in 1876 he visited Duxbury, and on one or two occasions young cousins visited Lexington.

Most of Lucy Brooke's brothers and sisters with their old-fashioned, biblical names lived into their seventies and eighties, but by the 1870s they were passing from the scene in rather rapid succession, hardworking, religious people to the end. Many of the children had moved from Duxbury, some to New York and Illinois, but most remained in Massachusetts. John Brooke was reluctant to see these family ties broken. And when he was seventy, still thinking along these lines, he wrote a cousin in Dorchester, Massachusetts, remarking, "I take great interest in all that relates to my mother's kindred, leaving Duxbury the successive generations scatter. I would like therefore to have some information as to their whereabouts. As time passes the lines will otherwise be broken."[36] Though Brooke had fought as hard as he knew how for the Confederacy, he was never ashamed of his Northern blood.

Hard up for cash, Brooke in May 1866, wrote attorneys in Leavenworth, Kansas, about 160 acres in the Delaware Trust Lands that he had bought on October 1, 1858. Taxes had been paid through 1860 and Brooke was anxious to learn if his land had been confiscated or sold.[37] He found that his land had not been disposed of but that it would cost $125–$150 to pay the delinquent taxes or buy the call certificates. The lawyers stated that there was no demand for prairie land at that time, but eventually Brooke's land would be worth $3–$5 an acre. An attempt was made to sell the land at the lower price, but there were no takers, for, as the lawyers pointed out, "money is scarce & times hard in

[35] Thomas to Brooke, 14 June 1865, BP.

[36] Brooke to Mrs. Ray Ripley, 4 March 1896 (copy), BP.

[37] Brooke to Messrs. J. A. & D. G. Holderman, 27 May 1866 (copy), BP. Although Brooke said the land had been purchased on 1 Oct. 1858, there is reason to believe he meant the date to be 1857.

Kansas."[38] Apparently unable to pay the delinquent taxes, Brooke early in 1868 sold the land for $75, or less than fifty-seven cents an acre, to the attorneys who assumed the back taxes.

Until 1864 John Brooke's personal life had revolved around Lizzie, and when she died after a lingering illness he had buried his grief in a mountain of work. When the Southern struggle for independence was lost, Brooke, unemployed and forced to confront himself, was torn by remorse for not having been a better husband. He began to draw into himself and concentrate his affections on Anna, his link with the painful yet wonderful past. In those sad days he received much comfort from Mrs. M. T. James of Gloucester, Virginia, whose husband owned a shipyard on the York River. Mrs. James had been a close friend of Lizzie's and understood John Brooke well. Gloucester served as a haven for Brooke during vacation periods, a place where he could relive the old days under a cloak of sympathy. And when in Lexington, Brooke wrote to Mrs. James and she responded—signing herself "your true friend"—giving advice when asked and sometimes trying subtly to redirect Brooke's thoughts when he was in a fit of depression. She showed the greatest interest in Anna and like Lizzie stressed the value of the Scriptures as a healing agent for wounded souls. On one occasion she reassured the lonely man that "no thing concerning Anna and yourself is too trivial to interest me."[39]

But as a widower Brooke found himself only half a person. He needed someone with him constantly to share his victories and defeats. Only forty in 1867, his passionate nature demanded companionship. Moreover, a wife could do things for Anna that Brooke could never do. Nowhere did Brooke explain more clearly his ideas on marriage than in a letter of advice he wrote in April 1867: "I would suggest to you, if you need suggestion, the inestimable advantage of adding to ambition the desire of promoting the happiness of some one who will sympathise with you, encourage you in trouble and share with you in trouble and share with you in success the events of life. In other words wear the colors of

[38] J. A. and D. B. Holderman to Brooke, 27 Sept. 1867, BP.
[39] James to Brooke, 29 May [1869], BP.

some fair lady and enter the lists to win her commendation."[40] By this time Brooke was prepared to take his own advice and had begun to look around for a new wife. This was no easy matter, for Brooke had high standards and knew exactly what kind of wife he wanted. Moody, introspective, sentimental, serious and reserved, yet brilliant and impatient, he was not an easy person to satisfy. While he was considering various possibilities, he could always, so long as brother William lived, count on a sympathetic ear. William never married but fell in and out of love a number of times and each time seemed to suffer a severe emotional jolt. He showed great interest in John's romantic pursuits, and drawing on his own experience he counseled his brother with a dash of levity.[41]

At one point Brooke's name was linked with that of Agnes Lee, a daughter of General Robert E. Lee. Certainly they took walks and went boating together on the North River. But it is hard to say whether it was a serious romance. Nonetheless, some people seemed to think that it was. In April 1867 Catesby Jones, in the midst of discussing affairs of the joint company, wrote Minor: "If Brooke has been so fortunate as to win Agnes Lee, he is indeed to be congratulated. She was one of my favorites."[42]

During this trying time for Brooke, no friend stood firmer than Bob Minor. While residing in Richmond the warmhearted Minor acted as a willing middleman, transmitting brief messages back and forth between his friend and Margaretta Wise, the witty and vivacious daughter of former Governor Henry A. Wise. One of the belles of the sixties, Margaretta, called Néné, had been born in Portugal when her father was United States minister there. The references to Néné were usually at the end of business letters and in a light vein. Brooke sent messages cloaked in nautical terminology and Néné responded in kind. Late in 1866 Minor wrote his friend: "I delivered your message to Miss Néné—

[40] Brooke to Morehead, 13 April 1867 (copy), BP. The contents of the letter indicate that Morehead was a young man who served with Brooke in the Confederacy.

[41] During the Civil War, William had worked in the Naval Office of Ordnance and Hydrography and had shown a keen interest in his brother's work. A clubfoot incapacitated him for field duty. After the war he secured a position as a tutor in Caroline County and remained there until his death in 1868 at age 37.

[42] Jones to Minor, 9 April 1867, Minor Papers, VHS. The North River is now called the Maury.

or rather she read that portion of your letter—at the whist table and her only reply was 'Capt Brooke is a humbug'—I called it 'your cable message'—but 'twas too deep for me. She is very clever—and very agreeable—and I like her very much—she laughed at the 'Store clothes' paragraph." The "store clothes" allusion related to a game Minor played. In many of his letters to Brooke over a five-year period, he jokingly mentioned the need for dress clothes at Brooke's wedding and he constantly asked when he might be called upon to use them. There is no doubt that Brooke liked Néné very much and found her to be highly amusing, but it is not clear how serious the romance was. Once she sent him a cake. If Néné and John had been able to see more of each other, events might have taken a different turn. In his letters to Minor, Brooke often mentioned how much he would like to see the Humbird, as he dubbed Néné. As it was, after a year and a half of bantering, Brooke noted in a letter to Minor: "I hear that Miss N——is engaged to be married, so our friends leave us."[43]

By early 1867 Brooke had focused his attention on Mrs. Kate Corbin Pendleton, twelve years younger than himself. She was the widow of Lieutenant Colonel Alexander Swift Pendleton, the only son of General William Nelson Pendleton, rector of Grace Episcopal Church in Lexington and General Lee's former chief of artillery. Colonel Pendleton, called "Sandy," had served in turn as adjutant general for Generals "Stonewall" Jackson, Richard Ewell, and Jubal Early, before being cut down at the Battle of Fisher's Hill in 1864.[44] After the war, in order to be near Sandy's family and in response to their urgent invitation, Kate had moved in with the Pendletons in Lexington, but later she obtained a position as governess at Clifton, the home of Colonel William Preston Johnston, a professor of Washington College.

It took Brooke a long time to wear down Kate's resistance, as the Pendletons offered subtle opposition and perhaps Kate sensed the captain would not be an easy man to live with.[45] But in 1869

[43] Minor to Brooke, 22 Dec. 1866, BP; Brooke to Minor, 31 March 1868, Minor Papers, VHS. Néné married William Carrington Mayo.

[44] See William Gleason Bean, *Stonewall's Man, Sandie Pendleton* (Chapel Hill, N.C., 1959).

[45] This opposition is revealed in Brooke's diary and in copies of the letters he wrote.

she finally consented. General Smith, the VMI superintendent, promised to take immediate steps to build a house for Brooke, and the latter began drawing sketches and floor plans for a suitable dwelling. But as delays piled up Brooke and Kate decided not to delay the wedding until the house was completed.

John Brooke and Kate Corbin Pendleton were married in Fredericksburg on March 14, 1871. The date must have been advanced for in the preceding December General Pendleton, who was on a fund-raising tour for the church, wrote that he had heard from Kate and she "hardly expects to be married before next summer." Mrs. James was caught off guard too, and when she heard Brooke was to be married momentarily, she dashed off a note explaining that she had understood he "would not be married for several months."[46] After his frantic courtship Brooke was almost casual in announcing his plans to Bob Minor, who was eager to stand up with him. Writing on February 6, he observed: "I shall probably be married in Fredericksburg, shall not, however, have any of those multitudinous gatherings which generally attend such affairs. At least that is what I understand to be the idea of the one who has the most say in regard to it."[47]

Back in Lexington after the church wedding, Brooke wrote Bob Minor that he had "come to an anchor with a prize under my lee." He explained that "there were no attendants except the family and the usual complement of spectators. Everything was right the parson tied us tight." The house was nearly ready for occupancy, "only delayed in accordance with Lexington usage." In a jovial mood, the new husband found that the VMI mechanics reminded him of "monkeys with paint pails." Minor, a good sport to the end, replied that he had been teased unmercifully because his "store clothes" had not been needed after all. In 1875 Brooke exercised an option to buy the house and lot. There was some doubt as to the authority of the Board of Visitors to give a clear title, but the board agreed that as soon as the legislature conferred

[46] Pendleton to his wife, 3 Dec. 1870, William Nelson Pendleton Papers, Southern Hist. Collection, UNC; Mrs. James to Brooke, 10 Feb. 1871, BP. She wrote letters both to Lexington and Fredericksburg to make sure Brooke would receive one promptly.

[47] Brooke to Minor, 6 Feb. 1871, Minor Papers, VHS.

the necessary power it would make a deed of sale upon Brooke's payment of $3,500 in Virginia bonds.[48]

Brooke's marriage to Kate, a devout Christian to whom formal religion meant much, had also solved for Brooke a problem that had long bothered him. Nine months before the wedding, doubtless to satisfy Kate, he had been confirmed in the Episcopal church.[49]

Kate had deliberated long and hard on her second marriage, but once she made up her mind she gave her life completely to her new husband. Perhaps she was not consumed by the flames of youthful passion, but she proved to have the abiding love and deep devotion that in the long run would count for more. Kate sensed John's need for her and hers for him. In the days of poverty and adversity that marked the Reconstruction years, they could put their individual tragedies behind them and shape together a new life of hope. They would be stronger for it. With an understanding wife and a stable home, John would enjoy the pleasures of home life which the navy, the war, and then the loss of his first wife had denied him. No longer need he dread orders that meant long and endless separations. And it was particularly comforting to him that the gentle Kate proved to be a very good stepmother to Anna, who was now in her teens. On May 17, 1875, a little more than four years after the wedding, George Mercer Brooke was born. As letters came in from relatives and friends, Brooke, now forty-eight, must have felt a glow of paternal pride. Over the years George would be very close to his mother, but with his father the relationship would be more formal. Though George would love and respect his father, the difference in age and Captain Brooke's sense of dignity aroused a feeling of awe.

A second child, Rosa Johnston, was born on October 29,

[48] Brooke to Minor, 23 March 1871, ibid.; Minor to Brooke, 30 March 1871, BP; Board of Visitors Minutes, VMI, 18 Jan. 1875. The property was sold to VMI by the Brooke family in 1950.

[49] The register of Grace (Episcopal) Church, now Robert E. Lee Memorial Church, shows that on Sunday, 12 June 1870 (Trinity Sunday), Brooke and Anna were confirmed. See also chap. VII, n. 88 above.

1876. She was named for Rosa Tucker Johnston, the wife of Colonel William Preston Johnston, in whose house Kate had worked. In time Rosa would marry Henry Parker Willis, a Washington and Lee University professor who became a prominent economist. A second son, Richard Corbin, was born in 1878 but soon died. This tragedy strengthened the ties in the little family, coming as it did so closely after a frantic period when young George, desperately ill, had nearly died.

Whenever Brooke was away from home, Kate, who called him Captain Brooke, wrote him affectionate letters describing the activities of the children in detail, and when the children grew old enough to visit, she tried to write them every day. It is clear that Kate was not only a good wife but a wonderful mother. Brooke, fifty years older than his children, was reserved in manner, but Kate made as warm a home life for him as he could have hoped for. In his letters to old friends, Brooke revealed pride and contentment with family life. When possible the old sailor sought to amuse the children, as in June 1885 when he took them to the boat race between the Harry Lees and the Albert Sydneys, boat crews at Washington and Lee University. Getting into the spirit of the occasion, he noted: "The Harry Lees won, but owing I think to an unlucky encounter of oars with overhanging tree boughs just before the finish. The Albert Sydneys had been ahead."[50] One can imagine young George, age ten, echoing his father's opinions.

In contrast to her husband, Kate's great interest was people rather than ideas. The letters she wrote to her family and friends in the 1860s suggest that she was well educated for a young lady of that day and had a mind of her own. She was noted for her charm, animation, and kindness. When casual callers dropped in, the captain, not interested in small talk or gossip, usually paid his respects and then retired to his study to wrestle with intellectual problems, while Kate entertained the guests—something she did very well. Understanding John's quirks, she arranged her routine to suit him. Of course, if an old friend like Hunter Davidson or Bob Minor came for a visit, Brooke always had a "shot in the

[50] Brooke's garden journal, 16 June 1885, BP.

locker," and no doubt there was vibrant conversation on a wide range of topics, past, present, and future, far into the night.

Kate was proud of her husband's scientific accomplishments, and quite early she seems to have decided that he had not received the recognition he was due. Except among a few navy men and scientists, his work was unsung. Kate knew that Brooke was a modest and retiring person who would not push himself ahead. Consequently, early in her marriage she began to record in a diary conversations with her husband about his past.

Meanwhile, Anna blossomed into a young lady. She was an apt student in school and read extensively. Affectionate and devoted to her family, she had a number of cadet beaus and on occasion visited friends and relatives in various parts of the state. The letters she dutifully wrote home when she was visiting are marked by precision and clarity. She called the children, who were twenty years her junior, "Brother" and "Dolly" and was very sweet with them. In 1885, just at the time she had accepted a position to teach in the schools of Abbeville, South Carolina, she became sick and had to resign the position. Sinking rapidly, she died in a few days at the age of twenty-eight. The whole family was greatly saddened, but for Brooke this sudden severance of a last link with the dim past was an especially cruel blow.

XII /

THREE DECADES

AT VIRGINIA MILITARY

INSTITUTE

A BRIGHT spot in Brooke's early years at the Institute was his renewed association with Matthew Fontaine Maury, who joined the
faculty in 1868. By unanimous resolution the Academic Board
had recommended "the appointment of Capt M F Maury as Prof.
of Meteorology." Commodore Maury's international reputation
stood firmly on his work as an oceanographer. But his letters show
that for many years he had been interested in building up agriculture through a scientific study of climatology and meteorology.
Like General Smith, Maury was eager to expand the economic
resources of the South, particularly Virginia.

When Maury's acceptance of the position at VMI was announced, Brooke, who had corresponded with him since the war, hastened to congratulate him and inform him that his acceptance had
"excited very lively emotions of pleasure." Brooke observed that it
was his understanding that the term *meteorology* in Maury's title
was "merely provisional." Commodore Maury's appointment
meant much to Brooke in a personal way. But it also affected his

official duties, because there was a danger of overlapping responsibilities. In announcing Maury's imminent arrival to the Board of Visitors, General Smith remarked that Maury would be in charge of the physical survey of Virginia for the purpose "of preparing a complete physical history of the state accompanied by an accurate geographical map." This was in fact the project to which General Custis Lee and Colonels McDonald and Brooke had been assigned the year before under Lee's supervision. Under Maury's direction, however, the undertaking was even more ambitious. As in the case of Custis Lee before him, Maury was supposed to receive the cooperation of other officers, including Brooke.[1]

The prospective arrival of Maury led to a careful reconsideration of the scientific courses offered at the Institute, for the superintendent believed that every department engaged in scientific research would "be stimulated by the energies of his fertile mind." One result was the decision to introduce a course in physics. It was proposed that this elementary course utilizing experiments should consider such topics as heat, light, sound, and electricity. It was to be given to second-year students (third classmen) to serve as an introduction to more advanced scientific courses offered the last two years so that students could more readily understand "physical laws and phenomena." Maury was designated professor of physics in the new department of that name, whereas Brooke remained head of his old department, redesignated the Department of Practical Astronomy, Physics, Descriptive Geography, and Geodesy. The older man was put in charge of general physics, while Brooke was made responsible for what was called special physics.[2] Actually, Maury gave his attention to the physical survey of Virginia while Brooke taught the new elementary course. When Brooke complained in 1871 of "the insufficient time given to physics," General Smith was sympathetic and proposed a way to give more attention to laboratory work.

In addition to his regular teaching duties, Captain Brooke gave Maury a hand with the physical survey of Virginia. At Maury's request he calculated the distances by the Great Circle in geo-

[1] Brooke to Maury, 10 May 1868 (copy), BP; Superintendent's Annual Report, VMI, 25 June 1868.
[2] Superintendent's Annual Report, VMI, 25 June 1868.

graphic miles and statute miles between Norfolk and Omaha, Norfolk and Kansas City, and Norfolk and the Lizard.[3] Later Maury asked Brooke to determine the Great Circle distances from New York and Norfolk to Memphis and the Red River terminus of the Southern Pacific Railway. The commercial implications are obvious. When Maury finished the preliminary survey in December 1868, General Smith had 20,000 copies printed at Institute expense. Copies were sent to various southern governors and mayors of southern cities.[4] Smith's purpose was to encourage the shipment of minerals and agricultural goods produced in the states of the interior to the Atlantic seaboard via Virginia.

As a result of General Smith's bold decision to rebuild the Institute, the decade of the seventies promised much. By 1870 the corps of cadets numbered 360, drawn from every southern state and some northern states. That year fifty-two cadets graduated, by far the largest number in the history of the school up to that time. In 1871 the president of the Board of Visitors asserted that the restored institution was "second to no military and scientific school in the United States," and that it was in a more prosperous condition than before the war. The apparent prosperity was reflected in rising faculty salaries, Brooke's pay for the school year 1870–71 being $1,800.[5] In 1872 the president of the Board of Visitors boasted that physically the Institute was "completely restored in all of its original proportions."[6] VMI's fame was spreading beyond the state's borders; in the class of 1873 only twenty-two of the fifty-two graduates were from Virginia.

The apparent prosperity of the Institute, unfortunately, turned out to be an illusion; the fine new buildings were built on sand. Progress ground to a halt as a combination of factors carried VMI to the brink of bankruptcy. For a time in 1872 faculty salaries were suspended, and in 1874, when 20 percent of faculty salaries was withheld, "the professors advanced $25,000 from

[3] Smith to Maury, 2 Oct. 1868 (copy), Maury Papers, VMI Archives.
[4] Copies of the letters transmitted to the mayor of Memphis and a southern governor can be found in the Maury Papers, UVa Lib. The letter to the governor is dated 16 Jan. 1869.
[5] Board of Visitors Annual Report, VMI, 5 Jan. 1871.
[6] Ibid., 5 July 1872.

their scanty means, in the way of loans, to help the credit of the school." At the end of June 1876, even though salaries had been cut 15 percent, Brooke wrote that he had not been paid since January.[7] A further reduction of 15 percent in 1878 put salaries below the level of 1860. The enrollment was down to 159, less than half of what it had been at the beginning of the decade, and the number of departments had dropped from fourteen to eight. Library holdings in 1877 totaled only 5,496 volumes. The general decline continued until 1883. In that doleful year only thirteen cadets graduated and but two books were purchased for the library.[8] Early in the crisis General Smith had begun to cut corners. One expedient was to induce professors to pick up sections in other disciplines, "thereby reducing the number of assistant professors."[9]

Despite financial vicissitudes the Institute was able to maintain a strong faculty with a core of twelve full professors, two of whom held master's degrees. But tradition was firmly entrenched. In a report to the board in 1871 the superintendent noted that education in America was passing through a period of rapid change and that there was much experimentation with the elective system. But he was convinced that "the experiments now being introduced have to be tested by experience." "We know," he wrote "that youths of sixteen and eighteen years of age are incapable of that judgment which is essential to a proper selection of the course of study to be pursued by them."[10]

Smith stressed that while the Academic Board was not unmindful of changes in other colleges, as a whole the members were convinced of the soundness of the VMI system. The superintendent was sure that in large measure the success of the school could be attributed "to a rigid system of military discipline, the effect of which is to impart *energy, system, subordination* and *self-reliance* to the young."[11] The use of textbooks, all of which had to

[7] Ibid., 5 July 1875, p. 5; Brooke to Munford, 30 June 1876 (copy), BP.

[8] These figures were obtained from annual reports and the *V.M.I. Register of Former Cadets, 1957.*

[9] Superintendent's Annual Report, VMI, 5 Jan. 1872.

[10] Ibid., 23 June 1871.

[11] Ibid., 23 Sept. 1874.

be approved by the Academic Board, was emphasized. A rigid curriculum, daily recitations, and the frequent submission of grades were aspects of the system. It was a method which placed a premium on hard and consistent work but offered little incentive to originality. Brooke with his imagination and creative talent found the monotony irksome.

As departments were consolidated in the 1870s Brooke's responsibilities increased. In 1873, following the death of Commodore Maury, the different physics courses were combined in Brooke's department, which was designated the Department of Practical Astronomy and Physics. When the veteran Colonel Blair, professor of Natural Philosophy, retired because of ill health, his department was broken up and Brooke was assigned his courses in mechanics. Simultaneously, the course in descriptive geography was transferred out of Brooke's department. Over the years Brooke usually had one or two assistants. These men were recent graduates of the Institute with good records who either were satisfying their two-year teaching obligations incurred as state cadets or were waiting for job opportunities commensurate with their abilities. Such appointments were made on an annual basis by the Academic Board. At one time or another Brooke taught physics, mechanics, practical astronomy, and physical geography. Also, when unexpected vacancies occurred he had to teach for short periods such diverse subjects as French and geology. His annual report to the superintendent was usually confined to a statement of courses taught, names of assistants, textbooks used, and perfunctory remarks about the conduct of the cadets.

A man with a curious mind and positive opinions like Brooke could be expected to have definite views on education. His views were far more flexible than those of the superintendent. While agreeing that the Institute had made a significant contribution to the state before the Civil War and had filled the needs "of a large part of the Southern youth," he insisted that the great changes that had occurred in America since 1865 made necessary substantial modification in the VMI curriculum. In 1871–72 Brooke led the faculty in a fruitless effort for changes in the curriculum. Sharp differences with General Smith's rigid position created a spirit of restlessness in Brooke, whose academic training had been tempered by practical scientific experience. In his view, changes in the undergraduate curriculum were essential if the superintendent really intended that the Institute's postgraduate courses in the special schools, "fit men for professional work."[12]

Nowhere did Brooke elaborate more clearly his ideas on VMI's educational function than in a memorandum he prepared in 1872. Noting the new economic developments in the United States, he observed that changes in class structure and occupations had resulted. It was essential, he felt, that the curriculum on the undergraduate level, which emphasized engineering and the military arts, be broadened to include courses that would be useful in the new industrial society. In Brooke's view, discoveries were "so numerous and so quickly applied" that a person without technical knowledge could not hope to secure employment in "industrial pursuits." Instruction on the undergraduate level should be coordinated with the graduate program. Brooke recommended that the Institute "preserve that which is good—the moral and gymnastic training—and . . . add technical knowledge."[13]

Brooke always emphasized the practical aspects of his courses. For a man of his broad experience, however, the repetition cannot have been exciting. Moreover, the lack of adequate equipment made it difficult to conduct original experiments. Brooke's formal education had been fragmentary; of the culminating year at Annopolis, he once remarked to John Rodgers: "I can't say I learned much there."[14] That he made every effort to keep up in those fields where he had achieved at least some recognition is shown by his voluminous correspondence with his old navy friends and the scientific articles he wrote. But he was self-taught and his scientific knowledge was specialized in the fields of practical astronomy, surveying, hydrography, navigation, and ordnance.

Under the circumstances it is not really surprising that Brooke during his thirty-four years as a professor made no significant contributions in scientific theory and won no particular acclaim in the academic community outside Lexington. As a teacher, there can

[12] Undated, signed draft written by John M. Brooke, c. Jan. 1872, BP.

[13] Ibid.

[14] Brooke to Rodgers, 1 June 1865, Rodgers Family Papers, Naval Hist. Foundation, MSS Div., LC.

be no doubt that he knew his subject. But he was not a professor by choice, and he lacked the magnetism of an inspired teacher. Technically competent, he was respected as an individual, but it is doubtful that his students were warmly attracted to him as a person. He was guided by high professional standards and serious purpose, though he lacked understanding for those who were limited in ability or motivation. It is not recorded that he indulged in jokes or laughter; however, as he grew older he learned patience. Writing to Bob Minor after the war, he confessed: "In looking back I can see very clearly in most instances that my troubles were for a good purpose, and now I try hard to do right and to have faith and certainly I have gained peace of mind."

In his navy days Brooke had had a few close friends and they stuck by him for life; but as he grew older he became increasingly reserved and tended to withdraw. Many of his navy friends called him a genius. It was a tragedy of the Civil War that in the somber days following the surrender the spark of genius never had a chance to glow. Though there were compensations in teaching at a small college, his postwar life was one of many disappointments.

The lack of a progressive spirit on the part of the administration and the low pay at the Institute frustrated Brooke in the 1870s and 1880s. He felt that he was leading a treadmill existence with no opportunity to develop his interests. As he saw the years slipping away, he remarked in his letters that he was tied down by his academic duties and had little time for anything else. The school year began early in September and did not end until the Fourth of July. Except for an occasional holiday, such as Christmas Day and New Market Day (May 15), there were no breaks in the routine. Nor was this condition likely to change. That the cadets hoped for a better day is revealed in the minutes of the Board of Visitors in 1877: "The Superintendent having stated that many applications were presented to him for furloughes from cadets who desired to visit home during Christmas, the Board directed the superintendent to issue an order re-affirming their decision, that no furloughes be granted during the period of active duty at the Institute."[15] This policy would remain unchanged until the 1920s.

[15] Board of Visitors Minutes, VMI, 18 Jan. 1877.

It is obvious that Brooke was discontented at VMI, despite his happy marriage and family, during some of his most productive years. It is not surprising, therefore, to learn that during the years 1868–85 he made strenuous efforts to find more congenial employment. Admirals John Rodgers and Daniel Ammen advised Brooke they could "probably" get him a job surveying the northern Japanese island of Hokkaido. Brooke expressed interest, but after dangling for some months the matter was dropped.[16] Perhaps the cautious Japanese never made a formal offer. Brazil was another possibility. Catesby Jones recommended Brooke to the Brazilian government as a torpedo expert. Admiral S. P. Lee, Captain Andrew W. Johnson, and Captain Edward Simpson, all of the United States Navy, also worked in Brooke's behalf, but a satisfactory contract could not be worked out. Brooke thought the terms ambiguous and the job not sufficiently challenging.[17] An offer from Argentina came through Brooke's Confederate comrade Hunter Davidson. Eager to secure Brooke's services, Davidson, who was in charge of the Torpedo and Hydrographic Division of the Argentine Republic, offered Brooke the post of chief of ordnance at a handsome salary. But conditions at the Institute were beginning to improve, so in the end Brooke felt duty-bound to decline the offer and remain in Lexington.[18]

In 1880 Brooke actively sought the presidency of the Virginia Agricultural and Mechanical College at Blacksburg that was established under the Morrill Act in 1872. Brooke enlisted the support of a number of influential people who wrote letters to William Henry Ruffner, chairman of the selection committee and state superintendent of public instruction.[19] But Ruffner, who was an ex-officio member of the Blacksburg board and one of the most distinguished educators in the South, informed Brooke that

[16] Rodgers to Brooke, 8 May 1873, BP.

[17] Jones to Brooke, 18 July 1874, Johnson to Brooke, 29 July, 18 Sept., 28 Sept. 1874, Simpson to Brooke, 1 Aug. 1874, Lee to Brooke, 1 Aug., 3 Sept. 1874, Brooke to Davidson, 25 Sept. 1874 (copy), A. J. deMello Tamborini to Brooke, 25 Sept. 1874, BP.

[18] Davidson to Brooke, 31 Aug., 8 Dec., 16 Dec. 1875, Brooke to Davidson, 20 March 1876 (copy), BP.

[19] Wilfred Emory Cutshaw to Brooke, 24 Nov. 1880, Brooke to Cutshaw, 26 Nov. 1880, William Preston Johnston to Ruffner, 14 Jan. 1881, William Nelson Pendleton to Ruffner, 7 Feb. 1881, BP. The original letters of recommendation are in the Brooke Papers because Brooke asked that they be sent to him when the matter was closed.

"owing to the want of such education heretofore in the southern states, we have no class of men, whose previous training has been just in the line wanted." Unwilling to hire a northerner, Ruffner noted, the board was in touch with a Canadian. When Brooke lost out in Blacksburg, his good friend William Preston Johnston, president of Louisiana State University, offered him the position of professor of natural history at that institution. Tempted though Brooke was, he turned down the offer because he thought the climate would be unhealthy for his children.[20]

The position Brooke wanted most was that of superintendent of the Coast Survey. When Superintendent Carlisle P. Patterson died in 1881, Commodore J. C. P. deKrafft, chief of the Bureau of Yards and Docks, wrote Brooke about the vacancy and proposed his candidacy. "The more we can do," wrote deKrafft, "to bring Southern men of ability forward in the conduct of affairs & in association with men of the North, the more we will do to cement the bonds of national brotherhood which should bind us inseperable together under the old flag which we all have reason to venerate." Brooke responded promptly that "no position could afford a better field or more congenial work."[21] As a result, four admirals, two commodores, and four senior captains made a concerted effort to secure the position for Brooke.[22] Many of these officers were on active service, and nearly all were Brooke's classmates or men he had served under. Some called directly on the president; others wrote letters in his behalf. John Rodgers delivered to President Chester Arthur a personal letter from the governor of Virginia, Frederick Holliday. In addition, one of Virginia's senators and all of its representatives in Congress but the two Readjusters rallied behind this effort to place a former Confederate in a high government post.[23] In the long run the effort failed when Arthur promoted the assistant superintendent to the higher position. But at

[20] Ruffner to Brooke, 31 Dec. 1880, Johnston to Brooke, 22 April 1881, Brooke to Johnston, 22 May 1881 (copy), BP.

[21] DeKrafft to Brooke, 18 Aug. 1881, Brooke to deKrafft, 20 Aug. 1881 (copy), BP.

[22] The admirals were Samuel Phillips Lee, John Rodgers, Thomas H. Stevens, and Daniel Ammen; deKrafft and Francis Asbury Roe were the commodores. The captains included Richard L. Law, Andrew W. Johnson, and Thomas Scott Fillebrown.

[23] The influential Readjuster Senator William Mahone, who was a VMI graduate, did not support Brooke's cause.

least Brooke could reflect how the friendships formed before the Civil War had weathered that bloody conflict.

Four years later the superintendency of the Coast Survey fell vacant again and a renewed effort was made by Brooke's old navy friends, bolstered by some younger officers who were familiar with Brooke's scientific achievements.[24] With Grover Cleveland, a Democrat, in the White House, hopes ran high. But this effort also failed. By this time Brooke seemed willing to accept his lot.

In the end Brooke adjusted himself to teaching. As an outlet, he maintained a passion for all that pertained to the navy, particularly ordnance and hydrography. For many years his friends supplied him with information and opinions so that he could keep abreast of developments. William Würdemann, the Washington instrument maker, who witnessed some of the artillery bombardment and destruction of the Franco-Prussian War, informed him that the German breechloaders were superior to the French muzzle-loaders in range and accuracy; moreover, fewer men were required to service them. Years later, in 1887 A. W. Johnson, who was one of Brooke's most faithful correspondents, asked Brooke what he thought "of the air balloon, now brought to perfection, for bombarding an Enemy's strong hold, and their vessels from aloft." Johnson noted that the weapon was under serious study in the Navy Department as a defensive weapon. C. A. McEvoy, who was still in London in 1901, described an apparatus for detecting the approach of submarines and noted that "there is something like a scare on now in Naval circles about the 'Submarines' which were made light of at first. My own strong impression is that they have a future."[25] This, of course, had been Brooke's view thirty years earlier.

Brooke's naval friends kept him supplied with all sorts of government reports from the Naval Observatory, Hydrographic Office, and Coast Survey, and he read those relating to ordnance, hydrography, and astronomical observations avidly. As late as 1886 he wrote Admiral Ammen that he had "been reading with

[24] The lead this time was taken by Adm. Thornton Jenkins, who had promised his support to another candidate in 1881 before he knew Brooke was interested. Among the younger officers were George E. Belknap and David B. Harmony.

[25] Johnson to Brooke, 28 April 1887, McEvoy to Brooke, 11 Dec. 1901, BP.

interest the report of the Senate Committee on Ordnance and Warships." In 1879 he was greatly pleased when notified that he had been elected an associate member of the United States Naval Institute by a unanimous vote. He read the proceedings and was himself urged to contribute articles, which he promised to do when he had time. In 1887 Brooke paid the $3 entrance fee to become a member of the newly formed United States Naval Academy Graduates Association. This organization was "for the purpose of promoting kindly feeling and social intercourse among its members, of fostering the memories of the Naval Academy, and of preserving the records of all the graduates." Brooke's friend Rear Admiral Edward Simpson was president.[26]

Despite the concern of some officers in improving the weapons and techniques of the navy, the twenty years following the Civil War marked a period of stagnation. The Navy Department was reluctant to test new ships, weapons, or equipment. Some officers, including S. P. Lee and A. W. Johnson, expressed their frustration to Brooke. Admiral Lee never reconciled himself to the policy of barring former Confederates from the service; it was, he believed, a manifestation of "wretched sectional despotism which unjustly deprives the Navy" of the services of some of its ablest men.[27]

For many months after the Civil War there was a lack of concern with deep-sea sounding in the United States Navy, but Brooke, after he had become settled in Lexington, turned his attention to such matters again. In November 1867, Thomas Scott Fillebrown in the Hydrographic Office informed Brooke that Commodore Jenkins, chief of the Bureau of Navigation, was having instrument maker Würdemann make two Brooke deep-sea leads and that Jenkins "intended to adopt them for the Navy and furnish all vessels with them."[28] Also, Brooke learned, the Hydrographic Office had just sent two of Brooke's registers to Commander John Irwin of the *Gettysburg* for surveys in the Caribbean Sea which Fillebrown presumed to be preliminary to the laying of

---

[26] Brooke to Ammen, 24 July 1886 (copy), BP; "Minutes of the First Annual Meeting," *The United States Naval Academy Graduates Association*, 11 June 1886, pp. 4–5.

[27] Lee to Brooke, 18 Aug. 1876, BP.

[28] Fillebrown to Brooke, 22 Nov. 1867, BP.

a cable between Santiago, Cuba, and Aspinwall.[29] Würdemann paid Brooke $125 from the sum he received for manufacturing the sounding registers for the Navy Department. In 1870 Brooke was asked to make suggestions for a book on hydrographic surveying being written by Captain William Jeffers. The book was to include a chapter on deep-sea sounding.[30]

In July 1873, with VMI slipping into the financial abyss, Brooke took advantage of his summer vacation to visit his wife's home in Fredericksburg. While there, his spirits must have been considerably lifted by a communication he received from T. S. and J. D. Negus, the New York instrument makers he had known since his exploring days in the Pacific. The Negus firm, writing that the Peruvian consul, J. C. Tracy, had asked them to supply six Brooke deep-sea sounding leads, wished to know where the leads could be obtained. The Peruvian government intended to make soundings between Panama and Paita, Peru, preliminary to the laying of a submarine cable.[31] Brooke informed the consul that his apparatus was "not manufactured by any person except to order" and proposed an interview in New York so that proper arrangements could be made for the exact type of equipment needed. Brooke's enthusiasm was indubitably dampened when the consul replied that the Peruvian government wanted the deep-sea sounding leads at once and could not wait to have any made.[32] The implication was that if Brooke leads were not available, Peru would get some leads that were. Six days later, after talking to Peruvian chargé d'affaires Villena, Consul Tracy moderated his position and asked how soon Brooke could furnish three of his leads and what the price would be. There is no further correspondence on the matter, so one cannot say whether Brooke filled the order. It is clear, however, that aside from the $5,000 paid him by the United States government shortly before the Civil War, Brooke's profits from the invention were modest.

Recognition among people whose opinion counted was another

---

[29] Fillebrown to Brooke, 20 March 1868, BP.

[30] Fillebrown to Brooke, 14 Jan. 1870, BP.

[31] Negus to Brooke, 25 July 1873, Tracy to Brooke, 13 Aug. 1873, BP.

[32] Brooke to Tracy, c. 5 Aug. 1873 (copy), Brooke to T. S. and J. D. Negus, 29 July 1873 (copy), Tracy to Brooke, 7 Aug. 1873, BP.

matter. In the late 1870s and early 1880s Brooke corresponded with two naval officers who were particularly distinguished for their work in deep-sea sounding, Captain George E. Belknap and Lieutenant Commander Charles D. Sigsbee. Belknap in the *Tuscarora* made 304 soundings with the Brooke lead in the Pacific Ocean of more than one thousand fathoms, of which nine were of four thousand fathoms or more.[33] Sigsbee at the Hydrographic Office developed a modification of the Brooke lead. These men and others gave full credit to Brooke in their writings.

John Brooke was not content to rest on his laurels. In a letter to Commodore Belknap in 1879 he suggested echo sounding with tuning forks as a way "to record the depth continuously as the ship runs."[34] It will be recalled echo sounding was a subject on which Brooke had written to Maury at the Naval Observatory in the 1850s and had himself conducted crude experiments in the Pacific. Although there was more correspondence between Brooke and Belknap, there is no further reference to echo sounding.

No subject attracted Captain Brooke more than big guns. His intense activity in that field during the Civil War left a lasting imprint upon him, as was shown in the years 1879–81 by a number of articles he published. The many clippings and notes in his papers are a constant reminder of his consuming interest in naval ordnance. Whenever he heard that a gun had burst, he tried to analyze why. In his writings he drew heavily on his practical Confederate experience, but also he kept up with the latest books and articles on ordnance published in the United States and abroad. This knowledge was augmented by a continuing correspondence with American ordnance experts.

A gun explosion that particularly fascinated him was that of the 38-ton, 12-inch Armstrong gun in the turret of H.M.S. *Thunderer* while the ship was engaged in routine target practice off Malta on January 2, 1879. In the tragedy eleven lives were lost. A committee of naval officers investigating the explosion reported that it was the result of an air space in the chamber of the gun.

---

[33] Daniel Ammen, abstracts from "Recent Improvements in Apparatus and Methods of Sounding Ocean Depths," *Proceedings of the American Association for the Advancement of Science* 33 (Sept. 1884).

[34] Brooke to Belknap, 1 April 1879 (copy), BP.

But this hypothesis was rejected by a joint army-navy committee meeting at Malta largely on the testimony of Captain Andrew Noble, physicist and ballistics expert, who was familiar with Brooke's experiments on the utility of the air space. The *Thunderer* incident stirred heated debates in Parliament, and on the basis of published reports of the discussion in the House of Lords on March 17, Brooke concluded that the gun had burst because fragments of an empty cast-iron shell had lodged in the steel barrel. The former Confederate ordnance chief wrote an article explaining his deductions and sent it to C. A. McEvoy with the hope of publishing it in a London newspaper. Meanwhile, the report of the Malta committee, which attributed the explosion to a double charge, was published. McEvoy, consequently, could not sell the article and in disgust so informed Brooke.

When his article was returned to him, Brooke published it in the July 1879 issue of the new *United Service Quarterly*. He agreed with the British that unless a rational explanation was found, public distrust of that type of weapon would supplant great expectations. But Brooke was not satisfied with the conclusion of either British committee as reported in the press. In his article, he wrote of the double charge: "This finding is not in accord with the evidence of witnesses, which goes to show that the gun contained but a single charge." He must have been reassured to receive a note from E. O. Matthews, now ordnance officer at the New York Navy Yard, stating: "Your theory (supported by your Experience) fully explains to my mind all the peculiarities attending the breaking of that [*Thunderer*] gun."[35]

In time, McEvoy was able to send Brooke a copy of the official Blue Book which contained the full report of the joint committee that had met at Malta. It was an impressive document.[36] The committee had agreed unanimously that a double charge was the cause of the burst. Brooke studied the committee's report carefully, making notes and calculations in the margin, but he re-

[35] John M. Brooke, "Probable Cause of the Explosion of the 38-Ton Gun on Board H.M.S. 'Thunderer,' " *United Service: A Quarterly Review of Military and Naval Affairs* 1 (July 1879): 449; Matthews to Brooke, 26 June 1879, BP.

[36] *Minutes of the Proceedings of the Thunderer Committee together with Appendix Presented to Both Houses of Parliament by Command of Her Majesty* (London, 1879).

mained unconvinced. In fact, he was prompted to write a second article, much longer than his first, in which he carefully analyzed the evidence. This highly technical article appeared in the January 1880 issue of the *United Service,* now a monthly. "It is proposed," he wrote, "to discuss the observed results of the explosion so fully given in these carefully prepared reports and diagrams, and to show that they are physically in accordance with the hypothesis of a single charge and a wedging shell." What Brooke maintained was not that a double charge could not have burst the barrel. Rather, he insisted that that was not the only reasonable explanation. After a close examination of the testimony of the witnesses, who were not of one mind, he concluded that the theory of a single charge and wedging shell offered a more reasonable and logical explanation than did a double charge. He implied that the British officers were so determined not to tarnish the reputation of the services that they strained in order to make the evidence fit a predetermined conclusion. Admiral John Rodgers, still on active service and now the senior rear admiral in the navy, thought Brooke's second article "hit the nail on the head."[37]

Although the Malta committee had handed down a unanimous opinion, some doubts lingered. At least that committee had urged that as a means of reassuring the public about the safety of such guns, a sister gun of the *Thunderer* be sent to England for tests. This was done, and the joint army-navy Ordnance Committee tested the gun with variations of air space, with a wad in the bore, and with a double charge. In its fourteen-page report it insisted that the tests gave "the strongest possible confirmation" of the findings of the Malta committee.[38] But in Brooke's view the bursting of the test gun at Woolwich was not conclusive. He was constrained to write a third article on the *Thunderer* gun explosion, this time analyzing the Ordnance Committee's conclusion as it was reported in the press. It is necessary, he wrote, "to compare the effects of a double charge with those produced by the cause of

[37] John M. Brooke, "Discussion of the Explosion of the 38-Ton Gun on Board H.M.S. 'Thunderer,' " *United Service: A Monthly Review of Military and Naval Affairs* 1 (Jan. 1880): 3; Rodgers to Brooke, 6 Feb. 1880, BP.

[38] *Report by the Special Committee on Ordnance on Experiments with a 12-inch R. M. L. Gun Returned from H.M.S.* Thunderer. *Presented to Both Houses of Parliament by Her Majesty* (London, 1880).

explosion of the gun in the turret." He concluded that the appearance of what was left of the tested gun was precisely what one would have expected from a double charge when one considered "distribution of metal, estimated strength of the gun, relative positions of projectiles and powder." But, the fact that the gun tested at Woolwich with a double charge had broken along the lines expected did not prove that the *Thunderer* gun, which had broken along different lines of strain, had burst from the same cause.[39]

Carried forward by the momentum of the *Thunderer* studies, Brooke in 1880 wrote two more articles for the *United Service* on ordnance. One of these, entitled "Heavy Guns and the Development of Their Power," traced in detail changes in such matters as breech loading, air space, and types of powder between 1843, when Baron Wahrendorf, the proprietor of the Aker Foundry in Sweden, first experimented with breech-loading cannon, and 1880, when Alfred Krupp, the German arms expert, demonstrated the extraordinary power of his new gun. This article showed that secluded as Brooke might be, he had kept abreast of the rapid international developments in the ordnance field since the Civil War. The second article was a seven-page review of a revised and enlarged textbook prepared for midshipmen at the Naval Academy. The book, *A Text-Book of Naval Ordnance and Gunnery*, was written by Commander Augustus Paul Cooke, U.S.N. In his review Brooke revealed a profound knowledge of the history of ordnance, explosives, and devices to determine the velocity of projectiles from the year 1840, "when a systematic course of investigation by officers of the Ordnance Corps was begun," until the time he wrote the review.[40]

Brooke's final contribution to the *United Service* was a twenty-eight-page review of *The War-Ships and Navies of the World* by Chief Engineer J. W. King. In this article he demonstrated a professional knowledge of ships and armaments not only in the United States and Europe but in China and Japan as well. In conclusion

[39] John M. Brooke, "The 'Thunderer' Gun Experiments," *United Service* 2 (May 1880): 635-38.

[40] John M. Brooke, "Heavy Guns and the Development of Their Power," ibid., 2 (March 1880): 289-309; Brooke, "Cooke's Naval Ordnance and Gunnery," ibid., 3 (Sept. 1880): 376-82.

the former Confederate urged a strengthening of the United States Navy: "Having given in 'War-Ships and Navies of the World' to the legislator all that is requisite to enable him to appreciate the material naval superiority of foreign powers, and to the architect a scale of power by which to proportion his ships, Chief Engineer King, warranted by the facts, presents his conclusions as to the needs of the United States navy. To those who believe that this great country needs in time of peace no preparation for war, it may be said that the influence of armament is like that of the lightning-rod, which by virtue of Franklin's 'power-of-points,' silently discharges the gathering cloud, and, if there be no time for that, turns aside the bolt."[41] Perhaps King's book and Brooke's plea had some part in promoting the resurgence of the American navy that began, although slowly, about that time.

With his nautical and scientific background it is natural that Brooke should have retained a lifelong interest in the weather and its scientific prediction. Shortly after he began work at the Virginia Military Institute he sought to determine the precise longitude of Lexington by observing meteoric showers. In this calculation he wished to work closely with his friends at the Naval Observatory, and he assured A. W. Johnson that he would have a chronometer "carefully rated and in readiness."[42] There survive in the Brooke Papers some meteorological notes Brooke kept between 1870 and 1875. He was concerned with such things as conditions of the sky, wind, temperature, and barometric pressure, and he drew conclusions from his observations. The notation for April 27, 1872, illustrates his method. "Smoky haze the sun setting as a round red ball. This I have observed to be attended always by serene dry weather." On June 29, 1873, he noted, "I think therefore a high barometer in June falling indicates rain without electrical disturbance." In Brooke's daily recording of precipitation he received the cooperation of his friend Professor John Lyle Campbell of Washington and Lee University. But Brooke did not confine his attention to weather in his own locale. Writing to Admiral Rodgers in January 1881, when the latter was head of the Naval Observatory, Brooke pondered the reasons for the se-

[41] John M. Brooke, "War-Ships and Navies of the World," ibid., 4 (Feb. 1881): 231.
[42] Brooke to Johnson, 18 Nov. 1866 (copy), BP.

verity of that winter and the heavy snowfall. He was positive that "some phenomenon of unusual occurrence" had preceded it, and he was eager to find out what it was. He suggested that one cause could be the "abnormally *high* temperature of the Northern lakes in December." Though he had little faith in "so called weather prophets," he thought much could be learned through observation and the proper interpretation of physical laws.[43]

Over the years Brooke received requests for information or assistance from many sources, including former colleagues, onetime cadets, family friends, and people engaged in particular activities. The diversity of requests is amazing. A relative asked Brooke to draw from memory a sketch of General Richard Brooke Garnett, who had been killed at Gettysburg, as no likeness had been found. Bob Minor requested that he draw plans for a small Episcopal church in Fauquier County. The artist Fred Volck, with whom he had worked in the Confederate navy, asked his assistance in arranging the sale in Lexington of Volck's equestrian statuette of General Robert E. Lee; Volck believed a subscription among students might raise $500. The widow of Brooke's Confederate comrade Beverley Kennon wanted him to prepare for publication a biographical memoir left by her husband. Judge Sam Houston Letcher, who was preparing a biographical sketch of his father, John Letcher, the wartime governor, asked Brooke for firsthand information about the governor's administration and character. Fred Volck's brother, A. A. Volck, who had been commissioned to paint a picture of General Lee's horse Traveller, asked Brooke a long series of questions about the horse's physical characteristics. When possible Brooke complied with these requests. As a former bureau chief in the Confederacy, Brooke was requested to write letters of recommendation by old employees, while as a professor, graduates of the Institute asked him for his endorsement. Brooke's letters of recommendation were brief and to the point. He stressed qualities such as zeal, determination, faithfulness, ability, and honor—qualities he prized himself.

In 1879 Brooke was appointed to the Board of Visitors of the Naval Academy. The idea originated with Brooke's classmates.[44]

[43] Brooke to Rodgers, Jan. 1881 (copy), BP.
[44] James Jouett to Brooke, 24 May 1879, BP.

Informing him of his appointment, the secretary of the navy requested that he witness the June examinations at the academy with other members of the board. Needless to say, Brooke accepted the honor "with great pleasure." The board met from June 2 to June 10, holding at least one session daily. Brooke was the only southerner on the eleven-member board, which included educators, writers, and three members of Congress among its nine civilian members. J. W. King, chief engineer, U.S.N., and Commodore Thomas H. Stevens, president of the board, were the two naval members. In reporting on those subjects with which Brooke was most conversant, the board found the instruction in the theory of gunnery "sufficient as it is." According to the board, physics instruction was "as extended as the time allotted permits," but it was recommended that more experimental equipment be acquired. Brooke was conscientious and must have been pleased with Stevens's comment to A. W. Johnson that he was "the brains of the Board."[45]

There is one further aspect of Brooke's trip to Annapolis that should be mentioned. The superintendent of the academy, Commodore Foxhall Alexander Parker, had been sick for some time and died at the end of the examination period. A funeral with full military honors was held at the academy on June 12, and Brooke was one of eight pallbearers; the others included two admirals, a commodore, two commanders, and a medical director.[46]

Such activities, of course, were peripheral. Until the end of the century Brooke would be primarily involved with what went on at the Institute. And for quite a few years nothing much seemed to happen. The school was in a rut. Financial pressures were partly responsible. But another reason is that the first superintendent held office for fifty years. Not only had General Francis H. Smith established the school, but after the Civil War when many were fainthearted, he had pressed steadily forward and it

[45] *Report* of the Board of Visitors, U.S. Naval Academy, 10 June 1879, and Johnson to Brooke, 14 July 1879, BP.
[46] Order No. 46, U.S. Naval Academy, 11 June 1879, BP. In 1880 Admiral Stevens and Capts. A. W. Johnson and R. L. Law tried to have Brooke appointed to the Board of Visitors at West Point but failed. Apparently it was too soon after his Annapolis duty.

was through his efforts that the Institute had risen from the ashes. Yet, in the 1880s some members of the Board of Visitors and faculty were becoming convinced that his continued presence at the helm was a major cause of the Institute's stagnation. Set in his ways, he resented change. What brought matters to a head was faculty salaries. In his annual message of 1886 the superintendent made a strong plea for raising salaries. The board did not act on the request because the small size of the corps meant low revenues. Smith resented the board's inaction.

In 1887 the superintendent took exception to seven statements in the annual report of the Board of Visitors and asked for an investigation by the legislature. At the time the president of the board was Brooke's friend General Thomas Munford, a VMI graduate. The investigation was described by its chairman as "long & tedious." It appears that Brooke testified against the superintendent. In a letter to Brooke written after Munford had retired from the board, the former president said: "Be assured that your friends felt that you were only showing the Virginia legislature that you were a Virginia gentleman ready to do your duty in & under all circumstances."[47] Although some improvements had been made in the Institute's financial condition by 1888, Brooke had little confidence in the school's future so long as General Smith remained superintendent.

The report of the joint legislative committee indicated its investigation had been thorough and fair. The committee found "that a manifest want of harmony existed between the last Board of Visitors and the superintendent, and they cannot, in all candor see why it may not continue under the [present] Board." While praising "the noble and heroic character" of the superintendent and making note "of his faithful and eminent" services, the committee endeavored to ease him out. Attempting to soothe the old man's feelings, it recommended that he retire at the end of the year, 1888, as superintendent emeritus on half pay. General Smith did not follow the recommendation at the time, but a year later he took advantage of the VMI Semicentennial, celebrated on

[47] Senator J. N. Stubbs, Chairman, Joint Committee, to Munford, 7 April 1888, Smith File, VMI Records; Munford to Brooke, 17 April 1889, BP.

the Fourth of July, to announce his resignation, effective January 1, 1890.[48]

As the new superintendent, the Board of Visitors elected Brigadier General Scott Shipp, an 1859 graduate who had led the cadets at the Battle of New Market in the Civil War and had been commandant of cadets for many years. Shipp, a strict disciplinarian with whom Brooke was congenial, would make changes, but he believed firmly in the traditions of the Institute. For example, in his annual report of 1893, after describing the rigid daily routine, he commented: "The general result is a trained body of energetic, self-reliant, practical men, who know how to turn to the best advantage all their endowments and attainments." Two years later, the superintendent noted that "success in life depends in a much greater degree upon moral force than upon intellectual brilliancy and scholastic attainment. Under military government one soon learns that there are other things to be taken into the account than his own rash will and selfish inclination." In words that sound strange in today's world, he proclaimed in his 1896 report that "divine law, human experience, both assert the absolute necessity of order, subordination, self-restraint, respect for constituted authority." Disciplinarian though he was, however, General Shipp did not lose sight of the Institute's academic goals, and he was fully convinced that military discipline could be made the handmaiden of intellectual achievement. VMI would move forward under his leadership, and Brooke would enjoy perhaps his happiest years as a professor.[49]

An augury of better times was the slowly climbing enrollment. The new superintendent reported in 1895 that the cadet corps was the largest since the school year 1871–72, and he reminded the Board that the period 1868–72, had been abnormal because of the temporary advantage VMI's rapid rebuilding program had given it. In 1895 there were 205 cadets on the rolls, of whom seventy-five were first-year men.[50] Since 1887 progress had been evident.

[48] Board of Visitors Minutes, VMI, 23 June 1888 (the report of the joint committee, Senate Document No. XXVII, is spread on the minutes); ibid., 1 July 1889.

[49] Superintendent's Annual Reports, VMI, 22 June 1893, p. 3; 20 June 1895, p. 4; 20 June 1896, p. 8.

[50] Ibid., 20 June 1895, 18 June 1897. The latter report gives detailed statistical information on enrollment for the period 1866–98.

With the recovery and expansion of other southern colleges, however, VMI's out-of-state enrollment steadily declined. In 1895 the Board of Visitors undertook an active recruitment program.[51] In two consecutive years General Shipp noted that some families traditionally sent their sons to VMI and that a considerable number of cadets were sons of alumni or younger brothers of cadets already enrolled.[52] These were manifestations of the strong spirit of school loyalty that has always been characteristic of the Institute. Despite his efforts to lift VMI from the doldrums, however, Shipp was no advocate of unlimited growth. In fact, he strove for an enrollment of about three hundred. Beyond that number, he believed the VMI system would break down and the cadets would lose the individual attention he deemed so important.

During the 1880s and 1890s the Academic Board, of which Brooke was a member, continued to determine academic policy and to give some attention to disciplinary matters under the direction of the superintendent. When General Shipp became superintendent he did not dominate the proceedings of the professors to the extent his predecessor had. Working through ad hoc committees the Academic Board devoted much of its time to routine matters. As in the earlier period, Brooke did not initiate many motions, but he did his share of important committee work and his opinions were respected.

Brooke continued to handle physics, while new courses in electrical engineering were taught by Major Francis Mallory, an 1889 graduate who had just finished three years of graduate work in physics and mathematics at Johns Hopkins University. By 1899 electrical engineering was drawing considerable numbers of cadets, and Brooke, who supervised the new offerings, had three assistant professors in his department. The subjects taught were expanded to include descriptive astronomy, descriptive mechanics, heat, thermodynamics, optics, sound, magnetism, and electricity.[53] This development had been made possible by a substantial

[51] Board of Visitors Minutes, VMI, 6 Feb. 1895; Shipp to John B. Purcell, Richmond, 1 June 1895, BP.

[52] Superintendent's Annual Reports, VMI, 20 June 1896, 18 June 1897.

[53] Ibid., 15 June 1899.

increase in scientific equipment beginning in 1887 which Brooke had secured largely through the efforts of General Munford, then president of the Board of Visitors.

There is no doubt that Brooke favored changes in the traditional order, and as he grew older he continued to maintain a flexible attitude in such matters. A summary of Brooke's views is given in his response to a query from the Academic Board as to the advisibility of revising and expanding the curriculum. It was his position that revision was "desirable" and enlargement, too, "if practicable." But, he noted, "enlargement would require a higher standard of admission than we now have." And, he added, "a change is needed in the allotment of time for study and preparation as compared with the time given to recitation." In his opinion there was too much pressure on second classmen (juniors) in physics. "Under existing arrangements," he noted, "the time given to study and preparation has ranged during the term between fifteen and thirty minutes." He informed the committee that the whole class concurred in his statement on inadequate study time.[54]

The appointment of General Shipp as superintendent brought changes in the personnel of the Academic Board. Three of the eight department heads resigned: Colonel Mark B. Hardin, chemistry; Colonel John W. Lyell, mathematics; and Colonel William M. Patton, engineering. These resignations made Colonel John M. Brooke the senior member of the faculty. As such, he presided at Academic Board meetings in the absence of the superintendent, and when it was necessary for General Shipp to be out of town, the latter appointed Brooke acting superintendent. The vacancies created by the resignations gave the Institute the opportunity to appoint its first Ph.D. to the faculty. The two other appointees were VMI graduates without graduate degrees. Because of its unique character, there remained a tendency for the Institute to be ingrown.

In Brooke's last years, when he was the senior faculty member, the maintenance of academic standards was a fundamental concern, not only of the Academic Board but of the superin-

[54] Brooke to Cols. Nichols and Pendleton, 14 May 1895, Academic Board Papers and Reports, VMI.

tendent and the Board of Visitors as well. In 1896 a complaint was made, remarkably similar to assertions heard today: "The neglect of English in the preparatory schools of the country renders it necessary that the first half of the first year be devoted exclusively to English Grammar." Brooke strongly supported this view. The same year Superintendent Shipp addressed himself to those "well-meaning friends" who suggested the VMI curriculum would be improved by adding such courses as "telegraphy, stenography, typewriting, book-keeping and many useful and subordinate arts." Shipp insisted that it was "much higher work to train the mind than the hand or the eye" and there was insufficient time to do both.[55] We can be sure that Brooke agreed with General Shipp.

Another matter of continuing concern was the library. Its recovery after the Civil War was slow. As late as 1885 it contained only 8,400 volumes, "including valuable unbound periodicals and pamphlets," of which 375 books had been added in the past year. By 1893 the library had 16,259 books and pamphlets and suffered from a lack of space for proper arrangement and classification. It was reported in 1896 that the library subscribed to twenty-two newspapers and periodicals, which were "scientific, technical, military, political, historical and literary in character." When the library moved into new and enlarged quarters in 1897, the superintendent boasted that it had "become a 'utility' and attraction it has never been before in the history of the school."[56] The librarian, who was a faculty member and received $100 a year for the extra job, was assisted by two cadets paid $50 apiece. Certainly the board, though loosening the purse strings, was not throwing its money around. As long as Brooke was at the Institute, his research must have been hampered by the weak library. In Brooke's last year of teaching the Library Committee called attention to the lack of chairs, which forced many cadets to sit on the windowsills and steps, and the "very bad" lighting which caused injury to the eyes.

The lack of adequate facilities was not confined to the library.

[55] Superintendent's Annual Report, VMI, 20 June 1896; Board of Visitors Minutes, VMI, 20 June 1896.
[56] Superintendent's Annual Reports, VMI, 20 June 1885, 18 June 1897. The growth of the library can be traced in the annual reports and the Board of Visitors Minutes.

The Committee on Hospital, Grounds, and Buildings in 1890 submitted a depressing report on classrooms and suggested that an "emphatic Memorial" be sent to the legislature apprising it of conditions. Brooke's rank gave him no preferred treatment, for in 1897, two years before his retirement, the board committee singled out his classrooms for comment. It found them "not suitable for the work done in them by reason of their size, arrangement and situation."[57]

Other matters considered by the authorities are of interest if one would understand the environment in which Brooke worked. The Board of Visitors in 1884 found that a petition from the corps "asking that all recitations be suspended on Saturdays" was inexpedient.[58] This question was still being debated ninety-five years later. Public speeches and articles were also a matter of concern. The Academic Board in 1885 ordered that no speech be given by a cadet in public nor any article be published in a magazine, pamphlet, or newspaper until examined and approved by a committee of the board. The following year the Board of Visitors took similar action with reference to the valedictory address, requiring that the address be submitted in advance to the superintendent and commandant.[59]

Intercollegiate athletics made an unobtrusive appearance in the 1890s. The first notice came in 1893 when the Board of Visitors acknowledged receipt of "a communication from the Cadets on the subject of football" requesting permission "to participate in games away from the Institute." The board declined on the ground that such a policy "would conflict with the discipline of the School." The Academic Board had at an earlier meeting split on the question. But the pressure kept up, and in 1898, a year before Colonel Brooke retired, the Board of Visitors granted the football team leaves of absence on Founders Day (November 11) and Thanksgiving Day, and a maximum of one day travel time preceding and succeeding each game. Similar permission was granted the baseball team for New Market Day (May 15). The

[57] Board of Visitors Minutes, VMI, 23 June 1890, 21 June 1897.

[58] Ibid., 18 Dec. 1884.

[59] Academic Board Minutes, VMI, 11 Sept. 1885, Board of Visitors Minutes, VMI, 28 June 1886.

board, however, wanted it "distinctly understood, that in granting this request, they have gone to the extreme limit of their purpose in granting absences for Athletic purposes."[60]

The Board of Visitors, particularly in the 1890s, was quite receptive to corps trips, generally to southern cities. This was in keeping with the spirit of the times when the "Lost Cause" was glorified. Moreover, the trips were a manifestation of state pride and a stimulus to enrollment. Often the trips were arranged to coincide with the end of the school year so that graduation ceremonies could be held in the city visited.[61] Brooke went on some of these trips and must have enjoyed the chance to reminisce with friends of long ago who had shared the trials of the Confederate war effort.

While VMI was doing its part to perpetuate the glories of the Confederacy and advertise the progress of the "New South," it was also drawing closer to the federal government. The "bloody shirt" was buried as the Civil War receded into the background. Indicative of the new spirit was the appointment of Scott Shipp, who had led the cadets at New Market, to the Board of Visitors of the United States Military Academy in 1890. Four years later he was appointed president of the Board of Visitors at the Naval Academy.[62] These appointments also reflected the high regard for VMI in the armed services. When Shipp, the longtime commandant, became superintendent, the Institute found it difficult to recruit a permanent replacement. It was impossible to find a VMI graduate possessing the necessary qualities of leadership and maturity who was willing to accept the post on a permanent basis for the low pay promised. Therefore, the Institute turned to the United States Army, which agreed to detail an experienced officer at the Institute as commandant for a limited tour of duty. This became the custom.

Links were forged with the Union in other ways. During the Spanish-American War the superintendent reminded the Board of

[60] Board of Visitors Minutes, VMI, 3 Feb. 1893, 19 Jan. 1898.

[61] Information on the trips can be found in the Superintendent's Annual Reports. See also C. Vann Woodward, *A History of the South*, vol. 9, *Origins of the New South* (Baton Rouge, La., Press, 1951), pp. 155–59.

[62] Jennings C. Wise, *Personal Memoir of the Life and Services of Scott Shipp* (privately printed, 1915), pp. 43–44.

Visitors that the war demonstrated the utility of the military training VMI offered, and he noted that the "Virginia contingent in the Federal Army is largely officered by graduates of this institution."[63] The next year, Brooke's last as a professor, Scott Shipp reported that 136 cadets had served as officers in the Spanish-American War and the Philippine insurrection. Twenty-four VMI men held commissions in the regular army and six in the navy. One of the former was Brooke's son, Lieutenant George Mercer Brooke, United States Infantry, who had entered the army in 1897 as a private and won his commission through competitive examination.[64] Young Brooke had graduated from VMI in 1896. John Brooke's life had come full circle. At seventy-two, it was time for him to retire.

The superintendent's annual report of June 17, 1899, included the following brief statement: "Colonel John M. Brooke, Professor of Physics and Astronomy, was relieved from active service and appointed Emeritus Professor." He had served the Institute thirty-four years, ten years more than his service in the United States and Confederate navies combined. Aside from General Shipp, Colonel Thomas Semmes, professor of modern languages, was the only old-timer from the Civil War era left on the faculty. The Board of Visitors passed a complimentary resolution sketching Brooke's life and awarded him a salary of $1,200 per year. General Munford promptly wrote Brooke how delighted he was with the board's action. Kate thanked the president of the Board of Visitors personally for the board's action in making financial provision for Brooke's retirement. Referring to her husband, she exclaimed: "In thus having a long borne anxiety laid to rest he feels a profound relief, which is shared in full by those nearest him."[65] Major Mallory, some forty years Brooke's junior, was promoted to colonel and professor of physics and astronomy to fill the vacancy at the same meeting of the board at which Brooke was retired.

[63] Superintendent's Annual Report, VMI, 18 June 1898.
[64] Ibid., 17 June 1899; Capt. Daniel Price, Sullivan's Island, S.C., to Brooke, 22 Sept. 1899, BP.
[65] Munford to Brooke, 5 July 1899, BP; Kate Brooke to Alexander Hamilton, president, Board of Visitors, 30 June 1899, Brooke File, VMI Records.

John Brooke lived for six and a half years after his VMI retirement, old age gradually sapping his strength. The days of feverish activity and endless writing were long since past. He did not keep many of his letters of the last period of his life, and one suspects he did not bother to answer his correspondence. Most of his close friends of the old days were gone; it was a time for reverie. We may assume that he walked, worked a little in his garden, which had earlier been a source of exercise and pleasure, and read. No doubt he liked to spend time in his study with such souvenirs from his travels as he had been able to save over the decades. One gentleman told the author how, as a young boy some seventy years earlier, he had been led up to Captain Brooke's study. He never ceased to wonder at the experience. By the time of the visit the captain had a very long white beard and he must have looked like the Ancient Mariner himself.

The year after Brooke's retirement, the Fortnightly Club was organized and the naval scientist was made an honorary member. The club, composed of a few established members of the two college faculties and representative townsmen, met to enjoy a good dinner and to hear and discuss a scholarly paper presented by a member. The farsightedness of the founders is proved by the fact that nearly eighty years later the club is in a flourishing condition. Brooke must have enjoyed it and looked forward to the meetings.

We have Kate's word that he had no interest in genealogy and never had known much about his family history.[66] But throughout his life he was always interested in the welfare and activities of contemporary family members. Above all, in his declining years Captain Brooke, as always, had the love and attention of Kate and of his daughter Rosa, who was still at home. In a life of turmoil, unending labor, anxiety, and frustration, some of the best years came at the end. He could thank Kate for that.

On December 14, 1906, the VMI surgeon notified General Shipp that Brooke was critically ill from a stroke of paralysis. Before the day was over, the old sailor had crossed the bar. He

---

[66] Kate Brooke to James Mercer Garnett, 19 April 1905, James Mercer Garnett Papers, William R. Perkins Library, Duke University.

was buried with full military honors in the Lexington cemetery. From the Episcopal church to the grave site the casket was accompanied by the corps of cadets, and the superintendent stipulated that "from the time the procession moves until the final volley at the grave, a gun will be fired at such intervals as the Commandant of Cadets may direct." What impressed the cadets most on that bleak December day was the rain. More than fifty years later, on separate occasions, at least three men who had been cadets in the procession recalled the rain that came down in torrents.[67]

The Academic Board prepared a fourteen-page printed memorial which sketched Brooke's life. But perhaps the best estimate of his character and worth was that given in the General Orders of the Virginia Military Institute announcing his death. In preparing its memorial the Academic Board utilized the character sketch of the General Order almost verbatim and acknowledged that it had been written by an old friend. Quite likely General Shipp was the author. The General Order said of Brooke: "He was of the stern old type of character and cherished high ideals. Unswerving in his loyalty to his friends, he was a good hater; intolerant of sham, pretense, and opportunism. He knew what he wanted, what he thought, what he felt, and while modest was not backward forcibly to assert himself when occasion demanded. There are few left who knew him well. By those few he was greatly loved and is greatly lamented."[68]

[67] General Orders No. 57, Headquarters, VMI, 16 Dec. 1906; conversations of the author with John E. Townes, Murray F. Edwards, and James R. Gilliam.
[68] General Orders No. 56, Headquarters, VMI, 15 Dec. 1906.

Index

Index /